No One's Ways

No One's Ways

An Essay on Infinite Naming

Daniel Heller-Roazen

ZONE BOOKS · NEW YORK

2017

© 2017 Daniel Heller-Roazen

ZONE BOOKS

633 Vanderbilt Street

Brooklyn, NY 11218

Printed in the United States of America.

Distributed by The MIT Press,
Cambridge, Massachusetts, and London, England

LCCN 2016043303

ISBN 978-1-935408-88-8

Contents

CHAPTER ONE

A Guest's Gift

"No one is altogether nameless," declares the king of an island at the fringes
of the world. He means less to state a principle than to issue a command
to the stranger who has arrived, uninvited, at his court: that man must
identify himself. Yet the seafarer knows how to elude the sovereign. Once
before, on another distant island, he vanquished a more fearsome host, a
brute who killed his guests and ate them raw. That one had also demanded
that his guest name himself. To him, the voyager spoke these famous lines:
"*Outis* is my name. My father and mother call me / *Outis*, as do all the others
who are my companions."[1]

Everyone knows what happened next. The host accepted the man's
words and, in exchange for them, presented his guest with a gift of his own.
He promised he would eat *Outis* last, after finishing off each of his companions. Yet the guest kept him from keeping his word. The seafarer had
given his host wine, taken from some of the unlucky people whom he and
his men had visited. The giant host knew nothing of its powers and, overcome by what he drank, fell asleep soon after uttering his promise — or his
threat. Then the men, united in a common cause, gouged out their captor's
eye with a burning stake. Woken in agony, the once indomitable host cried
out for help. His neighbors, alarmed, rushed to the edge of his cave, asking
what had befallen him. But now the wounded giant could not see his guest,
nor could he, as he discovered, truly name him.

The mariner had anticipated the terms by which the neighbors would
offer help to their friend.[2] Incredulous, they ask: "Surely no mortal against
your will can be driving your sleep off? / Surely none can be killing you by
force or treachery?"[3] The sightless host seeks to give them an answer, but

7

even as he summons his foe's name to his friends, its two syllables fall apart. He took *Outis* to be a name like any other, which refers to an individual. In repetition, however, it sounds as neither name nor noun but indefinite pronoun, composed of two words, which must lack any referent. *Oūtis*, in the Cyclops' mouth, becomes *oú tis*, "no one." In Homeric Greek, the idiom of the hero and the giant, the pseudo-name "No One" and the pronoun "no one," *Outis* and *oú tis*, are almost identical in sound. Only a difference in accentuation separates them. It is enough to save the wily guest.

Yet there is more to the deceit of *Outis* than this shifting of accents. When the neighbors wonder whether there could be anyone doing violence to their friend, they also echo the guest's words, although they cannot know it. Two parts of speech shift in a second movement, the inverse of the first. An indefinite pronoun calls to mind a noun and name. Asking whether there is "not someone" (*mḗ tis*) doing harm to their friend, the neighbors employ an interrogative expression that is nearly indistinguishable in sound from the word *mētis*, that is, "cunning."[4] Once again, a difference of accentuation alone separates these two expressions. The visitor thus reveals himself to be worthy of his self-made mask. To the blind host who stands before him as to those who are too distant to see him, the seafarer, by the cunning of words alone, renders himself positively nameless.

The ruse combines several meanings that are, in form and force, distinct. In the simplest sense, the word — or non-word — *Outis* effectively denies two complete propositions. When the neighbors hear this term uttered by their wounded friend, they draw a valid, if erroneous, inference. They conclude that the following sentences are true: it is not the case that someone has woken their friend; it is not the case that someone is "killing" him "by force or by treachery."[5] It is as if, in response to their hypotheses, their friend had merely exclaimed: "No!" But the word or nonword *Outis* also works by a second means. It can be heard as the denial of not two statements but a single predicate. The maimed giant also suggests this much. "Good friends," he exclaims, "*Oú tis* [that is, No One] is killing me!" Those assembled outside his cave can hardly be faulted for concluding that the property of "being harmed" does not apply to him. Yet the expression can also be perceived in a further sense. *Outis* alludes to a third possibility of language: the assertion of a present lack, or a privation. There

8

is not anyone, in this sense, behind the giant's cries, the cause of his pain being missing.

Yet the meaning of the pseudonym is also simpler and more extreme. Beyond the invalidation of the proposition, the negation of the predicate and the suggestion of a privation, a fourth layer of speech may be discerned in it. It is that enclosed in the expression *oú tis* when understood, in the most literal, if barely grammatical, sense, as the refusal of the indefinite article "a" or "one": as "not-any," "not-one," or "non-one." Everything follows from this act of language, which constitutes the most minimal and extreme of affirmations, as well as the most far-reaching and excessive of negations. Long before being received at the island court and being called upon to reveal his unknown name, the guest has monstrously distorted the monarch's apparently self-evident thesis that "no one [*oú . . . tis*] is altogether nameless." Nameless because called "No One," the seafarer has shown that proposition to be both true and false. He may well, then, satisfy the king's explicit demand. He has already revealed its foundation to be insecure.

The man's response so perfectly overturns the sovereign principle of identification that one may wonder whether he did not, in fact, invent the tale of *Outis* in response to the king's insistent demand that he reveal himself. The guest, of course, presents the story of his voyages as no more than a recollection. Yet no one survives to attest to its truth or falsity, and when the man finally reveals his famous name, only he himself can judge its worth. The son of Laertes alone knows when and why he chose to twist *Odysseus* into *Outis*. What is certain is that the man of many ways claims to have accomplished a great deed: becoming positively anonymous while continuing to bear a name, if not, in fact, while bearing the dismembered parts of his own name, *Outis* being perhaps a distortion of the syllables of *Odysseus*.[6] The ingenious hero would have saved himself by a single act of speech: adding the particle "no," "not-," or "non-" (*ou*) to the indefinite pronoun "a," "one," or "someone" (*tis*). This act is simple yet profoundly perplexing in sense and effects. In it, an entire company of linguistic shadows comes loose. They are the most indeterminate of spoken beings: meanings more tenuous and more fleeting even than that of being "a" or "one," for that, precisely, they are not.

In its extreme uncertainty, the name *Outis* illustrates a fundamental rule of language. Every time the particle "not-" or "non-" is attached to a given word, the same event in speech may be discerned. One term is denied; its denotations are suppressed. Yet in that refusal, a realm of sense is also disclosed: one that has no positive designation, although it is delimited. Something is named, yet the nature of the naming remains opaque. Among the many tidings that Odysseus brings back from his twenty years of wanderings at sea, there is the news of this strange possibility of speech, which lends a word, by the most minimal of changes, an unfamiliar form. To exhaust its indefinite meanings, one would need to traverse the entire domain of signification that a given expression implicitly excludes. Perhaps a god could do it. Yet in the non-man's cave, as at the king's court, none is present.

The thinkers who came after Odysseus did not forget the lesson in naming that he taught. From Aristotle and his commentators in Greek and Arabic, in Latin and in more modern languages, to the masters of the medieval universities and their early modern successors, from Kant and Hegel to those who sought to explore the possibility of cognition after them, thinkers would return to the power that the seafarer made his own: to designate by naming "indistinctly" or "indefinitely," as Aristotle would hold, or to reason by judging "infinitely," as Kant and his followers would maintain. In many tongues, and in implicit and explicit reference to diverse grammars, philosophers would assess the power of a particle as modest as *ou, mē, lā, ghayr, nicht-,* or *non-*. In the theory of such expressions of affirmative refusal, speech and thought would find themselves at disconcerting crossings. Words, becoming non-words, seem to evoke beings that are, in themselves, barely definable; thinking, striving to catch up with the rulebound faculty of speech that always accompanies it, runs the risk of losing itself in the subtleties of grammar. But in lingering on the possibility of speaking by speaking of the *non-*, philosophers would reach many of their most far-reaching inventions. These include the doctrines of affirmation and negation, contrariety and contradiction; the theory of the types and orders of predicable properties; the concept of the merely thought "thing," in its distinction to being and non-being alike; an account of a judgment from which the possibility of absolute knowledge may be derived; and a logic of cognition in which Being itself originates in a point graspable solely as "non-nothing."

The adventures of the *non-* in philosophy deserve to be reconstructed because of their intrinsic historical importance. Yet there is also more. In their complications, their tensions and their equivocations, the theories of non-words illustrate the ways in which the facts of natural grammars may be an incitement for thinking. Speaking without being aware of the rules by which we speak, reasoning in given languages without reflecting on the logics that they imply, we are able to make use of a capacity that is obscure to us, without examining it as such. But we are also capable of bending our thinking back upon its idiom, listening to the system of constraints that our words and phrases exhibit. That is the way of *Outis*. It consists in grasping hold of a language, albeit in part and in particles, rendering its structural equivocations and consequences explicit, while putting them to a new use. If this path has long attracted thinkers, it is because it promises, in earnestness or in treachery, a major accomplishment: to cast light on the central and unsurpassable presupposition of reason, which, without knowing exactly what we name, we designate as "language." The fable of the guest's gift to his host is also exemplary in this respect. In it, no more — and no less — than an analysis of speech allows a speaker to elude captivity and death. A thinking use of grammar leads out of the cave.

Whether deception or resource, trick or treasure, the guest's gift draws on a possibility that persists, in different ways, in every language. Non-'s sense is lodged in our reason and our speech, as if in accordance with some unknown law of logic or grammar, if not both. This, too, is why it demands scrutiny, even if it threatens those who would attend to it, like the hero's foes, with the many dangers of its snares.

CHAPTER TWO

In the Voice

The book by Aristotle known today as *On Interpretation* opens with a simple but perplexing claim: there are "things in the voice [*ta en tē phōnē*]," the reader learns, that stand in need of study.[1] One might wonder about the "voice" that Aristotle evokes. What is it, one could ask, and how has it come to contain what the philosopher perceives in it? Aristotle's subsequent reflections, however, bear not on the container but its contents. His very first words suggest that he will treat the terms now called "parts of speech," for he states that he will define the "noun" or "name" (*onoma*) and the "verb" (*rhēma*). Yet he then declares that he intends to investigate four more complex beings: "negation, affirmation, statement and sentence."[2] On their own, he argues, words are signs of soundless "impressions" (*pathēmata*) made upon the soul.[3] Aristotle observes that he has explored this subject elsewhere. His reference appears to be to his psychological writings, which offer studies of sensible impressions of various kinds; yet the reader also knows that in the *Categories*, Aristotle explored the varieties of names, enumerating the ways in which things can be said to be. Now his task will be to show how it is that, from individual nouns and verbs, whole phrases can be formed. For the first time in his works on language, Aristotle will treat a fundamental question: truth and falsity. In isolation, a name or verb may signify something, but it "has no truth or falsity to it [*oute gar pseudos oute alēthes pō*]." Only when incorporated into a sentence, in "combination and division," can a "thing in the voice" be considered true or false.[4]

Sentences are to constitute the ultimate subjects of this treatise. To reach them, however, Aristotle must first clear the field of inquiry of troublesome elements of speech. There is, it seems, vocal clutter to be set aside. The philosopher begins at the beginning, offering a summary account of the types of words. Then he advances to the level of the sentence (*logos*), considered as "a significant spoken sound some part of which is significant in separation."[5] He is quick to add that not all sentences need occupy his attention, since only some of their number may be said to be either true or false. "Every sentence is significant," he reasons, "but not every sentence is a statement-making [*apophantikos*] sentence." Only in "statement-making sentences" is there truth and falsity.[6] A prayer, for instance, "is a sentence, but it is neither true or false."[7] Aristotle gives no other examples of sentences shorn of truth or falsity, but he suggests that there are many more. He points, in passing, to "rhetoric" and "poetics," which study such sentences in detail. Soon he takes a further step. He reveals that the "statement-making sentence" is a kind of genus, of which there are two species: affirmation (*kataphasis*) and negation (*apophasis*). "An affirmation is a statement affirming something of something; a negation is a statement denying something of something."[8] Aristotle thus defines the statement as the composition of two major units. The first signifies a certain thing; the second points to a property that the thing does, or does not, possess. In the terminology imposed on a long tradition by Aristotle and his successors, the statement consists of a subject and a predicate. In an affirmation, the predicate is affirmed of the subject; in a negation, the predicate is denied of it.

On Interpretation develops a theory of such predicative statements. With the *Categories*, it lays the foundation for an elaborate doctrine of the forms of argument and the possibilities of reasoned demonstration. From the *Prior Analytics* to the *Posterior Analytics* and the *Sophistical Refutations*, an entire system of deduction is constructed on the basis of the principles laid down in this discussion of "things in the voice." In time, it was to become perhaps the single most lasting and influential account of the forms of certain proof ever to be conceived. For centuries, scientific arguments advanced in the traditions deriving from Greek culture would strive to adhere to it. That the field of Aristotelian demonstration is limited becomes apparent early in this book. Implicitly, the philosopher suggests that affirmations and negations will be formulated in the present tense and in the third person. Certain types of terms, moreover, will be excluded as a rule from the phrases contained in Aristotle's proofs. The philosopher's paradigmatic demonstrations, unlike those of many of his successors, will include neither proper names, such as "Plato," "Socrates," or "Callias," nor demonstrative pronouns, such as "here," "then," "that," or "this."[9] Singular terms, in principle, cannot be parts of Aristotle's proofs.[10] Conversely, terms whose meanings are so general that they cannot be defined by more expansive properties also exceed the limits of this system.[11] There is, in other words, not only a lower but also an upper edge to Aristotle's proofs. Their argumentation must advance within the domain set out by two borders, renouncing recourse to terms that designate things that are either unique or absolutely general. Demonstration must content itself with "things in the voice" of an intermediary nature.

There is a reason for this restriction, and it follows from the aims of the system in which the theory of the statement-making sentence is a part. Aristotle's aspiration in his works on language and demonstration is to provide a doctrine of not the single phrase but the ordered sequence of related phrases; his interest, that is, lies in not the *logismos*, or "reasoning" in itself, but the *sullogismos*, syllogism, "joined reasoning," or chain of propositions. In this chain, there are, he writes, to be three predicative statements, bound together by one relation of formally necessary implication. As a first example, one may evoke the first and simplest of the syllogistic "figures" (*skhēmata*) enumerated by the philosopher. This is the form of argumentation known to the logical tradition by the name of "Barbara," and that may be exemplified by an Aristotelian reasoning on the nature of certain vegetative things: "If every broad-leafed plant is deciduous and every vine is broad-leafed, then every vine is deciduous."[12] Aristotle also proposes an abstract account of this form of deduction, in which single letters take the place of entire terms: "If A is predicated of every B, and B is predicated of every C, then A is predicated of every C."[13] Here, a single hypothetical particle ("If") and two paratactic conjunctions ("and" and "then") frame three predications: (1) A is predicated of every B; (2) B is predicated of every C; (3) A is predicated of every C.

It has been observed that "in formulating syllogisms with the help of letters, Aristotle always puts the predicate in the first place and the subject in the second. He never says 'All *B* is *A*,' but uses instead the expression '*A* is predicated of all *B*' or more often '*A* belongs to all *B*.'"[14] Were one to place the subject in the first position in the statement, one would obtain a more immediately comprehensible logical theorem: "If all *B* is *A*, and all *C* is *B*, then all *C* is *A*." Less obvious are the shifting roles that logical terms play in the three steps of this syllogism. A moment's attention suffices to observe, however, that the term that, in the first sentence, is in the place of subject (namely, *B*) passes, in the second sentence, to the place of predicate. In other words, from "every broad-leafed plant is deciduous" to "every vine is broad-leaved," the same expression — "broad-leafed" — changes logical position. This is not a curiosity of the first syllogistic figure but a constant in this type of classical reasoning. Each of the three forms of Aristotelian deduction demands such a variety of displacement; there is always one term that must appear first as a subject and, later, as a predicate.[15] Such movements, however, come at a price. The terms included in syllogisms must, by nature, be neutral with respect to their possible positions, in the sense that they must be able to function both as subjects and as predicates. Homogeneity between subject and predicate is a formal necessity.[16]

From this principle, one may infer the rule that dictates that singular and absolutely general terms must be excluded from the field of proof. A proper name, such as "Socrates," may appear as the subject of a statement, as when one asserts, "Socrates possesses wisdom." Yet the proper name of Plato's teacher may not function as a predicate. One cannot claim that the property of being "Socrates" belongs to any class of beings, because the proper name, by nature, designates an individual, rather than some characteristic shared by many things. This is also why expressions of exceptional generality must lie beyond the domain of syllogistic reasoning. "Substance," for example, might be considered to be a term of this kind. Although it may be predicated of anything that exists, "substance" cannot easily be defined with respect to some greater idea of which it would be a species. By definition, a highest genus cannot exhibit features more general than itself, and one therefore has no ground to transfer such a term, in a deduction, from the position of predicate to that of subject. Like proper names, the designations of the most universal of things must therefore exceed the reach of ordered "statement-making sentences."

When Aristotle sets out to consider what is "in the voice" in *On Interpretation*, his aim is to account for the ways in which words may enter into predicative assertions that respect such formal limitations. At first glance, the difference between nouns (or names) and verbs might appear to pose certain difficulties for his theory, for a simple reason: in the symbolic form in which Aristotle presents the types of syllogistic reasoning, the terms in the position of subject and predicate are all nouns, or adjectives easily transformable into nouns when necessary. "Broad-leafed plant" and "deciduous" are both susceptible to being treated as the subjects of sentences; one may assert either that "every broad-leafed plant" possesses a certain quality, or that "every deciduous plant" exhibits a certain property. One might consider verbs, however, to be of a fundamentally different nature. In the statement, "Every man walks," for instance, one may discern a subject ("every man") and a predicate ("walks"); but the predicate is not of such a kind as to be immediately convertible, in English or in classical Greek, into a subject. Our grammar forbids us from forming a sentence in which "walks" would, in turn, become the subject of the verb, for (barring discourse about terms placed in quotation marks) one cannot say: "Every walks is. . . ."

Aristotle suggests a solution to this problem, arguing that the grammatical asymmetry of noun and verb belies a logical homogeneity. "There is no difference," he argues, "between saying 'a man walks' [*anthrōpon badizei*] and 'a man is walking' [*anthrōpon badizonta einai*]."[17] Then it is but a step to a second glossing, which may be taken to be logically equivalent to the first, even if its grammatical form would appear to be distinct. "A man is walking" can be understood to be synonymous with the statement "a man is a walking thing," or the predicative claim, "a man is something that walks." In his *Metaphysics*, Aristotle repeats this argument. "There is no difference between 'a man is ailing' and 'a man ails,' nor between 'a man is walking' (or 'cutting') and 'a man walks' (or 'cuts'); and similarly in the other cases."[18] Beneath apparent grammatical diversity, there is, therefore, an identity of thought content that the philosopher brings to light. Once again, "a man ails" may be taken as synonymous with "a man is ailing" and, by extension, "a man is a thing that ails," just as "a man cuts" can be taken as shorthand for "a man is cutting" and "a man is a cutting thing." Through this analysis, two-term assertions can be rewritten as three-term ones. A sentence composed of a noun and a verb can be rephrased as one with two nouns, linked by the joining verb, or "copula," "is."[19] Within the noun-verb phrase, Aristotle, in short, locates a structure of tacit predication. Even where there appears to be only a subject and a verb, two terms lie concealed. One is the subject; the other is the predicate. A "statement-making sentence" may be present in implicit as well as explicit form.

In considering the varieties of subjects and predicates, however, Aristotle encounters a perplexing phenomenon of speech. He observes that there are some things "in the voice" for which there exists no name: anonymous beings, which he will soon succeed in naming. To recover the conditions of their appearance, one must recall the treatise's argument. In the second chapter of *On Interpretation*, Aristotle distinguishes nouns, verbs, and conjunctions from "the inarticulate noises [*agrammatoi psophoi*] of beasts." He notes that whereas linguistic sounds are significant "by convention," animal cries are meaningful "by nature."[20] He adds that, within the field of spoken sounds, one may divide the class of nouns (or names) into the simple, such as "boat," and the complex, such as "pirate-boat." If one examines these expressions closely, one will observe that both are composite in character, in that they consist of a multitude of lesser sounds. Yet there is a notable difference between them. Whereas the parts of complex designations (such as the units "pirate" and "boat") are meaningful in isolation, the parts of simple names have no significance in themselves.[21] One may ask after the nature of the "part" (*meros*) that Aristotle here evokes. His argument seems to hold both for individual syllables and for those "smallest parts of the voice" that the ancient grammarians would define as "letters."[22] Without lingering on these details, however, Aristotle passes from names to verbs. In his third chapter, he presents the verb as similar in meaning to the name, while manifesting a supplementary feature: that of signifying a certain time, or, as the scholars of language would later say, exhibiting a tense.[23]

Yet Aristotle now makes an unexpected concession. He admits that there are certain expressions that defy the analysis that he proposes: words that would appear to be names and verbs and yet that cannot be viewed as either one or the other. His example for the class of names is the queer term "not-man" or "non-man" (*ouk anthrōpos*). There is no reason to assume that such an expression was any more customary in Aristotle's language than it is today in English. The question of the reasons that prompt the philosopher to summon it, therefore, is difficult to answer. Evoking the expression "non-man," Aristotle comments: "It is not a name, nor is there any correct name for it. It is neither a phrase nor a negation. Let us call it an indefinite name [*onoma aoriston*]."[24] Aristotle's reasoning is worth unfolding. He first suggests that one might consider the strange term "non-man" to be a name. Perhaps this is because "non-man" does not belong to either of the two parts of speech that Aristotle posits, in addition to names, in *On Interpretation*. "Non-man" is not a particle (*syndesmos*), for it will not bind two words, as would a conjunction or a preposition; nor may it be considered a verb, for it fails to signify any "time," not being tensed. Nonetheless, Aristotle's first point is clear: "non-man" is no name. Such a consideration might lead one to view "non-man" as shorthand for a statement of negation, if one takes into account three grammatical features of the ancient Greek language in which Aristotle wrote his work. First, a subject, if implied, need not be explicitly stated; second, one may construct a full sentence by purely nominal means, simply by joining subject and predicate, without any mention of the verb "to be"; and, third, in the absence of a single word for the indefinite article in ancient Greek, the sense of the English word "a" can be implicit where its presence is not explicitly marked. Aristotle's first public might have taken the utterance "not-man" to abbreviate a complete sentence, such as "[He is] not [a] man," or "[It is] not [a] man." Aristotle, however, also expressly excludes this interpretation: "not-man" or "non-man," he states, "is neither a phrase nor a negation." Yet, after having asserted that "non-man is not a name [*to de ouk anthrōpos ouk onoma*]," he corrects himself, declaring this expression to be some variety of name, for which there is no "correct name," and which he now distinguishes by virtue of being "indeterminate" or "indefinite" (*aoriston*).[25]

The reader of *On Interpretation* soon learns that such indefiniteness is not restricted to the field of names. In the chapter of his treatise dedicated to verbs, Aristotle calls to mind similar expressions, writing: "'non-recovers' [*oukh' hygainei*] and 'non-ails' [*ou kamnei*] I do not call verbs. For though they additionally signify time and always hold of something, yet there is a difference — for which there is no name. Let us call them indefinite verbs [*aoriston rhēma*]."²⁶ Once more, the reader might be forgiven for taking such utterances as "non-recovers" (which might also translated as "not-recovers") and "non-ails" (or "not-ails") as verbs, for they are manifestly neither particles nor nouns, and Aristotle has not allowed for any parts of speech beyond these three. The philosopher also admits that such terms, while functioning to designate, do "additionally signify time," making of them verbs of a kind. Yet they exhibit a "difference" (*diaphora*) for which "there is," he repeats, "no name." Speakers of Greek might again take such utterances, despite their brevity, as phrases; "non-recovers" or "not-recovers," for example, might well be a complete sentence, which one might render into English as "[He] does not recover," and the Greek "non-ails" or "not-ails" might be taken to be synonymous with "[He] does not ail." Yet it appears that Aristotle has a different interpretation in mind. Even as he treated "non-man" as a single "indefinite name," so he now advances that "non-recovers" (or "not-recovers") and "non-ails" (or "not-ails") are examples of a category of speech that has yet to be discerned: that of the indeterminate or "indefinite verb."

There are several ways to address the difficulties raised by such terms. The simplest would be to ask about their sense, or — to evoke a term whose form reflects the question it is to name — their non-sense. One could, in other words, examine Aristotle's language, and the languages that we still, at least in part, employ today, posing a simple question. Under what conditions may one call anything a "non-man"? What does one mean in speaking of "non-healing" and "non-ailing"? This would be to take the path of grammatical inquiry. Another possibility is to put such questions to Aristotle himself. For what reason does he take such terms to be remarkable? One may recall that the aim of *On Interpretation* is hardly "interpretative" in any narrow sense, and the examples of indefinite words Aristotle offers are not citations of any identifiable discourse. If such expressions matter to him, one might surmise, it is for reasons pertaining to the architecture of his doctrine. Noting that the ultimate object of this work is the "statement-making sentence," one could wager that the indefinite name and verb are best situated in the theory of proof that Aristotle means to found.

Perhaps expressions such as "non-man" and "non-heals" are to be elements in a system containing statements of many types, some of which will involve indefinite terms. The argument seems plausible, but Aristotle's own books would appear to belie it. Soon after Aristotle names the unnamed name and the unnamed verb, he sets them aside. When, in his more advanced works on demonstration, he presents the forms of valid reasoning, he offers many examples of statements embedded in three-part syllogisms; but those statements, as a rule, include no indefinite expressions.[27] The Aristotelian branches of philosophy respect this limitation. Neither the philosopher's biology nor his astronomy, neither his doctrine of the virtues nor his theory of the natural world appears to bear, in any major way, on things namable solely by non-names and non-verbs. It is all the more remarkable, for this reason, that in his book on what is "in the voice," Aristotle should have drawn such attention to these designations. It seems that he found something to be pondered in the words to which, for the sake of his new science, he was soon to bid farewell. He summoned their indefiniteness to the ear and to the mind, even if he could not dispel it, as if anticipating that it would linger yet.

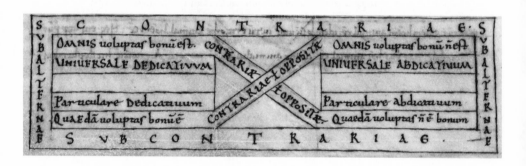

Apuleian Square of Opposition, ninth
century (University of Pennsylvania
Libraries, Lawrence J. Schoenberg
Collection, LJS 101, fol 54v).

CHAPTER THREE

Square Necessities

A reader of *On Interpretation* might well anticipate that Aristotle's first treatment of indefinite terms would also be his last. Yet long after their appearance and disappearance has receded from view, words such as "non-man" and "non-ails" return in the philosopher's first book on sentences. Having discussed the name and verb in isolation, Aristotle offers an account of their combinations in the affirmation and the negation, proposing certain principles that he takes to be fundamental in valid reasoning. He explains that where an affirmation and a negation bear on the same subject, considered with respect to the same predicate, they enter into the relationship of contradiction (*antiphasis*). "For every affirmation, there is an opposite negation; for every negation, there is an opposite affirmation. Let us call an affirmation and a negation which are opposite a contradiction."[1] Appealing to the rule of thinking that would in the modern age be called "the principle of bivalence," Aristotle stipulates that whenever a statement, whether affirmative or negative, bears on general subjects belonging to the past or present, it must necessarily be either true or false.[2] Next he formulates the related principle that would later be known as the "law of the excluded middle": where two statements are contradictory among themselves, "it is always necessary for one to be true and the other to be false."[3] Having established these basic points, Aristotle concedes, however, that contradiction is not always easily identifiable, for speech contains several varieties of opposition. Misled by language, one might take one kind of contrariety for another.

To ward off the possibility of confusion, Aristotle offers a systematic account of the relations that obtain between opposing sentences. His discussion was to constitute a crucial chapter in the history of the theory of the statement. By late antiquity, it acquired a fixed shape. The principles of *On Interpretation* were to be projected, for the purposes of teaching, onto the surface of an imagined square. The earliest recorded account of this geometrical figure dates from the second century CE, when the teachings of Aristotle were transmitted in a simple and abbreviated form. A Latin treatise, *On Interpretation*, traditionally attributed to the rhetorician and poet Apuleius of Madaura, proposes a simple paradigm for the predicative statement: "Every pleasure is good" (*Omnis voluptas bonum est*). Following Aristotle, the Roman author observes that one may relate this assertion to three others: "Every pleasure is not good" (*Omnis voluptas bonum non est*); "Some pleasure is good" (*Quaedam voluptas bonum est*); "Some pleasure is not good" (*Quaedam voluptas bonum non est*). He then comments:

> Now it is time to discuss how those four propositions are related to one another — and it is useful to consider them in a squared figure. So, as is written below, let there be affirmative and negative universals on the top line, e.g., "Every pleasure is good," "Every pleasure is not good." These may be said to be inconsistent [*incongruae*] with one another. Likewise on the bottom line, under each of them, let the particulars be written, e.g., "Some pleasure is good," "Some pleasure is not good." These may be said to be nearly equal to one another. Then let the oblique angular lines be drawn, one stretching from the universal dedicative to the particular abdicative, the other from the particular dedicative to the universal abdicative. Those [pairs of propositions], which are opposite to one another in both quantity and quality, may be called alternates [*alterutrae*], because it is indeed necessary that one or the other be true, which is said to be a complete and total conflict.[4]

The late antique author's "squared figure" exhibits several noteworthy traits. In each of its four right angles, a predicative assertion is to be inscribed. The two upper vertices will contain two universal statements: that is, two sentences bearing on a subject qualified by the determiner "every." "Every pleasure is good" will be written in the upper left, and "Every pleasure is not good" in the upper right. The two lower vertices of the square exhibit statements that will be considered to be "particular" in the sense that they bear on an indeterminate quantity of subjects, a quantity to be designated by the determiner "some." The sentence, "Some pleasure is good," will be inscribed in the lower left corner, and "Some pleasure is not good" will then be written to its right. The horizontal lines of the square will thus trace a movement in quality, from "is" (*est*) to "is not" (*non est*), or, in other words, from affirmation to negation. The vertical lines of the square will convey a passage in quantity: from universal to particular, that is, from "every" (*omnis*) to "some" (*quaedam*).

The Greek and Latin traditions, as they are preserved today, contain no earlier example of such a square of logical opposition. Galen's *Institutio logica*, a handbook contemporaneous with the Roman *On Interpretation*, presents similar teachings; but in it, the geometrical figure is lacking.[5] There are certainly points of detail and terminology that distinguish the theory of the Latin *On Interpretation* from that presented in Aristotle's distant model. Whereas the Greek philosopher speaks of "affirmation" and "negation," the Roman calls to mind "dedicative" and "abdicative" "propositions."[6] Moreover, as a universal negative statement, Aristotle proposed a sentence of the form: "No pleasure is good." The Roman author maintains that the universal negative statement exhibits a different structure: "Every pleasure is not good." What may be most consequential is that the Roman author recasts the grammatical form of the particular negative statement that is inscribed in the square's bottom right corner, thus deciding, to a large degree, on the logical syntax by which it would be subsequently known. Where Aristotle would have written, "Not some pleasure is good," Apuleius suggests instead "Some pleasure is not good."[7] Nonetheless, the Roman square illustrates the fundamental lineaments of the Aristotelian doctrine, and the quadrilateral figure attributed to Apuleius was to become a standard element in the instruction of philosophy for centuries to come.

Later it would become common practice to assign to each vertex of the square a single letter, drawn from the vowels of the Latin words *affirmo* and *nego*, "I state" and "I deny." Moving from left to right and from top to bottom, one would then read four alphabetic symbols: A, E, I, and O. The relations that hold between sentences could be written, in abbreviated form, as correspondences between letters. For the link exhibited by the vertical lines tying A and I, on the one hand, and E and O, on the other,

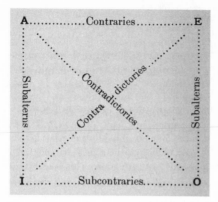

A .... Contraries .... E

Subalterns

Contradictories

Contra

Subalterns

I .... Subcontraries .... O

Square of Opposition, from John Neville Keynes, *Studies and Exercises in Formal Logic* (London: MacMillan & Co., 1884).

the philosophers of the Latin tradition would speak of "subalternation." They would argue that, in each case, a lower or "subaltern" sentence, such as I or O, is true if the corresponding higher or "superaltern," such as A or E, is also true; furthermore, they would reason, if the superaltern is true, the subaltern, too, must also be true. For the relation exhibited by the two diagonals — A and O on the one hand, and E and I on the other — philosophers would speak of "contradiction." Of each such pairs of sentences, one must be true and one must be false. These are, in Roman terms, the two sets of "alternate" propositions in a relation of "complete and total conflict." Finally, it would be maintained that the horizontal lines of the square represent relations between two logical varieties of contrariety (*enantiōsis*, or *oppositio contraria*). A and E would be considered "contrary" sentences in the narrow sense, while I and O would rather be qualified as "subcontraries." It would be said that by nature, two contraries cannot both be true, although they may both be false. Symmetrically, one would add, two subcontraries cannot both be false, although they may both be true.[8]

There can be little doubt that this geometrical figure possesses one pedagogical virtue: it renders the logical relation of contradiction unmistakable to the eye. A glance at the square's lines suffices to identify the special variety of opposition that defines the two contrasting statements of which only one is true and only one is false — and to observe that this opposition holds solely between sentences linked by the shape's diagonals. To this degree, the diagram proposed in the Roman treatise well serves to present the teachings contained in Aristotle's *On Interpretation*. But the geometrical figure is also faithful to its distant source in a less obvious sense. If contradiction is readily identifiable on its reasoned surface, it is because of its difference with respect to contrariety and subcontrariety. Contradiction, in other words, emerges from a background of other oppositions. Necessity may well dictate, as Aristotle maintains, that for every affirmation, there is a corresponding negation, and that for every negation, there is a corresponding affirmation. The figure's four lines suggest that such necessities presuppose a further principle, which remains unspoken. Contradiction, to be immediately intelligible, requires the definition of contrariety. Visibly, if silently, the horizontal beams support the two diagonals.

This fact is troubling to the theory of the predicative statement, for a simple reason that is nowhere exhibited on the surface of this square: contrariety is a concept far more difficult to master than contradiction. One may well consider the sentences "Every pleasure is good" and "Every pleasure is not good" to be exemplary contraries, if one defines them, as does Aristotle, as two sentences that cannot both be true. One may also concede, with the Greek philosopher, that there is a different but related form of opposition linking two sentences that cannot both be false, that is, the "subcontraries" I and O: in the Roman square, "Some pleasure is good" and "Some pleasure is not good." Nonetheless, there are also more obscure types of contrariety. Even if one accepts the constraints of the Aristotelian exercise and refuses to introduce any fundamentally new terms into the exemplary predicative assertions, one can summon a type of opposition that is absent from the square. To do so, one need interfere neither with the movement in quantity from "every" to "some" nor with the passage in quality from affirmation to negation. A simpler act suffices to evoke a contrariety on which the Roman logician does not linger. One need only introduce a "non-" or "not-" (non-) before subjects and predicates. For example, one may place "non-" or "not-" before the term "pleasure" and the term "good." Then one will produce two new, if perplexing, contraries of the sentence "Every pleasure is good": "Every non-pleasure is good" and "Every pleasure is non-good."

A reader of Aristotle's *On Interpretation* might have expected the ancient philosopher to deny the sense of such predicative statements, or to say nothing of them, even if they are grammatically admissible in Greek. Aristotle's initial remarks on indefinite names and verbs seem to be conclusive. Yet several chapters later, the philosopher's argument takes a new turn. Appearing to restate a point already proposed and defended, he observes: "Now, an affirmation signifies something about something, this last being either a name, or a non-name [or 'not-name']; and what is affirmed must be one thing about one thing."[9] As if to explain the curious term "non-name" (*to anōnymon*), Aristotle adds: "Names and non-names have already been discussed. For I do not call 'non-man' a name but an indefinite name — for what it signifies is in a way one thing, but indefinite — just as I do not call 'non-recover' [or 'not-recovers or 'does-not-recover'] a verb, but an indefinite verb."[10] Without underlining the fact, Aristotle now specifies that an affirmation may bear on indefinite as well as definite predicates. Yet lest the point be lost on his readership, he continues: "Every affirmation and negation consists of a name and a verb, or an indefinite name and a verb."[11] That is a new proposition in the argument of the treatise, and Aristotle, as if aware of the bewilderment it might provoke, hastens to offer some examples. He explains that the sentence "Man is just" has its negation in its contradictory: "Man is not just." Yet "Man is just" also has a contrary in the sentence "Man is non-just," a sentence that, in turn, has its own contradictory in the statement: "Man is not non-just."

Aristotle explains the matter further in Book I of the *Prior Analytics*. "In establishing or refuting," he then writes, "it makes some difference whether we suppose the expressions 'not to be this' and 'to be non-this' are identical or different in meaning, e.g., 'not to be white' and 'to be non-white.'"[12] As if anticipating the perplexity of his readers, he settles the question: "They do not mean the same thing, nor is 'to be non-white' the negation of 'to be white,' for that is 'not to be white.'"[13] Chapter 10 of *On Interpretation* contains a systematic classification and enumeration of the correlated sentences that illustrate this principle. After having propounded the theses from which the Roman author would draw his square diagram, Aristotle furnishes the elements of another order of related predicative statements. It has been observed that they compose a second set of propositional relations, which may also be projected onto a figure: a square of logical negation.[14]

Again, four predicative assertions will be inscribed in four vertices. "Man is just" will be written the position of A, in the upper left corner. To its right, one can then notate E, its contrary: "Man is non-just." In the lower left corner, one can then place I: "Man is not non-just." To its right, finally, one will find O, its contrary: "Man is not just." Once again, two "oblique angular lines" will draw out two relations of contradiction: "Man is just" (A) has its contradictory in "Man is not just" (O); "Man is non-just" (E) has its contradictory in "Man is not non-just" (I). Contrariety, a second time, will be exhibited by the square's two horizontal lines. Yet the truth is that the possibilities of contrariety are more numerous and more polymorphic than such a square of negation would suggest. The reason is simple: one may also place "not" or "non" before the subject, in addition to the predicate. Then, as Aristotle explains, one obtains more predicative statements. Indefiniteness begins to flower. Once one admits "non-names" in the position of subject and predicate, a total of six sentences can be formed: "Man is non-just," "Man is not non-just," "Non-man is just," "Non-man is not just," "Non-man is not-just," and "Non-man is not non-just."

One might object that in such developments, Aristotle's clarity of reasoning is equaled only by the obscurity of his paradigmatic statements. For what, exactly, does the sentence "Non-man is not non-just" mean? Aristotle offers no answer to this question, and for a reason. His aim is not to explain the meaning of such an assertion on its own but to establish its relations to the other statements that variously oppose it. He concentrates, therefore, on the regularities of sense that contrasting sentences will exhibit by virtue of their logical structure. He continues to argue for the distinction between contradiction and contrariety, enjoining the reader not to mistake negation for the affirmation of an indefinite predicate. "*A* is not *B*" must not be confused with "*A* is non-*B*"; the statement "Man is not just" must not be mistaken, in other words, for "Man is non-just." Their difference comes to light when one compares the statement "Man is just" to "Man is non-just," or "Non-man is just."

Between the truth conditions of such sentences, a relation may be observed. An affirmation of an indefinite predicate, such as "Man is non-just" (*S is non-P*) implies the truth of what one might call its "propositional contrary," that is, the negation, "Man is not just" (*S is not P*). As Aristotle explains in the *Prior Analytics*, "If it is true to say 'it is non-white,' it is true to say 'it is not white'; for it is impossible that a thing should simultaneously be white and be non-white; consequently, if the affirmation does not belong, the denial must belong."[15] The converse, however, does not hold. From the denial that a thing possesses a definite property, one may not derive the affirmation of the correspondingly indefinite property, since one cannot be certain that, if "It is not white," then "It is non-white," or "It is not non-white." According to the "subaltern" relation of contraries, a thing may be neither "white" nor "non-white," yet it cannot possess both such properties at once. Lawrence Horn has noted that this distinction between the consequences of not possessing a property and possessing a non-property, in addition to being in itself "insightful and internally consistent," has been echoed often in modern attempts to grasp the order of natural languages, from Jespersen's distinction between "nexal negation" (*not happy*) and "special negation" (*unhappy*) to Von Wright's opposition of "weak" negation, which implies a contradictory, and "strong" negation, which implies a contrary, and "Jackendorff's semantic revision of Klima's categories of sentential vs. constituent negation."[16]

Following Aristotle, the classical Roman square of logical opposition, articulated in its four propositions of "Every ... is," "No ... is," "Some ... is" and "Some is not ... ," refrains from offering a full account of indefinite predicative assertions. The contrarieties that such sentences exhibit are both simpler and more obscure than those exhibited on the classical square, which limits itself to contrasting such statements as "Every ... is" and "No ... is," and "Some is ... " and "Some ... is not." One might argue that indefinite properties, being producible by the mere affixation of a *non-* to subject or to predicate, constitute the source of a contrariety so simple that the philosopher need hardly consider them in detail. Yet the minimalism of the "non-" or "not-" (*ou* or *non*) conceals a logical question of great magnitude. What is the exact nature of the relation between such statements as "Some pleasure is good" and "Some pleasure is non-good," or between "Some non-pleasure is good" and "Some non-pleasure is non-good"? It cannot be negation, as Aristotle declares. "It is clear," he writes in the *Prior Analytics*, "that 'it is non-good' is not the negation of 'it is good.'"[17] The negation would be "It is not good." There then remains the question of what exactly the predicate "non-good" may mean and, more generally, of what relation a predicative statement bears to the contraries that indefinitely oppose it.

Matters would be simpler were it possible, for the purposes of reasoning, to set aside all indefinite terms, be they "names" or "verbs." Beyond the theory of contrariety and contradiction, however, such expressions return again in this doctrine of the statement-making sentence. As evidence, it suffices to consider the rules that logicians treat as principles of "obversion." These rules dictate that from statements of the kinds exhibited on the square of opposition, one may draw certain inferences, such that the truth of consequent will follow necessarily from that of the antecedent. From a proposition such as "Every pleasure is good," one may infer the proposition "No pleasure is non-good": from a universal affirmative (A), one may, that is, derive a universal negative (E). In the same way, one may infer a universal affirmative (A) from a universal negative (E), since from the statement, "No pleasure is evil," one may deduce this fact: "Every pleasure is non-evil." One can also treat particular or "indefinite" propositions in such a manner, at least if one admits a restricted interpretation of "some," meaning "some, but not all." If it is true that only "some pleasure is good," then it is also true that "some pleasure is non-good"; if it is the case that only "some pleasure is non-good," then it is the case that "some pleasure is good."[18] Such "immediate consequences" reveal the existence of hidden links tying statements with definite terms to statements with indefinite ones.[19] Any clear separation between the two forms, therefore, grows uncertain. Even where sentences bearing on such subjects as "non-pleasure," "non-man" and "non-just" would appear to be absent, statements about such indefinite terms may still legitimately be inferred.

Despite his recurrent attention to such varieties of speech in his work on words, statements, truth, and the forms of certain proof, Aristotle retreats from proposing a full analysis of indefinite terms. Strictly speaking, he advances only a single affirmative thesis about them. It is striking that he does so almost as an afterthought and in passing. "What an indefinite name [or noun] signifies," he writes, "is, in some manner, a single thing" (*hen gar sēmainei kai to aoriston*).[20] Aristotle offers no evidence in support of this claim, nor does he provide a commentary upon it. This principle appears as something like an axiom in his argument, allowing him to include such terms as "non-man," "non-just," "non-ails," and "non-recovers" in a theory from which they might otherwise have been excluded. That the indefinite term signifies something, and that the "something" in question is, "in some manner," one, remains a decisive yet obscure postulate, which ushers into this doctrine a logical matter whose exact nature is far from clear. It is telling that the name given by Aristotle to such terms seems to illustrate the very difficulty it must designate. The attribute "indefinite" (*aoriston*) is almost indefinite in form. One might wager that it constitutes a name for the "non-definite": some contrary of the definite, which does not, however, entail its negation.

The truth is that in *On Interpretation*, the word "indefinite" constitutes less the name of a concept than the index of a difficulty, which troubles the theory of terms, sentences, and the regularities of truth and falsity that are to hold between forms of stated opposition. As a double of the name and verb that compose the statement, as an undefined variation of the contrariety illustrated on the square of opposition, as an uncertain term in a consequent, which is derivable from the simplest antecedent, the indefinite term — whether noun or verb, non-subject or non-predicate — exhibits the same impenetrability. It certainly cannot be placed outside the domain of rational language, like animal noises, which are significant by nature; nor can it be excluded, like the prayer and the exclamation, from the field of utterances that philosophy, being concerned with true sayings, takes into account. Indefinite expressions therefore appear and reappear in Aristotle's theory, being the witnesses to a possibility of speech that he neither fully integrates nor altogether excludes. The philosopher, of course, was not the first to have noted the indeterminacy of such words. Centuries before he evoked the difficulty of defining the meaning of an expression as "non-man," a nameless bard had sung of the glory and the cunning of a man of many ways, who, to save his life, knew to name himself "non-one," "not one," or "no one." Odysseus, as every Greek well knew, had truncated his own name and twisted it into *Outis*. In listening attentively to what is in the voice, however, Aristotle made of that strange mask the subject of a new question for thinking. Drawing out the troubling consequences of the existence of non-words, he became the first to name the indefiniteness that he heard, to transcribe it and to interpret it. He was not to be the last.

CHAPTER FOUR

Varieties of Indefiniteness

The place of indefinite names and verbs in Aristotle's doctrine of language is modest, yet it is precisely defined. When the philosopher calls to mind such expressions as "non-man" and "non-just," it is to clarify related logical matters, such as the theory of contradiction and the types of contrariety, and to account for the relations among well-formed statements. Aristotle's followers were long to respect this delimitation of the spoken indefinite. In Greek and, later, in Syriac, Arabic, Hebrew, and Latin, they evoked such terms above all in the theory of the predicative statement. Thanks to their labors, indefinite terms would acquire a definite position on the squares of logical opposition and in the principles that they were to illustrate. Behind the systematic inquiry into the regularities of logical form, however, there lurked a persistent question: what does it mean for a term to be "indefinite"? Aristotle's word for this uncertain state is *aoriston*, which can be opposed to *horismenos*, as "limitless," "boundless," or "unenclosed," may be distinguished from "limited," "bounded," and "enclosed." It is perhaps in this sense that Thucydides recounted that the Athenians accused the Megarians of "pushing their cultivation into . . . unenclosed land on the border," or, as Hobbes has it, "having tilled . . . ground unset out with bounds"; the territory designated as "unenclosed," or "unset out with bounds," in Greek, is *aoriston*.[1] It is certain that, when Aristotle employs this expression, he summons the "indeterminate" condition of being without any perceptible boundary. Yet the vanishing of a contour brings several possibilities into view.

Aristotle's works furnish precious tools for the definition of the indefinite. They are not all present in the treatise on sentences in which indefinite names and verbs come fleetingly to light, but if one considers the Aristotelian corpus as a whole, a set of regular distinctions may be discerned. Long ago, H. A. Wolfson proposed a luminous reconstruction of the Aristotelian typology of absent things.[2] He showed that one may distinguish among three types of logical terms in the philosopher's works, which would seem to imply three conditions of non-being. There are, first, the expressions employed in "negation" (*apophasis*), in the sense that Aristotle gives to this term. This is the denial that a certain predicate may be attributed to some subject, or, metaphysically stated, that a certain property belongs to some substance. To evoke an Aristotelian sentence discussed in detail by Aristotle's greatest early commentator, Alexander of Aphrodisias, in the late second or early third century, one may take the following utterance as exemplary of such "negation": "The wall does not see [*oukh' horai*]." In this case, the verbal predicate, "seeing," is denied to the nominal subject, "the wall," and the sign of the negation is the word "not" (*oukh*), placed before the predicate.[3]

Such statements of negation may be distinguished from assertions including terms that express a "privation" (*sterēsis*). A corresponding example of such a statement may be simply given: "The blind man does not see [*oukh' horai*]."[4] In its grammatical shape, such a predicate is indistinguishable from that attributed to the wall; but for Aristotle, a fundamental logical and metaphysical difference separates them. The not seeing of the wall is "negative" in structure; the not seeing of the blind man, by contrast, is "privative." The negative term signifies the absence of a certain property in a subject, even where that subject would never be expected to possess it. It is in this sense that one may assert that the wall "does not see," without suggesting that the situation might be otherwise. The privative term does more; it suggests that the subject has been "deprived" of some attribute that it might also have possessed.[5] In this case, one asserts, in other words, that a property is positively "lacking."[6] A privative predicate, unlike a negative one, can therefore be affirmed of a being only if one might also attribute to it the corresponding contrary predicate, that is, its "possession" (*hexis*, *habitus*, "habit" or "having"). As Aristotle explains, "*privation* and *possession* are spoken of in connection with the same thing, for example sight and blindness in connection with the eye."[7]

"Indefinite" terms would seem to point toward a third sort of non-determination, distinct from negation as well as privation. Were one to hold to the philosopher's example of "seeing," "not seeing," and "blindness" to designate respectively a property, its negation, and its privation, a correspondingly indefinite expression would take the form of an attribute such as "non-seeing" or "non-blind." Where exactly one ought to situate such indefinite terms with respect to negative and privative expressions, however, is less than clear. Aristotle fails to provide a comprehensive analysis of these three types of variously "negative" terms, and certain important problems, as a consequence, remain unsolved. Reconstructing the philosopher's doctrine of these three related terms, Wolfson pointedly remarked: "The question may therefore be raised whether according to Aristotle the term 'not-seeing' [or 'non-seeing'] could be predicated of a wall."[8]

Matters are complicated by the fact that one cannot know with certainty, from the mere form of a word, whether it is negative or privative. The distinctions of logic and grammar may diverge. Aristotle is well aware that some privative expressions seem stamped, in their morphology, by an indubitable sign of their sense. The alpha that he named "privative" constitutes one example of this apparent correspondence between logical status and word structure, for where an alpha is attached to a Greek expression, it often signifies that some substance or attribute is unexpectedly lacking. In a similar way, the English language possesses the privative nominal suffix "-*less*." Words such as "toothless," "headless," or "homeless" evoke absences belonging only to subjects that might possess, in principle, the corresponding contrary traits. Only a mouth that could contain teeth can be "toothless"; only an animal endowed with a head may be "headless"; only a being who may lay claim to some residence can be "homeless." Yet there are also certain terms that would seem positive in form and yet that name privations; examples in English include the words "blind," "deaf," and "bald." In this respect, the ancient Greek language is no different from our own. It furnishes no unequivocal criterion for deciding whether a given word expresses a negative or privative attribute.

To these difficulties, the philosopher adds those entailed by the fact that absence comes in many kinds, all of which leave their traces on words. In his *Metaphysics*, Aristotle makes clear that the blindness of a man is but the first variety of privation. There are far more complex cases. Take the blindness of the mole, an animal "deprived of sight in a different sense"; while the species in question is lacking in vision, the genus to which it belongs does, as a rule, have the ability to see. Even within the sphere of human sightlessness, Aristotle adds, privation is of several types. "One is not blind at any and every age, but only if one has not sight at the age at which one would normally have it," or if one lacks it in the circumstances in which one would have been expected to possess it.[9]

There are further subtleties in the names of missing properties. Aristotle comments that a man who is said to be "footless" may, in fact, have one or two feet; their "imperfection" may suffice for him to be said to be as if "without" them. Similarly, "a privative term may be employed because the thing at issue has little of the attribute," or because what it does have of it is of a poor quality. Something may be called "indivisible" not only because it truly cannot be divided, but also because it cannot "easily be divided or divided well."[10] Yet Aristotle also concedes that the names of privation are more polymorphic than this initial summary would suggest. Sometimes it is not what has little of a certain attribute but rather what has none of it that is said to be "deprived" of it; in this sense, "it is not the one-eyed man but he who is sightless who is called blind."[11] In his *Metaphysics*, Aristotle offers an extended account of the matter, going so far as to propose an enumeration of four distinct senses in which one speaks of privation. It is striking that, in this list, only one meaning corresponds to the kind of privation that Aristotle opposes to negation in his works on the logic of terms.[12] Most startling, however, is that as soon as the philosopher completes his classification, he adds that, in truth, it is incomplete. "There are just as many kinds of privations as there are of words with negative prefixes," he comments, leaving the matter unresolved.[13]

Throughout his discussion of privative and negative expressions, Aristotle makes no mention of indefinite terms, either by name or by example. One can only wonder where exactly he would situate their specific variety of non-determination. What is lacking to the "non-man"? What may one deny to his imaginable non-qualities? The least one may conclude is that the logical and metaphysical distinctions that Aristotle proposes, however clear in principle, prove difficult to untangle in the field of speech. One might also infer that the "non-determination" that marks the indefinite seems itself curiously resistant to definition.

Naming is another matter. Within a generation of Aristotle, the terms that had once been "anonymous" and to which *On Interpretation* gave a new and obscure technical designation were to receive another. Theophrastus of Eresus, Aristotle's successor at the Lyceum, advanced a new expression for the terms for which his teacher had used the word "indefinite." Today, Theophrastus's works survive solely in fragments, but among the remaining sources, several texts testify to the same terminological invention. Pseudo-Magentius records that while Aristotle employed the word *aoriston* for statements containing a term such as "non-man," his followers had a different habit. The propositions that "Aristotle himself called 'indefinite'" would come to be known, "by his pupils and those associated with Theophrastus," as "transposed propositions," or "propositions from transposition [*ek metatheseōs*]."[14] This expression was soon to become standard usage among philosophers writing in Greek. After Theophrastus, it can regularly be found among the Hellenistic commentators of Aristotle. Later, the philosophers of classical Islam, reading Aristotle and his commentators in translation while writing in Arabic, evoked terms and propositions said, in this sense, to be "deviated" or "deflected" (*maʿdūl*), rather than "simple" (*basīṭ*).[15]

Talk of "transposed," "deviated" and "deflected" expressions and statements seems to have provoked some perplexity in antiquity, for the sources suggest at least two explanations of these terms. According to the first account, the "transposition" involves the movement of a single Greek particle: *ou* (or *ouk* or *oukhʾ*), which one may render in English "not" or "non." This logical operator would have been "deflected" from its place in a negative predicate, such as "is not just," to its place in an indefinite predicate, such as "is non-just." In the first case, it would precede the verb "to be" (*ouk esti dikaios anthrōpos*, "Man is not just"); in the second, it would follow it (*estin ou dikaios anthrōpos*, "Man is non-just"). One syllable, in short, would be "deviated"; the proposition would consequently be "transposed." Relating this explanation, Pseudo-Magentius observes: "The diphthong *ou* does not remain with its own terms."[16] In the words of Stephanus of Alexandria, "the negative 'not' is transposed away from the 'is.'"[17] According to a second interpretation, however, the "deviation" comes to pass not in the order of speech but on the imagined surface of a square. Ammonius, writing in the fifth or sixth century CE, explains that Theophrastus spoke of "deflection" because he referred to a diagram in which one might replace or "transpose" (*metatithenai*) definite terms by indefinite ones, thereby recasting the geometrical figure of opposition.[18]

Deflected terms and propositions introduce new characteristics into the ancient doctrine of the indefinite. The most important among them involves the fact that the "transposed" expression, for some thinkers, may apply both to things that exist and to things that do not. Ammonius explains in his commentary on Aristotle's *On Interpretation* that Aristotle wrote of indefinite terms "because he saw that such vocal sounds too were often included in assertions, as when we say, 'Non-man walks' [*ouk anthrō-pos peripatei*], although they were not accorded any name by the ancients."[19] The exegete holds that in this sentence, "non-man" might well "be suspected of being a name [or noun, *onoma*]"; he even concedes that it may be one, by the standards of grammar. Yet the perspectives of logic and language, we learn, must be distinguished. Philosophical analysis must go further than grammar, accounting not only for the order of words but also for the implications of their sense.

Ammonius teaches that, for the purposes of logic, a term such as "non-man" cannot be viewed as a name, at least in the primary sense that philosophers attribute to that type of expression:

> A name signifies one nature, that of the thing named. Yet each such vocal sound [as an indefinite name] destroys one thing, namely, what is signified by the name said without the negative <particle>, and also introduces all the other things beside that, both those which are and those which are not. For "non-man" is not just said of a man, but also of a horse or dog, or of a goat-stag or centaur, and of absolutely all things which are or are not. For this reason he [Aristotle] bids us call them, this whole class, "indefinite names": "names," on the one hand, because ... they signify one thing in a way, namely everything beside the definite thing considered as one, e.g. "non-man" signifies everything besides man as being one in just this respect, that all have in common their not being just what a man is; but "indefinite" because what is signified by them does not signify the particular existence of any thing, which is the

rule among names, but rather a non-existence which applies equally to things which are and which are not [*aorista de, dioti to hyp'autōn sēmainomenon oukh' hyparxin tina pragmatos sēmainei, hoper tois onomasin ethos, all'anuparxian ousi te homoiōs kai mē ousin epharmozousan*].[20]

Aristotle himself had not explicitly treated the question of whether a term such as "non-man" signifies "the particular existence of any thing" or a "non-existence." Yet it is the Aristotelian terminology that allows this metaphysical distinction to be drawn. Ammonius reasons in terms of negation and privation. He supposes that there are certain negative expressions that may be truly predicated, even when they signify properties that do not exist; the example is the wall that "does not see." Then, as he knows well, there are terms signifying privations, such as that of which one makes use in stating that the blind man "does not see"; in this case, the validity of the term depends on a state of virtual possession.[21] Recalling the distinction between the implications of negation and privation, Ammonius resolves an old problem by a single gesture: he sets indefinite names among negations. He then introduces a new specification. Whereas an ordinary negative term merely denies a certain quality, a "transposed" designation, as he defines it, has a double function. By its "non-," it first "destroys one thing." Then, from that initial elimination, it "introduces" a panoply of non-existences: "everything beside the definite thing" that has been evoked. For Ammonius, an indefinite name thus un-names and names at once. The term "non-man" indicates that the subject of which it is predicated is "not man," even as it conjures up the indistinct nature that is common to horse and dog, goat-stag and centaur.

Ammonius appears to have drawn the elements for his argument from a remark made by Aristotle concerning indefinite verbs, rather than names. Discussing such predicates as "non-ails [or 'does-not-ail']" and "non-recovers [or 'does-not-recover']," Aristotle had stated that such verbs "hold indifferently of anything, whether existent or non-existent" (*homoiōs eph' hotououn hyparkhei, kai ontos kai mē ontos*).[22] If "non-recovers" can signify both something existent and something non-existent, the commentator seems to have reasoned, so, too, may "non-man" signify both a real and an imaginary animal; it can, then, designate "absolutely all things," with the exception of "man." The examples Ammonius offers of such an unlimited range of things, however, belie his claim. Despite their real and imaginary diversity, horse, dog, goat-stag, and centaur, although admittedly both existent and non-existent, share a common trait. They belong to the same genus of which "man" is a species. They are all, quite simply, animals. "Absolutely all things" might well have included a stranger collection; its members could have contained among them such things as plants, numbers, Athens, and propositions. The excess of Ammonius's "deflected" name seems, therefore, less than absolute. "Non-man" may "destroy" the signification of "man," but it nevertheless appears to preserve the unity of a single genus. As R. Petrilli has remarked, the Greek commentator has, perhaps unwillingly, introduced a "restriction" on the rule that he proposes.[23] His semantic "non-determination," however vast its potential field of reference, remains obstinately, if tacitly, determinate.

In this respect, Ammonius's treatment concords with the two monuments of the late antique philosophy of language that are Boethius's *Commentaries on On Interpretation*.[24] Completed in the second decade of the sixth century, these works were to become vastly influential in the parts of Europe in which Latin remained in use. For centuries, they accompanied Boethius's own translation of Aristotle's first books on the rules of reasoning, which every student pupil of philosophy, from the Middle Ages through the Renaissance, would study. Like Ammonius, who was his contemporary, Boethius explains that, according to Aristotle, an indefinite name signifies by effecting a process of semantic "removal." As Boethius writes in his first commentary on the Aristotelian treatise, "He who says 'non-man' removes 'man' [*Qui vero dicit non-homo hominem tollit*]."[25] In his more extended second interpretation, he likewise declares: "What is meant by 'non-man' is whatever is outside 'man,' once 'man' has been annulled [*Sublatio enim homine quidquid praeter hominem est, hoc significat non-homo*]."[26] Boethius's remarks make clear that he would accept Ammonius's thesis that an indefinite name possesses a status close to that of the negative term, which signifies "a non-existence which applies equally to things which are and which are not." As if to illustrate this point, Boethius offers, as a first example of such a name of a "non-man," "Sulla," the designation of the historic Roman dictator: a "man," one might reason, who, being long dead, is "no man" now.[27] Yet Boethius also takes a further step, for he suggests that an indefinite term's meaning points beyond the genus to which its correspondingly definite name pertains. For Boethius, *non-homo* can be said not only of a dead man, or an animal, real or imaginary, but also "of a stone, or of a log of wood, or of other things [*de lapide vel de ligno vel de aliis*]."[28]

For this reason, Boethius explains, there was once a debate, "among the ancients," as to whether such a term could be called a "name" (*nomen*) in any sense. One party maintained that, to be a name, an expression must possess a "well-delimited meaning" (*est circumscriptivae significationis*), "definitely" (*definite*) signifying whatever it is that it designates. It is certain that, by such standards, *non-homo* cannot be called a *nomen*. A second party, however, stretched the linguistic and logical category of the name, distinguishing between the *nomen* in this primary and simple sense (*simpliciter*) and the *nomen* in a secondary acceptation. This group reasoned that, when grasped in an attenuated form, the category of name applies to any term that signifies without reference to time (or tense), even if such signification occurs "indefinitely" (*indefinite*).[29] Boethius's own doctrine combines these two positions. He holds fast to the classical theory that, strictly speaking, "every name definitely signifies the thing it names."[30] For the philosopher, if not the grammarian, therefore, "non-man" cannot be considered a real name. Yet Boethius admits that, in a secondary meaning, one may also speak of names when evoking expressions that signify "indefinitely," by means of an act of "removal" and "annulment."

Boethius takes special measures to ensure that such indeterminate designations not be confused with "names" in the ordinary sense. With a terminological decision whose consequences were to resonate in Europe for centuries, Boethius forges a single Latin expression for Aristotle's "indefinite" words, Theophrastus's "transposed" terms, and the propositions containing them. Boethius translates the Greek *aoriston*, "indefinite," by the Latin *infinitum*, adding, by way of explanation: "for it signifies many things, indeed infinite things" (*quoniam plura et ea infinita significant*).[31] In the next chapter of his commentary, Boethius extends such reasoning to the theory of verbs. In place of the Greek "indefinite verb" (*rhēma aoriston*), he proposes the Latin "infinite verb" (*verbum infinitum*). "Non-runs" (*non currit*) and "non-works" (*non laborat*), he argues, in fidelity to Aristotle and in accord with Ammonius, may be said of "what is and of what is not" (*quod est vel quod non est*). One may apply such verbal predicates to existing subjects, such as the horse, and to inexistent ones, such as dead Sulla or the centaur. While earlier Aristotelians had been familiar with "indefinite" expressions and statements, Boethius henceforth reasons in "infinite" terms and propositions.

Boethius's decision to conceive the "infinite name" and "infinite verb" is more than an expedient of Graeco-Roman translation, though it is also that. The term "indefinite" was otherwise expressible in Latin and, had he so wished, Boethius might have evoked a *nomen* and *verbum indefinitum*, employing an attribute that he uses elsewhere in his logical works.[32] Returning, after Ammonius and Theophrastus, to the opacity of the terms evoked by Aristotle, Boethius proposes, instead, an original rendition, which abbreviates a new definition of the logic and metaphysics of the *aoriston*. Building on the theories of his predecessors, Boethius suggests that, in the "deflection" of a sign of negation, in the passage from a *non est* to an *est non-*, a particular mode of being — or non-being — comes to light: that which Boethius, almost without comment, designates as "infinite."

Such "infinity" is different from any we are accustomed to imagining. It is certainly not reducible to an unbounded presence, being not a datum but the product of an act of semantic "destruction": the exclusion of a "well-delimited meaning" by the mere addition of a "non-" to a given term. Yet the signification of a *nomen infinitum* also differs from those of privative and negative terms. Unlike a privative expression, an infinite name does not designate a property that is lacking in the sense that, while absent, it could also have been present. An infinite name need not refer, in other words, to natural potentialities. "Non-man" may be said of a stone, a log, a deceased sovereign, and a centaur. The meaning of an infinite name, however, is also irreducible to that of a negative term, which asserts that a certain property does not belong to a certain subject. Boethius's infinite expression at once condenses and reorders the traits variously discernible in the ancient typology of negative and privative terms. As he defines it, *non-homo* resembles a negative term in being capable of signifying a non-existence; but it draws close to the privative term in being structurally double in its signification. To state that something is a "non-man" is not only, in a negative manner, to deny that it is a man. It is also to posit a being, in a form reminiscent of the privation, advancing that it is "many things, indeed infinite things" other than man. To utter an infinite name is, in this sense, both to refuse a finitude and to affirm the infinitude that exceeds it.

With the modest inventiveness of a master commentator, Boethius hardly calls attention to the fact that, by means of translation and renaming, he has both solved a thorny problem in the ancient philosophy of language and grasped an event of speech that was perhaps never before defined: the naming of a pure non-existence, "unenclosed" and "unset out," in distinction from both negation and privation, as Aristotle had presented them. In such a naming, one may discern a double act of meaning: both "destruction" and "introduction," denial and affirmation. In the passage from "man" to "non-man," from "just" to "non-just," from "works" to "non-works," limitation and position, conjoined in a single utterance, engender an unknown boundlessness. An infinity of sense arises from the negation of a finite being or deed. That Boethius considered the idea of such infinity to be little more than a gloss on a dark passage in the classics can be gleaned from the speed with which he advances his concept and moves on to other matters. After pausing to explain the sense and specificity of infinite expressions, after admitting that such words may be "names" and "verbs" for the grammarian, but not the logician, Boethius dismisses them from his book, as if in fidelity to the principle that philosophy, a science of the definite, admits exclusively terms of "well-delimited meaning."[33] This was his way of following Aristotle, and many after him were to adopt it. Yet other paths led out of the Greek, and some also circumvented the "infinity" that he conceived. In time and in translation, it would become ever clearer that there are different ways to transpose one language of thinking into another, and to parse the varieties of indefiniteness.

CHAPTER FIVE

An Imported Irregularity

Latin was not the only tongue into which Aristotle's works on language and the forms of argument were translated in antiquity. Starting in the third century CE, the Greek philosopher's books came to be taught in Asia Minor as well as Europe, at such centers of Eastern Christianity as Nisibis and Antioch. There, read in Syriac, Aristotle's treatises became basic elements in a course of study in theology that included training in the art of dialectic and the varieties of proof.[1] Several centuries later, the ancient philosopher's works came into contact with a younger Semitic tongue. After the Islamic conquest of the Near East and, later, with the establishment of the Abbasid Caliphate in Baghdad in 750, a movement of translation into Arabic began. Books were culled from libraries and centers of learning across the Levant, the Mediterranean and Near East, and Aristotle's thought acquired a new idiom. Isḥāq ibn Ḥunayn, a Nestorian, produced an Arabic *On Interpretation* in the latter part of the ninth, or early tenth, century, perhaps on the basis of a Syriac version made by his father, Ḥunayn ibn Isḥāq.[2] First "severely tampered with by second and third hands," later augmented by interlinear glosses by successive readers, Isḥāq's rendition assumed a fixed textual shape by the second half of the tenth century.[3] Philosophers reading and writing in Arabic, from Central Asia across the Levant to North Africa and Andalusia, would for centuries know this version of the ancient treatise.

Certain aspects of Aristotle's book resisted translation. There were, first, questions of vocabulary that were difficult to resolve: technical expressions of Greek and Syriac logic for which it was incumbent upon Isḥāq to devise Arabic equivalents. Al-Farabi, known in the Arabic tradition as the "second master" after Aristotle alone, was acutely aware of

this fact. In his *Book of Letters*, written close to the age of the great translation movement, the tenth-century thinker recalls to his readers that
"the philosophy that now exists among the Arabs has been transferred to
them from the Greeks."[4] From that "transfer," he deduces certain general
principles concerning the transmission of philosophy. Just as the thinkers
of ancient Greece employed ordinary Greek expressions to denote their
new technical concepts, Al-Farabi reasons, so their Arabic followers were
confronted with the task of naming unfamiliar notions by familiar words.
The transition between languages presupposes, in each case, a movement
within the lexicon of a single tongue. For Greek to pass into Arabic, a
"transfer" from non-philosophical to philosophical vocabulary must be
accomplished within the second language, as it had once been achieved in
the first.

Al-Farabi observes that this is far from easy to accomplish. Wherever
philosophy is translated, speakers of the second tongue "may find that
there are philosophical concepts for which the first nation transferred
words from popular concepts unknown to the second nation, and for which
they have no words." Nonetheless, if one follows certain rules, solutions
will be found. "If those same concepts resemble other popular concepts
known to the second nation and for which they do have expressions, then
it is better to cast aside the words of the first nation and to look for those
that are most similar among their own popular concepts. They should take
those expressions and use them to designate philosophical concepts." Even
if "there are concepts for which the second nation does not have similar
popular concepts in the first place," expedients may be devised. Speakers
of a second language, in such cases, can "do one of three things: 1) invent
words from their own letters; 2) express other concepts with them in some
way or another, using existing words in a different sense; 3) or, they must
use the expressions of the first nation, once they have altered them in such
a way as to enable the second nation to utter them with ease."[5] Al-Farabi
concedes that a concept forged by such means "will be very strange to the
people of a second nation, for they will not have had it before, or anything
similar to it." In time, they may, however, come to accept it.[6]

Yet Al-Farabi knows that any project to transfer philosophy from
Greek must run up against more formidable barriers than the limits of

vocabularies. Syntax can also play a role. There is perhaps no more striking example than that of the form of the predicative proposition. In the European tradition, Aristotle's "statement-bearing sentence" was long analyzed as containing three terms: a subject, a predicate, and a lesser linking term, commonly known, after the Latin Middle Ages, as a "copula."[7] In "every man is mortal," teachers would long explain, "every man" is the subject, "mortal" is the predicate, and "is" is the copula, which unites the two categorical terms of the proposition. Such a parsing of the predicative statement can be applied to many tongues, Latin as well as Greek, English, German, and Italian. The situation, however, is markedly different in Arabic, for a simple reason: there, the "is" is lacking.

Al-Farabi discusses this curious grammatical circumstance at length in his *Book of Letters*. "In many languages," he observes, "for example, in Persian, [in Greek], in Syriac and in Sogdian, there is a word that is employed to designate all things, without thereby specifying any one thing as opposed to any other, a word that signifies the linking of an attribute to the subject of attribution. This is a word that ties the predicate to the subject whenever the predicate is a noun, or one wishes it to be tied to a subject by an absolute link, without any signification of time."[8] For such a term, Al-Farabi explains, one says *hast* in Persian, *astin* (or *estin*) in Greek, and *asti* in Sogdian.[9] "Yet there exists no word in Arabic, since its beginnings, that occupies this place." Al-Farabi takes this to be a fault of the younger language, to be remedied by technical means. There is, for him, no way around the missing "is": "One necessarily needs it for theoretical sciences and for the art of logic."[10]

Such a term matters for reasoning not in itself but in the ordered series that is the statement. Latin authors could presuppose the presence of the copula in the sentence and, without pausing to consider its necessity or contingency, orient their distinctions of logical form with respect to it. It was for them a fixed point of reference, which enabled them to call attention to the separation of the negative statement from the indefinite. In the Latin of the Scholastic philosophers, the difference between these two varieties of propositions rests, most clearly, on the syntagmatic position of the "is." In the negative proposition "Every man is not mortal," the Latin equivalent of the English particle "not" precedes the copula: *Omnis homo non est mortalis.* By contrast, in the indefinite or "metathetic" proposition, "Every man is non-mortal," the same negative particle follows the copula: *Omnis homo est non-mortalis.* A difference of syntax, in short, exhibits a distinction of logical form. In this respect, the Latin phrasing follows the Greek. It suffices to observe the sequence of terms to judge whether a given statement is negative or indefinite in shape. In the absence of the copula, however, this clear line of demarcation vanishes. It becomes difficult, if not impossible, to tell a sentence in which an act of predication is negated (*is not* . . .) from one in which the predicate itself, through the addition of a particle, is rendered indeterminate (*is non-* . . .). Logical "deviation" and its absence fade from view.

The Hellenistic Aristotelians distinguished three types of propositions, which, expressed in classical Arabic, grow perilously difficult to tell apart. Developing his logic in the language that he spoke and wrote, Aristotle had appealed to differences of form that any speaker of Greek could apprehend. They may be illustrated by three classical examples of predicative assertions treated in Aristotle's works: "Man is blind [*esti typhlos anthrōpos*]"; "Man is not just [*ouk esti dikaios anthrōpos*]"; "Man is non-just [*estin ou dikaios anthrōpos*]."[11] Ammonius, ordering his master's doctrine in canonical terms, called these three propositions "privative" (*sterētikē*), "negative" (*apophatikē*) and "indefinite" (*aoristos*), respectively.[12] Committed to reproducing the logical form of the Greek in their language, the Arabic thinkers devised means to remedy the apparent absence of the linking "is." They would employ a personal pronoun, such as "he" or "it" (*huwa*), or a technical term, such as "being" or "entity" (*mawjūd*), to signify the copula.[13] In principle, if only in the special idiom that they had devised, Arabic philosophers could then distinguish between a negative proposition, such as "Man is not just," and a privative or indefinite one, such as "Man is unjust" and "Man is non-just."[14] Yet a further fact of grammar would then trouble the transfer of the indefinite. After vocabulary and syntax, morphology, too, proved an obstacle. The laws of word formation in Arabic confronted the philosophers with a barrier that they could not easily surmount.

A language such as English contains prefixes and affixes that, when joined to words, possess the power to change their meaning, turning the designation of a state of possession into the naming of a condition of lack. It can suffice to add an "a-" or an "un-" to a word's beginning, or a "-less" to its end, to mark it as privative in sense: from "typical," one thus moves to "atypical," from "aesthetic" to "anesthetic," "interested" to "uninterested," "penny" to "penniless." Greek, as well as Latin, contained such inseparable parts of words, the English prefix "a-" being often the remnant of the old "alpha privative." These elements in word structure played a notable, if subtle, role in Aristotle's account of the kinds of predicable terms. In Greek and Latin as in English, such morphemes often allow for a formal distinction between privative words, such as "eyeless," and indefinite words, such as "non-just." Yet a further fundamental fact about the relation of grammatical possibilities to logical distinctions is also worthy of note. The very existence of indefinite expressions, as Aristotle presents them in *On Interpretation*, rests on a single morphological means: the power to add a prefix, such as "non-" (Greek *ou* or Latin *non-*) to a term.

Classical Arabic contains no elements of this kind. Neither *non-* nor *a-*, neither *un-* nor *-less*, has any formal grammatical counterparts in it. As H. A. Wolfson observed, in Arabic "no distinction can be made between an infinite term, such as 'not-seeing,' and a term which is privative in form, such as 'unseeing.' Both of them are expressed by a separable negative particle followed by the participle in question."[15] This circumstance can also be positively described by stating that one Arabic sentence can suggest more varieties of meaning than any of the types of proposition that Aristotle took to be primary. A clear example can be found in a sentence such as *Zayid lā baṣīr*, which was to become a common paradigm among philosophers in the Arabic tradition. The laws of Arabic grammar dictate that such a chain of words can mean "Zayid is not seeing," a statement that the Greek philosopher would have considered to be a negative, or "Zayid is unseeing," which would be privative, or "Zayid is non-seeing," which would be indefinite.[16]

Faithful to the sources that they received, the Arabic philosophers distinguished between these three varieties of propositions. In their treatments of the doctrine of the statement, they followed the account proposed by Aristotle and his commentators, careful not to confuse negative propositions with the privative. They also developed technical terms for the indefinite statement. They named it *ghayr muḥaṣṣal*, "not defined," or *maʿdūl*, that is, after Theophrastus and his commentators, "metathetic": "deviated," "deflected," or "transposed."[17] Knowledge of the meaning of these logical expressions was almost certainly restricted to classical Arabic philosophers. Such terms belonged to Al-Farabi's influential jargon, of which F. W. Zimmermann has commented: "It is almost entirely informed by alien models. The occasional borrowing from neighboring disciplines (such as grammar) apart, virtually all ... technical expressions are inherited from the Graeco-Syriac tradition of logic. . . . Al-Farabi's jargon derives from texts not translated by himself, not by a single author, not by indigenous writers of Arabic, and not immediately from Greek."[18]

The "indefinite" was doubtless an odd category in Greek, but it was to be, for all these reasons, an even stranger thing in classical Arabic. In the short treatise that he devoted to *On Interpretation*, Al-Farabi recalls that according to Aristotle, "a name can be definite or indefinite," a definite name becoming "indefinite when the negative particle, that is, the particle 'not,' is linked to it in such a way that together the two words assume the shape of a single expression." As if in concession to the perplexity of his readers, the philosopher followed those remarks with a commentary of a different kind, admitting that such a variety of name is difficult to conceive: "This hardly exists in the Arabic language, except as an imported irregularity [*shayʾan dhā muʾakkadan*], as in 'a non-one man' [*insānun lā aḥadun*] and 'a non-thing drachma' [*dirhaman lā shayʾun*].'"[19] The sense of these examples is anything but clear; the most recent editor of the text, in reproducing them, comments that "non-one man" and "non-thing drachma," in particular, "are so irregular that their meaning is totally obscure."[20] They may well have struck Al-Farabi's readers as idiosyncrasies inherited from the mother tongue of philosophy. Perhaps for this reason, Al-Farabi adds that the importance of this "imported irregularity" ought not be diminished. He warns his reader: "This <theory> of the widest sense <of indefinite or infinite names> is a principle of enormous benefit to science and one it is tremendously harmful to neglect. You should, therefore, give it your attention and exercise."[21]

In the long commentary that he devoted to Aristotle's *On Interpretation*, Al-Farabi explains first of all that indefinite names, although composed of a name and a particle of negation, constitute "single expressions."[22] He admits in his short treatise on Aristotle's logic that one might be tempted to take such terms to be phrases, rather than names, "on the ground that they consist of two expressions." "But," he adds, "the communities that use them do not count them as phrases; indeed, to them their shapes are the same as those of single expressions: they behave like single expressions and they inflect like single expressions."[23] In meaning, indefinite names are close to compound names, such as "Abd-al-Malik," "the king's servant"; they are linguistically composite yet signify one thing.[24] Indefinite expressions, in other words, are names in logic, even if not in grammar. To this degree, Al-Farabi can be said to promulgate an Aristotelian principle, as best he can, in Arabic. He also breaks with the Hellenistic commentators in one fundamental respect. Al-Farabi notes that most of the ancient philosopher's exegetes believe an indefinite expression to "signify any random thing, no matter whether existent or non-existent."[25] That allusion may be to Ammonius, who taught that a term such as "non-man" may be "not just said of a man, but also of a horse or dog, or of a goat-stag or centaur, and of absolutely all things which are or are not." Al-Farabi's claim holds also for Boethius, who held the indefinite term to signify a domain of things so vast as to be "infinite" in expanse. Al-Farabi, by contrast, maintains that the meaning of such terms points to one variety of absence alone: that which Aristotle and his pupils call "privation" (sterēsis, or 'adam).[26]

This thesis is of considerable philosophical importance. It dictates that to be "non-something" is not "not to be something," but to be in the specific mode by which a thing is positively missing — to be, in short, "lacking in something." Two of the three varieties of propositions distinguished by the ancient Aristotelians fade, then, into a single type. A relation of synonymy can be said to hold between sentences such as "The man is non-seeing" and "The man is blind." According to this doctrine, there is merely a formal distinction between the privative and the indefinite proposition. If one enumerates the varieties of proposition other than the affirmative, one may also simply distinguish two kinds, opposing the negative statement to the indefinite or to the privative, the last two being logically equivalent.

In his short treatise on Aristotle's On Interpretation, Al-Farabi sets forth a richer doctrine. He explains that indefinite names (al-asmā' ghayr al-

muḥaṣṣala) possess three meanings, of which privation is but the first. The second is "broader." The philosopher writes that it brings about a particular kind of indeterminate "elimination": "It eliminates [*rafaʿa*] something from an existing thing designed to have the eliminated thing inhering in itself or in its species or in its genus, of necessity or of possibility."[27] When one declares certain numbers to be odd or "non-even," one accomplishes a "deviated affirmation" in this sense, "eliminating 'even' from something which (or some of which) is designed to be even of necessity."[28] So, too, he adds, when one distinguishes, among living creatures, between the rational and the non-rational, one signifies, first, by naming in the simple sense ("rational") and, second, by naming indefinitely ("non-rational"), even as one eliminates from a portion of the genus "living creature" the possible property of being "rational."[29] The third meaning of the indefinite is "broader still." This meaning may be employed in theology. "It eliminates from an existing thing something which is not designed to be in some or all of it in the first place, as when we say of the divine that it is non-mortal and non-fading."[30]

Al-Farabi's elucidation of the indefinite was, in certain respects, to dominate the Arabic tradition in the philosophy of language that succeeded him. To be sure, Avicenna, writing a century later, offers his own account of indefinite expressions.[31] While Al-Farabi held the term "non-man" to be in structure like the name ʿAbd al-Malik, built of parts not significant in themselves, Avicenna observes that the indefinite name can be broken down into constituents that are meaningful in isolation; for, in its Arabic form, an indefinite name is composed of a name and a separate particle of negation, *lā*, *laysa*, or *ghayr*.[32] To this degree, Avicenna argues, the indefinite term is closest not to "'Abd al-Malik," but to a composite phrase predicated of a subject, such as "in the house" in the sentence "Zayd is in the house."[33] Despite this innovation, however, Avicenna follows Al-Farabi's in grasping indefinite expressions as primarily signifying privations. "By non-sighted," Avicenna explains in the section of his *Remarks and Admonitions* dedicated to logic, "we intend 'blind,' or some concept more general than that."[34]

One might have anticipated that a type of term as remote in origin and as odd in form as "non-seeing" would have lived a short life in philosophical translation. Yet two centuries after Avicenna, Averroes pauses more than once, as did his predecessors, to explain the structure of the indefinite name, its significations, and its applications in logic. Following the "second master," Averroes identifies the indefinite with the privative. "Among names," we read in his *Middle Commentary* to Aristotle's *On Interpretation*, "some are definite and some are indefinite. Definite names designate states of possessions [*malakāt*] — for example, 'man' or 'horse.' Indefinite names are composed of the name of the possession and the particle 'non-' or "not" [*lā*], in those languages where this kind of name is used, as when we say 'non-man' and 'non-horse.'"[35] In his short commentary on the Aristotelian treatise, Averroes lingers longer on such names, following Aristotle in showing particular attention to statements that contain them in the position of the predicate. "Some propositions are transposed, and these are those propositions in which the predicate is an indefinite name or verb, as when we say, 'Socrates is non-well.'" But this, the philosopher adds, occurs only "in propositions that are not used in the Arabic language. . . . The force of the indefinite terms in those languages in which they are used is the force of privative terms, for, when we say, 'non-' and 'seeing,' it is of the same order as when we say 'blind'; similarly, when we say 'non-' and 'well,' it is of the same order as when we say 'sick.'"[36]

Despite the doctrinal differences they exhibit, these works of Arabic philosophy present a coherent reading of their ancient source. They are united, first, in maintaining that terms constructed by the addition of the words "no," "not" or "non-" (*lā*, *laysa* or *ghayr*), are privative in sense. Several consequences follow from this fact. The first involves the truth conditions that define the valid use of such expressions in predicative propositions. If the indefinite term is grasped as signifying something that is lacking, it holds if and only if the subject of which it is predicated exists, for a simple reason: only an existent thing can be in a state of lack with respect to a possible possession.[37] It is solely of a man who is alive, for example, that the property of blindness may meaningfully be affirmed or denied; no dead person can be said to be lacking or not lacking in the faculty of sight, and with respect to a chimera, a square circle, or other non-existent things, the predication of privation as well as its denial are senseless. To this degree, the privative predicable differs from the negative, which may be truly affirmed and denied of both what is and what is not.

A second consequence concerns the limitation in the range of meanings that indefinite terms then may have. "Non-seeing," for Ammonius and Boethius, points to the endless domain of things other than seeing: things within the same genus as "seeing," as one might infer, for Ammonius, such as hearing, smelling, and tasting, and, for Boethius, any things whatsoever except seeing — in principle, even a coin, a figure, or a mythic beast. Yet once the indefinite expression is identified with the privative, the scope of its virtual meanings diminishes considerably. "Non-seeing" will then signify the lack of sight, which is blindness, and no more. Finally, the philosophers of the Arabic tradition show little hesitation, for this reason, in maintaining that such terms, despite their relative indeterminacy, have a valid function in logic, even if they are irregular in grammar. Since, as privations, they point to observable states, since they signify not "any random thing, no matter whether existent or non-existent," but a precisely definable and existent state of deprivation, they may have a place in the philosophical theory of terms and argument.

The Arabic readings of the indefinite may be contrasted, on all these counts, to those offered by the Latin Scholastic philosophers of the twelfth and thirteenth centuries. The masters of the medieval European universities were in part familiar with the works of the Arabic thinkers, especially the commentaries that Averroes dedicated to Aristotle's *On Interpretation*.[38] Boethius, however, never ceased to be a persistent and powerful force in the Latin West. For more than a millennium, indefinite names were known in Latin as "infinite," and from this fact of terminology an entire doctrine is derivable. For much of the Scholastic tradition, such expressions as "non-man" and "non-seeing" designate not privations but negations. The consequences of this position, once again, are multiple. First, indefinite terms hold of both being and non-being. Second, the meaning of such terms, unbound from any existing things, ranges over an "infinite" expanse of senses, "non-seeing" denoting anything at all but "seeing," "non-man" signifying anything conceivable but "man." For this reason, infinite terms were to strike many Latin thinkers as too tenuous in their meaning, too extensible in their applications, to be of any real use in a field of knowledge, such as philosophy. Some Schoolmen went so far as to lend these terms a status that was, in fact, symmetrically opposed to the one that the Arabic philosophers had accorded them. Both traditions admitted a distinction between grammar, defined as the study of the parts of speech, and logic, understood as the science of the order of true statements. Yet whereas the Arabic thinkers tended to see Aristotle's indefinite expressions as "names" in the field of logic, if not in that of grammar, the Latin authors often adopted an inverse position, taking "infinite names" to pertain to the domain of grammar but not logic.[39]

In his paraphrase of *On Interpretation*, Albert the Great would thus teach that the "infinite name" is "deficient" in that, unlike a finite expression, it does not signify any particular "substance with quality." "As to grammar," he concludes, it therefore "falls under the definition of the noun," but as to logic, it "is excluded from its perfect definition."[40] Later in the thirteenth century, the English philosopher and commentator Simon of Faversham expressed a similar position in more detail. He set infinite words beyond the limits of the proposition (*enuntiatio*) that philosophers must take into account:

> Note that the infinite name and the infinite verb are excluded from the consideration of the logician because the name and verb which the logician considers should be parts of the proposition. But infinite names are not part of the proposition, because everything that can be a part of the proposition must signify some concept of the mind, for the proposition is principally for the sake of truth. But we cannot have truth except through that which expresses a determinate concept. For [the infinite name and verb] are said indifferently of being and non-being; they are therefore neither verbs nor names for the logician, and thus they are not his concern. They are not, however, excluded from the grammarian's consideration, because they do possess those accidents of the name and verb by means of which they can be composed with one another.[41]

The contrast between the Arabic and the Latin appropriations of Aristotle's indefinite expressions is striking. It is, however, hardly surprising. The truth is that it responds to an equivocation in the treatment of the question in *On Interpretation*. Toward the inception of his treatise, Aristotle calls to mind such terms as "non-man" and "non-heals"; he states that they are neither names nor verbs, being, rather, "indefinite" expressions. From that brief discussion and that apparent gesture of dismissal, one might infer, as do the Latin thinkers, that such terms have no real place in the philosophical analysis of language, being too indeterminate to be integrated in the statements of science. Toward the conclusion of the same treatise, however, Aristotle again evokes such terms as "non-man" and "non-just." There he defines them as the contraries of "man" and "just," proposing a table of statements in which "man" and "non-man," "just" and "non-just," are related as contraries, distinct from contradictories. From that more rigorous discussion of the types of opposition, one might conclude, as do the Arabic thinkers, that indefinite terms do constitute elements in the theory of the proposition. In their discord, the two exegetical traditions are, in this sense, faithful to their ancient source. Together, they amplify a single uncertainty. So, too, in alternately assimilating the indefinite statement to the negative statement or to the privative, and in drawing out, each time, the semantic and logical consequences that such a decision implies, the Arabic and the Latin commentators make of the classical philosopher's silence the condition of their own disquisitions.

The Arabo-Latin exegetical dispute also implies a grammatical dimension that is no less remarkable than the doctrinal. From Greek to Latin, Aristotle's treatise passed between two languages in which it is possible to form any number of words by the addition of an inseparable "not" or "non- ." Translated into Arabic, however, Aristotle's indefinite term acquires a form far more difficult to reproduce and define. One might expect, therefore, that the Arabic thinkers would have retreated before the concepts of the indefinite name and verb; in their awareness of the grammatical differences between Greek and Arabic, the philosophers of the classical age of Islam might have chosen to omit such expressions from their logic, attributing them to the contingencies of linguistic difference. Yet precisely this did not occur. Instead, it was a Roman thinker, Boethius, who defined indefinite words, with which he was familiar in non-philosophical Latin and Greek, in a new and technical meaning. It was Boethius who maintained that the indeterminate names and verbs that Aristotle discussed signify an "infinite" range of significations. Thanks to his commentary and translation, the *onoma aoriston,* renamed as the *nomen infinitum*, would, in its strictly endless field of meanings, drift slowly but surely toward the outer edges of philosophy. From there it was to be but a step for some Schoolmen to judge that such a term belonged to the distinctions of grammar rather than to logic.

Approaching Aristotle's book from a greater distance, the Arabic philosophers staked out a different path. Indefinite terms were for them a crucial component in the logic they inherited from the Greek tradition. They viewed the oddities of the more ancient language as worthy of recovery in translation and transposition. Al-Farabi would seek to render a new and technical Arabic prose homogenous, in its terms and syntax, with its predecessor in philosophy, even at the price of distorting its classical shape. Yet in their fidelity to their sources, in their aim to transfer an ancient doctrine to a young nation, the Arabic thinkers also proposed a new interpretation, which casts a bright light on the indefinite expressions that the grammar of their tongue lacked. Commenting on the ancient mode of forming names and verbs, Al-Farabi and his successors brought to light one sense of the indefinite that is grammatically indubitable, yet which no commentator before him appears to have specified as such. This is, simply, the sense of signifying a privation. In the languages that do possess an inseparable prefix such as "not-" or "non-," its addition to a word often means that in some crucial respect, the thing that has been named is missing. Consider, as examples, an act that is said to be "non-violent" because it is devoid of the violence that might accompany it; or an expression judged to be "nonsensical," in that it could, but does not, contain any admissible meaning; or, finally, the "non-sequitur," which, in argument, should follow but does not.

At first glance, these contemporary English examples would seem to illustrate the definition of the indefinite proposed by the Arabic thinkers, not the Scholastic. The curious fact is that Boethius wrote in a language in which indefinite terms could be readily both formed and employed. His Latin contained such expressions as *non liquet* and *non rationalis*, each of which could be said, in a way, to denote an existent thing in a state of deprivation. Yet in his influential commentaries, Boethius declared that, in logic, if not in language, indefinite names and verbs fulfill a stranger function: that of signifying the infinite domain of everything — possible or impossible, existent or non-existent — that the meaning of a term does not entail. Could a single expression, one wonders, ever say so little, or so much? With poorer means, in this particular respect, in a tongue that lacked the possibility of constructing terms by the mere addition of a "non-" to them, the Arabic authors accomplished something that Boethius did not, for they grasped a major role that "indefinite" words do play in speech. The philosophers of the "young nation" intuited a law of sense, which holds for many of the languages that they themselves did not speak. Without ever having explicitly stated as much, the "second master" and his disciples appear to have been certain that, if speakers construct words such as those that Aristotle evoked, naming non-things and non-actions, it is to designate conditions of deprivation, pointing to states of poverty, rather than excess. This was the major insight contained in the Arabic treatment of the indefinite. Simplifying Aristotle's doctrine of the proposition, the thinkers of the age of classical Islam succeeded in offering of the indefinite an account faithful to this usage. From Greek to Syriac, from Syriac to Arabic, the ancient philosophical category thus acquired a new linguistic exactitude. A transfer was achieved. Glossed by the masters of this second nation, the "imported irregularity" marked out a circuitous but certain path toward a rule of speech. The later Latins were to take another.

CHAPTER SIX

Ways of Indeterminacy

Several kinds of infinite names were known in the medieval Latin schools, and in the monastery and university, students in the liberal arts would be introduced to their complexities more than once. In the first and most elementary of the language arts, grammar, "infinity" was held to be a quality proper to many varieties of words. This was, in part, an inheritance from the classical age. The ancient Greek grammatical term *aoriston*, which one might render as "indefinite" or "indeterminate," was translated into Latin as *infinitum*, assuring that attribute a permanent place in the study of language.[1] As early as the first century CE, two Roman grammarians, Palaemon and Probus, both argued that, when considering the types of designations, one must distinguish between the finite and the infinite. These qualifications, for the Romans, applied above all to a single part of speech: the set of special names or nouns that are regularly employed "in place of" (*pro-*) other designations, and that an ancient tradition of linguistic analysis, which is alive and well today, defines as "pronouns."

According to Palaemon, a *pronomen* is "finite" (*finitus*) if it signifies a "certain person" (*certam personam*), by "designation" (*designatio*) or clear reference to a speaking subject. The word *ego*, "I," illustrates this principle. As soon as it is spoken, it points to the being who has uttered it. The meaning of "you," for Palaemon, is of another kind, because it can signify any speaking subject who, while present in the moment of speech, happens to be silent. For the reference of "you" to become definite, a further indication may be required; it can be necessary to point, or to avail oneself of some other gesture of the hand. Palaemon reasons, therefore, that the word "you" (*tu*) is "less than finite" (*minus quam finitus*). For him, there also exist terms of lesser "finitude." To this class belong pronouns of the third person, such as "it," "he," "she," and "they." Not even a supplementary indication can fully dispel their indeterminacy. Aware of the poverty of their meaning, Palaemon calls such expressions "infinite" (*infinita*). Probus of Berytus, his contemporary, presents a similar account, yet with a difference. For Probus, the "finitude" (*finitudo*) of words corresponds not to the certainty of their actual reference, but to the definition of their virtual signification: the degree to which their lexical sense can be established independent of context.[2] According to this conception of the finitude and infinitude of speech, a proper noun, such as "Cato," will be said to be more definite than a demonstrative pronoun, such as "this," and a phrase such as "I, Nero," will be considered to be of a greater "finitude" than the word "I."

In his great treatise on the Roman language, *De lingua latina*, Varro draws on these distinctions, even as he proposes a more complex account of designations. "The kinds of naming," he writes, "are four": subordinate pronouns (*provocabula*), such as "which"; common nouns (*vocabula*), such as "shield" or "sword"; proper nouns (*nomina*), such as "Romulus" and "Remus"; and demonstrative pronouns (*pronomina*), such as "that" and "this."[3] Varro orders these varieties of names with respect to one model of determinacy: "The first class is infinite (*infinitum*); the second is almost infinite (*ut infinitum*); the third is almost finite (*ut finitum*); the fourth is finite (*finitum*)." This scale, like the terminology of Palaemon and Probus, implies one point that may seem surprising today. "Finitude," not "infinitude," is the positive and primary term. This fact alone explains why the grammarians consider the infinite to be "less than finite" and not, as one might have anticipated, "more" than it. "Finitude," for them, is the model for the signification of all names. From the heights of its definition — whether it is of reference or of sense, mere pointing or lexical meaning — one descends to the level of the "almost finite"; from there, in turn, one passes to the stage of the "almost infinite." At a further remove, one reaches the most minimal degree of expression, for which the word "infinite" is apt.

Later scholars of the Latin tongue build on these foundations. Donatus, Charisius, and Servius all teach, in different ways, that nouns and pronouns are to be classified in hierarchical ranks of finitude. Donatus, in the fourth century, explains that designations are of a "bipartite quality," being divided between the "finite" and the "infinite." "I," "you," and "he" or "she" are "finite" words, which signify "persons"; by contrast, coordinating expressions, such as "that" and "which," are "infinite" words, which signify persons and non-persons.[4] In fidelity to the old tripartition, however, Donatus also adds in passing that there are also certain pronouns that are "less than finite" (*minus quam finita*); as examples, he cites *ipse*, "him-, her-, or itself," and *iste*, "this."[5] In the late fourth or early fifth century, Servius relates a similar typology. He declares "all pronouns" to be either *finita* or *infinita*, before admitting, as a supplement, a category of the "less than finite." "Finite" pronouns, for him, designate persons. The words "I," "you," "he," and "she" all satisfy this condition. Infinite pronouns signify "any person whatsoever," according to six linguistic forms: "who; of such a kind as; such that; of such quantity that; as large as; of such a number that; all." "Less than finite" pronouns, finally, point to a "well-known" but unspecified person, as when one alludes to someone by employing such indefinite expressions as "him," "himself," "that one," or "to himself."[6]

The grammatical authority most studied in the Latin West, Priscian, transmits a simplified account of these classifications in the books of his *Institutiones grammaticae*, composed in the sixth century. He argues that there exists a class of names signifying some "general substance," "quality," "quantity," or "number," without any further definition. Such designations are termed "infinite," because they indefinitely subsume all the species of whatever they designate.[7] Words such as "'who,' 'that,' 'which,' 'such,' 'how much,' and the like" belong to this class of indefinite expressions. For Priscian, they are more akin to nouns than to pronouns. Unlike *pronomina* such as "he" and "she," they cannot always take the place of proper nouns in sentences, nor do they necessarily signify persons. These "infinite names" express substances and qualities, like other names; but they possess the additional characteristic of being "infinite" and "general" in meaning.[8]

To these assorted nouns and pronouns, the philosophers of the twelfth century add a further variety of indefinite words. While the ancient and medieval grammarians are concerned with parts of speech, in their diversity and regularity, the philosophers of the twelfth century, like their predecessors, concentrate on terms: parts of sentences and, more precisely,

"statement-making sentences" with which Aristotle identified the predicative assertion. A first task for those aiming to grasp the form of propositions and the laws of their relations is to analyze the types of subjects
and predicates, as well as the conditions in which they may be validly
employed. Aristotle remains the distant model for the thinkers who set
out on this path of inquiry. It may be recalled that his doctrine of the syllogism demands that all logical terms be employable both as subjects and
as predicates. If one holds to this stricture, proper names cannot easily be
incorporated in syllogistic reasoning, for although they may function as
subjects, they can hardly be employed as predicates; one may well state
"Socrates is Greek," but it is difficult to ascertain how one could say of
anything that it is "a Socrates." Yet there also exist logical expressions that
pose an inverse problem, their meaning being, so to speak, too vast, rather
than too narrow, to be predicated as properties, at least in any ordinary
manner. The twelfth-century philosophers show particular interest for
this type of term. They struggle to understand its "infinitude," as well as
its place in the theory of the statement and the conditions of its truth.

One may take, as an example, the late twelfth or early thirteenth-cen-
tury logic book known today as the *Tractatus Anagnini*. Its anonymous
authors declare that there exist certain words whose application is limitless: "terms," as they call them, "that contain everything" (*termina omnia
continentes*).[9] The first examples of such terms offered in this treatise are the
expressions "something" (*aliquid*) and "thing" (*res*). The medieval thinkers'
claim seems difficult to reject. Whatever can be said to be is "something";
one may also reason that it is necessarily one "thing" or another. Other
philosophers from the period also allude to this set of unbounded designations. To the terms "something" and "thing," they add expressions that are
no less capacious. The authors of the *Ars Meliduna*, from the second half of
the twelfth century, argue that the term "being" (*ens*) is of a like nature; it,
too, "contains everything."[10] Such a claim cannot easily be rejected, for it
would seem that if something is something, it must also be a "being"; otherwise it is nothing. A commentary on Priscian from the mid-twelfth century contains a longer list of such terms. One finds in it not only "being,"
"something," and "thing," but also "one" (*unum*) and "discrete" (*discretum*).[11]
Again, the reasons for the proposal can be reconstructed. Whatever is a

"thing," a "something," or a "being" must be "one"; yet to be intelligible as "one," it must also be distinct and, therefore, "discrete."

Such terms pertain more directly to the doctrine of the proposition than do the infinite words of the ancient grammarians. Personal pronouns such as "I," or "you," reflexive pronouns such as "myself" and "herself," relative pronouns, such as "that" and "which," anaphoric pronouns, which pick up to earlier designations, replacing them by simpler terms, such as "it," or "him," are usually absent from Aristotle's syllogisms. Their complex signifying and referential structures become important objects of philosophical study in the Middle Ages; but it is at a relatively late date, and once the more elementary bases of medieval logic have been laid.[12] "Terms that contain everything," by contrast, are remarkably simple in form and seem, at first glance, perfectly suited to playing major roles in predicative assertions. But how may one define a subject such as "being," whose meaning embraces everything that is? And what can one mean in asserting of anything that it is "something," or that it possesses the property of being "discrete"? Such terms appear to defy the logic of the statement that they serve. Grammatically, they may well appear as both subjects and predicates; they nonetheless signify in a manner that remains obscure. As predicates, in particular, "terms that contain everything" raise questions for which the medieval thinkers could find no answers in their ancient sources.

At the end of the classical age, Porphyry, Plotinus's pupil, wrote a treatise called *Eisagōgē* or *Introduction*, in which he enumerated the distinct ways in which properties might be attributed to subjects. Medieval philosophers knew this book well; for them, it constituted the first treatise in the fundamental collection of books on logic that they called the *Organon*. After Porphyry, "predicables," or expressions capable of being said of many things, would be called "universals" (*predicamenta*). Thinkers would follow Porphyry in distinguishing between five types among them: those which name a genus, such as "animal"; those which name a species, such as "man"; those which name a difference, such as "rational"; those which name a property, such as "capable of laughter"; and those which name an accident, such as "sitting," "standing," or being "in a certain place." Porphyry ordered these five types of terms according to their degree of universality. He showed how, from the most general of all genera in view ("animal," in this case), one might pass to the most special of the species considered ("man," in the same example). An elementary pictorial representation, in the Middle Ages, would illustrate this logical descent. It would be an inverted tree, whose "special" fruits, placed below, would rise up to their roots, leading to their most general properties. Gazing at the logical body, one would observe a ramified and hierarchically ordered series of predicable terms.

The problem is where to place "terms that contain everything." That such expressions appear to be "predicables" can hardly be contested. But exactly what kind of predicate does one affirm in simply stating, "Man is something," "Man is a being," "Man is one," "Man is discrete"? Aware of the difficulties of the question, the authors of the *Ars Meliduna* offer a deceptively simple answer. They maintain that "terms that contain everything" have no place whatsoever on Porphyry's tree: "No name that belongs to every thing, such as 'thing,' 'something,' 'being,' or 'one,' signifies a universal [*Nullum nomen conveniens cuilibet rei significant universal, ut 'res', 'aliquid', 'ens' et 'unum'*]."[13] They could signify a universal only if there were some genus common to all things; but this Aristotle expressly excludes, arguing that "Being" is not a genus.[14] There is, in other words, neither a genus nor a species derivable from properties such as "being something," "being a being," and "being one." That may seem a startling proposition; but it implies another, which is no less remarkable. Aristotle posited a set of supreme genera, by which all things can be characterized. These are the "categories," which designate the properties that one may evoke to define whatever is. In the second chapter of his *Categories*, Aristotle maintains that such fundamental genera are ten in number: "substance; quantity; qualification; a relative; where; when; or being-in-a-position; having; doing; being-affected." He illustrated each one: "To give a rough idea, examples of substance are man, horse; of quantity: four-foot, five-foot; of qualification: white, grammatical; of a relative: double, half, larger; of where: in the Lyceum, in the market-place; of when: yesterday, last year; of being-in-a-position: is-lying, is-sitting; of having: has-shoes-on, has-armor-on; of doing: cutting, burning; of being-affected, being-cut, being-burned."[15]

Faithful to their principles, the medieval authors affirm the consequence that is entailed by their thesis that "terms that contain everything" signify no genera. It may be simply stated: such terms pertain to none of the categories. Or perhaps they pertain to none of them in particular. Several possibilities, in fact, may be envisaged. According to the authors of a collection of glosses on Priscian dating to the mid-twelfth century, "terms that contain everything" may be employed to express a categorical meaning. In other words, one might predicate unity, or being, or discretion, in defining the nature of a certain thing. Yet what exactly such terms signify, what species and genera they evoke, can still only be decided with reference to the context of their use, their meaning being by nature "equivocal."[16] The authors of the *Ars Meliduna* advance a different argument. For them, "terms that contain everything" may be stated of each of the categories and determine no specific natures. They are not, however, utterly meaningless. Although they may not determine that which exactly a being is, they can, nonetheless, indicate a fact: the fact, namely, that what they are predicated of necessarily exists. A "term that contains everything," points to not "*what a thing itself is*, but simply *that it is* [*non ostendit de aliquo quid ipsum sit, sed simpliciter quod sit*]."[17]

The *Dialectica Monacensis*, a treatise from the second half of the twelfth century, proposes a technical designation for such expressions.[18] "Terms that contain everything," we read, are "transcendent names" (*nomina transcendentia*). The attribute "transcendent" in this phrase points to the fact that such designations "step beyond" or "exceed" the categories known to Aristotle and his ancient pupils. Such "transcendence," for the medieval authors, seems easily expressible, for the list of these terms is long and open. Among them one may count such names as "'thing' [*res*], 'being' [*ens*], 'one' [*unum*], 'universal' [*universale*], 'possible' [*possibile*], 'contingent' [*contingens*], 'the same' [*idem*], 'different' [*diuersum*], and so forth."[19] It does not take long to realize that such names are not only difficult to avoid; they are also prevalent in certain domains of thought, such as philosophy. Whenever one claims that a certain predicable term is a universal, whenever one states that it is different from another, or the same as it, that it is necessary, possible, impossible or contingent, reasoning not only by means of predication but concerning predicates and predicable expressions, one ceases to deliberate in the language of genera, species, and ordered properties. One steps, rather, beyond the categories, and speaks in "transcendent names."

Today, students of the history of philosophy are less familiar with such terms than with the "transcendental" properties of later medieval thought. These have long been believed to appear for the first time in Philip the Chancellor's *Summa de Bono*, a work dated between 1225 and 1228. It is in this treatise that the Parisian poet and theologian argues that there exist certain attributes that may be affirmed of all things. Philip calls them "the most common" (*communissima*) of all properties, maintaining, moreover, that they are four in number: "being, one, true, and good."[20] His thesis would soon become an accepted proposition in the philosophy of the Latin universities. "Anything that is," a Scholastic adage after him would state, "is a being, is one, is true and is good [*Quodlibet est ens, unuum, verum, bonum*]." Drawing on the metaphysics of the Arabic tradition, which had begun to be rendered into Latin in his day, as well as Aristotelian and Neoplatonic sources newly accessible in Europe in the thirteenth century, Philip laid the foundations for a new theory of the most basic of all metaphysical determinations: attributes said to be "transcendental" in the precise sense that, exceeding the range of each of the predicable terms discussed in Porphyry's *Introduction*, they surpass the domains of the ten categories known to the Aristotelian tradition.

From the thirteenth through the sixteenth century, the philosophers of the Latin universities would investigate the nature of these "overstepping" attributes. Soon it would be an established point of doctrine among Scholastics that Being is "convertible" with any of the other transcendental terms. This means simply that if anything can be said to be, it can also be said to be "good," or "one," or "true"; conversely, whatever partakes of one of these properties can also be said to "be." Important questions, of course, would remain to be resolved. There was the problem of the exact number of transcendentals. Are they three, four, or perhaps more? Can one establish their number with certainty? There was also the thorny problem of the relations between these various terms, which are at once distinct in sense and yet identical in actual reference. Several solutions would be proposed. Some thinkers claimed that transcendental terms are "the same in reality, yet distinct in concept" (*idem subiecto, differunt ratione*). That answer also raises questions.[21] Gradually, however, a new and general branch of theology and philosophy would emerge from the doctrine of the transcendental determinations. This was to be a foundational domain of medieval science and philosophy: metaphysics, the "first science," conceived, after Aristotle, by his Greek, Arabic, and Latin readers, as the study of "being qua being" (*ens qua ens*), discernible in the set of "most common" properties.

The *nomina transcendentia* discussed by the twelfth-century grammarians and logicians appear to be more modest entities by comparison. Those who deliberate about their kind are less concerned with the nature of substance, or the relation of divine to created being, than a curious but undeniable logico-linguistic circumstance: speaking beings are in the habit of affirming properties that, however obvious they may appear, defy all definition, at least if one understands "definition" as implying some limitation by opposition. Yet in questioning such puzzling customs of speech, in investigating "terms that contain everything," the earlier medieval thinkers run up against many of the matters that will later occupy the more systematic Scholastic metaphysicians. By the early thirteenth century, it becomes necessary for the grammarians and the logicians to define the "equivocal" meaning proper to "transcendent names." That problem leads them to contemplate a difficulty that the Scholastic theologians would also be forced to consider. Reading the *Metaphysics* of Aristotle, Avicenna, Averroes, the thirteenth- and fourteenth-century doctors would ask about the sense in which Being can be predicated both of a first cause and that which it causes. How can a single term, they would wonder, be affirmed of both a unique uncreated substance and many created beings? So, too, the twelfth-century thinkers seek to explain how terms such as "thing" and "one" may run across the range of each and every categorical determination, being somehow predicable of whatever is said to be.

In the twelfth century, philosophers posed and responded to this question in logical and linguistic terms. A number of solutions were advanced. Perhaps the most innovative and complete is that adopted by the anonymous authors of the *Summe Metensis*, which dates from the early thirteenth century. These thinkers reason that even if a transcendent name can be stated of any genus, it is said primarily of one, and only secondarily of others. The term "equivocation," they argue, is itself equivocal; one can, and indeed must, distinguish its multiple senses. A first equivocation is that which affects terms that signify a multitude of things, such that no particular order or hierarchy obtains between their meanings. A second equivocation is that which affects terms that signify one thing in a primary sense, and others in a secondary and derived sense.[22] Transcendent names are "equivocal" in the second, "general" (*communiter*) meaning of the term. They are to be attributed "according to the prior and the posterior," *secundum prius et posterius*. To employ a term that announced a notion to have the greatest fortune in later theology, words that contain everything are, in short, "analogical."[23]

At the threshold of the thirteenth century, the question that appears most to preoccupy the philosophers, however, is not that of the relation between the transcendent terms of logic and the transcendental properties of metaphysics. There is a different distinction that needs to be repeatedly recalled and defended: that which separates words that contain everything from an older set of designations, which, while predicable, also exceed all genera. Transcendent terms are to be distinguished from infinite names. This is so not only for formal reasons, because, in other words, the definition of the first class of designations is distinct, in medieval doctrine, from the second. It is true that the infinitude of a term that contains everything arises from its capacity to name an unlimited expanse, without distinction. "Being" thus designates anything and everything that can be said to be; it steps across all the categories by virtue of the indeterminate positivity of its sense. The "infinitude" of a *nomen infinitum*, however, is of a different nature, for it is tied to an expanse of meaning that, however vast, is limited by definition. The term "non-man," in Boethius's account, posits and affirms the endless field of things that are not man; but it does so solely on condition of excluding whatever is meant by the word "man." Yet there is a further and more important reason for which the medieval thinkers repeatedly seek to distinguish transcendent names from infinite words. If not kept strictly separate from the odd expressions conceived by Aristotle in his treatise *On Interpretation*, a danger threatens terms that contain everything. It is the peril of what the medieval thinkers call *infinitatio*, "becoming infinite," or, to wager a technical English word as odd as the Latin, "infinitization."

One must begin by noting the fundamental differences that separate the "term that contains everything" from the *nomen infinitum*. A transcendent name is a word that, present in the vocabulary of a language, signifies an unlimited domain of things. By contrast, an "infinite name" is, in its form, a learned construction, which acquires its "infinitude" by a technical means: the addition of the Latin prefix *non-* to it. One may ask how many transcendent names there are and if, indeed, they are of such a nature as to be enumerable in a given language. That question can hardly be raised concerning "infinite names," for a simple reason: it would seem that *any* name can be rendered "infinite," through the mere affixation of a certain negative particle to it. That fact, however, implies a theoretical danger of which the medieval thinkers are well aware. To retain their structure and remain "transcendent," terms that contain everything must be protected from virtual "infinitization."

The earliest recorded discussions of transcendent names already contain this prohibition: such terms must not be subject to *infinitatio*.[24] The treatise known as *Introductiones Montane minores*, which dates from approximately 1130, argues this point forcefully. The authors appeal to the established logical principle known as "contraposition." The reader is enjoined to contemplate a paradigmatic proposition: "Every man is a thing" (*omnis homo est res*). "This statement," the authors of the book explain, "is true."[25] They then observe that, according to Aristotle and his pupils, one may "convert" it by contraposition, thereby obtaining a second statement: "No non-thing is a man," or "what is not a thing is also not a man," and, affirmatively, "every non-thing is not a man" (*omnis non-res non est homo*). The rules of logic dictate that a contraposition does not change the truth or falsity of a proposition. Therefore, if the first statement is true, so, too, the second must be true. Now, though, the authors evoke a further logico-metaphysical rule that is accepted by many philosophers in this period. Nothing can be truly predicated of a non-existent subject; positively stated, for any true predicative statement, it may be assumed that the subject of the proposition exists. If one holds that "Every non-thing is not a man," one must, consequently, also grant the thesis: "A non-thing is" (*non-res est*).

That sentence challenges the very possibility of a term that contains everything. For if one accepts that "a non-thing is," what, then, will one say of the stated "non-thing": is it itself a "thing" (*res*)? If one answers in the negative, the comprehensiveness of the predicable "thing" will be diminished, since there will be at least one thing that is "not a thing." The term "thing," in short, will not "contain everything"; the first transcendent name will not be "transcendent," or it will be so only in part. Yet if, instead, one answers in the affirmative, the conclusion will be equally troubling. For if it is true that a "non-thing" is indeed a "thing," the predicate "thing" becomes logically incoherent, comprehending in its scope both "things" and "non-things." To avoid such consequences, the authors of the *Tractatus Anagnani*, a little later in the century, decree: "Terms that contain everything may not be infinitized [*termini omnia continentes non possunt infinitari*]."[26] In principle, the philosophers formally exclude the possibility of propositions such as "non-thing is not a man," even if, for reasons of pedagogical clarity, they still evoke the terms they banish: "'Non-something is' and 'non-thing is,'" the authors conclude, "are hence as nothing [*Unde nichil est 'non-aliquid est,' 'non res est'*]."[27]

Faced with such difficulties, a number of authors of the period reach similar conclusions. Already at the end of the eleventh century, Garlandus Compotista, arguing with unnamed contemporaries, refuses to concede that the designation *non-substantia*, "non-substance," may meaningfully be employed or assigned any determinate sense. "It is impossible," he asserts, "to give a meaning to anything except what was or what will be," and "non-substance" fulfills neither of these conditions. Were one to grant the admissibility of the term "non-substance," one would also be compelled to accept such statements as "non-substance is a non-man" (*non-substantia est non-homo*); according to such reasoning, one would then also be obligated to admit such a proposition as "nothing is something" (*nichil est aliquid*).[28] The grammarian Robert of Paris, in the second half of the twelfth century, concurs: "Names that contain everything [*nomina quae conueniunt omnia*]," he writes, giving as examples the terms "being" (*ens*), "one" (*unum*), and "something" (*aliquid*), "may not be infinitized [*non possunt infinitari*]. Therefore, we do not accept statements such as 'Socrates is a non-being' [*Socrates est non-ens*]."[29] Abelard, as C. H. Knepkens has observed, "also entered the discussion on this subject, and turned out to be very reluctant to admit this kind of infinite noun. In the *Logica 'Ingredientibus'* he claimed that if one accepts the infinite term '*non-res*,' the consequence is that the finite noun '*res*' can be employed only to speak about existing things, whereas in the *Dialectica* he expressly said that '*res*' and '*aliquid*' are also nouns which can be used to speak of non-existing things."[30]

Such stipulations may seem excessive in the detail of their precautions. Yet they respond to a logical peril that is contained in the expressions that Aristotle conceived. The truth is that of the varieties of infinitude known to the medieval scholars of language, none is as potentially destructive as that engendered by "infinitization." This is why the philosophers seek to delimit the field of its application. Were it to go unchecked, the force of *infinitatio* would consume all the infinite words known to the study of language, altering their place in grammar and philosophy and making of them examples of words such as Aristotle's "non-man." Grammatical *nomina infinita* would be the first to be undone. "Infinite" and "less than finite" pronouns, as well as nouns designating "general substance," can also be rendered otherwise indeterminate if one adds a *non-* to them. After "non-man" and "non-just," there would be other indeterminate ideas, produced by the affixation of *non-* to the "infinite names" of the grammarians. Later writers would not hesitate to evoke them: Nicholas of Cusa would present God as the "non-Other" (*non aliud*); Fichte would summon a *not-I* or *non-I* (*Nicht-ich*), structurally opposed to the *I*; Beckett would title a late dramatic piece *Not-I*; Lacan would return insistently to a quantity that, forcing French grammar, he would designate as "the not-all" (*le pas-tout*).[31] Yet the "infinitization" considered in detail by the twelfth-century thinkers was perhaps most threatening to transcendent names and metaphysically transcendental properties. Such terms and notions might well possess a boundless potential application, in sense or reference, containing everything, extending across all genera, uniting all beings in a set of primary substantial determinations. Still, they would not survive the force of Aristotle's "indefinite."

It suffices to consider, as an illustration, the oldest member of the set: "non-man." If one admits that this word has a sense, it is because it implies an exclusive, disjunctive opposition: that between "man" and "non-man." Once posited, such an opposition may be referred to any and to all beings. To this degree, the range of its signification may recall that of the other "infinite names" investigated in the medieval schools. But the similarity between these varieties of indeterminate expressions belies fundamental differences. According to the grammarians, a part of speech such as a relative or subordinate pronoun, "that" or "which," can potentially mean all things, being substitutable, in an acceptable syntax, for any stated common noun. According to the medieval philosophers, a term that contains everything, such as "being," "thing," or "one," can signify all subjects, being predicable, if equivocally, beyond the limits of the species, genera, and categories known to the tradition. Yet the opposition suggested by an expression such as "non-man" possesses a different boundlessness. It is more extreme.

In their generality, the infinite words of the grammarians and the terms that contain everything of the philosophers evoke expanses of things that can be said: universes of signification, conceived in their virtual endlessness. The *nomen infinitum* transmitted to the Middle Ages by Boethius signifies otherwise. If it refers to any domain of meaning, it is by drawing out a line that traverses it. Nothing to which such a term applies can escape its divisive force. It may be recalled that Aristotle's doctrine of oppositions stipulates that a property and its indefinite contrary cannot both apply to a single subject, at least in the same respect and at the same time. From that stricture, one may infer a simple rule of exclusive disjunctive reasoning: for any pair of terms such as "non-man" and "man," if the first holds, then the second does not, and conversely. This reasoning applies to every case in which an infinite term is truly stated. If one takes as an example the expression "non-circular," one may consider every geometrical figure, certain that if this attribute pertains to it, "circular" does not; in the same way, of the natural numbers familiar to classical and medieval mathematics, one may assert, without hesitation, that each is either "non-even" (that is, odd) or "even," and if it is one, then it is not the other; for it cannot be both.

The force of indefinite expressions of the Aristotelian variety remains, in any case, unchanged. Under the divisive power of such an infinite name, a range of sense or reference splits in two. Whatever the domain of the things that one refers it to, be it massive or minute, real or imaginary, the *nomen infinitum* in the Aristotelian-Boethian sense inscribes its cut in it. Unlike the infinite words of grammar and the comprehensive predicable terms of twelfth-century philosophy, an expression such as "non-man," "non-just" or "non-thing" does more than evoke an indefinite expanse of signification. It also fractures it. It is, therefore, the ruin of the transcendent and the transcendental. Against the universality of grammatical indefiniteness and against the universality of total predicable containment, the "infinite name" sets its own: a universality of extensive and intensive partition. Exploring the ways of indeterminacy, the early medieval thinkers saw this fact keenly. In their theories of the varieties of spoken infinity, they sought to avoid the divisiveness that the infinite name necessarily announced. Their successors in philosophy would depart from this point. Some would follow in the steps of their teachers, limiting the field of infinite naming to secure the integrity of transcendent terms and transcendental properties. Others would defy the old prohibitions, venturing into unexplored terrains of speech and thought. There, in new logics and metaphysics, non-things never glimpsed before would distinctly, if at times impossibly, come into view.

CHAPTER SEVEN

From Empty Words

Philosophy has long understood itself as a practice that aims to establish order amid the disarray of our multiple and conflicting representations. Yet it has also often found itself, as if on an unexpected detour, occupied with a lesser task: disciplining our use of words. The reckoning with speech, by turns destructive and constructive, has taken several shapes. Thinkers have often sought to demonstrate that certain forms of reasoning and theses are confused, or intrinsically misleading; at other times, they have also taken to advancing arguments and propositions in their stead. Philosophers have concentrated on individual statements as well as the relations that bind them in chains of inference. But they have also attended to individual words — nouns, adjectives and verbs — even when the subjects in question, at least superficially, seem hardly of a linguistic nature. A number of Plato's dialogues might be characterized as seeking to establish the conditions under which certain common expressions are best employed. As examples, one might cite the discussions of the senses of "just" in the *Republic*, "pious" in the *Euthyphro*, "speech" in the *Phaedrus*, or "learning" in the *Meno*. To succeed in the projects that they set themselves, defining the nature of these qualities and substances, these dialogues must resolve problems of vocabulary. The clarification of thinking does not advance far without a treatment — if not a therapy — of speech.

From its inception in Greece, however, philosophy has also found itself drawn into a stranger relation to language. In addition to deliberating about the correct uses of given words, thinkers have felt the need to devise expressions that none before them knew. In this domain, as in many others, the rise of knowledge has been accompanied by the emergence of jargon. Among numerous famous cases, one might evoke Democritus's introduction of the cosmic "swerve" or *parenklisis*, Aristotle's coining of the word *energeia*, which we now know as "energy," or the Sceptics' introduction of the technical term *adoxastōs*, "beliefless," to name their new ideal of philosophic activity. Yet there are also examples of a different nature, which testify to a confrontation with speech that is more extreme and telling.

Classical sources suggest that the Greek Stoics were perhaps the first thinkers to invent a curious set of technical expressions: "empty words."[1] The oldest recorded examples of such locutions are the terms *blityri* and *skindapsos*. These words resemble ones contained in the ancient Greek language, and the philologists who have studied them have shown that they are susceptible to lexical analysis of a kind. Both expressions seem to "derive from the musical domain and, in particular, the domain of strings."[2] *Blityri* evokes the twanging of a harp; *skindapsos* summons to the mind the sound of some stringed instrument. The philosophical works in which one encounters these words leave little doubt as to the function that they serve. Each of them is a learned barbarism invented for a single purpose: to show that it is possible to distinguish a unit of speech, or word (*lexis*), from a unit of sense, or definition (*logos*).

According to Diogenes Laertius, these expressions are the work of one of the founders of the Stoic school, Zeno of Citium, who evoked them as examples of terms that, while words, are "without meaning" (*asēmos*).[3] Galen, an authority on logic as on medicine, is also familiar with this usage.[4] Sextus Empiricus records both expressions in his *Adversus mathematicos*, even as he notes: "The [true] cannot be found in what has no meaning, such as *blityri* and *skindapsos*."[5] In the fifth or sixth century CE, Ammonius introduces them into his commentary on Aristotle's *Prior Analytics*, adding to their number a third word: *knax*. Explaining this set of three, the Alexandrian scholar remarks that they are "sounds" or "words" "without meaning"" (*asēmoi phōnai*).[6] These expressions were to have a long, if modest, life in logic. In the fifth century CE, Syrianus, the head of Plato's Academy in Athens, refers in a commentary on Aristotle's *Metaphysics* to "the much-discussed *skindapsos*," as a word signifying a "thing that may not exist in any way at all."[7]

Such terms were also to be transmitted, with classical logic, to posterity. Never belonging properly to one language, they could not, however, be transferred to another. The ancient barbarisms thus persisted in Roman transliteration, where they came to be known to the Latin authors as technical terms that were both foreign and meaningless. Boethius would write in his commentary on Aristotle's *De interpretatione* of "words that are composed of letters and syllables, but have no signification, such as *blituri*."[8] In the Middle Ages, the role assigned to these expressions was often attributed to other locutions, such as *buff* and *buffbaff*, which were to be similarly defined as "non-significant sounds [or words]" (*voces non significativae*).[9] *Blityri* and *skindapsos*, however, never fell entirely out of use, at least among scholars doing commerce in the technical terms of philosophy. In Jean Leclerc's *Ontologia, sive de ente in genere* of 1698, both expressions may be found. There the reader learns that they are "words signifying nothing."[10] In the eighteenth century, Leibniz alludes to them more than once. In his *Essays on Theodicy*, which date to 1710, he recalls: "The old schools gave the names *Scindapsus* or *Blityri* to words empty of sense [*vuides de sens*]."[11] Elsewhere he assigns to the second of these empty words a curiously positive role. "*Nothing*," Leibniz remarks in a logical fragment, "is what can be named but not conceived, like *blitiri* [*Nihil est quod nominari potest, sed cogitare non potest, ut Blitiri*]".[12]

The paradox, of course, is that as soon as they were introduced, *blityri*, *skindapsos*, and *knax* acquired an established meaning, at least for philosophers. Those learned in the arts of language would know that these are "non-signifying expressions" (*voces non-significativae*): clear signs of the absence of sense. A difficult problem still remained, however, to be solved. What exactly does the attribute "non-signifying" (*asēmos*, or *non significativum*), in such settings, signify? The indefiniteness of this quality admits of several interpretations: being "without any meaning whatsoever," "without meaning in some usual sense," "without definite meaning," "without reference," and, not least, "without such a meaning that, when employed in a sentence, will yield truth or falsity." The semantic void marked by these terms can be filled in many ways and, if one is to employ them fruitfully, one has little choice but to choose among their variously sterile senses.

It is likely that in its first appearances, every technical expression exhibits something of the obscurity of a *blityri*, or a *skindapsos*, and some of the most august of philosophic terms may well have once displayed the opacity of such a word as *knax*. If a new expression is favourably received, the jarring sound of its first unfamiliarity tends to be soon forgotten. With a certain historical remove, examples, however, are not difficult to identify.

When, close to the year 1150, the Toledan translator Dominicus Gundissalinus composes his treatise on the organization of knowledge, *De divisione philosophie*, he introduces into philosophical discourse a word that may have struck his first readers as a perplexingly obscure noun: *metaphysica*. To the learned, that expression was not, of course, entirely unknown. As early as the first century CE, Adronicus of Rhodes employed the Greek phrase "after the physics" (*meta ta physika*) in his edition of Aristotle. He thereby designated the position of several treatises that, in his ordering of the Philosopher's works, followed the books known as the *Physics*. This was to be an influential choice of terms. Later Greek Aristotelians, from Alexander of Aphrodisias to Themistius and Ammonius, followed his usage; for them, *metaphysica* was a phrase denoting a set of Aristotle's books.[13] The Latin and Arabic readers of Aristotle would also know the expression in this sense. Boethius employs the term *metaphysica* as the title of certain works by Aristotle. The Philosopher's Arabic readers also wrote of a group of texts that they called, in transliteration from the Greek, *mâtâtâfîsîqâ* or, in Arabic translation, *ba'd al-ṭabi'īyāt*, that is, "After the Physics."[14] None of the ancient commentators, whether Greek, Latin or Arabic, seems to have been familiar with "metaphysics" as a generic designation of a field of study, rather than a title. Precisely this was to be the innovation of Gundissalinus's usage. In terms that are in appearances traditional, being based on a Boethian classification, Gundissalinus divides the theoretical sciences into three parts, which he orders by nobility.[15] First there is physics (*physica*), or natural science (*scientia naturalis*), the "lowest"; next comes mathematics (*mathematica*); and third and last is "theology" (*theologia*), which may be called "first science" (*scientia prima*), "first philosophy" (*philosophia prima*), or — as the author now wagers — "metaphysics" (*metaphysica*).[16]

Gundissalinus's designation was to have a bright future. From the thirteenth century to the end of the Middle Ages, from the early modern period through to the twenty-first century, "metaphysics," universally employed as a common noun, has retained the status he bestowed on it. Yet the nature of the field of inquiry that this word designates has also remained a question. It is certain that Aristotle himself had no single designation for the domain of study to which he dedicated his treatises "after the *Physics*." Pierre Aubenque has written that in their origins, the investigations carried out in the work known to posterity as Aristotle's *Metaphysics* belong to a "nameless science."[17] Aristotle, for his part, repeatedly evokes a "science" he "searched after" (*epistēmē zētoumenē*).[18] That search was not to be completed quickly. Two millennia after the redaction of the books "After the *Physics*," Leibniz observed that "metaphysics, which Aristotle called *zētoumenē*, belongs to those sciences that are still pursued."[19]

The truth is that the discussions collected in the texts of Aristotle's so-called *Metaphysics* contain developments that can be represented in several ways. In the eyes of the Philosopher's classical readers, these works provided the founding contribution to the field of investigation that they knew by at least three titles, in Greek, in Arabic as in Latin: "wisdom," "first philosophy," and "theology." The diversity of those designations is no accident. It bespeaks a major theoretical uncertainty, which concerns above all one troubled point: the place, in this doctrine of being and beings, of the highest and noblest of beings said to be — that is, God. The history of medieval "metaphysics" after Gundissalinus is in large part that of philosophers' answers to the question of the unity of this field of study. The solutions proposed by the Scholastics of the Latin West were crucially informed by the works of Avicenna and Averroes, who discussed the "subject" (*mawḍūʿ*) of Aristotle's unnamed science in treatises and in commentaries on Aristotle read in European universities starting in the twelfth century. In the early eleventh century of the Christian era, Avicenna argues in his *Healing* (*Al-Shifāʾ*) that the subject of the theoretical science inaugurated by Aristotle must be "being as being" (*al-mawjūd bi-mā huwa mawjūd, ens inquantum est ens*), rather than divinity.[20] The reason for Avicenna's exclusion of God from the subject of first philosophy can be simply stated. Aristotle himself stipulates that each science presupposes its proper subject. Now, in "first philosophy," Avicenna reasons, divine existence is to be demonstrated; therefore, it cannot be assumed. Accepting principles no less Aristotelian, Averroes, in the twelfth century, reaches an opposing position, arguing that it is the task of physics to prove God's existence. "After the *Physics*," then, one may presuppose it, studying its nature in detail.

The Scholastic philosophers of the medieval West proposed their own answers to the question of the unity of metaphysics, combining these two positions in new ways. Among many discussions carried out in the thirteenth and fourteenth centuries in Europe, three paths may be discerned, as Albert Zimmermann has shown.[21] The first position, espoused by Roger Bacon, William of Aspall, and Aegedius of Rome, holds that "metaphysics" is a science of several subjects: being, substance, and God. According to this view, "first philosophy" lacks any formal unity of definition, although it may be that everything studied in its domain is ultimately reducible to a single cause.[22] Albert the Great, Richard Rufus, and Thomas Aquinas express a second view. According to these thinkers, the subject of metaphysics possesses a formal unity in God, insofar as He is the cause of "being in general" (*ens in communi*).[23] The third position is discernible in Roger Kilwardby, Henry of Ghent, and Duns Scotus. It consists in claiming that the subject of metaphysics is "being as being" (*ens qua ens*), such that God himself, defined as the supreme being, falls within its domain.[24]

After Gundissalinus, "metaphysics," however, would also concern itself with matters more minimal than God, being, or the nature of substance. At times, philosophers would even look to what might seem the most unremarkable of things for the solution to the problem of "being as being." When, at the end of the thirteenth century, Henry of Ghent aims to clarify the subject of metaphysics, setting out the nature of being in its "most common" sense, he thus orients his discussion with respect to one notion that seems so elementary that few thinkers before him might have thought it worthy of systematic exposition: the notion, namely, of "the thing" (*res*). "The thing, or the something [*res, sive aliquid*]," Henry declares in his Seventh Quodlibet, "is the most common of all [*omnium communissimum*], that which contains everything in an analogous scope."[25] Here the terms "the thing, or something," are employed in an undeniably technical acceptation, and to be understood in its full force, Henry's thesis requires some commentary. His proposition stipulates that existing "things," whether material or intelligible, constitute only portions of what there is. With a terminological decision of the greatest consequences, Henry employs the name "thing, or something" (*res, sive aliquid*) for anything to which one might attach some positive properties: "*any thought content, whether or not it corresponds to an object.*"[26] In Henry's parlance, "the term *res*," as J. F. Courtine notes, "designates the content of any representation whatsoever, abstracted from its being 'outside the intellect' [*extra intellectum*]."[27]

Henry avails himself of the history of the Latin tongue to make his thesis clear. Evoking a thesis familiar to several thinkers of his time, he explains that the term *res* or "thing" is ambiguous by virtue of its etymology. In one sense, a "thing" (*res*) is so-called on account of its *ratitudo*, or "ratitude"; in other words, it partakes of a certain stability, being firmly established in some "reality" outside the mind. In another sense, however, a "thing" draws its nature from the activity named by *reor, reris*, "to opine," "think," and "believe"; in this meaning, a "thing" pertains solely to some individual's mind, being no more than the object of an "opinion."[28] Of these two senses of "thing" (*res*), Henry reasons, the second is the vaster. The philosopher maintains that the category of "the thing according to opinion" (*res secundum opinionem*) embraces being as such, without distinction, since whatever can be said to be is such that it can be "according to opinion." Whether alive or dead, real or fictitious, a man, for example, is always such a "thing."

Yet so, too, Henry adds, is the fabled "goat-stag" (*tragelaphos*, or *hirco-cervus*). Aristotle had introduced this odd animal into his logical works as a thing that one can name, although it does not exist.[29] Henry admits that such a creature is fantastical, but he argues that it is nonetheless hardly "nothing." Even if it is to be found nowhere outside the thinker's mind, it possesses certain properties, most notably that of being of a bipartite animal nature: "half goat, half stag." This alone distinguishes it from being nothing, since nothing, as an ancient tradition holds, possesses no properties. The "goat-stag," in short, is a perfect "thing," as would be, for that matter, a "goat-man," or a "stag-man," were one to conceive them. It is safe to venture that all such creatures are largely unattested in the order of nature, at least as we know it. One might add that, like the "chimera," they are even impossible in it. Nonetheless, these various non-men can be, and indeed have been, opined.

"Things" of this kind have no clear place in Aristotle's books of *Meta-physics*. Such *res* are closely related, however, to a concept proposed by

Avicenna in his divine science. In the fifth chapter of Book One of his "first philosophy" (*philosophia prima*), as it would be known in Latin, Avicenna identifies a set of "intentions" (*maʿānī*, known to the Latins as *intentiones*) or "concepts" (*taṣawwurāt, imaginationes*) that are so fundamental as to be indefinable, except by notions less simple than they.[30] The first two of these intentions are "the existent" or "being" (*al-mawjūd, ens*) and "the thing" (*al-shay, res*). All languages, Avicenna writes, distinguish these two concepts, even if, in certain uses, their differences may recede from view.[31] Avicenna first explains that the "existent" is "established" (*muthbat*) and "realized" or "determinate" (*muḥaṣṣal*)." Its being may be of two varieties, referable either to singular items (*fī-l-ʿiyān, in singularibus*) or to the soul (*fī-n-nafs, in anima*).[32] Next Avicenna offers a double account of the "thing," which he presents as no less "established" and "realized" than the existent. The thing is, first, susceptible to becoming the subject of speech, being "that on which true discourse bears [*huwa alladī yuṣaḥḥu ʿanhu-l khabar, de quo potest aliquid vere enuntiari*]."[33] Second, it possesses a "certain stability" (*ḥaqīqa khaṣṣa, certitudo propria*) on which its definition or "what-ness" (*māhiyya, quidditas*) rests.[34] A thing is, in other words, some "something," with a fixed nature that can be identified. While the "existent" draws its essence from being in singular things and in the mind, the "thing," by contrast, can be present solely in the soul. In this sense, a "thing" may, in fact, be said to be "inexistent" (*maʿdūm, quod dicitur non esse*), not because it is nothing at all — for to be stated or posited it must still be conceived as such — but because it is present only in the mind that lays hold of it.[35]

A century before Avicenna, Al-Farabi, in a text unknown to the Latin West, proposed a similarly fundamental distinction between the "existent" or "being" (*al-mawjūd*) and the "thing" (*al-shay*). In his *Book of Letters*, Al-Farabi explained that "'thing' is said of anything that has a given whatness [quiddity, or *māhiyya*]," "whether it be outside the soul or the object of representation of any kind." To state of something that it is a "thing" is therefore to affirm that it possesses a nature that can be defined. To state of something that it is an "existent" is to make a different claim, because it is to posit that the "thing" in question can be found somewhere outside the intellect. To this degree, Al-Farabi explains, "the thing is more general than the existent [*a'amma min al-mawjūd*]."[36] Even the "impossible," as he points out, is called a "thing," but one would not go so far as to maintain that it is "existent."[37]

Several scholars have related these distinctions in classical Arabic metaphysics to theological debates carried out in the first centuries of Islam. Early on, the adepts of the Islamic thought known as the *kalām* were divided on two important doctrinal points: whether the different divine attributes, such as "all-merciful," "all-knowing," and "all-powerful," are truly "things," and whether God may himself be called either a "thing" or an "existent."[38] Yet it was not only the theory of the divine nature that required that these concepts be rendered clear and distinct. The Islamic account of creation may also have demanded it. It is striking that, according to the Qur'ān, God creates by conferring existence upon what, later, will have been his creation. Unlike the divinity of the Book of Genesis, he does not say, "Let there be . . ." Twice, he simply utters an imperative: "Be!" (*kun*).[39] The structure of that act of speech suggests that, before creation, there are "things" somehow known to God: "things" such as the ideas of uncreated creatures, which are still inexistent.

According to an early witness, Fakhr al-Dīn al-Rāzī, the theologians of the Mu'atazila taught that in saying "Be!" God speaks, in fact, to "inexistent possible beings." These, the theologians would have held, are "essences [*dawāt, a'yān, ḥaqā'iq*] before entering into existence; the divine Agent does not make essences, but rather makes them exist."[40] The authors associated with the school of the tenth-century thinker Abū Hāshim al-Jubbā'i go so far as to hold that, even for mortal minds, the autonomy of the notion of the "thing" follows from the fact that we can discuss what does not exist. Several arguments support this view. According to Ibn Muttawayh, "If anyone claims that 'thing' corresponds to 'existent,' he is mistaken. For one says such things as: 'I have conceived an existing thing.' But then [if the 'thing' corresponds to 'existent'], this is redundant."[41] A perfectly complementary reasoning of the apagogic form has been attributed to Abū Hāshim himself. He is reputed to have maintained that, "If the name ['thing'] were restricted to [signifying] the existent, then whoever said, 'I have conceived an inexistent thing' would be caught in a contradiction, as if he had in fact said, 'I have conceived an existent inexistent'; and if this is absurd, then it must be known that the name ['thing'] can be attributed both to the inexistent and to the existent."[42] As Ahmed Alami concludes, "the identification of thingness with existence leads either to redundancy or to contradiction. Such an identification is thus absurd, and the doctrine of the Bahšāmians is therefore that 'when someone says *I have conceived a thing*, one cannot know if he has conceived an existent or an inexistent.'"[43]

Neutral with respect to the distinction between existence and inexistence, this "thing" differs markedly from the "things" known to the Greeks and Romans. The classical Latin idea of *res*, which in many settings translates the Greek *pragma*, seems to derive from the field of goods (*bona*), in which the "thing" is securely present.[44] Nonetheless, there is one case in which the concept of a classical Roman "something" draws close to the neutral mode of existence (or non-existence) that the classical Islamic philosophers attributed to their thought "things." In expounding the doctrines of his Greek teachers to his friend Lucilius, Seneca emphasizes a point on which the Stoics differ from the students of the Academy. Plato, he reports, holds that there is a "supreme genus," identifiable with existence, being, or the fact "that something is" (*quod est*). By contrast, "some Stoics" teach that there is a genus that is "even higher" (*magis genus*):

> In their opinion, the first genus is the "something" [or "the what?": *quid*]. I will explain to you the reason for their holding this opinion. They say that in nature there are things that are [*quaedam sunt*] and things that are not [*quaedam non sunt*]; and even those that are not are incorporated in nature. These are things that present themselves to the mind [*quae animo succurrunt*], such as centaurs, giants and all that which, having issued from false thinking [*falsa cogitatione formarum*], has ended up taking on some imagistic consistency [*habere aliquam imaginem coepit*], despite having no existence [*quamvis non habeat substantiam*].[45]

Seneca's account of the position of "some Stoics" (*quibusdam Stoicis*) raises several questions, both in its own terms and in relation to other ancient presentations of the Hellenistic doctrine. Several classical sources do suggest that the Stoics believed there to be a "supreme genus," beyond that of "being" or "substance" (*ousia*), a genus identifiable with a single, indefinite Greek pronoun that corresponds exactly to the Latin *quid*: *ti*, "something."[46] As a rule, however, this category accounts not so much for "false" imaginings, as Seneca writes, as for a type of bodiless things that the Stoics introduced into thinking: the "incorporeals" — time, void, place and the expressible — which "subsist" (*hyparchein*), in the absence of bodily existence (*ousia*).[47] Seneca's category of the "something" or "what" seems, instead, to function in a manner close to that of the "thing" of the medieval Latin philosophers. Like the *res* evoked by Henry, which applies no less to the goat-stag than to the goat and to the stag, the Roman thinker's *quid* holds for a living man, a centaur and a giant. In the genus of this supreme "something," the difference between man and non-man, being and non-being, fades from view.

It is striking that even before encountering Avicenna's works of divine science, the Latin authors of Christian Europe began to complicate the senses of *res*. In a passage of his *De doctrina christiana*, Augustine employs the word "thing" in a novel fashion: it is, for him, a name for the unity of the Trinity that he affirms.[48] In the eleventh century, Anselm of Canterbury suggests in his letter on the incarnation of the Word that one may give the name *res* to a purely linguistic being: the "thing stated" (*res enuntiata*).[49] Such usages become the subject of sustained discussion in the twelfth century, when Abelard devotes attention to defining the term "thing" (*res*) in logic.[50] In one passage, Abelard argues against those who believe predicable universal terms to be "things" (*res*). He explains, in a "non-realist" manner, that universals are merely "words" (*voces*), which signify things and bear witness to a common "essence" (*esse*), or *status*.[51]

Elsewhere Abelard discusses the use of the term "thing" for the signification not of a single term, such as a predicable, but of a complete proposition. "Socrates is mortal," for instance, signifies one complex thought that is irreducible to each of the units of signification of which it is composed. Is the whole meaning of the statement, in distinction to its many parts, a *res*? Abelard's answer is that it is not; he argues that the signification of a sentence is not a "thing" but a "saying" (*dictum*), which expresses "the manner in which the things stated relate to each other" (*modus rerum se habendi ad invicem*). Yet the truth is that philosopher's own usage is more equivocal than his declarations allow, as Jean Jolivet has shown.[52] Although Abelard explicitly recommends that the term "thing" be restricted to physical beings (*physicae res*), he also employs *res* to signify an intensely discursive being. In such cases, he writes of the "signified thing" (*res . . . ceterorum praedicamentorum*), "the thing under the word, the subject of the word" (*rerum subjectarum decem nominibus*), and "the things contained in predicable terms" (*res . . . quae in praedicamentis continentur*).[53]

In their debates concerning words "that contain everything," Abelard's contemporaries are also led to distinguish the uncertain senses of a "thing." *Res* features in the early enumerations of "terms that contain everything," which cut across all categories and apply to everything that is. It is therefore unsurprising that, in wondering whether such comprehensive names may be submitted to *infinitatio*, the twelfth-century thinkers also run up against the question of the distinction between "thing" and "being." They come to it, in blithe ignorance of Avicenna, through the application of the principle of "contraposition." It may be recalled that this rule dictates that an affirmative proposition (A) of the form *Every X is Y* may be immediately converted, without any change in truth or falsity, into a negative proposition (E) of the form *No non-Y is X*. From "Every man is a thing" (*omnis homo est res*), one may, in short, infer that "No non-thing is a man" (*Nulla non-res est homo*). From that sentence, one may deduce a further universal affirmative statement: "Every non-thing is a non-man" (*Omnis non-res est non-homo*). If that statement is true, however, then its subject must also necessarily exist; one may maintain that "every non-thing is," or "every non-thing exists." The authors of the twelfth century had faced the consequences of that strange statement. Were it true, the term "thing" would no longer "contain everything," since there would be at least one thing — that is, the "non-thing" — that escaped it. Moreover, the contents of "thing" and "being" would also no longer correspond. For now "being" would belong to the "non-thing," no less than to the "thing." It was to avoid the possibility of such a cleavage between infinite words, to ward off the danger of a partition between "being" and "thing," that the twelfth-century thinkers forbade the application of the rule of contraposition to any propositions including "terms that contains everything."[54] This stricture alone was to protect the unity of "thing" and "being," *res* and *ens*.

That measure was not to last long. As soon as Avicenna's first philosophy came to be widely known in the Latin West, the question returned with new force. A shifting of the problem can already be detected in the early development of the theory of transcendental terms. In Philip the Chancellor's introduction of "the most common" (*communissima*) of all properties, no mention is made of the term "thing." The first Scholastic "transcendentals" are but four: "being, one, true and good" (*ens, unum verum, et bonum*).[55] Faithful to the Chancellor, Alexander of Hales, Bonaventure and Albert the Great restrict their enumerations of transcendentals to these four transcategorical properties. Thirty years after Philip's *Summa de bono*, however, "the picture changes."[56] Thomas Aquinas proposes the most extensive systematic treatment of the transcendentals in the thirteenth century, identifying six basic determinations. He now adds to the old quartet "thing" (*res*) and "something" (*aliquid*).[57] That Avicenna's doctrine plays a role in his choice is certain. Yet "thing" and "something" occupy an uneasy place in Thomistic metaphysics. Thomas understands being as actuality and, following Phillip, he presents the transcendentals as the names of the most basic attributes of being (*esse*). But he also knows that for Avicenna, whose *Metaphysica* he takes as a crucial source, the "thing," unlike the "existent" (*ens*), possesses a "what-ness" or a "quiddity" (*quidditas*) that is distinct from being, or existence (*esse*). In this presentation of the transcendentals, the term "thing" remains, therefore, something of an outlier. "It is difficult to see," Jan A. Aertsen has observed, "how *res*," for Thomas, "can be said to be a 'property' of being."[58]

By the early fourteenth century, a new and decisive step is taken. Francis of Marchia devotes the third Quodlibet of his commentary on Peter Lombard's *Sentences* to resolving the difficulty bequeathed by Avicenna: "Whether the intention of the 'existent' is more primary than the intention of the 'thing.'"[59] By posing the question of the relation between "being" and "thing" in explicit and programmatic form, Francis contests a metaphysical principle that for centuries had been viewed as in no need of explanation. This is the principle that "the concept of 'being' has a primary position with respect to all other concepts," that *ens*, in other words, "designates the most general, and therefore the primordial and foundational, manner of the being of things *in themselves*."[60] But Francis does more than to turn an axiom into a question, for he also answers it in a form that is perhaps unprecedented. Reversing the traditional order of the transcendental properties, Francis sets the idea of the "thing" (*res*) before that of "being" (*ens*). Then he goes so far as to derive the determinations of being, being one, being true, and being good from the property of being "something." To be in any way, he explains, is to be a certain *res* and, therefore, to be conceivable by means of the general concept presupposed by the thing: "somethingness" (*aliquitas*). Hence his conclusion: "It appears that one must say that the concept of 'somethingness' [*conceptus aliquitatis*] is the most comprehensive concept [*conceptus latissimus*] of all concepts, for no concept is as comprehensive or as wide as it; rather, it is absolutely more comprehensive and more universal than any other. And this [concept of somethingness] is the first object of the intellect — not 'being' [*ens*], 'one' [*unum*], or 'good' [*bonum*]."[61]

Francis's words are worth unfolding. The idea of "somethingness," he holds, is "absolutely more comprehensive and universal" than any other. Taken in isolation, however, this thesis, however clear, runs the risk of concealing the full force of the new concept that Francis posits. "Somethingness" is not only "more comprehensive and wider" than any other concept. It also draws close to the inconceivable, and for a simple reason: by definition, this concept stands against the emptiest of all notions, which is hardly an idea at all. Francis explains himself by means of an extended reasoning in infinite names. He observes that the notion of "man" is opposed to that of "non-man" (*non-homo*). So, too, he writes, the idea of "one" is opposed to "non-one" (*non-unum*); and "being" or "existent" (*ens*) is opposed to "non-existent" or "non-being" (*non-ens*). All these terms, however obscure, are united signifying "something." Even "non-beings," he recalls, may be conceived, as the example of impossible creatures and constructions indicate; despite their faulty modes of existence, they partake of "somethingness." Yet the term "something" (*aliquid*) itself is opposed only to "nothing" (*nihil*): that, namely, which is "not something positive" (*non sit aliquid positiuum*).[62] To be "something" (*aliquid*), for Francis, is thus to be anything that is not nothing; conversely, to be anything that is not nothing is to be "something." But "to be anything that is not nothing" is to be in elusively complex ways. Whatever can be defined as "non-man," "non-one," or "non-being" — and all the other shadowy essences that Francis likewise admits — lays claim to that minimal "being," or, as one ought perhaps better say, that "non-being." Anything that is something, anything that can be something, as long as it is more than nothing, and even if it is not existent and will never be existent, will be a "thing." Therefore, it will fall under the supreme concept of "somethingness."

Existent or inexistent, actual, possible or impossible, laying claim only to a certain "what-ness," *res*, in such terms, are peculiar "things" indeed. One might argue that, in the language of this late medieval philosopher, the most familiar of words designates the most abstract and tenuous of all concepts. *Res* are, one might infer, anything but "goods," fungible or tangible objects. But the means by which the old and common Latin word *res* acquires this perplexing technical signification is also remarkable in itself. Unlike *blituri* or *skindapsos*, which lived long lives in meaning by "meaning nothing," and unlike *metaphysica*, which briefly lost its exact textual reference to acquire a new sense, *res*, in the lexicon of the first philosophers of the Latin West, fulfils its calling in freeing itself of the elementary meanings it long possessed. Transferred from ordinary speech to the idiom of medieval first philosophy, translated from Greek to Latin, by means of Arabic, the scope of meaning of the new Scholastic "thing" reaches beyond that of any older word. It comes to signify the concept that sustains all naming by means of *non-*, whether the *non-* in question be one of opposition or contrariety, fantasy or falsehood, simple privation or necessary inexistence. *Res* is, in each case, what enables the non-man — centaur, giant, chimera or goat-stag — to be thought, even if, being unattested or impossible, he, she, or it cannot also be said to exist. "Something" intelligible, even if it is so precisely in being impossible, such a *res* thus points to a limit of conception, which must somehow be conceived. Yet however fleeting its form may have been, however extreme its articulations, the fringe of this "thing, or something" would also be surpassed. Those who came after Avicenna, Henry and Francis would extend the edge of *metaphysica* further. Aiming to order their representations, philosophers would find new words to evoke the expanses of sense that they envisaged, and they would empty, ever more intensely, the expressions that they received.

CHAPTER EIGHT

Toward the Object in General

The early modern age was a time of new things in logic and metaphysics. Terms defined in the universities of medieval Europe were put to unexpected uses, and notions once rooted in the principles of Scholasticism came to play roles outside the fields of their first elaboration. Implicitly and explicitly, thinkers set medieval concepts against the aims for which they had been formed. Lorenzo Valla, humanist, grammarian and polemicist, provides an instructive example. In his *Dialectical Disputations*, whose first edition dates to 1439, Valla sets out to offer a "re-ploughing" (*ripastinatio*), "repairing" (*reconcinnatio*), and "revision" (*retractatio*) of logic, which he grasps, in rhetorical terms, as the theory of argument. To this end, he begins by offering a critical analysis of the "basic principles" (*primordia*) of traditional philosophy. These he takes to be twofold: the ten categories enumerated by Aristotle and the extracategorical terms known as the transcendental properties, which, according to the Scholastic doctrine, apply to everything that is. Condemning the obscurities of thinking to which the abuse of Latin led the doctors of the universities, Valla recalls the medieval theories of the "thing," arguing forcefully that they be revised. Evoking the set of transcendental terms as Thomas Aquinas knew them, Valla remarks that these universal properties are considered to be six in number: "being, something, thing, one, true, and good [*ens, aliquid, res, unum, verum, bonum*]." That plurality strikes him as unfounded. Likening the field of namable things to a dominion in need of a ruler, he writes: "Let us ask which of these terms, or which signification of the term, is emperor and king of them all — the most inclusive of any that God, the Son of God, gave to us."[1]

Valla knows that the Scholastic Aristotelians and readers of the Arabic philosophers would bestow the rank of preeminent transcendental property on the first term in their series: *ens*, that is, "being" or "existent." Yet he objects to this choice. He recalls that, by its form, the word *ens* is "a participle of every gender, but when it changes into a noun it is neuter only." To determine what this neuter signifies, one must consider its morphology. Valla reminds his reader that, in Latin, every participial form condenses the meanings of a relative or antecedent pronoun and an indicative verb, conjugated in the present tense. The term *accidens*, "happening," means "that which happens," *id quod accidit*, just as *amans*, "loving," refers to the person, man or woman, "who loves" (*qui et quae amat*), and *consequens* and *antecedens* signify "that which follows" and "that which precedes" (*id quod consequitur, id quod antecedit*).[2] Valla reasons that the meaning of the participial expression *ens*, "existent" or "being," also adheres to this pattern. It is shorthand for a more customary expression: "that which exists" (*id quod est*), "that which is," or, more generally, is said to be.

The property of "being" (*ens*), therefore, expresses this meaning: "that which is." But what, then, is "that"? Valla holds that none of the three subsequent transcendental terms, "one, true and good," can furnish a satisfactory answer, for as abstract substantives built from adjectives, they all depend in their meaning on the noun to which they are referred. One might answer that the crucial term among the six is "something" (*aliquid*). Yet Valla argues that the meaning of this word, too, can be resolved into a simpler form: "something" (*aliquid*) is simply "some thing" (*aliqua res*). It thereby points to the "thing" (*res*): the sole word among the six that, for Valla, deserves the rights of supremacy.[3]

Valla defines *res* in a new sense, in distinction to both quiddity and existence. With attention to the varieties of classical usage and in fidelity to the rhetorical tradition, Valla understands the Latin "thing," in each of its many senses, to signify a discursive being: the matter at issue in speech. As evidence, Valla evokes such expressions as *res privata* and *res publica*, which point to private and public "matters," and such formulaic expressions as *de re rustica, de re uxoria, de re navali*, and *de re militari*, "things" of farming, marriage, the navy and the army.[4] The "thing," in such cases, signifies no single concept; rather, it constitutes "a function of signification, which assures a minimal unit of reference," as Fosca Mariani Zini has observed.[5] It is by naming that which is at stake in discourse that *res* reveals itself, each time, to be "the most comprehensive [*capacissima*] of all words," *rex* and *imperator*, and the source of the "transcendental" terms."[6]

Even as Valla roots the transcategorical properties of being in the word "thing," *res* also acquires a different meaning in the early modern period. Despite its novelty, this sense also derives, in part, from a medieval invention. Classical Arabic culture witnessed the rise of a new field of mathematics, which treats not only the definite magnitudes and multitudes known to ancient arithmetic and geometry but also a new quantity: one that is unknown in itself but that, by virtue of the relations it bears to others, can be defined when submitted to calculation. The name of this field of study remains in use today: "algebra," a Latinized form of the Arabic word *al-jabr,* which Muḥammad ibn Mūsā al-Khwārizmī employs in the title of the book with which he sets out his new technique.[7] The European works of mathematics that draw on al-Khwārizmī's invention put Latin and Romance names for the "thing" to a new use. It has been observed that "in the Latin translations of Arabic algebra by John of Seville, Gerard of Cremona and Leonard of Pisa, that is, from the beginning of the thirteenth century, the word chosen to designate the unknown is *res*, and at the end of the fifteenth century, Luca Pacioli's *Summa de Arithmetica* (Venice, 1494) introduces the term *Cosa*, 'thing,' into the vernacular, almost systematically and in the same sense."[8]

This usage quickly becomes standard in works of Italian mathematics. From Cardano to Tartaglia, the "thing" is the unknown quantity to be defined. This terminology is soon adopted in other languages, such as German, where the technical terms *Cosa, Cossa*, and *Coss* are soon also standard.[9] When expounding the elementary algebraic "rule of three," for example, which allows one to determine the value of an unknown quantity, if one knows that a first quantity bears the same relation to a second quantity that a third bears to it, scholars would present the unknown quantity as the "thing" sought, *la cosa che lhomo vol sapere*, as Pacioli writes.[10] The problems of early modern algebra may appear to be far removed from the questions of medieval metaphysics. Yet scholars have argued for the existence of historical and conceptual links between the "thing" of Arabic thought and the notion of the algebraic *cosa*.[11] Alternately distinct from being without being nothing, and distinct from being a known quantity without, for that matter, being no quantity whatsoever, *res*, in metaphysics and mathematics, acquires a new and persistently problematic status in epistemology.

Soon the "thing" of logic and first philosophy would also be reconceived. The attribute of being thing-like or, to use the more usual Latinate expression, "real," plays a crucial role in Francisco Suárez's *Metaphysical Disputations* of 1597, where it defines the subject of the science envisaged by this influential early modern Scholastic. Rewriting the terms by which Aristotle presents his theory "after the *Physics*" and by which Avicenna characterizes the subject of his own investigations into divine knowledge, Suárez argues that the "adequate object" of *metaphysica* is not "being insofar as it is being" (*ens inquantum ens*) but "being insofar as it is *real* being" (*ens inquantum ens reale*).[12] The attribute "real," in this phrase, extends the domain of first philosophy, at least compared to that of the Aristotelian tradition. Metaphysics, for Suárez, bears not only on what exists in actuality and therefore can be said to "be" in the most fully realized sense of the term; it also takes into account "things" that are in no way actual and yet still possess some intrinsic aptitude (*apititudo*) to exist: "possible essences."[13] Nonetheless, for Suárez, the field of metaphysics remains bounded. Beyond its limits, he maintains, there are also things that, while possessing properties, cannot be said to be "real." These are "beings of reason" or "rational beings" (*entia rationis*): things that can be and are conceived by the mind, without, however, being of such a nature as to exist in any sense, whether in actuality or even in potentiality.

Suárez defines the nature of such things, in technical terms, as "represented being" (*esse objective*) or "known being" (*esse cognitum*). He specifies that "beings of reason" possess "being only objectively in the intellect" (*habent esse objective tantum in intellectum*) or by virtue of being "thought by reason as existing" (*a ratione cogitatur ut ens*).[14] "Beings of reason" form a motley company of thought things. "Logical intentions," such as the essence of genus, species, subject and predicate, antecedent and consequent, belong to their number. Yet so, too, do fictitious and impossible things, such as the fabled chimera and the "flying ox" (*bos volans*).[15]

Privations, such as muteness and blindness, partake of this minimal mode of being. One may say the same for negations, in their varied forms, and for "infinitations." The conditions of "not being a man" and "being a non-man," the states of "not being a chimera" and "being a non-chimera," are therefore all "beings of reason."[16] Suárez maintains that, while lacking in existence, such things may be truly affirmed. Aristotle himself believed the proposition "a non-being is a non-being [*to mē on einai mē on*]" to be true.[17] Suárez reasons that if Aristotle was correct, then the proposition "a chimaera is a non-being" must also be true, although it refers to two beings of reason.[18] Nonetheless, the properties of being truly said (or being susceptible to being truly said) and being existent (or being capable of being existent) remain formally distinct. Beings of reason, Suárez writes, are not "true, real beings, because they are not capable of real and true existence, nor do they have any likeness with real beings."[19] Between "real being" (*ens reale*) and "rational being" (*ens rationis*), a commonality of the mere name "being," and not its concept, holds.[20]

In this respect, Suárez argues tacitly against near-predecessors and contemporaries. Some thinkers close to him had gone so far as to propose a concept of being so expansive as to include both the "real" and the "rational." They drew often on Avicenna, whose theory of the fundamental status of the "thing" (*res*) — as Henry of Ghent and Francis of Marchia, each in his own way, had shown — suggested a path beyond the category of "existence," whether actual or possible. As early as the first part of the fourteenth century, the English author Walter Burley, philosopher, logician, and reader of the Arabic metaphysicians, advanced the notion of "maximally transcendent" being (*ut est maxime transcendens*), defined as being (*esse*) that is "common to everything that is intelligible and identical with the adequate object of the intellect."[21] "Distinct from being as possible or actual, maximally transcendent being is said to be 'in the intellect,' which is to say *objectively* in the intellect. Burley identifies this maximally transcendent being as 'the intelligible' and traces his doctrine in its regard to Avicenna's *Metaphysics*."[22] The attribute of "maximally transcendent" points to the fact that this concept exceeds or "transcends," to the greatest possible degree, the divisions between types of being, including that between "being" and "represented being." Walter Burley's "maximally transcendent being," in other words, transgresses the border separating "real being" and "being of reason."

In the early sixteenth century, the Spanish philosopher and theologian Domingo de Soto gave a new name to such a "maximal" expanse of being. Evoking the medieval designation for properties that hold for all actual beings, beyond categorical differences, Soto avails himself of a term coined to signify being in its greatest generality, being both "real and "rational": "supertranscendental" (*supratranscendens*). Just as the Scholastic "transcendental" exceeds the ten categories, applying to them all, so the "supertranscendental" steps beyond the distinction between real being and beings of reason, being common to them both. Domingo de Soto offers only one example of a supertranscendental property. It is that of being "imaginable" (*imaginabilis*).[23] His reasoning is clear. Regardless of whether a thing is truly "real" or merely "rational," actual, potential, or in fact by nature impossible, it may be imagined. "Imaginability" holds of both being, in the sense of actuality, and "objective" or merely representable being.

In the same years in which Suárez completes his *Disputationes*, the Portuguese philosopher Pedro da Fonseca develops this suggestion. He proposes a notion of a "something" (*aliquid*) so vast as to include anything of which one can think or speak, be it real or merely present in the mind. Moreover, he goes so far as to identify three "supertranscendental" predicable properties that belong to this "something": being "opinionable" (*opinabilis*), being "thinkable" (*cogitabilis*) and being "apprehensible" (*apprehensibilis*).[24] From Philip the Chancellor to Thomas Aquinas, from Duns Scotus to Suárez, the transcendental properties apply to being, grasped according to the form of actuality and potentiality. The supertranscendentals envisaged by Domingo de Soto and Pedro da Fonseca, by contrast, hold both of being and non-being. Exceeding the difference between the real and the fictitious, the possible and the impossible, they define the properties of a mere "something," which may be the object of an "opinion" even if, inexistent, it cannot be known.

Although they are largely forgotten today, supertranscendental terms play a role in European logic and metaphysics throughout the seventeenth century, as John P. Doyle has shown. Certain thinkers, such as John of St. Thomas (or John Poinsot [1589–1644]), evoke the doctrine of the supertranscendental without developing it. Others refine and amplify the theory of these most universal of predicable properties. "Antonio Bernaldo de Quiros (1613–68) thinks that logic prescinds from real being and being of reason, and in this context he refers to 'loveable' (*amabile*), 'knowable' (*cognoscibile*) and 'intelligible' as terms which are super-transcendent. Richard Lynch (1610–1676) does the same and adds 'imaginable' and 'willable' (*volibile*) to his list. Silvester Mauro (1619–1687) uses 'super-transcendental' as synonymous with 'intelligible' or 'knowable' (*cognoscibile*) which he says includes impossible things and 'nothing itself' (*ipsum nihil*)."[25] In 1674, the French Jesuit André Semery dedicates a portion of his logic course to these terms, his examples being "intelligible," "knowable," and "thinkable." "The adequate object of the intellect, he tells us, is not transcendental being but rather super-transcendental being, which includes the impossible as well as the possible. Prior to both the impossible and the possible, super-transcendental being equates with 'something' in the broadest sense, and is the equivalent of simply being an object of understanding."[26]

The consequences of these inventions are far-reaching. Not only do the theorists of the supertranscendental explicitly maintain that both the art of reasoning and the doctrine of first philosophy must take into account the "real" and the "rational," in their "maximal" commonality as well as in their obvious distinction. These philosophers also clearly, if tacitly, suggest that outside the domain of philosophical construction, one may distinguish several modes of non-theoretical access to supertranscendental being. Imagination is but the first among them. According to these authors, "the 'something' in the broadest sense" first envisaged by Domingo can be willed, and it may also be loved. Just as one imagines what can and could never be, so, too, they suggest, may one will the inexistent and the impossible, and desire them. To hold this proposition is to grant a striking principle: that the faculty of the will and the passion of love, like the imagination, are receptive to inexistence, being sensitive to things that are not. In volition and in desire, one can, then, intend "nothing itself" (*ipsum nihil*): some "'something' in the broadest sense" that remains intelligible, in its supertranscendence, even if, lacking in being, it can hardly be said to be an "entity."

The diffusion of the doctrine of the supertranscendental was not restricted to works written in the language of the Church and schools.

It was also espoused in the vernacular. In 1638, in Paris, Jean Salabert publishes his treatise *Of Perfect Reasoning, in Which One Discovers the Treasures of French Logic, and the Ruses of Several Sophisms*.[27] In the section of his book dedicated to the "Categories of Accidents," Salabert introduces and explains the ten predicable terms enumerated by Aristotle. Having completed his summary of the classical doctrine, Salabert observes: "There exist other words, which may be attributed indifferently to all the Categorical terms." "These," he specifies, "are called *transcendental* terms." To explain himself, the learned author offers a long list of those vastly predicable properties: "being, thing, one, true, good, perfect, possible, and those like them." Yet he also takes a further step, drawing on more recent works of logic and metaphysics, as well as the French usage of his day. "Moreover," he continues,

> there are some terms that are called *supertranscendental* [*sur-transcendants*], because they are attributed not only to real and positive terms, but even to those that are negative, fictitious, and chimerical, such as 'intelligible,' 'imaginable,' 'knowable,' 'imaginary.' Thus one may say, 'The chimera is intelligible'... 'Privation is knowable.' In our French language, we attribute this term, 'thing' not only to true things, but even to signs, privations, and impossible things, for we often say, 'that's an imaginary thing' [*c'est une chose feinte*], 'that's an impossible thing' [*c'est chose impossible*]. The word 'thing' is therefore a supertranscendental term.[28]

Inevitably, the theorists of these all-encompassing predicable words are led to confront an old and troubling question: may such terms be submitted to *infinitatio*? Once one grants such a property as the "intelligible," can one not oppose it to its indefinite double, the "non-intelligible" or "unintelligible"? Admittedly, the utility of such an expression is less than clear, not least because, in being intelligible as such, it appears to contradict the property of "non-intelligibility" that it is to signify. The seventeenth-century Scholastics recognize that the matter demands careful treatment.[29] Silvester Mauro argues that since expressions such as "intelligible" and "knowable" may be affirmed of everything, both being and non-being, there is nothing that their indefinite forms could signify; in principle, one may therefore set the possibility of infinite supertranscendental names aside. A term such as *intelligibile*, he writes, can be infinitated, yet only in speech (*verbaliter*), for no intention will ever correspond to such an expression as *non-intelligibile*.[30] Luis de Lossada (1681–1748) and José Aguilar (1652–1708) maintain similar positions. The first explains that if it holds at all, the term "non-thinkable" (*non-cogitatibile*) must apply to some object that is affirmed in speech and, therefore, thought; but then it refutes itself, holding of none.[31] Echoing the twelfth-century bans on the *infinitatio* of "terms containing everything," José Aguilar issues this monition to his readers: "Know that supertranscendental terms may not be infinitated [*infinitari non posse*]," and no subject may be known to be "non-knowable" (*non-cognoscibile*).[32]

Other philosophers of the early modern age, however, respond to the question affirmatively, in ways that are more subtle and surprising. Richard Lynch argues that it is legitimate to subject supertranscendentals to *infinitatio*, albeit solely on condition of representing to oneself a universe of being and thinking which, while conceivable, is in itself impossible. "If, *per impossibile*," he conjectures, "it were the case that there were an infinity of concepts, of which none were being, taken with however greater universality, none imaginable, or none willable, then certainly each of these concepts would be non-being [*non ens*], and each would be something non-imaginable [*quid non imaginabile*] and non-willable [*non volibile*]."[33] Antonio Bernaldo de Quiros offers a different justification of the admissibility of such infinitations. Drawing on no less an authority than Aristotle, he recalls that the author of the first *Metaphysica* wrote that "non-being is non-being," or "the non-existent is the non-existent." This, he comments, suggests that, although one cannot know the "non-intelligible" (*non-intelligibile*) in itself, one may "indirectly" glean some knowledge of those things to which it pertains, for it must apply to the non-existent (*non-ens*), which is nothing.[34]

The richest and most impressive defense of the intelligibility of the "non-intelligible" is that offered by the Catalan philosopher Miguel Viñas (1642–1718). Sent by his brethren to Peru and later Chile, Viñas taught theology and philosophy in the Santiago of the New World. In his *Philosophia Scholastica*, he devotes extraordinary care to the question of whether the supertranscendental property "intelligible" may be "infinitated." He evokes eight objections to the notion of the *non-intelligibile* and methodically refutes them, one by one.[35] First, he observes, it might be said that a false symmetry obtains between infinite names in the usual sense, which are doubtless admissible, and infinite supertranscendental names. Boethius had argued that a term such as "non-man" removes the meaning of "man" and signifies everything that remains after its destruction. Viñas's imagined opponent now declares: once one has eliminated the sense of the "intelligible" by a like procedure, there is "nothing that the term *non intelligibile* can signify."[36] Viñas responds that "non-intelligible" might still signify something other than the absence of the intelligible. Were this so, this term would be meaningful, even if it could not be said to be true or false: "What is represented by the term *non intelligibile* is as such neither true nor false but simply diverse from the meaning of the term 'intelligible.'"[37] Such a representation might be mistaken, but in its error it would possess positive properties.

Similarly, one might think that a term such as "knowable" (*cognoscibile*) cannot be "infinitated," except by signifying an idea that is knowable, such that it contradicts itself. Viñas replies that although "the term 'non-knowable' represents some object, which is in fact knowable, it does not represent it as knowable, but rather as distinct from what is represented by the term 'knowable.'"[38] As refutations follow objections in the unfolding of the disputation, the subtlety of the senses of non-intelligibility increases. A single argument, nevertheless, may be discerned in this treatment of the infinite supertranscendental predicable property. Submitted to *infinitatio*, the term "intelligible" continues to signify, without, however, signifying anything that can be either actual or possible. It points, in diverse ways, to the being of a false representation: something hybrid or confused, which partakes, impossibly, yet not inconceivably, of quiddity and inexistence. Yet however mistaken the thought of such a non-intelligible may be, it remains, for Viñas, distinct from nothing. Therefore, it is not absolutely shorn of sense.

The infinite supertranscendental name is a curious subject of first philosophy. Recalling Viñas's own journey to the westernmost edge of the Spanish New World, Doyle has likened it to "a kind of philosophical Finisterre" of metaphysics, a point which thinking runs up against "an extrinsic boundary for what can be signified and expressed."[39] When one follows Viñas through his defense of the infinite supertranscendental, one reaches the limit of the "non-intelligible," a term which, properly understood, "negates not only all existing things, but also all possible things, and even more strikingly, all impossible things, however one conceives or reaches them or it."[40] This land's end in philosophy may never have been surpassed. Yet there are echoes of such a charting of the fringes of the nameable and the thinkable elsewhere in the early modern period, echoes that both recall the Jesuits and annouce major developments that are to come.

As early as 1604, the German Calvinist Clemens Timpler (1567–1624) dedicates the opening of his *Metaphysicae systema methodicum* to a persistent "problem" in his field: that of "the proper and adequate subject" of first philosophy.[41] Timpler claims that his predecessors have responded to this question by proposing four solutions, which concern objects classifiable in degrees of ascending amplitude. Metaphysics may be concerned, first, with the highest of all real beings, namely God; second, with incorporeal substance, in which one may include both the divine and the spiritual substance more generally; third, with "real being," after the Suárezian fashion; fourth, with both "real being" and "beings of reason," in a manner that recalls the early theorists of supertranscendental being, such as Domingo de Soto. Timpler himself proposes a fifth solution to the problem. It implies a subject of still greater comprehensiveness: "every intelligible" (*omne intelligibile*). Such a subject, Timpler argues, spans the entire stretch of the thinkable, running from "something" to "nothing." Timpler suggests, in other words, that "nothing" is itself somehow intelligible. Therefore, it falls within the domain of metaphysics — or, to use the term of art employed in these years by Rodolphus Goclenius (1572–1621), "ontology."[42] Later in the seventeenth century, Leibniz proposes an account of first philosophy that rests on similar foundations. Without employing the term "supertranscendental," he evokes its central notion, making of the "thinkable" (*cogitabile*) the subject of the knowledge that he envisages. "General science," he writes in his *Introduction to a Secret Encyclopedia*, which dates to 1683–85, "is nothing other than the science of the universal Thinkable as such," which includes "Ontology, or the Science of Something and Nothing, Being and Non-Being, the Thing and the Mode of the Thing, Substance and Accident."[43]

Only if one recalls the aims of such a "science of Something and Nothing" (*scientia de Aliquo et Nihilo*) can one measure the sense and consequences of Kant's definition of the object of "transcendental philosophy" in his *Critique of Pure Reason* of 1781. In the concluding paragraphs of his presentation of the "Transcendental Doctrine of the Power of Judgment," Kant recalls that those before him devoted considerable attention to determining the subject of their systems of metaphysics. "The highest concept with which one is accustomed to begin a transcendental philosophy," he notes, "is usually the division between the possible and the impossible."[44] His allusion is clearly to Leibniz's disciples, Wolff and Baumgarten, whose doctrines Kant knew well.[45] In his *Metaphysica* of 1757, Baumgarten opened his treatise of ontology with an account of the "possible." The opposition between "something" and "nothing," Baumgarten argues, rests upon the more elementary distinction between the "possible" and the "impossible." "Something" (*aliquid*, or *Etwas*) is definable as "non-nothing" (*non-nihil*), that is, a "representable thing that does not imply contradiction" (*repraesentabile, quidquid non involvit contradictionem*). For this reason, "something" is also "possible" (*possibile, Möglich*).[46] In the *Critique*, Kant argues that Baumgarten's partition is inadequate because it is incomplete. It presupposes a concept that remains unidentified. Evoking the "customary" division between the possible and the impossible, Kant remarks: "Since every division presupposes a concept that is to be divided, a still higher one must be given, and this is the concept of an object in general [*der Begriff von einem Gegenstande überhaupt*] (taken problematically, leaving undecided whether it is something or nothing)."[47]

This "concept of an object in general" implies a thought of extreme abstraction. "Higher" than the notions of the possible and the impossible, which are in turn more primordial than the ideas of the something and the nothing, Kant's "object in general" constitutes the supreme notion of transcendental philosophy, which is "requisite" (*erfoderlich*), as Kant notes, for the completeness of the system of critical philosophy. By definition, one cannot say of such an "object in general" that it is possible or impossible, for it is the ground of that alternative. By specification, in other words, such an "object" may be defined as possible or impossible and, consequently, as "something" or as "nothing." In itself it is neither. Irreducible to being and to non-being, it must be "taken problematically [*problematisch genommen*]." Here "problematic" names a striking status, which may well be unique. Elsewhere Kant stipulates that as a rule, thoughts can be correlated with "objects" of a more classical variety: "Considered subjectively," he writes in a fragment of metaphysics, "as representation, before it is analyzed, subjective thinking always has an object [*Object*]. Every such object of thinking is either Something or Nothing [*Ein jeder Object des Denkens ist entweder Etwas oder Nichts*]."[48] Every object, that is, except "the object in general," for in its sovereign status, this "object" refuses the exclusive alternative of being "either something or nothing," preceding the division between the possible and the impossible, as the concept from which all logical and metaphysical oppositions may be deduced. Although Kant refrains from stating it explicitly, the consequence of the "problematic" status of the object in general is radical. It cannot be the "object" (*Objekt*) of any representation whatsoever, at least "considered subjectively" and for "subjective thinking."

The irony, of course, is that Kant's specifications, like this very qualification, demonstrate that this supreme "object" (*Gegenstand*) can, nonetheless, be represented, if one takes "representation" to imply definition. That is an old irony, which marks every notion that aims, as does this highest concept, to set out a limit in speech and thought. One might well compare the "object in general," in this sense, to the supreme Stoic genus of the "something" or the "what" (*ti* or *quid*), which, as Seneca explained to Lucilius, holds of things that are and things that are not. Strictly speaking, it is neither existent nor inexistent, yet it is "something." One might also liken Kant's sovereign "object" to the ideas signified by infinite supertranscendental names, such as "non-intelligible," or "non-thinkable," whose meaning seems, at least at first glance, to refute itself.[49] Each of these notions demands that one conceive of some "maximally transcendent" thing that, without being reducible to anything that truly is, is not simply nothing.

It is remarkable that, from Henry of Ghent to Francis of Marchia, from Suárez to Baumgarten, it is one indefinite property that defines the fundamental "thing" of first philosophy: being "non-nothing" (*non-nihil*). "The name *res*," Duns Scotus states, in his Third Quodlibet, "can be taken in the most common manner, to the degree to which it applies to everything that is not nothing [or "non-nothing": *non nihil*]."[50] Introducing the "possible" such that it can be qualified as "something" (*Etwas*), Baumgarten departs from exactly these terms: "Non-nothing [*Nonnihil*]," he writes, "is something (*aliquid*), a representable [thing], which does not involve contradiction, and which is not A and non-A."[51] Despite its novelties, the "object in general," in its irreducibility to the possible and the impossible, remains a "non-nothing." The proof is that one may state of such an "object" precisely what the philosophers from the Middle Ages through the early modern period, employing a strictly infinite verb, affirmed of their primordial "thing": in itself, *non repugnat esse*, it "does not exclude being," or, as one might write, forcing a translation, it "non-excludes being." Baumgarten assumes in his *Metaphsyica* that such a "non-exclusion" must take the form of an absence of contradiction, which, being convertible with possibility, leads inevitably to the position of "something." Kant is more cautious. Beginning with neither the possible nor the impossible but the notion of which they are but modifications, he holds to a first concept that is, in a sense, closer to the infinite supertranscendental terms of the Iberian Scholastics than to the notion from which Baumgarten's ontology departs. The "object in general," like the "non-intelligible," or the "non-knowable," straddles the divide between what can and will and what cannot and will not be. To conceive of such an "object," one must envisage a single condition of being something and nothing, at once in disjunction and in conjunction.

Such a conception is more than difficult. It brings thinking up against a limit of representation, while demanding also that it be represented as such. In this sense, Kant's concept at once recalls and reverses an older innovation: that of the thinkers who introduced "non-signifying terms" into philosophy. The authors who devised such words as *blituri*, *skindapsos*, and *knax* proposed names for a single impossibility of representation: a point that, while reached in thinking, also remains external to it, involving terms that "signify nothing." Kant, like Miguel Viñas before him, invents a limit concept of an inverse kind. The "object in general" points to a border that is not only conceived in thinking but is also defined in such a way as to be structurally internal to it. Like any limit, the land's end of conceptuality can be viewed from two sides: as a *blituri,* which names the first "non-signifying" intention, just beyond the intelligible, or as a *Gegenstand überhaupt*, which names the last determinable, if "non-intelligible" concept, from which all other concepts must be deduced. From empty words to the object in general, these edges always belong, however, to some *res*: what is in question in speech, as Valla might have argued, that is, as his algebraist contemporaries could have added, unknown quantities, definable by being submitted to new operations in thought. From the non-significant to the nonexistent, from the possible and the impossible and to their condition in an object that is neither, it is by reasoning in infinite names and verbs that thinking draws near such "problematic" things. The indefinite alone is adequate to these thought objects. First philosophy becomes the science of "Something and Nothing, Being and Non-Being, the Thing and the Mode of the Thing, Substance and Accident," by reckoning repeatedly with the powers of the *non-*, on the winding path that leads from the centaur and the goat-stag to the chimera and the flying ox.

CHAPTER NINE

The Infinite Judgment

In contrast to modern science and mathematics, which have often reckoned in terms of problems and solutions, philosophy, starting with Kant, sets out to confront questions that are unavoidable and in part unanswerable. The *Critique of Pure Reason* of 1781 announces this bold project. In the preface to the first edition of his book, Kant writes that human reason is "burdened" by "questions that it cannot dismiss, for they are given to it by the nature of reason itself, and that it also cannot answer, for they exceed all the powers of human reason."[1] From this "peculiar fate" follow certain perplexities, which Kant sets before his readers. He recalls that, to reach certain knowledge, thinking departs from "principles whose use is unavoidable in the course of experience." Soon it rises to "more remote conditions," for which mere experience provides no indubitable rules. To continue in the use of its faculties, reason finds itself forced "to take refuge in principles that overstep all possible use in experience, and yet that seem so unsuspicious that even ordinary common sense agrees with them." Thinking, as a result, falls helplessly into "obscurities and contradictions." Struggles ensue, played out on the "battlefield" that Kant calls metaphysics.

The dissensions of modern philosophy belong to this contested terrain. "Dogmatists" and "skeptics" vie for dominion over its presumed resources. The first party, laying claim to an incontrovertible knowledge of things independent of experience and its conditions, sets up "despotic" doctrines. The second party, composed of "nomads who abhor all permanent cultivation of the soul," periodically shatters "civil unity" with its doubt, without accomplishing more. Evoking Locke's *Essay Concerning Human Understanding*, Kant notes that "in recent times," it seemed that "an end would be put to all these controversies, and the lawfulness of all the competing claims would be completely decided, through a certain physiology of the human understanding." That promise, however, soon showed itself to be empty. "Now, after all paths (as we persuade ourselves) have been tried in vain, what rules is tedium and complete indifferentism, the mother of chaos and night in the sciences, but at the same time also the origin, or at least the prelude, of their incipient transformation and enlightenment, when through ill-applied effort they have become obscure, confused, and useless."[2]

The "incipient transformation and enlightenment" is critique. Kant specifies, however, that he understands the term "critique" in a new sense. His inquiry into the mind is not "a critique of books and systems, but a critique of the faculty of reason in general, in respect of all the cognitions after which reason might strive *independently of all experience*, and hence the decision about the possibility or impossibility of a metaphysics in general, and the determination of its sources, as well as its extent and boundaries, all, however, from principles."[3] "Critique" will respond in a new manner to the question from which philosophy departs: "How is the faculty of think-ing itself possible?"[4] Faithful to a long tradition in the theory of knowledge, Kant grasps "thinking" as the formulation, analysis and ordering of true judgments. He can therefore consider the question of the possibility of thinking to be synonymous with another: how are true judgments possi-ble? The *Critique of Pure Reason* will be a study of the conditions and validity of judgments concerning sensible and non-sensible objects, a study that will also explain how human reason, in failing to examine itself, falls prey to its own illusions. Kant sets out to establish the claims that the mind can make and to delimit the borders beyond which its judgments, if they are to be sound, may not venture. He promises that, after this preliminary treatise, he will provide a "system of pure (speculative) reason," a "Meta-physics of Nature." It "will be not half so extensive but incomparably richer in content than this critique, which had first to display the sources and conditions of its possibility, and needed to clear and level a ground that was completely overgrown."[5] Before reaching that work, however, the reader is called upon to show "the patience and impartiality of a judge," as the claims of the reason appear before the tribunal of reason.

To establish a new lawfulness in the domain of judgment, Kant resolves to adopt an unfamiliar perspective on the activity of thinking. He likens the change in point of view that he suggests to the "revolution" that Copernicus brought about in astronomy when, for the sake of a simpler calculation, he supposed the Sun to be situated where the Earth had been thought to lie. The change that Kant proposes concerns the relation that the mind bears to that which it knows. "Up to now," Kant explains in the preface to the second edition of his book, which dates to 1787, "it has been assumed that all our cognition must conform to the objects; but all attempts to find out something about the *a priori* through concepts that would extend our cognition have, on this presupposition, come to nothing. Hence let us once try whether we do not get farther with the problems of metaphysics by assuming that the objects must conform to our cognition, which would agree better with the requested possibility of an *a priori* cognition of them, which is to establish something about objects before they are given to us."[6] "Dogmatic" and "skeptical" thinkers, as Kant presents them, have been united in assuming that knowledge is founded on the correspondence of a representation with its object, a correspondence for which they have provided no ground other than a harmony guaranteed by nature or God. The *Critique of Pure Reason* sets out to proceed otherwise. Its "Copernican Revolution" doubles that of the early modern Polish scientist by reversing it. Whereas the author of *De Revolutionibus* proceeded from the hypothesis that it is the Sun, and not the Earth, that stands still among the motions of the heavenly bodies, Kant suggests that it is the mind of the observer, rather than the observed, that is immobile. Unchanging in its faculties and axioms, its principles and concepts, human reason now appears as a power that legislates, as if from the center of the universe, to its objects.

A reordering of the elements of philosophy ensues. Following Aristotle and his successors, the Scholastic thinkers reckoned with a set of ten categories, or "predicaments" (*praedicamenta*); they took these terms to provide the fundamental concepts by which beings, in their diversity, may be defined and known. For this reason, the thinkers of the tradition also understood the categories to furnish a class of expressions employable in forming true judgments about what there is. The *Critique of Pure Reason* follows a fundamentally different path. It investigates the principles of the mind before exploring the characteristics of the objects that it encounters. Instead of deriving the elements of logic from the categories, as many had done before him, Kant begins with the rules of thinking, functions, or "forms of judgment," and seeks to deduce the categories from them. A new logic becomes the organ of an unprecedented philosophy.

Kant builds his critical system from an elementary thesis. Human knowledge, he maintains, springs from two sources: intuition and understanding, or sensibility and thought. The mind, he teaches, is never related directly to objects; rather, it is affected by representations, which are given immediately in intuition and cognized through the mediation of concepts. The order of the *Critique of Pure Reason* follows from these principles. Kant begins his treatise with a "Transcendental Aesthetic," which defines the two a priori formal conditions of intuition — space and time — under which objects are given to the mind in sensibility. Having established the elements of this Transcendental Aesthetic, Kant sets forth a Transcendental Analytic, which seeks to show by what concepts the mind grasps intuition in its representations. First Kant sets out a Table of Judgments, which defines "the logical functions of the understanding in judgment"; next, he proposes a Table of Categories. The first Table, he twice remarks, is to provide the "guiding thread" (*Leitfaden*) for the second.[7] The two tables are isomorphic in that each displays the same divisions, or "titles": Quantity, Quality, Relation, and Modality. Each of these titles is also composed of the same three "moments," in which two antithetical terms are followed by a third, which combines them. In Kant's presentation, twelve categories, which specify the modes by which things may be said to be, emerge as the correlates of twelve functions of judgment, which define the ways in which things are conceived by thought.

It may seem that, in this account, the old relation between the elements of metaphysics and logic has simply been reversed. The expressions of logic are not founded in the nature of things; rather, all types of properties derive from operations of the mind. But the categories and the forms of judgment now acquire a new sense. A major innovation is already perceptible in the second triad of Kant's table of the moments of thinking, which presents the "qualities" of judgments. Kant departs from the opposition between the "affirmative" assertion, which states that a predicate belongs to a subject, and the "negative" assertion, which denies that attribution. The German Scholastic philosophers of the eighteenth century had related these forms to the two determinations of a "thing" (*res*): "reality" (*realitas*) and "negation" (*negatio*). "What is posited in a thing to determine it (marks and predicates)," Baumgarten wrote in his influential *Metaphysica*, "are its *determinations* [*determinationes*]; these are either positive and affirmative — and if they are truly so, they are *realities* — or negative — and if they are truly so, are *negations*."[8] G. W. F. Meier amplified this doctrine in his own *Metaphysics* of 1752, which Kant employed, with Baumgarten's, in his teaching. "If one justifiably asserts something about a thing," Meier reasoned, "then this something belongs to and is contained in the thing. A reality is therefore a genuine addition to a thing, through which it in fact receives something and is broadened or enlarged.... If one denies something about a thing, one thinks that this something is lacking. Consequently, a negation is in fact a diminishment, and a thing is diminished when it is subjected to a negation."[9]

Kant upholds the correlation between perfection and privation, on the one hand, and, on the other, the affirmation and the negation of a predicate. Yet he also reconfigures it. Under the second title of his Table of Categories, he presents a triad of quality, which echoes that of the Table of the Judgments. To the logical distinction between affirmative and negative assertions, there corresponds the categorical distinction between "reality" and "negation."[10] As Béatrice Longuenesse observes, however, Kant "transforms the meaning of this correspondence." Two forms of predication, when related to sensible intuition, are now cast as the sources of two metaphysical determinations. "Reality" appears as "the concept of an object in general, by means of which the intuition of this object is regarded as determined *in respect of the logical function of affirmation in a judgment*"; negation emerges as "the concept of an object in general, by means of which the intuition of this object is regarded as determined *in respect of the logical function of negation in a judgment*."[11] Perfection and privation will now be derived from the logical operations of pure reason; the determinations of the "thing" (*res*) that is the object of knowledge acquire a new foundation in the typology of propositions that will bear upon it. In short, Kant deduces metaphysical "realities" and "negations" from two functions of judgment: affirmation and negation.

The *Critique of Pure Reason* thereby provides a new basis for the Scholastic concept of the "thing" (*res*), grasped as a quiddity or "what-ness," consisting of a set of specifiable determinations or "realities" (*realitates*). But the first two qualities of judgment alone cannot provide a sufficient ground for the cognition of a "thing," for reasons of which Kant is well aware. Affirmation and negation, as Kant understands them, give rise to "perfections" and "privations." The "thing," moreover, is more than a mass of determinations. For Kant as for his Scholastic forerunners, the "thing" is, rather, a totality; *res* names a complete set of positive and negative characteristics.

The rationalist thinkers of the early modern age had made of this thesis a first principle of sorts, which they did not think it necessary to justify. They proceeded "dogmatically," in Kant's terms, in assuming each *res* to be a whole. To be faithful to his critical project, Kant cannot follow in their footsteps; he must derive the idea of the thing, as a complete set of properties, from some operation of our understanding. Kant makes clear that, to this end, traditional rules of thinking are of little assistance. He reminds his readers of the "principle of contradiction" transmitted by the Aristotelian tradition. This rule stipulates that, of two contradictorily opposed predicates, such as "*is A*" and "*is not A*," considered in the same respect and at the same time, no more than one may hold for a given subject.[12] At first glance, it might seem that this principle could furnish Kant with the law that he requires, assuring that, of such contradictory properties, one holds for any given thing. But this, Kant argues, would be to misunderstand the nature of the principle of contradiction, confusing it with a different and more far-reaching rule of the understanding. That a property and its contradictory cannot hold at once of one subject is, for Kant, an "analytic" principle of reason, equivalent to an axiom of logic. Yet to be certain that any given property can always be affirmed or denied of any thing, one must first resolve a troubling question. Could a "thing" not be indeterminate with respect to the property and its negation? Could it not be, quite simply, neither one nor the other?

Some objects might well be said to be neutral with respect to certain attributes, in that one can say of them that they do not possess a certain characteristic and also that they do not, for that matter, *not* possess it either. "Vague" things, situated at the edge of borders, could be of this variety. They might be strictly indeterminate. Consider the points of transition where an object crosses the threshold separating two states, being neither one nor the other. C. S. Peirce once called this "line of demarcation" to mind: "A drop of ink has fallen upon the paper and I have walled it round. Now every point of the area within the wall is either black or white; and no point is both black and white. That is plain. The black is, however, all in one spot or blot; it is within bounds. There is a line of demarcation between the black and the white. Now I ask about the points of this line, are they black or white?"[13] One could multiply examples of such states and objects. Amos Funkenstein has evoked the irrational number in this regard. Unlike a rational number, it cannot be constructed by two integers. It may be constructed to any desired position, in the sense that, "to the question 'is the nth number after the digit the number four?' the answer is always yes or no; I can construct the irrational number up to (n) and determine its value." Nonetheless, such a number remains non-constructible, that is, indeterminate, in its totality.[14] Similarly, "to the question whether Napoleon had a Muslim ancestor, the answer is already determined as yes or no, even if in practice I may never be able to ascertain it. But the same question asked about Stendhal's Julien Sorel is neither yes nor no until I asked and answered it arbitrarily, because Stendhal was mute on that point."[15] In all these cases, certain subjects appear to be susceptible to determination, but no more. They are, in Kant's technical terms, merely "determinable," rather than definitely "determined."

Kant maintains that such "determinability" pertains solely to concepts. "Every concept, in regard to what is not contained in it, is indeterminate, and stands under the principle of determinability: that of every two contradictorily opposed predicates only one can apply to it, which rests on the principle of contradiction and hence is a merely logical principle, which abstracts from the content of cognition, and has in view nothing but the logical form of cognition." For him, "things," however, are of a different nature. They are "thoroughly determined." Kant's Leibnizian predecessors had made of this thesis a fundamental principle in their metaphysics. "Whatever exists," Wolff declared, "is determined in every way" (*omnimode determinatum*).[16] Wolff held the law of "total" or "thoroughgoing determination" (*principium omnimodae determinationis*) to be equivalent to the principle of individuation; for him, every singular thing is a determined thing, an "individual," according to Leibniz, being "thoroughly determined" in the entirety of its properties.[17] As Anneliese Maier has shown, Baumgarten took a further step when he made of this principle of determination a consequence of the concept of existence. "Not only is everything that exists thoroughly determined. Rather, for Baumgarten, the inverse holds: everything that is thoroughly determined exists. Thoroughgoing inner determination belongs to the concept of existence; it is by virtue of this determination that a real thing is distinct from a merely possible thing and also contains more than a merely possible thing."[18]

Kant appropriates this principle in the *Critique of Pure Reason*, arguing that all things are submitted to the force of a "total determination," or, as he writes, *omnimoda determinatio*. "Every thing, as to its possibility, stands under the principle of thoroughgoing determination; according to which, among all possible predicates of things, insofar as they are compared with their opposites, one must apply to it."[19] Kant asserts that, unlike the "principle of determinability" that holds for concepts, the principle of thoroughgoing determination "does not rest merely on the principle of contradiction, for besides considering every thing in relation to contradictorily conflicting predicates, it considers every thing further in relation to *the whole of possibility*, as the sum total of all predicates of things in general; and by presupposing that as a condition *a priori*, it represents every thing as deriving its own possibility from the share it has in that whole of possibility."[20]

Defined in such terms, the principle is far-reaching in its consequences. It stipulates more than that each thing is related, in its predicates, to the predicates that all actual things possess. It also asserts that each thing is related "to the whole of possibility," being linked to the entirety of the properties that possible beings, as well as actual beings, might possess. "What this means," Kant explains, "is that in order to cognize a thing completely, one has to cognize everything possible and determine the thing through it, whether affirmatively or negatively."[21] Yet to "cognize everything possible" is to conceive of a notion that outstrips intuition in time and space. It is to apprehend nothing less than the idea of "sum total of all possibility, insofar as it grounds every thing as the condition of its thoroughgoing determination in regard to the predicates which may constitute the thing."[22] Recalling the terms of his predecessors, Kant writes that this "sum total of all possibility" may also be called the "supreme being" (ens summum), the "original being" (ens originarium), or the "being of beings" (ens entium)."[23] Such a being contains "all predicates as regards their transcendental content not merely *under* itself, but *within itself*," such that all other beings are derivable from it, in that they possess some of its perfections.[24] Each thing, in other words, can be defined as a "limitation" (Einschränkung) of the idea of this "sum of possibility," since in its own set of properties, it contains some subclass of the "perfection" belonging to the "supreme being." "Some of it is ascribed to the thing, and the rest is excluded from it."[25] An individual thing is but a restriction of the whole of reality. Its determination is the limitation of the sum total of possibility.

In the *Critique of Pure Reason*, Kant leaves no doubt as to the status that the idea of such a "sum total of possibility" possesses for a finite mind, such as ours, whose cognition depends on the union of sensible intuitions and rational concepts. The "being of beings," for us, is a "transcendental ideal," derivable from the principle of thoroughgoing determination. "Reason does not presuppose the existence of a being conforming to the ideal," Kant specifies, "but only the idea of such a being, in order to derive from an unconditioned totality of thoroughgoing determination the conditioned totality, i.e., that of the limited. For reason the ideal is thus the image (*prototypon*) of all things, which all together, as defective copies (*ectypa*), take from it the matter for their possibility, and yet although they approach more or less nearly to it, they always fall infinitely short of reaching it."[26] Kant is aware that one might well seek to draw substantial theological consequences from this principle, "hypostatizing" this ideal: "If we pursue this idea of ours so far as to hypostatize it, then we will be able to determine original being through the mere concept of the highest reality as a being that is singular, simple, all-sufficient, eternal, etc., in a word, we will be able to determine it in its unconditioned completeness through all predications. The concept of such a being is that of *God* thought of in a transcendental sense, and thus the ideal of pure reason is the object of a transcendental theology."[27] Kant's own position, however, is clear. "This use of the transcendental idea would be overstepping the boundaries of its vocation and its permissibility." The notion of "all reality" is "a mere fiction, through which we encompass and realize the manifold of our idea in an ideal."

If we make of this transcendental ideal the basis for a theology, there-fore, we deceive ourselves, falling prey to illusions of our own making. To find in the law of thoroughgoing determination the ground of a real divinity, we must, in fact, not only "hypostatize the idea of the sum total of reality," taking a concept of pure reason as the basis for a false inference. Such a "hypostatization" rests in turn on a confusion of two types of unity: that which we encounter in our every use of the faculty of reason, which is "distributed" in a plurality of cognitions, and that to which we could lay claim were we acquainted with a "collective" experience, grasped as a totality. Laying bare the source of our misunderstandings, Kant explains: "We dialectically transform the *distributive* unity of the use of the under-standing in experience into the *collective* unity of a whole experience; and from this whole of appearance we think up an individual containing in itself all empirical reality, which then — by means of a transcendental sub-reption we have already thought — is confused with the concept of a thing that stands at the summit of the possibility of all things, providing the real conditions for their thoroughgoing determination."[28] Confusions follow confusions, Kant adds, when, after making the "mere representation" of "All of reality" into an object and after having "hypostatized" it as an exist-ing thing, we go so far as to "personify" it as a god formed in our image.[29]

Kant's strictures are clear enough, but there remains a simple question, which he must confront. By what right may the critical philosopher appeal to "thoroughgoing determination"? What transcendental ground may he claim for the idea of the thing, grasped as a totality of positive and privative properties? A "dogmatic" thinker, such as Leibniz, Wolff, or Baumgarten, could make of the concept of thoroughgoing determination a fundamental element of metaphysics, without considering the grounds on which they might posit it. It has been observed that, in a number of writings that pre-date the "Copernican Revolution" of his critical philosophy, Kant himself does likewise, evoking the principle of total determination in his proof of divine existence.[30] In the *Critique of Pure Reason*, however, he cannot

follow that path. His philosophy requires that he account for thoroughgoing determination with reference to the forms and functions of our
understanding.

The critical philosopher meets the challenge that he sets himself,
although he does so in terms that his readers have not always fully grasped.
Kant finds a basis for the principle of thoroughgoing determination in a
propositional quality that has often been lost from view. This is the quality
in his Table of Judgments that follows the affirmative and the negative,
combining and superseding them in one "moment." Here Kant introduces
a type of assertion that seems to be at once affirmative in its grammatical
and logical structure and yet negative in its sense and consequences. Kant,
however, argues forcefully that it is neither one nor the other. For him, it is
a third type of statement. He names it the "infinite judgment."

From his lectures on logic to the exposition of his doctrine of the mind
in the *Critique of Pure Reason*, Kant calls attention to this variety of assertion, which complicates the typology of statements. Kant distinguishes
it rigorously from affirmation and negation. The transcripts of Kant's
logic courses offer precious material for understanding its structure and
interpreting the terms of the *Critique*. In the so-called *Vienna Logic*, which
represents an account of lectures given around 1780, Kant explains that
"*quality*" may be defined as "the relation of concepts insofar as they stand
in the relation of unity with one another."[31] One such relation is discernible when a first concept is positively combined with a second, as in the
affirmative proposition: "Men are mortal." Analyzing this statement, Kant
writes: "Here I affirm mortality of men, or I think men as they stand under
the concept of mortality."

A second relation between concepts arises in the moment in which one
concept is separated from another, as in the negative proposition: "No man
is mortal." Kant explains: "Here I deny mortality of man. If I think man, I
think him as he is distinct from all that which is mortal."[32] A clear syntactic
difference separates such statements. "When the copula *est* [that is, "is"]
occurs *simpliciter*," Kant observes, commenting on Latin usage, "it signifies
the connection of two concepts; when the copula *est* is affected with the
non [as in *non est*, 'is not'], it signifies the opposition of the two concepts
and indicates that the one concept does not belong to the other, or is not

contained in the sphere of the other. E.g., 'the soul is not mortal' (*anima non est mortalis*); here I represent that mortality does not include the soul."[33] In the so-called *Jäsche Logic*, which derives from Kant's late lectures, this doctrine of the qualities of judgment appears in an abbreviated form: "In the *affirmative* judgment, the subject is thought *under* the sphere of a predicate; in the *negative* it is posited *outside* the sphere of the latter."[34]

Only if one keeps in mind this account of the "qualitative" relations of concepts can one understand the structure of the infinite judgment as it appears in the *Critique of Pure Reason*. Kant's paradigm for this judgment remains that of his courses: "The soul is non-mortal" (*anima est non mortalis*, or, as he also writes, *die Seele ist nichtsterblich*).[35] Such a predicative statement appears to be negative, for it indicates that the subject ("the soul") does not belong to the sphere of the predicate ("mortality"). Kant maintains, however, that this proposition does more than to negate. "If I say . . . 'the soul is non-mortal' (*anima est non mortalis*)," he writes in the *Vienna Logic*, "then I say not merely that the soul contains nothing mortal, but also that it is contained in the sphere of everything that is not mortal. In this case something special is said, then, namely, that I do not merely exclude one concept from the sphere of another concept, but also think the concept under the whole remaining sphere, which does not belong under the concept that is excluded." Kant hastens to add that, in addition to not being negative, such a proposition is also not affirmative: "I do not actually say, 'is immortal' (*est immortalis*), but instead I say that the soul can be counted among all the concepts in general that may be thought outside the concept of mortality."[36] Yet even as it denies that a certain property belongs to a given subject, this judgment brings about a fundamental affirmation. For Kant, it also posits its subject: "In the infinite judgment, the subject is posited in the sphere of a concept that lies outside the sphere of another" (*im unendlichen wird es in die Sphäre eines Begriffs, die außerhalb der Sphäre eines andern liegt, gesetzt*).[37]

The Transcendental Analytic of the *Critique of Pure Reason* presents the theory of this third "quality" of predicative judgment in condensed form. "If I had said of the soul that it is not mortal," Kant writes, evoking the example employed in his logic courses, "then I would at least have avoided an error by means of a negative judgment." He asks that the reader follow him as he passes from the negative quality to the infinite: "The soul is non-mortal."[38] "As far as logical form is concerned," Kant remarks, "I have certainly made an actual affirmation, for I have placed the soul within the unlimited domain of non-mortal things."[39] The "non-mortal" is "unlimited" (*unbeschränkt*), in other words, despite being engendered by a partition. "What is mortal contains one part of the whole domain of possible beings; that which is non-mortal contains the other. Nothing is said by my proposition ["The soul is non-mortal"] but that the soul is one of the infinite multitude of things that remain if I take away everything that is mortal." Kant's reasoning appears to rest on an unstated axiom concerning an "infinite multitude" — namely, that, unlike a finite arithmetical quantity, it remains equal to itself no matter how much is removed from it. In its quantity and its quality, an "infinite multitude" is unaltered, therefore, by the logical "exception" (*Ausnahme*) that the infinite judgment decrees: "The infinite sphere of the possible is thereby limited only to the extent that that which is mortal is separated from it, and the soul is played in the remaining space of its domain. But even with this exception, this space still remains infinite, and more parts could be taken away from it without the concept of the soul growing in the least and being affirmatively determined."[40]

That the Kantian doctrine of the infinite judgment owes a debt to previous teachings in logic is certain. Kant himself was the first to stress the lasting value of the classical theory of the proposition, famously (or infamously) noting, in the preface to the second edition of his *Critique*, that "since the time of Aristotle," logic had neither regressed nor progressed.[41] Kant's third moment in the quality of judgment clearly recalls one possibility envisaged by Aristotle in his doctrine of sentences: the statement containing an indefinite or "infinite" predicate. The early modern scholars of logic knew such propositions well. As a rule, they classified them as affirmations, for the same reason for which Kant himself holds them to be, formally speaking, "actual affirmations": the copula, "*is*," is not negated in them. In 1663, Johannes Micraelius explained this point in his *Lexicon Philosophicum*: "If the particle *non* is a part of the subject or the predicate, this is not a negation but, rather, remains an affirmation. It is, however, called an *infinite affirmation*, as in the statement 'Whoever does not believe [or 'whoever non-believes'] will be damned' [*Qui non credit damnatur*])."[42]

The German Scholastic philosophers of the early modern age reserved a place in their logical theories for such sentences. In his *Philosophia ratio-nalis, sive logica*, which dates to 1728, Wolff remarks that "If the particle of negation [that is, the Latin *non*] is not referred to the copula, but to the predicate, or the subject, then it is not a negative proposition, but another, which has a nature of its own." He adds that such a proposition, "which appears to be negative," is in fact affirmative, before specifying: "It is called *infinite*."[43] Baumgarten proposes a like doctrine, as do Emil Arnoldt, Christian August Crusius, and Johann Heinrich Lambert.[44] Friedrich Christian Baumeister offers examples that could not be clearer: "Adam could *non-sin*. Adam could *non-die*. These statements are infinite, yet they are true. They are distinct from the following propositions: Adam could not sin; Adam could not die. Those statements, instead, are negative and false."[45] Lest their readers mistake the nature of the "infinite proposition," some authors of the period have recourse to a new expression. They designate such a statement as an "apparent negation" (*negatio apparens*). "A sentence by which one links two concepts is affirmative (*affirmans*)," explains Hermann Friedrich Kahrel in his *Denckkunst* of 1755; "when the sentence separates these concepts, one speaks of a sentence that is negative (*negans*). When, however, the particle *not* [or *non-*] belongs to the subject or the predicate, one has a *pseudo-negation* [*eine Scheinverneinung*], which is in fact an affirmative sentence."[46]

In the *Critique of Pure Reason,* Kant does more than to recall such doctrines. He gives to the "infinite proposition" or "pseudo-negation" a new function, which casts a bright light on a fundamental innovation of his philosophy. Kant introduces a distinction between received accounts of the statement, which he considers to belong to "General Logic," and a domain of study that he is the first to define. This is his "Transcendental Logic." He explains the difference: "General logic abstracts from all content of the predicate (even if it is negative), and considers only whether it is attributed to the subject or opposed to it. Transcendental logic, however, also considers the value or content of the logical affirmation made in a judgment by means of a merely negative predicate, and what sort of gain this yields for the whole of cognition."[47] "General" logic is, in other words, purely formal; it bears on the shape of propositions and their relations, abstracted from what they assert.[48] "Transcendental logic," by contrast, considers the "value or content" of a statement, understood, as Van der Kuijlen observes, "in a very specific way": transcendentally, that is, as pure a priori knowledge, which pertains neither to objects nor to their properties, but to the conditions of knowledge.[49] Kant's definition of transcendental logic in these lines of the *Critique* is designed to take the infinite judgment into account. Looking beyond the form of propositions and, more exactly, beyond the opposition of affirmative and negative statements, transcendental logic registers three qualities of propositions. Unlike "general logic," it apprehends what distinguishes the moment of "infinity" from that of "affirmation" and "negation." Transcendental logic alone measures its yield for "the whole of cognition."

Had Kant limited himself to considerations of general logic, he would have understood the sentence "The soul is non-mortal" to be a "pseudo-negation," or an affirmative statement, equivalent to the sentence, "The soul is immortal." He would, then, have maintained that the infinite judgment "thinks" one concept "under another." Kant argues, however, that the infinite judgment does more. Even as it excludes one concept from the sphere of another, it posits it, setting it in a domain that is defined by the infinitude of the expanse left over once the sphere belonging to a concept is removed or "excepted" from it. Kant draws close, in this respect, to a friend and correspondent. A decade before the *Critique*, Johann Heinrich Lambert wrote in his *Anlage zur Architectonic* that "when one says 'A is non-B,' what one signifies is that, 'A is something other than B.'"[50] Transcendental logic makes of this interpretation of the indefinite predicate the condition for its concept of the infinite judgment. As Fumiyasu Ishikawa has stressed, "non-A," for Kant, means not so much "not A," as "something outside A"; it is, in other words, "not A" [*nicht* A] only on condition of being "*rather* [*sondern*] something else."[51] In the infinite judgment, this "something else" is thus posited as a thing: as totally determined, even if the judging mind, by virtue of the limits of its faculties, cannot entirely grasp it.

In a logical fragment, Kant emphasizes the bipartite structure that characterizes his third quality of judgment. "The infinite judgment not only indicates that a subject is not included in the sphere of the predicate; rather, it indicates that it lies outside that sphere, in some infinite somewhere [*Das unendliche Urteil zeigt nicht bloß an, daß ein Subjekt unter der Sphäre nicht enthalten ist, sondern daß es außer der Sphäre desselben in dem unendlichen irgendwo sei*]. Consequently, it represents the sphere of the predicate as restricted [*beschränkt*]."[52] The so-called *Jäsche Logic* goes further in positively characterizing the expanse of this "restricted" yet "infinite somewhere." Elucidating the nature of a property such as "*non-A*," Kant gives, yet again, the example of being "non-mortal," specifying that this property signifies the logical expanse "outside" mortality. Yet he adds that this domain is "really no sphere at all but only *a sphere's sharing of a limit with the infinite,* or the *limiting itself* [die Angrenzung einer Sphäre an das Unendliche *oder die* Begrenzung selbst]."[53]

Kant considers such a "sharing of a limit with the infinite, or limiting itself" to be not a variety of negation but an affirmative determination. "Although exclusion is a negation," he writes, "the restriction of a concept is still a positive act. Therefore, limits are positive concepts of restricted objects."[54] In excluding a thing from a defined sphere, the infinite judgment is negative; but in restricting a concept, by contrast, it is affirmative. For Kant, the *non-* of *non-A* is for this reason productive. By its form, it projects, by "limitation," the "space" or "room" belonging to the "infinity of spheres" of everything that is not *A*: "Outside the sphere of a concept, there is room for an infinity of spheres [*außer der Sphaera eines Begriffes ist Raum zu einer Unendlichkeit von Sphäris*]."[55] The judgment that contains a predicate such as *non-a* is therefore "infinite" not only in the old sense, in that it involves an indefinite logical expression. It is also "infinite" on account of the domain that it engenders, for in the "positive act" of restricting the sphere of a concept, it affirms the logical expanse of total determination. As Béatrice Longuenesse has argued, infinite judgment is in this sense a crucial structure; it allows the mind to "generate," through its own "discursive activity," "the complete logical space in which to think everything that is or may be."[56] It thereby constitutes the logical source of the transcendental ideal. This is also why Kant calls the infinite judgment a "judgment of determination" in a note in which he insists, more explicitly than he does in the First *Critique,* on the structural relation between this type of statement and the transcendental ideal: "The proposition 'the soul is non-mortal' [*anima est non-mortalis*] is a judgment of determination

[*Bestimmungsurteil*], which says that of two opposed predicates, *a* and *non-a*, the latter applies to the soul. Judgments of determination are all infinite, in order to determine a thing thoroughly, not merely to indicate the relation of connection or opposition."[57]

In a "judgment of determination," human reason takes a first step toward the total determination that characterizes the reality of every thing. Defining a thing as being, in some respect, *non-A*, it not only indicates the "opposition" between the sphere of the thing and that of a positive predicate, such as *A*; it apprehends one of the thing's properties and thereby posits the thing as a "thing," that is, as determined. The step, to be sure, is modest. For a thing to be known in the totality of its determinations, a further logical activity would then be required. As Kant explains, one would need to apply the threefold mode of reasoning known as the "disjunctive syllogism," which derives a negation from an "indefinite" property. The steps of this syllogism may be easily stated: for any object, denoted as X, one may assert, (1) X is either A or *non-A*; (2) but X is *non-A*; (3) therefore, X is not A. Infinite judgment furnishes the minor premise in this reasoned sequence, yielding some knowledge of the thing in question — with respect to a single property. To cognize a thing in the totality of its determinations, this procedure would need to be repeated, with respect to the total set of the possible properties that a thing might possess. Such a reasoning, of course, outstrips the capacities of a finite mind, such as our own, which knows things not as they are in themselves, but only as they appear to us, according to the two forms of intuition, in time and space. A divine intellect could do more. Kant suggests that he does exactly that — and, indeed, no more than that. According to the "odd and particularly ironic" thesis of theology proposed by the *Critique*, God is, as Deleuze remarked, but the "master of the disjunctive syllogism," the ground and agent of total determination.[58]

Kant's method of exposition in the *Critique of Pure Reason* is telling in this regard. When he passes from the Table of Judgments to the Table of Categories, deducing the concepts of the understanding from the operations of logic, Kant draws from the affirmative judgment the category of "reality," which consists in the determination of a thing, and he deduces from the negative judgment the category of "negation." From the "infinite judgment," he derives a concept of the understanding no less crucial for his systematic purposes: "limitation" (*Limitation*).[59] This is the category of which Kant avails himself in his discussion of the transcendental ideal, when he argues that "the thoroughgoing determination of every thing rests on the limitation of this All of reality [*auf der Einschränkung dieses All der Realität*], in that some of it is ascribed to the thing and the rest excluded from it."[60] Every determination, as he tells his reader there, may be grasped as a "limitation" of a "sum total of possibility." Yet this can be so only once reason has found its way to the idea of a "sum total of possibility" by the practice of conceptual "restriction," and once it has given itself the means to define every thing by an "exception" or "exclusion" with respect to the totality of possible properties. This is what the infinite judgment accomplishes, and this is why a logic that delineates the conditions of a priori knowledge must take it into account.

Kant's attachment to the third moment in the quality of judgment has often been considered a weak point in his doctrine of the functions of reason. It is not difficult to see why. When abstracted from the field of transcendental logic, the thesis that "The soul is non-mortal" is a judgment of a specific type, irreducible to "The soul is immortal," is certainly contestable. In the interpretation of the First *Critique*, there is a long tradition of treating the infinite judgment as little more than a symptom of Kant's desire for a tidy Table of Judgments. This tradition begins with Schopenhauer, who observed that Kant gave his "whole philosophy" a "logical basis" in the Table of Judgments, before seeking spuriously to derive the categories from it: "From this Table he deduces an exact dozen of categories, symmetrically arranged under four heads, which afterwards becomes the fearful procrustean bed into which Kant violently forces all things in the world and all that goes on in man, shrinking from no violence and disdaining no sophistry if only he is able to repeat everywhere the symmetry of that table."[61] To the affirmative and negative qualities of judgment, Schopenhauer noted, Kant "adds the infinite judgment, making use of a crotchet of the old scholastics, an ingeniously invented stop-gap [*eine Grille der alten Scholastiker, einen spitzfindig erdachten Lückenbüßer*], which does not even require to be explained, a blind window, such as many others he made for the sake of his architectonic symmetry."[62]

Almost a century later, and from a fundamentally different perspective, Peirce expressed a perspective close to Schopenhauer's. Writing of Kant's alleged "third quality of judgments, additional to affirmative and negative," Peirce observed, not without severity: "It is one of the numerous cases in which accidents of language have affected accepted logical forms without any good reason. . . . Kant adopted it because it rounded out his triad of categories of quality."[63] Later scholars of the *Critique* have often echoed this opinion. To Kemp Smith, the infinite judgment constitutes "a very artificial and somewhat arbitrary manner" of announcing "the 'discovery' of the category of limitation."[64] A more recent scholar, pausing to consider Kant's third quality of judgment, has similarly concluded: "This really won't do. The case for denying that *Henry is non-mortal* is a case for saying that it is negative. It is uncharacteristic of Kant to say that the two sentences 'Henry is non-mortal' and 'Henry is not mortal,' which do the same work in almost the same way, nevertheless express different kinds of judgment just because they differ in a minor verbal detail. I fear that part of the reason for this mistake is that Kant wants four-times-three indispensable kinds of judgment and needs infinite judgments to make up the complement."[65]

Such interpreters share more than their dissatisfaction with the Kantian account of the assertion "The soul is non-mortal." They also assume that the theory of the infinite judgment may be extracted from its place in the doctrine of the *Critique*, to be considered as one variety of assertion. Evaluating Kant's claims about the infinite judgment as a type of proposition, the commentators conclude that it is inadequate; as a consequence, they reason, it hardly belongs in the Table of Judgments, except as an ornament, crafted to "round off" a triad and preserve some semblance of symmetry. Such critics end by reproaching Kant for not having held to the perspective of "general logic," in which there are but two types of judgment: the affirmative and the negative. Yet Kant held the proposition "The soul is non-mortal" to differ from that of "The soul is immortal" not in its logical form but in its transcendental content. In the *Critique*, the infinite judgment matters not merely as a sentence that exhibits a structure common to certain assertions, but as a judgment that articulates a double act: the restriction of the sphere of predication and the positing of a thing in the infinite logical space of its total determination. The *Critique* is clear on this point: "general" or formal logic has no need of the infinite judgment. It is solely from the point of view of transcendental logic that one may discern the reason for its inclusion in the Transcendental Analytic. Responding to the needs of the critical philosophy, the infinite judgment alone grounds the rule of *omnimoda determinatio* in a function of the understanding.

As Kant develops this theory in the years following the publication of the First *Critique*, the infinite judgment and the principle of total determination continue to occupy him. In his logic lectures, he comments regularly on the third moment of quality. After the *Critique*, he introduces it in the *Prolegomena to Any Future Metaphysics*. He returns to it in his last notes.[66] At the same time, he amplifies his treatment of the transcendental ideal. In "What Does It Mean to Orient Oneself in Thinking," an essay published in 1786, Kant once again evokes the steps that lead reason to posit a "first *original* being as a supreme intelligence and at the same time a highest good."[67] Now he treats this positing, however, not as an illusory "hypostasis," but as a legitimate response to a "need of reason" (*Bedürfnis der Vernunft*), which furnishes a "subjective ground" for the assumption of "something which reason may not presume to know through objective grounds."[68] "Not only does our reason already feel a need to take the *concept* of the unlimited as the ground of the concepts of all limited things — hence of all other things — but this need even goes so far as the presupposition of its *existence*, without which one can provide no satisfactory ground at all for the contingency of the existence of things in the world, let alone for the purposiveness and order which is encountered everywhere in such a wondrous degree."[69]

In a note, Kant explains himself. He argues that, without mistaking the object of such a "necessary presupposition" for the content of a "free insight," our reason may legitimately derive the idea of a supreme and original being from the thought of the "reality" necessary for all things:

> Since reason needs to presuppose reality as given for the possibility of all things and considers the differences between things only as limitations arising through the negations attaching to them, it sees itself necessitated to take as a ground one single possibility, namely that of an unlimited being, to consider it as original and all others as derived. Since also the thoroughgoing possibility

of every thing must be encountered within existence as a whole — or at least since this is the only way in which the principle of thoroughgoing determination makes it possible for our reason to distinguish between the possible and the actual — we find a subjective ground of necessity, that is, a need in our reason itself to take the existence of a most real (*highest*) being as the ground of all possibility.[70]

The notion of such a "subjective ground of necessity" was absent from the discussion of the transcendental ideal in the *Critique* of 1781. In introducing it in 1786, Kant stresses its difference with respect to the idea of an "objective ground," such as that evoked by Descartes in his "dogmatic" proof of divine being. Kant holds that a "need of reason" assures nothing as to actual existence. It furnishes no more than an "advantageous" point of orientation in thinking: the supposition that, to the idea of an "All of reality," there corresponds an "intelligible author," creator of the world.

These are not Kant's last words on the thoroughgoing determination that the cognition of things must presuppose. Kant's *Opus Postumum* returns repeatedly to the problem of a "sum total of possibility," which it refers to the question of the unity of "One experience." In the fascicles of this unfinished work, Kant continues to depart from the doctrines of his "dogmatic" forerunners:

> Existence is thoroughgoing determination (*existentia est omnimoda determinatio*), Christian Wolff says, and so also conversely: thoroughgoing determination is existence [*omnimoda determinatio est existentia*], as a relationship of equivalent concepts. But the thoroughgoing determination that is here *thought* cannot be *given*; for it extends to an infinity of empirical determinations. Only in the concept of One object of *possible experience* — which is not derived from any experience, but rather, itself makes it possible — is objective reality (this *omnimoda determinatio*) necessarily granted to the [outer sense-object], not synthetically, but analytically, according to the principle of identity.[71]

After the transcendental ideal and the critique of its "hypostasis" in the idea of a divinity, after his theory of the "subjective ground of necessity" for the postulate of a "sum total of possibility," Kant now sets out in a new direction. He finds the properly "collective" unity of experience in a material continuously distributed throughout space, which he calls the "ether," or "caloric" (*Wärmestoff*). After deriving twelve categories from twelve logical functions of judgment, he deduces the "All of reality" from the irreducibly simple "knowledge of oneself through self-determination in space and time."[72] This "knowledge" now takes the form of a "positing" (*Setzung*). Unlike the thesis of the infinite judgment, however, this "positing" seems to have no "restricting" force. In the last fascicles of this work, Kant proposes a new founding proposition: "I am: this is the logical act which precedes all representation of the object; it is a *verbum* by which I posit myself. I exist in space and time and thoroughly determine my existence in space and time (*omnimoda determinatio est existentia*) as appearances according to the formal conditions for the connection of the manifold in intuition; I am both an outer and inner object for myself."[73]

These remarks announce a project that Kant did not live to complete. They also testify to his commitment to the principle of determination that his logic binds to the infinite judgment. Through to his last works, *omnimoda determinatio* grounds, for him, the conditions in which things experienced may be known in a rigorous sense: known, that is, in their complete positive and privative "realities" and known, therefore, if only partly, and in endless approximation, with respect to a "sum total of possibility," which Kant also takes to be wholly determined in the set of its infinite properties. That his accounts of the genesis and status of the ideal of total determination vary, from the *Critique of Pure Reason* to the works that follow its first edition, and from those works to his *Opus Postumum*, may be taken as signs of an objective instability of doctrine or a subjective uncertainty, if not both. One might also conclude, however, that these divergences testify to the intractability of the questions raised by the *Critique*. They may be of such a kind as to be not only unavoidable but also, as Kant foresaw, in part unanswerable.

What is certain is that, in reworking the notions of total determination and the infinite proposition, Kant transforms two questions that he received from his Scholastic predecessors. The contrast between them is stark. One is of indubitable doctrinal significance; the other, involving little more than an "accident of language," seems minor, if not minuscule, in its implications. Seeking to identify the ground of the idea of complete determination, Kant sets out to establish the conditions and limits in which a "thing" may be known. Striving to give an account of the "value and content" that infinite propositions possess for knowledge, he gives a new sense to one fact of speech: the possibility of affixing a *non-* to a term and making it into the predicate in an affirmative statement. The first question concerns nothing less than the complete intelligibility of realities, defined as quiddities: the distinct sets of metaphysical affirmations and negations that constitute varying limitations of one "sum total of possibility," being of beings, or God. The second question asks about no more than the knowledge that may be gleaned from the shape of some sentences spoken in a language, such as German, whose grammar allows for such words as "non-mortal" and "non-man." Kant posed these two questions and showed, in his *Critique*, how they could be systematically interlaced. The weave that he proposed was fragile, as well as subtle, and would hardly last beyond his work. By the beginning of the nineteenth century, it would come loose. Long after the first decades of his Copernican Revolution, however, bright threads would remain from its unraveling.

CHAPTER TEN

Zero Logic

Few documents offer a sharper image of the unstable aftermath of Kant's Copernican Revolution than the letter that the nineteen-year-old Schelling sends his slightly older friend, Hegel, on January 5, 1795. "Philosophy," Schelling declares, "is not yet at an end. Kant has provided the results. The premises are still missing. And who can understand the results without the premises?"[1] That Schelling should credit the architect of the critical system with having laid the foundations of a theory still incomplete is hardly surprising. Kant himself states more than once that the project inaugurated by his *Critique of Pure Reason* is preliminary in the sense of aiming to clear a field for the elaboration of doctrines of metaphysics, law, virtue, and natural science that are still to come. By Kant's own admission, some "results," therefore, lie beyond his *Critiques*. In his letter, however, Schelling gives a different sense to the limitations of the critical philosophy. The Kant that Schelling evokes has provided not a ground but "the results"; yet, in the absence of the premises, such results are unknowable. Neither the inception nor the conclusion of philosophy, therefore, is secure. To reach its "end," Schelling suggests, thinking must begin anew, tending toward an unseen point of speculation.

Poised between premises that are lacking and results that, being furnished in advance of their foundation, cannot but be inconclusive, the endeavor announced by Schelling in his letter is structurally complex. It must be one of fulfillment and initiation and, more exactly, fulfillment in reinitiation. In its ambition to remain faithful to the accomplishment of the transcendental system of cognition in surpassing it, however, Schelling's project is not unique. It bears the unmistakable marks of the last years of the eighteenth century, when many thinkers sought, in diverse and often contradictory ways, to draw out the theses entailed by Kant's critique by recasting its foundations. In his long unpublished but not unknown *Opus Postumum*, Kant himself had led the way toward such attempts. He suggested that, to achieve the project that he began in 1781, he might need to lay new grounds for his transcendental system of knowledge. Beginnings proliferate in this last work. From the nineteenth century to today, readers have found in its pages such diverse doctrinal matters as a solution to a "gap" that Kant claims to have belatedly discovered in his critical system; a transcendental deduction of the physical substance that fills the universe; a new theory of the act by which the I, in thinking, "affects itself"; and multiple accounts of the transition from critical philosophy to the metaphysics of modern natural science.

Kant's early readers soon reached conclusions that, while distinct from his own, were united in their aim to affirm the validity of the critical philosophy in surpassing it. Karl Leonhard Reinhold, who held the first Chair of Critical Philosophy at the University of Jena, proposed that Kant's philosophy could be maintained as a consistent whole only if it referred to a single, self-evident, and fundamental principle. Kant himself had failed to formulate it. Reinhold dubbed this rule the "principle of consciousness" and defined it in the following terms: "In consciousness, the subject distinguishes the representation from the subject and the object and relates the representation to both."[2] Only with the addition of a "theory of representation" founded on this principle, Reinhold argued, could critical philosophy achieve the coherence to which it laid claim. Dissenting voices were soon heard. The most notable was that of Gottlob Ernst Schulze, who claimed in his 1792 *Aenesidemus* that Reinhold had failed to save Kant's system from its fundamental inconsistencies and epistemological uncertainties.[3] Schulze maintained that the critical project, in its classical as in its reconstructed form, could not disprove the skepticism that it sought to set aside. Schulze's argument was novel, but in its conclusion, it recalled the negative position to which Friedrich Heinrich Jacobi had been led several years earlier. In his 1787 study of Kant's "transcendental idealism," Jacobi had argued that, when properly understood, the critical system refutes itself, by virtue less of a principle that it lacks than a concept that it contains: the problematic concept, that is, of the "thing in itself," which, for Kant, could not be known or observed in phenomena, yet must still be posited. "*Without* this presupposition," Jacobi pointedly remarked, "I cannot enter into the system; yet *with* this presupposition, I cannot remain within it."[4]

Among Kant's early readers and revisers, Salomon Maimon was perhaps the one who most forcefully confronted the premises and results of the "Copernican Revolution" in philosophy. His account of the critical system and its instabilities is exemplary, and the solutions that he proposes to resolve its tensions are, in more than one respect, exceptional in their originality. They were also to exert a profound, if forgotten, influence on later philosophers. As has often been observed, Maimon was an outsider among post-Kantians. Reinhold, Schulze, Fichte, Schelling, and Hegel all were and would be, as Wolff and Kant had been, teachers of philosophy in German schools and universities. Maimon was born into a traditional Jewish community in a village of the Polish Lithuanian Commonwealth, where he received the traditional training of a rabbi and Talmudist. As a young man, he taught himself German and philosophy; only in his last years did he begin to publish, having made a difficult and often interrupted voyage westward to Prussia from the "woods of Lithuania," in which, as he once wrote, he had been "condemned at birth to live out the best years" of his life.[5] As Maimon would explain in his remarkable *Autobiography*, he came to write his first work of philosophy while studying Kant's *Critique of Pure Reason* in a "very peculiar manner": "At a first reading, I only arrived at an obscure idea of each part. I then tried to render it distinct by thinking it for myself, and thus tried to enter into the spirit of the author. . . . As I had already appropriated the systems of Spinoza, Hume and Leibniz in the same way, it was natural that I sought to find a system agreeing with all these systems — a coalition-system. And in fact I found it and established it in the form of comments and explanations of the *Critique of Pure Reason*, which finally gave birth to my *Essay on Transcendental Philosophy*."[6]

Today, the felicitous destiny of Maimon's *Essay* is well known. In April 1789, Maimon's friend, Marcus Herz, transmitted the text of Maimon's first book to his friend Kant, who was then at work on the last drafts of his *Critique of Judgment*. "Herr Salomon Maimon," Herz wrote to Kant, by way of introduction, "formerly one of the crudest of Polish Jews, has managed to educate himself in the last few years to an extraordinary degree. By means of his genius, shrewdness and diligence, he has achieved a command of virtually all the higher disciplines and especially, just lately, a command of your philosophy, or at least your manner of philosophizing."[7] In his response to Herz from May 26, 1789, Kant admits that, observing such a weighty bundle of unsolicited papers in his mail, he was at first dismayed, "half deciding" to "send the manuscript back immediately." "But one glance at the work," he writes, "made me realize its excellence and that not only had none of my critics understood me and the main questions as well as Herr Maimon does but also very few men possess so much acumen for such deep investigations as he; and this moved me to lay his book aside till I might have a few moments of leisure."[8] Encouraged by Kant's favorable judgment, Maimon published his *Essay* in 1790. It was to be followed by five books, which assured Maimon a distinguished place in the esteem of his slightly younger and influential contemporary, Fichte, if not in all subsequent accounts of German philosophy. In a letter to Reinhold from March/April 1795, Fichte writes: "My respect for Maimon's talents knows no bounds. I firmly believe that he has completely overturned the entire Kantian philosophy as it has been understood by everyone until now, including you, and I am prepared to prove it. No one noticed what he has done; they had looked down on him from their heights. I believe that future centuries will mock us bitterly."[9]

Maimon never fails to situate his thought in relation to Kant's. Yet like many of his contemporaries, he questions whether the author of the *Critique of Pure Reason* has grasped the full force and consequences of the system that he devised. As Maimon observes at the beginning of his 1797 *Critical Investigations on the Human Mind*, the "Copernican Revolution" itself can be interpreted in several senses, suggesting different and indeed opposing accounts of the conditions of our knowledge. "I ask: In what does the difference between the Ptolemaic and the Copernican world system consist? What does it mean that in the first, the Sun moves around the Earth, while in the second, it is the other way round, the Earth moving along its axis or around the Sun?"[10] Maimon seeks to answer this question with new certitude. He begins by noting that, in the two systems, the relative motions of Sun and Earth are the same; the difference between them concerns the nature of the movement that is considered to be absolute. Absolute motion, however, is definable in several ways.

In a first sense, Maimon notes, a movement may be considered to be absolute after the fashion of a body that passes through empty space. Such a motion may be conceived in thought; but, by definition, it cannot be known, for there are no other bodies by which one might perceive it. It therefore cannot determine the difference between the two world systems, which must rest on some certain knowledge. In a second meaning, motion can be called "absolute" in the manner of a boat that, traveling along a river, moves in relation to a relative space, such as the riverbank. The boat is in movement with respect to the bank, but the inverse does not hold, "because," Maimon explains, "the boat does not move relative to single objects but to all the objects on the bank, while these objects remain stationary in their relation to one another only with respect to the boat."[11] Yet this account of absolute motion cannot capture the difference between the Ptolemaic and the Copernican systems, for according to both, the Earth moves daily with respect to all celestial bodies, while the Sun changes position solely with respect to the Earth.

Maimon then evokes a third position. Absolute motion can be defined as a change of place determined by a general a priori law, such as gravity. A stone falling from a tower moves with respect to the tower; this motion can be called "absolute," while the change of position of the tower with respect to the falling stone is merely relative. Yet the truth is that the law of gravity determines the position of the tower no less than of the stone; and, on its own, this basic law of physics affords no means to distinguish between their respective motions. Maimon therefore proposes a fourth and final account of absolute motion. A movement can now be called "absolute" if it is determined a priori, "so that in its universal application the motion of each object is recognized and distinguished from the motion of the correlative object. Even though the phenomenon as a whole of the two moving bodies in their relation to each other is one, and the motion of one is equal to that of the other, yet when the change of place of each of them is considered separately, it is differently determined."[12] Here Maimon appeals to Newton's law of general attraction. Given two mutually attracting masses, designated as A and B, B will determine A's change of position, and conversely. As Samuel Hugo Bergman observes, reconstructing Maimon's argument, "the rate of motion of *B* with respect to *A* is equal to the motion of *A* with respect to it. But although the motion is relative and reciprocal and the motion of *A* to *B* is equal to that of *B* to *A*, we can still distinguish between the primary and the secondary motion. The motion *A* insofar as it is determined by the attractive mass of *B* is primary and hence absolute, and the motion of *B*, although equal to *A*, is secondary and hence relative."[13]

Just as there are four known interpretations of absolute motion, Maimon explains, so there are four possible accounts of the relation that obtains between the knowing subject and the known object in cognition. What separates the views of the philosophers is not a discordance about the fact of knowledge itself; on this they concur, even as the Ptolemaic and Copernican systems accord with respect to the relative movements of Earth and Sun. The divisive question is that of the conditions of knowledge. According to traditional or "dogmatic" philosophers, the cause of knowledge lies absolutely in the object, the subject being but its relative cause. Maimon reasons that such a claim is no more demonstrable than the thesis that absolute motion is identifiable with the passage of a body through empty space. Just as such a movement cannot be known, so the appeal to an object utterly disjoined from a subject yields no insight into the origins of cognition. In a manner reminiscent of the second interpretation of absolute motion, some thinkers, by contrast, attribute to the mind a priori structures that define the subject's relation to its object. Even as the boat's motion along the river would determine the relative movement of the objects on the shoreline, such structures would then condition the possibility of knowledge. Yet this account of cognition is no more satisfactory than the second presentation of absolute motion. Just as that doctrine could not explain the difference between the Ptolemaic and Copernican systems, so this interpretation cannot justify the validity of a priori rules. It may do no more than allege some subjective cause for them, in a manner as arbitrary as the dogmatic appeal to an indemonstrable source of cognition.

Maimon suggests that to the third interpretation of absolute movement, there corresponds Kant's own transcendental doctrine in the *Critique of Pure Reason*. Just as the stone, in its fall from the tower, moves in accordance with the law of gravity, so, for Kant, the mind, in its sensations and concepts, acts in accordance with a priori laws determining its relations to objects. In other words, in the Kantian system, the "principle of the possibility of experience" occupies the place of the law of gravitation in physics. Gravity determines the stone's fall as "absolute" motion with respect to the tower; likewise, Kant conceives of the subject as the ground of a priori concepts.[14] Yet even as Maimon judges the third interpretation of absolute motion to be unsatisfactory, so he must reject this Kantian solution to the problem of cognition. In seeking to explain the difference between the two world systems, the third account fails to offer any reason for its attribution of the law of gravity to the stone, rather than to the tower. In the same way, the theory of Kant's *Critique* cannot justify its identification of a priori principles with the subject of knowledge; nor can it propose any answer to the question of why one a priori law, rather than another, applies to a given phenomenon.[15] The fourth interpretation alone affords a means to delineate the true relation of subject and object in knowledge. Newton, Maimon recalls, discovered a single law that holds for two masses, defined reciprocally in their different rates of motion. In the same way, a Copernican philosophy must establish one rule, which applies to subject and object, determining their necessary correspondence.

The doctrine of such a "Copernican Revolution" entails a fundamental revision of critical epistemology and metaphysics. Kant maintained that philosophy must leave room for a "thing in itself," as a cause of sensation that exceeds subjective conditions of experience: a "noumenon," as Kant wrote, beyond perceived phenomena. Maimon's theory leads directly to the elimination of that obscure thing. An object that is given simultaneously with the subject, like mass B placed in relation to mass A, can be no thing in itself, at least insofar as that "thing" is, as Kant held, removed from all experience. The thing in itself emerges, rather, as a function of reason, or a correlate of the mind. "When we speak of a thing in itself," Maimon writes, "we do not mean a thing by which consciousness is affected, but something that consciousness contains."[16] Jacobi's objection against the philosophy of "transcendental idealism" is then unjustified; the noumenon ceases to differ from the phenomenon, except in degree, and with respect to our intellect, which is limited by nature. In his *Essay on Transcendental*

Philosophy, Maimon offers an example. What the "thing" (*Ding*) gold is "in itself" remains, for us, "an unknown essence [*ein unbekanntes Wesen*]"; what we perceive are its properties, such as its color, its weight, and its hardness, assembled in a unity by our imagination, not understanding. "Our concept of gold is constituted by the synthesis of the properties, and this concept is distinguished from the thing itself only because of its formal incompleteness (the lack of insight into the objective connection of these properties)."[17] Degree of conceptual completeness alone grounds the difference between appearances and things. "The representation of the object or its concept is one and the same as the thing."[18] They differ solely in the intensity of their definition.

Such a "Copernican" principle transforms Kant's doctrine. Yet it is but an element in Maimon's "coalition system," which reconceives of the branches of transcendental philosophy. Logic looms prominently among them. It will be recalled that in the *Critique of Pure Reason*, Kant distinguishes "general" from "transcendental logic." The first treats of the forms of statements and their relations, independent of their content, while the second takes into account two "transcendental" matters: the a priori rules by which we may conceive of objects as such, and the meaning of judgments. As Nathan Rotenstreich observes, Kant thus introduces a "fundamental duality in the spheres of Logic, because we distinguish between thought that has no relationship to a given object and thought that does stand in relation to given data and classifies these data and fashions lawful objects out of them."[19] General logic appears to provide transcendental logic with its simplest formal terms, that is, subject and predicate, and with the set of the possible relations of conjunction, disjunction, and entailment that hold between propositions. General logic, to this degree, conditions transcendental logic.

Faithful to the outer lineaments of the Kantian system, Maimon retains the critical distinction between general and transcendental logic. Yet he redefines of the sense of this partition, for reasons that follow directly from his understanding of the Copernican Revolution in philosophy. Once object and subject of knowledge are submitted to a single law, such that the "thing in itself" becomes no more than a limit internal to human reason, the border separating formal and transcendental logic shifts. In a system that grants the validity of objects independent of the conditions of subjective experience, the criterion for the objectivity of thought may be external to thinking; a purely formal logic, which abstracts from the content of judgments and their origins, can play a major role. But for Maimon, as for many of his immediate and later idealistic successors, "the objectivity of things is derived from thought itself, which is the criterion of objectivity."[20] The relations of formal and transcendental logic therefore change. "Overturning" Kant's doctrine, as Fichte noted, Maimon advances several claims for the priority of "transcendental" over "general" logic.[21]

Maimon begins by observing that general logic "necessarily presupposes transcendental concepts and principles, without which its forms have no meaning." His examples are logical "affirmation" and "negation," which, he argues, reversing the course of Kant's own critical method, necessarily presuppose the "transcendental concepts of reality and negation."[22] Next, Maimon declares that the forms of reason, in themselves, constitute only possible relations; to acquire a real foundation, they must be rendered actual by some content, which by definition exceeds them. Finally, he maintains that even the most "analytic" of logical principles depends on a synthesis of consciousness, which only a non-formal act of thinking can provide. He calls to mind what is perhaps the simplest principle of thought: the principle of contradiction, which in his terms dictates that, if a thing possesses a certain property, it cannot, at the same time and in the same respect, possess its contrary. Maimon holds that even to formulate this law of thought, one must determine some content by an act of synthesis: to state, "if A is B, A is not non-B," one must conceive of A as defined by B.[23] Such a definition, however, exceeds mere form; it involves the matter of thinking.

Even as he redefines the nature and extent of formal logic, Maimon offers a new presentation of transcendental logic. Kant identified its highest principle with the "unity of apperception." "No cognitions can occur in us, no connection and unity among them," Kant explained in the *Critique of Pure Reason*, "without that unity of consciousness that precedes all data of the intuitions, and in relation to which all representation of objects is alone possible. This pure, original, unchanging consciousness I will now name *transcendental apperception*."[24] This is Kant's subjective condition for all thoughts: "The *I think* must *be able* to accompany all my representations."[25] Maimon responds that, on its own, such a principle cannot ground transcendental logic. It is necessary but insufficient. In his *Critical Investigations*, Maimon declares, recalling the First *Critique*: "I am only conscious of myself, as one with myself, in different representations, under the condition that my many different representations, belonging to a (synthetic) *unity of consciousness*, are *knowable*." Kant is correct when he maintains that, to unite two concepts in a judgment, holding *S is P*, the mind that thinks *S* must be the same mind that thinks *P*; and, for the mind to distinguish itself from what it thinks, there must, then, be a synthesis not only in the contents of thought, but also in thinking itself. A further question must still be posed and answered: "According to what principle are representations *knowable* as such *before real thinking*?"[26]

Maimon foresees the perplexity that his question may provoke. "You ask for the impossible!" Crito, the interlocutor in his dialogic *Investigations*, responds. "How can I know that representations belong to the unity of consciousness before I unite them in consciousness, that is, before I think of them?" Maimon believes he can offer a conclusive response by appealing to a new principle of transcendental logic, which furnishes an objective ground for the possibility of the relation of two representations in a synthesis. This is, in Maimon's words, the "highest principle of all real thought,"[27] and "the highest principle of all synthetic knowledge that determines objects."[28] It is "the principle of determinability" (*der Satz von Bestimmbarkeit*). From his *Essay on Transcendental Philosophy* through to his last works, Maimon places it at the center of his system of philosophy. It furnishes the foundation of predication, or real synthesis in consciousness. "We recognize that a synthesis is not merely symbolic but real," he explains, "because one part of it can be thought without the other (thought in itself), but not the reverse; but none of these parts can be presented in itself, as an abstract concept in intuition, so we cannot know whether one of them can be thought in itself unless we actually present it in intuition by means of different syntheses."[29] Two elements compose a synthesis of the first and simplest variety. One may be "thought without the other." This Maimon considers the "determinable" (*Bestimmbares*); it corresponds, in traditional logic, to the subject. The other, by contrast, cannot be thought "in itself." Maimon defines it as the "determinant" (*Bestimmung*); it corresponds to the predicate. The union of the two produces a "real synthesis": a new concept.

Maimon consistently draws his examples of such syntheses from mathematics, and he does so for a fundamental reason. Breaking with Kant, he argues that it is only in mathematics that the human mind can grasp the propositions whose legitimacy the *Critique of Pure Reason* sought to secure: "a priori synthetic judgments," which relate two concepts in such a way that the predicate lies "entirely outside the concept" of the subject, the conjunction of concepts being independent of any empirically given object.[30] In the proposition, "The triangle is right-angled or oblique-angled," for example, "triangle" is the "determinable"; one may conceive of it, in itself, without, however, specifying whether it is either right-angled or oblique-angled. "Right-angled or oblique-angled" is the "determinant," which cannot be represented on its own: "*Triangle* is the subject, but *being right- or oblique-angled* is the predicate, and the concept this synthesis gives rise to is an absolute concept."[31] The principle of determinability provides the a priori ground of this synthesis. It is because "triangle" is of such a nature as to be either "oblique-angled" or "right-angled," and because "right-angled or oblique-angled" is of such a nature as to be a property of a triangle, that, without regard to experience, one may know that this synthesis is possible. Lacking the logical terms of this analysis of judgment, Kant could not hope to solve the problem of cognition that he posed in his *Critique of Pure Reason*. Maimon explains:

> Kant revealed the subjective condition (of the thinker) as well as the objective condition (of what is thought), but he failed to see that the unity of the synthesis itself of what is thought depends on certain conditions and must be determined by itself under a priori conditions which . . . reside in the principle of determinability. The synthesis 'a is b' is possible because the predicate is dependent on the subject and cannot be thought without it. It follows, then, that if I think *b*, I must also think *a* since *b* can only be thought in combination with *a*; without such a combination thinking itself would be impossible.[32]

In his *Essay of Transcendental Philosophy*, Maimon appeals to grammatical features to illustrate this most basic principle in his thought. Just as a speaker of a given language can tell an adjective from a noun, specifying the order in which they may be combined, so, too, the mind may distinguish determinant from determinable, according to the a priori principle of their union:

> Linguistic usage already shows that each part of a synthesis cannot be treated as subject and as predicate in relation to the other part at the same time. For example, we can say 'a square table,' but not 'a table square,' 'a black line,' but not 'a line black,' etc. What is the reason for this? Will it be said (as is in fact claimed) that the *universal* is the predicate, and the *particular* the subject of a synthesis? But why is square more universal than table? Perhaps because it is not only a table but also a door, a window, etc. that can be square; however it is not only a square, but also a circle, a triangle etc. that can be a table; and it is the same with the second example: 'black' can be attributed to more things than lines, but 'line' can also be attributed to more things than black. So the reason [or ground, *Grund*] must be the one I give, namely, this: the subject comprises that part of a synthesis that also constitutes a synthesis in itself; as a result, it can also be thought in itself as an object without relation to the other part. By contrast, the predicate comprises the other part, the one that does not constitute a synthesis in itself; as a result it can be thought only as a constituent part of a synthesis, not in itself as an object.[33]

The lawful distinctions of grammar illustrate a rule of thought, and syntax, in its most elementary features, recapitulates transcendental logic.

In his 1794 treatise, *On Aristotle's Categories*, Maimon shows also that the principle of determinability founds the threefold distinction among the qualities of judgment that Kant sets forth in his *Critique*. First, Maimon reasons, an affirmation contains the "reason" for the union of subject and predicate: namely, that these concepts may enter into a relation of determination. His example is the statement: "A triangle can be right-angled." From the synthesis of subject and predicate, "a new object emerges, that is, a right-angled triangle. This is therefore an affirmative judgment."[34] Next Maimon considers the negative judgment: "An equilateral triangle cannot be right-angled." No new object emerges from the union of its subject and predicate, because there can be no object corresponding to the synthesis "an equilateral right-angled triangle." But being "right-angled" is a possible determination of a two-dimensional geometrical figure, and this judgment, like the preceding one, issues in a determination: "The predicate eliminates [*hebt auf*] a determination (the equality of the sides) thought in the subject."[35] Lest his doctrine of predicative judgments be misunderstood, Maimon avails himself of an unequivocal means of symbolic illustration. "Affirmation is equal to the *plus*, +, in algebra. The number + 3, for example, does not eliminate the number + 5; rather, through the union of + 5 and + 3, a new number emerges: +8." So, too, Maimon continues, "negation [*Verneinung*] is equivalent to the minus, –, in algebra: 5–3, by which + 2 is eliminated."

Maimon knows well that Kant also proposed a third quality of judgment. There exists, he therefore continues, a third variety of synthesis; but although its form is valid, it issues in no determination. "Virtue is quadrilateral" is Maimon's example for this third quality.[36] A reader familiar with Kant's logic and the history of the treatment of "the infinite proposition" and "pseudo-negation" (*Scheinverneinung*) would be astonished by this example, for a simple reason: it lacks any grammatically or logically "indefinite" expression. While Kant's examples of the "third quality" all involve predicates prefixed by a *non-*, no such affix appears in Maimon's example. Its logical syntax would appear to be perfectly affirmative, consisting in the union of a determinant, "quadrilateral," and a determinable, "virtue." Here transcendental logical and general logic, however, diverge. Despite its apparently regular syntactic form, "Virtue is quadrilateral" is a statement whose concepts, when thought as such, admit of no real synthesis. In such a proposition, "no new object is determined," yet "it is also true that nothing thought in *virtue* is eliminated." Maimon concludes: "In the third judgment, subject and predicate determine no new object." In algebraic terms, the infinite judgment combines concepts without effecting an arithmetical operation of addition or subtraction. "In a single consciousness," the elements of this judgment merely cancel each other out. They are, Maimon writes, "equivalent to o [*gleich* o]."[37]

In his 1794 *Essay on New Logic*, Maimon proposes a slightly different account of the algebraic structure of judgments. But he holds fast to his zero. "With respect to quality," he writes,

an affirmation — whose meaning is that a predicate is contained in a subject — can be designated by the sign of *equality*, =. The correspondence in the object can be designated by plus, +; negation, by minus, –, and *infinity* [*die Unendlichkeit*], by o. Accordingly, *a + b* is an *affirmative* judgment, and means that *a* and *b* can be linked in the unity of consciousness. *a–b* is a *negative* judgment, and means that *a* and *b* cancel each other in the same consciousness, and therefore cannot be linked in the unity of consciousness. *a o b* is an *infinite* judgment, and means that *a* and *b* correspond as little in the determination of an object as they are opposed; therefore, they remain after the union as they were before it. This union attaches no new properties to them; it also takes none away from them. It is in this regard = o.[38]

Maimon is the first to draw attention to the novelty of his analysis of the infinite judgment. He recalls that, "in their usual symbolic game [*Zeichenspiel*]," past logicians distinguished the infinite judgment from the negative on the grounds that, in the infinite proposition, "the sign of negation is removed from the copula and attached to the predicate." In all other respects, however, traditional philosophers took the difference between these qualities of judgment to be "indifferent" (*gleichgültig*). Maimon states: "I, however, have found an essential difference between the two varieties of judgment."[39] It follows from the principle of determinability, which allows the distinction between the negative and the infinite judgment to be newly and clearly drawn. In negation, there is a reason [*Grund*] for "the elimination of position [*die Hebung der Position*]"; in an infinite judgment, there is "merely a lack of reason of position" [*bloß der Mangel eines Grundes der Position*]." One might well wonder about the marks that might differentiate such states of non-being. Without responding directly to the question, Maimon, alluding to Kant's theory of negative magnitudes, offers an example, drawn from physics, to dispel any confusion: "It is exactly like the difference between the rest that is caused by two forces moving in opposition, and the rest that follows, according to the law of inertia, from the absence of any moving force."[40]

Maimon argues that, as obvious as it may seem once formulated, the distinction between these two logical immobilities eluded earlier thinkers. Lacking the principle of determinability, they could not tell the zero of "elimination" from the zero of "a lack of reason of position." The difference between such nothings, to them, was as nothing. Maimon concedes that, if pressed as to the a priori principle for the possibility of real synthesis, a traditional philosopher might be made to grant the existence of a problem; with the tools of merely general logic, however, he would be incapable of resolving it. "If one asks a philosopher: 'Can virtue be quadrilateral?' He will laugh you away [*so wird er Euch auslachen*]. Ask him further: 'Why not? The possible is everything that does not contain a contradiction. A quadri-lateral virtue contains no contradiction; therefore, a quadrilateral virtue is entirely possible.' Then the philosopher will be at a loss as to what he should answer."[41] Here the difference between the basic principles of general logic and transcendental logic comes fully to light. Each fundamental law of thinking establishes a criterion for the affirmation of logical possibility. The logical possibilities in question, however, are distinct. The possibility of general logic is formal, being reducible to the absence of contradiction: S can be P if S is not *non-P*. What remains to be decided, however, is the admissibility of either synthesis: the a priori determinability of S by either P or *non-P*.

A criterion for real — that is, determinable — possibility is required. This is the criterion that comes to light in Maimon's theory of infinite judgments. "If they are not simply to belong to the logical ornaments, but to have a meaning that is as distinct from the affirmative as from the nega-tive judgments," we read, later in the same treatise, "then so-called infinite judgments may be said to be those whose subject contains as little reason for the affirmation as for the negation of the predicate," that is, those "in which the predicate and its contrary can result in no possible determina-tion of the subject."[42] As an example, Maimon now evokes the judgment: "Virtue is non-quadrilateral" (or "Virtue is not quadrilateral," *Die Tugend ist nicht viereckig*). That example has much to startle Maimon's reader. Ear-lier in the same treatise, the infinite judgment appears in the seemingly simple affirmative form: "Virtue is quadrilateral." Now it would seem to be interchangeable with its apparent negation, or with its indefinite contrary. The propositions "Virtue is quadrilateral" and "Virtue is not (or non-) quadrilateral" would appear, in short, to be strictly indistinguishable.

How might two sentences so punctually opposed be taken as synony-mous? Classical logic, in its dependence on the principle of contradiction, would exclude their equivalence, and it would do so on absolutely a priori grounds. But in Maimon's new logic, apparent facts of syntax acquire a new sense. Formal relations of contrariety and contradiction are no longer conclusive in themselves. The opposition between "Virtue is quadrilateral" and "Virtue is not (or non-) quadrilateral" would be decisive if these sentences constituted the assertion and the negation of one subject's predicative determination. Yet they do not. Their opposition, therefore, is merely formal; in other words, it is illusory. Maimon explains: "Four-sidedness cannot result in a possible determination of virtue any more than non-four-sidedness. Both are determinations of space, which has no common concept with virtue. They are judgments in which, through a subjective unity of consciousness, the reason for affirmation and negation alike is denied [verneint]. They therefore express the concept of nothingness [Nichts] — not, however, the nothingness that emerges from contradiction or opposing constructions, but the nothingness that is thought as the lack of a reason for synthesis."[43]

Far from being an "ornament" of doctrine, the infinite judgment plays, therefore, a crucial role in the exposition of Maimon's critical philosophy. It exhibits the difference that separates his logic from that of his predecessors. Maimon's relatively few commentators have, for this reason, lingered on its origins and consequences. In his 1964 study of Maimon's philosophy, Samuel Atlas went so far as to reverse the order of the philosopher's own presentation in Aristotle's *Categories*. Atlas argued that it was the theory of the logical zero of the infinite judgment that first suggested to Maimon the principle of determinability, rather than the reverse.[44] That Maimon was intimately familiar with the logical problem of statements in which subject and predicate are incongruent can be inferred from his close familiarity with the work of the philosopher from whom he drew his self-fashioned surname, Mūsa ibn Maimūn, or, as he is more often known today, Maimonides. In the first part of his *Guide of the Perplexed*, Maimonides devotes several chapters to considering the meaning of the biblical expressions employed to characterize the nature of divinity. They appear to suggest that God possesses positive attributes belonging to beings such as ourselves. Repeatedly, Scripture seems to indicate that God is "living," "powerful," and "wise." Maimonides warns his readers, however, that before interpreting such expressions as affirmations of predicates in the usual sense, one must consider whether the Creator is of such a nature as to possess the same properties as His creation. Only a commonality of essence could justify the interpretation of these expressions as predicative determinations.

In the avowedly recondite chapters on divine attributes of his *Guide*, Maimonides leaves little doubt as to his own position on this question:

> Those who believe that there are essential attributes [*ṣifāt dhātiya*] that may be predicated of the Creator—namely, that He is existent, living, possessing power, knowing, and willing—ought to understand that these notions are not ascribed to Him and to us in the same sense. According to what they think, the difference between these attributes and ours lies in the former being greater, more perfect, more permanent, or more durable than ours, so that His existence is more durable than our existence, His life more permanent than our life, His power greater than our power, His knowledge more perfect than our knowledge, and His will more perfect than our will.[45]

Such interpreters fail to grasp that if comparisons of this kind are legitimate, it can only be because the virtues of the Creator and His creations share a common definition—because they are, in a word, alike. Such similarity, however, is in truth no more than the effect of an equivocation, or homonymy: "It is clear to all those who understand the meaning of being alike that the term 'existent' is predicated of Him, may He be exalted, and of everything that is other than He, in a purely equivocal sense. Similarly, the terms 'knowledge,' 'power,' 'will' and 'life,' as applied to Him, may He be exalted, and to all those possessing knowledge, power, will, and life, are purely equivocal [*bi-štirāk al-maḥḍ*], so that the meaning when they are predicated of Him is in no way like their meaning in other applications." It is by homonymy alone that properties known to belong to the created can be stated of the Creator. The meaning of the attributes ascribed to God and the meaning of the attributions known to human beings, Maimonides concludes, "have nothing in common in any respect or in any mode; these attributions have in common only the name and nothing else [*fī-l ism lā ghayr*]. This conception is of immense sublimity according to those who know. Keep it in memory."[46]

147

In his *Guide*, Maimonides proceeds to argue that, when properly understood, every description of God in Scripture either refers to one of His
actions or, if it denotes a property of His nature, signifies a negative attribute. Yet he adds that "negation" must here be taken in a particular sense.
"Negations [*as-suālb*] are not used with reference to or applied to Him, may
He be exalted, except from the following point of view, which you know:
one sometimes denies with reference to a thing something that cannot
fittingly exist in it. Thus we say of a wall that it is not endowed with sight
[or 'is non-seeing,' *lā baṣīr*]."[47] Such a "negation" (*salb*) therefore, corresponds to no imperfection. In a dense but decisive passage, Maimonides
writes that the negative propositions to be inferred of God deny not only
the affirmation of an attribute but also the affirmation of its privation:
"Every attribute that we predicate of Him is an attribute of action or, if
the attribute is intended for the apprehension of His essence and not of His
action, it signifies the negation of the privation [*salb 'adam*] of the attribute
in question."[48] To say that the wall is "not seeing" (or non-seeing), in this
sense, is to deny both that it possesses the property of sight and that it is
blind.[49] A negation of this kind does not, Maimonides suggests, provide a
definition; it merely posits a non-correspondence between the subject and
a predicate and its logical contrary. "Accordingly we say that the heavens
are neither light nor heavy nor acted upon and consequently not receptive
to external impressions, that they have no taste and no smell; and we make
other negations of this kind. All this is due to our ignorance with regard to
that matter."[50]

Maimon wrote two commentaries on the *Guide* that leave little doubt
as to the esteem in which he held the medieval treatise.[51] He published the
first of his accounts of Maimonides's doctrine in German, as a portion of
his own *Autobiography*. Here he explains how Maimonides "demonstrates"
that it is illegitimate to predicate existence of God as an attribute, "for
God's existence — necessary being — is already inherent in his essence
and therefore cannot be imputed to him as an attribute. God therefore
exists without existence, and it is the same with his other attributes."[52]
Maimon observes that, in a later chapter, Maimonides "goes even further,
explaining that exclusively negations of negations [*bloß Verneinungen der
Verneinungen*] can be predicated of God."[53] Such "negations of negations"

allude unmistakably to the particular variety of "negation" presented by Maimonides as the "negation of the privation of the attribute in question."

It is in his second commentary on the *Guide*, which he composed in Hebrew, that Maimon most exactly reconstructs the detail of the Maimonidean argument, integrating it into his own transcendental logic. Maimonides had raised the question of the "similarity" (*al-shibhiya*) between Creator and created, alleging that it alone could found the univocal sense of divine and human attributes. Only if God's being and human being shared some common definition might one claim that divine existence is "more durable than our existence." "Similarity" implies the shared belonging to a concept, and, Maimon writes, "if there is no common belonging, there can be no similarity." For this principle Maimon offers the following "explanation" in Hebrew, punctuated by supplements of Kantian terminology in German:

> Every concept of the understanding is composed of a subject and a predicate. The subject is that which is given to sensibility (*was der Sinnlichkeit gegeben wird*), while the predicate determines the subject insofar as it is posited by the understanding. For example, the concept of a triangle is composed of a subject and a predicate. The first is space; the second is the limitation of this space by threes sides. It is necessary that the subject be a general concept (*eine allgemeine Vorstellung*) and that the predicate a special determination of it, for if both were equal (in extension), they could not be combined into an intellectual synthesis, just as we could not conceive, for example, "a sweet line," since "line" and "sweet" have an equal extension; we can, however, conceive of a "straight line," since "line" is more comprehensive than "straight" and also of a "crooked line," for a "line" need not always be "straight"; but "straight" can refer only to a line; so that it is possible for us to represent a line that is not straight but it is impossible to represent "straight" without a "line." Hence, if we wish to represent a straight line, we must represent it as predicated of "line" and that is the ground of the synthesis "straight line," which is not so in the case of "sweet line."[54]

Here the terms of Maimon's law of determinability are unmistakably present. That "it is clear to all those who understand the meaning of being alike" that Creator and creation are not alike means no more and no less than this: the "life" or "wisdom" that is a "determinant" of divine being is no "determinant" of human being. Their logical expanses simply do not over-lap. One may conclude, a priori, that every statement uniting the subject "God" with a predicate known to human beings possesses the logical struc-ture of a judgment such as "the line is sweet," which is to say, in the terms of Aristotle's *Categories*, that of a judgment such as "virtue is quadrilateral," "virtue is not quadrilateral" or "virtue is non-quadrilateral." More exactly, that "God is wise" means, "God is not foolish," or "God is non-foolish," that is, "God" and "foolish," when combined, compose no synthesis. That "God is existent" means, "God is not inexistent," or "God is non-existent"; to put matters differently, "inexistence" is no determinant of the determinable "God." In these statements, nothing in God is defined, by addition or by subtraction. Such judgments, structurally "inert," are all at rest.

Maimon at times suggests that, to the degree to which the infinite judgment signifies "a lack of correspondence [*Mangel der Übereinstimmung*] between subject and predicate," it can be considered to be a variety of "negation."[55] But such a non-correspondence also possesses an undeniably affirmative force. Like Kant, albeit for reasons distinct from his, Mai-mon maintains that the "third quality" of judgment is irreducible to the second. Kant conceives of judgment as the act by which two concepts are related; negation appears to him as the mere denial that the "sphere" of one concept falls within that of another. By contrast, for Kant, to state, "The soul is non-mortal" is to refuse the subsumption of the concept "soul" by the concept "mortality" and, at the same time, to set it "in some infinite somewhere." Since, for Kant, such a logical "somewhere" is susceptible to further determination, the judgment that places an object in this infinite expanse is a "judgment of determination" (*Bestimmungsurteil*). Although he follows Kant in maintaining the independence of the infinite judg-ment from the negative, Maimon's doctrine, in a sense, could be no fur-ther removed from that of the founder of transcendental logic. Maimon's infinite judgment is one of "non-determination." It establishes that the subject is of such as nature as to be indefinable by the predicate.

Recalling the distant origins of the theory of non-words in logic, one might say that Maimon thereby retrieves the first sense of such expres-sions: that of being *aorista*, that is, less "infinite" than "indefinite" and, more exactly, "indeterminate." To this degree, he also departs from Kant's theory. In the third quality of Kantian judgments, it is the predicate that is "infinite." It limits the "sum total of possibility" attributable to the subject, even as the copula establishes that the subject, although thus delimited, constitutes a "thing." In the third quality of Maimonian judgments, by contrast, it is the entire proposition that is "infinite," in the sense that it establishes the real absence of a ground of determination. To the extent that it denies the correspondence between predicate and subject, the Maimonian infinite judgment is merely negative; but in not issuing even in a negative determination of the subject, it differs from a negation. The infinite judgment denies that a predicate and its contrary may apply to the subject, thereby establishing an a priori impossibility of determination. This variety of judgment leaves the subject intact, and indefinable — like God, as Maimonides maintains, or, as Maimon writes, for shorthand, like zero.

To this degree, Maimon's third quality of judgment is almost none at all, at least if one recalls his own definition of this discursive form of thought. According to his transcendental logic, a judgment is not merely the linking of a subject and a predicate. More fundamentally, it is the establishment of a real relation of determinability. Does non-determinability, one might ask, belong to the set of such relations? Implicitly, Maimon answers in the affirmative. The third quality seems, to him, some manner of "determination." As Friedrich Kuntze observed, Maimon's infinite judgment constitutes the "securing of the indeterminacy" (*die Versicherung der Unbestimmbarkeit*) of the subject.[56] Removing the subject from the relation of predication, whether affirmative or negative, it posits it as an indeterminate — and perhaps indeterminable — object of thought. One might well view this positing as distinct from any "determination." The inertial state of Maimon's zero of affirmation could be considered to articulate a form of thinking beyond judgment, effecting a withdrawal from the predicative relation and a suspension of all determination. This, at least, would be the interpretation toward which the transcendental philosophies of Maimon's three most illustrious speculative readers would lead. In different ways, Fichte, Schelling, and Hegel would find in Maimon's zero logic less than an outer edge than a border, which opens onto new accounts of the possibility of cognition. After Kant and after Maimon, they would draw more radical consequences still from the Copernican Revolution in philosophy, loosening transcendental logic ever more from its dependence on the forms of predicative reasoning. Striving simultaneously to complete the critical system and to found it anew, they would therefore also devise new means to define natures indeterminable because unconditioned — starting with that of the being who says "I."

CHAPTER ELEVEN

Non-I and I

Although it is little known today, Salomon Maimon's transcendental logic of the zero was not lost on his immediate successors. One may even go so far as to assert that it played a significant, if implicit, role in their theories of judgment, which revised the *Critique of Pure Reason* in fundamental ways. After Kant and often against him, the philosophers of the end of the eighteenth century sought to define the conditions and limits of human knowledge. To this end, they came to reconsider the nature of a priori synthetic judgments, the distinctions between the a priori and the a posteriori and the analytic and the synthetic, and the form of judgment. Long before the modern era, Aristotle had defined the affirmative assertion as a predicative proposition stating "one thing of another thing." In his logic, Kant reformulated this principle, defining the first quality of judgment as an act by which one concept "is placed in the sphere of another." Questioning the coherence and completeness of the critical system, philosophers after Kant came to contest this apparently simple definition. They were soon led to consider the possibility of new judgments, in which subject and predicate enter into relations hardly glimpsed by Kant.

"The most notable of such new judgments makes its appearance in the opening pages of the first introduction to Fichte's *On the Concept of the Science of Knowledge*, or *Wissenschaftslehre*. That Fichte himself understood his thought to owe a debt to the author of the *Essay on Transcendental Philosophy*, of course, is well known. Not only did Fichte express himself on this subject privately, in the letter to Reinhold in which he evoked his "limitless" esteem for Maimon. The first sentence of the preface to the first edition of the *Science of Knowledge*, from 1794, also stresses this point, crediting "the remarkable Maimonian writings [*die vortreffliche Maimonschen Schriften*]," along with Schulze's *Aenesidemus*, with having rendered possible the raising of philosophy, after Kant, "to the rank of one of the uncontested sciences."[1] Yet the legacy of the "remarkable Maimonian writings" is also detectable in a manner more limited and precise, which casts an unexpected light on Fichte's system of idealism.

Starting with the first edition of the *Doctrine of Knowledge*, Fichte sets out, in Reinhold's steps, to render the project of transcendental philosophy secure by grounding it in a single self-evident principle. Fichte aims, in his words, to "*discover* the primordial, absolutely unconditional first principle of all human knowledge," which, as "an absolutely primary principle," "can be neither *proved* nor *defined*."[2] Fichte holds that this primary proposition will exhibit an unprecedented logical form. By way of introduction, he reminds his readers of the types of statements known to traditional logic. They are two: the "synthetic," as he writes, and the "antithetical." Each variety of judgment relates two concepts by presupposing a double ground: "firstly of conjunction, and secondly of distinction, of which both could be exhibited, and both would *have* to be exhibited, if the judgment is to be warranted sound."[3] Fichte offers an example for each type:

> A bird is an animal: here the ground of conjunction we reflect upon is the specific concept of an animal, that it consists of matter, of organic matter, of animate living matter; while the grounds of distinction, which we disregard, consist of the specific differences among the various kinds of animal, whether they are bipeds or quadrupeds, and have feathers, scales or hairy skin. Again, a plant is not animal: here the ground of distinction we reflect upon is the specific difference between plant and animal; while the ground of conjunction we disregard is the fact of organization in general.[4]

Both such judgments are analyzable into the asymmetrical logical elements that are subject and predicate. In the "synthetic" judgment, the mind affirms the identity between two thought concepts; in the "antithetical" judgment, instead, it grasps their difference. Now, however, Fichte asks his reader to conceive of a third variety of statement. This is a judgment from which the relation of subject and predicate appears, at least at first, to be lacking. Its form is therefore unique. In this statement, Fichte explains, "something is asserted, not to be like anything else or opposed to anything else, but simply to be identical with itself: thus it could presuppose no ground of conjunction or distinction at all." It is by such a proposition that Fichte proposes to found all knowledge.

Fichte calls this the "thetic judgment," for in his doctrine, it achieves a pure *thesis*, in the Greek sense of the word, that is, a "positing," and no more. Fichte explains: "The first and foremost judgment of this type is 'I am.'"[5] One might wonder whether the term "judgment" is adequate to such a sentence. Fichte himself maintains that in the words "I am," a predicative form can hardly be discerned. In a crucial passage of the 1794 edition, he specifies that, in this statement, "nothing whatever is affirmed of the self, the place of the predicate being left infinitely empty for its possible determination [*die Stelle des Prädikats für die mögliche Bestimmung des Ich ins Unendliche leer gelassen wird*]." In the words "I am," a subject is to posit itself, in the absence of all predicates. This is an "absolute" positing, in the sense that it presupposes nothing before itself; moreover, for Fichte, it is a fundamental positing, since all theses and concepts in the "doctrine of knowledge" are derivable from it.[6] Yet Fichte adds that the thetic judgment can take more than a single form. "I am" is but the most minimal of its expressions. The reader learns that there exists an entire class of thetic sentences, some of which seem to bear on things other than the *I* and on matters other than the essence of the self. To grasp the belonging of such statements to the set of thetic judgments, one must look beyond their merely grammatical syntax. One must grasp them in their transcendental logic, understanding their content as well as their form. Then, Fichte wagers, certain apparently predicative assertions will reveal themselves to state nothing but the pure positing of the *I*.

As a first example of such thetic judgments in seemingly predicative form, Fichte offers the statement "Man is free." He observes that one would run into difficulties in defining this judgment in traditional terms, as an affirmation or a synthesis. According to the Kantian doctrine, an affirmative judgment subsumes the sphere of one concept under another. Were "Man is free" to be an affirmative judgment, it would, then, subordinate the sphere of "man" to that of "free beings generally." Fichte, however, responds: no such higher concept exists, because among beings, man alone is free. For this reason, one might, at a second stage, strive to define the proposition "Man is free" as a negative statement, that is, an "antithetical judgment." To do so clearly and distinctly, however, one would need to contrast man's nature with that of beings subject to the laws of natural necessity. "Then we should have to give the ground of distinction between the necessary and the not necessary," Fichte reasons, "and it would have to be shown that the former is not contained in the concept of man, whereas it is in that of the contrasted beings; and at the same time a respect would have to be pointed out in which they both concurred." Such a "respect," however, is inconceivable. Insofar as he is free, man is unique; he "has nothing whatsoever in common with natural beings, and hence is not contrasted to them either."[7] The truth is that the judgment "Man is free" effects neither a synthesis nor an antithesis. It means simply: "There is freedom," or, to put matters differently, "I am," the freedom stated in the verb "I am" being, then, left "infinitely empty for its possible determination."

Fichte grants that the thetic judgment recalls a form of discursive thought defined in transcendental logic before his *Doctrine of Knowledge*. "Kant and his followers," Fichte observes, "have very properly described these judgments as *infinite*. But no one, as far as I know, has explained them in a clear and determinate manner."[8] One can only wonder as to the identity of the unnamed Kantian "followers" that Fichte evokes with these words. Kant's infinite judgment and Maimon's, for example, are in crucial respects distinct. Where does Fichte's thetic judgment stand with respect to them? Fichte gives one sign that he has in mind "infinite judgments" less Kantian than Maimonian. In their syntax, the Fichtean thetic judgments, despite their variety, are affirmative: grammatical marks of "negation" or "indeterminacy," such as *nicht*, whether "not" or "non-," are lacking from them. This makes them unlikely examples of "infinite judgments" in any strictly Kantian sense. No "follower" of Kant would give the name "infinite" to a grammatically affirmative sentence, such as "Man is free"—none, that is, but Maimon, for whom "Virtue is quadrilateral" constitutes as legitimate an example of an infinite judgment as "Virtue is non-quadrilateral." What is crucial in Maimon's doctrine of the third quality of judgment is not syntactic form but the presence or absence, in the subject, of an a priori ground of determination. In unshackling the infinite judgment from its Kantian syntax, Fichte would seem to follow Maimon.

In its structure and in its consequences for both practical and theoretical philosophy, "the thetic judgment," however, is unprecedented. The key to its novelty lies in the manner in which, as Fichte writes, it leaves the place of the predicate "infinitely empty for its possible determination." In the assertion "I am," the philosopher discerns the mere positing of a subject, in the absence of all predicates. It would be an error to grasp such a sentence as an "absolute positing" in Kant's sense, that is, as a judgment of existence, which asserts the actuality of its subject.[9] Fichte's "I am" is not synonymous with such propositions as "I exist," "The *I* exists," or "The self exists," nor can it be adequately rephrased as an "analytic-speculative judgment of identity," such as "I am *I* and not non-I." Such readings, in deducing a complete judgment from the words "I am," close the "possible determination" that Fichte's first principle leaves "infinitely" open. Depriving the first principle of its essential indeterminacy, they transform "I am" into a complete "synthesis," or an affirmation.

If one takes Fichte at his word, one must conclude that, according to the classical standards of the predicative assertion, the thetic judgment that founds the *Doctrine of Knowledge* is structurally incomplete. As Wolfgang Janke has remarked, it is less a proposition than a "half-proposition without predicative completion."[10] "I am" means, in short: "I am—," or "I am ..." without that syntagma being completed. One might call it a transcendental fragment, or a speculative aposiopesis. Fichte's striking—and strikingly anarchic—philosophical decision is to make of such a "half-proposition" the fundamental principle of all cognition. "Science" or "knowledge" (*Wissenschaft*), as he understands it, begins with this act of truncation. Before every derived proposition of the *Doctrine of Knowledge*, there lies not only a first principle, which affirms the self-positing of a subject; there also lies concealed an ellipsis, which, in opening onto to a logical space that must be affirmed in its "emptiness," affirms the indeterminacy of the free self. The first principle sets out a ground that is, in this sense, abyssal. Fichte's positing "de-poses" knowledge even as it founds it.[11]

As a second example of a thetic proposition expressed in seemingly predicative form, Fichte evokes the judgment of taste. He explains: "*A* is beautiful (so far as *A* contains a feature also present in the ideal of beauty) is likewise a thetic judgment; for I cannot compare this feature with the ideal, since the latter is unknown to me."[12] Once again, were this judgment to possess a predicative form, it would, in Kantian terms, subsume the object *A* within the logical domain of the concept of the beautiful. Likewise, were it to be affirmative, according to Maimon's "new logic," it would state the determinability of the subject *A* by the predicate "beautiful," effecting a real synthesis of these two concepts in consciousness. Yet Fichte maintains that such logical analyses would both be faulty, and for a simple reason: the "feature" (*Merkmal*) by which *A* is said to be beautiful cannot be compared with the "ideal of beauty," for the aesthetic "ideal" remains unknowable to us. Any attempt to understand such a thesis in "antithetical" terms would therefore also fail. It suffices to consider the form that a correspondingly negative propositional paraphrase would take. To state, "*A* is unlike all things that are not beautiful," one would need, as in the preceding example, to define the ground of the distinction between the beautiful and the non-beautiful, demonstrating that the concept of the beautiful is not contained in the concept of *A*, although it is contained in that of the beings with which one would contrast it. At the same time, some "respect" in which the beautiful and non-beautiful "concurred" would be required. Yet the "respect" would again be lacking. "*A* is beautiful," means, then, not so much, as in the Kantian doctrine of reflective aesthetic judgment, "I judge that *A* is beautiful." More exactly, it means "I judge that *A* is —," or "I judge that *A* is . . ." the "place of the predicate being left infinitely empty for its possible determination."

For Fichte, such thetic judgments are not only syntactically incomplete. Properly understood, they also express a practical demand, which the judging subject places on itself. To state "I am" is not merely to posit an indeterminate subjective principle. It is also to issue an imperative: that the *I* "determine" itself by its own practical activity. As the young Hegel would pointedly remark, for Fichte, "Ego=Ego is transformed into the principle, 'Ego *ought* to be equal to Ego.'"[13] This exigency is crucial. Commenting on the statement, "Man is free," Fichte writes: "The logical form of the judgment, which is positive, requires that both concepts [*man* and *freedom*] should be united; yet they cannot be combined in any concept whatever, but only in the idea of self whose consciousness has been determined by nothing outside itself, it being rather its own mere consciousness which determines everything outside it." In the thetic judgment, a "requirement" thus comes to light, which exceeds pure thought. In its freedom, the self outstrips the domain of any determinable idea; it cannot, for this reason, be conjoined in a synthesis with another concept. "Man is free" is a proposition whose meaning may be realized only outside thinking — in the domain of action. Recalling Kant and revising him at once, Fichte thus declares: "Man must approximate, *ad infinitum*, to a freedom he can never, in principle, attain."[14] So, too, in judging something to be beautiful, the mind sets itself the endless "task" of striving to attain the ideal of beauty that must always elude it. In this case, "it is a task of my mind [*eine Aufgabe meines Geistes*] derived from the positing of myself, to discover this ideal, though it is a task that could only be discharged after a completed approximation to the infinite."[15] Man's practical vocation alone responds to the task set by the indeterminable incompletion of the thetic judgment.

In 1795, barely a year after the publication of Fichte's first *Doctrine of Knowledge*, Schelling proposes his first major system of transcendental philosophy. After Fichte and after Maimon, Schelling turns, in a new fashion, to the doctrine of the infinite judgment. Schelling's essay bears the programmatic title *On the I as the Principle of Philosophy, or On the Unconditional in Human Knowledge*. In his preface, Schelling presents his work in simple terms, which recall those of his critical predecessors: "The whole investigation deals with principles and hence can be tested only by principles. I have tried to depict the results of critical philosophy in its regression to the last principles of all knowledge. The only question, then, which the reader of this essay has to answer is the following: whether these principles are true or false, and (be they true or false) whether the results of critical philosophy are really based on them."[16] Following in the path cleared by Reinhold before Fichte, Schelling seeks to establish the single "fundamental principle" (*Grundlage*) of critical philosophy. For knowledge to have reality (*Realität*), he argues, it must be referred to a "primary ground" (*Urgrund*), "in which everything that is reaches existence, everything that is being thought reaches reality, and thought itself reaches the form of unity and immutability."[17]

Schelling argues that this "primary ground" must be "unconditioned." Exploiting the possibilities of the German language, he defines such a nature as literally no "thing." The "unconditioned" (*das Unbedingte*), he explains, is "what is not turned into a thing, and cannot in any way become a thing [*was gar nicht zum Ding* gemacht *ist, gar nicht zum Ding werden kann*]."[18] Schelling argues that there exists but one such unconditioned "something." This is a "something" (*etwas*) "that cannot be thought of as a thing at all": the self, or *I*, grasped in its "absoluteness," insofar as it "precedes all thinking and imagining." Schelling thus reaches his own primary proposition, from which all others are to be derived. While Fichte's first principle, "I am —," was a "half-proposition," Schelling's possesses the syntax of an exclamation: "*I am!* My *I* contains a being which precedes all thinking and imagining. It *is* by being thought, and it is thought because it *is*; and this is so, because it only is, it is only thought, insofar as it thinks *itself*. Thus it is, because it alone thinks *itself*, and it alone thinks itself, because it is. It produces itself by its own thinking — out of absolute *causality. I am!* It is by this alone that it announces itself in the unconditioned power of itself [*Selbstmacht*]."[19]

Schelling proceeds to argue that, once the *I* is defined as the "unconditional in human knowledge," "the entire content of all knowledge must be determinable through the *I* itself, and through opposition to the *I*."[20] There are consequently two, and only two, beginning points for philosophy. The first is that which stands in antithetical "opposition to the *I*"; the second is the *I* itself. The choice of the first point constitutes the defining trait of "dogmatism"; the choice of the second, instead, is the hallmark of "criticism." "The principle of dogmatism is a *non-I* posited as antecedent to any *I* [*ein vor allem Ich gesetztes Nicht-Ich*]; the principle of criticism is an *I* posited as antecedent to all [that is] *non-I* and as exclusive of any *I* [*ein vor allem Nicht-Ich, und mit Ausschliessung alles Nicht-Ichs gesetztes Ich*]."[21]

Schelling argues that the choice of a dogmatic beginning point is unfounded. Even Spinoza, its greatest representative, "has not proved anywhere that the unconditional could and should lie in the *non-I*. Rather, led only by his concept of the absolute, he straightaway posits it in an absolute object, and he does so as if he presupposed that everybody who conceded him his concept of the unconditional would follow him automatically that, of necessity, it had to be posited in a non-I."[22] Schelling maintains that Spinoza began as he did for an obvious reason; he wished to root knowledge in some unconditioned "fact" (*Thatsache*), and he found it in nature. With the critical philosophy, however, it became clear that such a "fact" lies nowhere but in the thinking *I*. "The perfect system of knowledge proceeds from the absolute *I*, excluding everything that stands in contrast to it."[23] After Fichte, Schelling argues that philosophy must begin from the *I* and that, more exactly, from a judgment that is "thetic" in form: "The *I* posits itself absolutely, and it posits all reality within itself. It posits everything as pure identity, that is, equal to itself. Thereby the *material primal form* [*materialer Urform*] of the *I* is the unity of its positing, insofar as it posits everything as equal to itself. The absolute *I* never steps outside of itself."[24]

Schelling concedes that a major theoretical difficulty remains. Philosophy, as he presents it, is to begin with the absoluteness of the self; but it is also, then, to lay the foundations for positive and conditioned knowledge. Yet how will thinking, once rooted in this subjective principle, succeed in accounting for the non-subjective — for everything, that is, that is not itself? Fichte first posed this question in terms that Schelling now recalls. The 1794 *Doctrine of Knowledge* maintained that, after the primary and indeterminable thetic judgment of the *I*, a second transcendental principle must be posited. By this second principle, Fichte argued, the *I* sets against itself a being as indefinite as itself, although opposed to it: a reality that checks and limits it. To designate this limiting principle, Fichte forged a new and technical name. In its grammatical and logical form, it is strictly "indefinite" or "infinite." Fichte designated that which is opposed to the *I* as the *non-I* (*nicht-Ich*).[25] After reconstructing the primal positing of the *I*, he sought to retrace the steps by which thinking runs up against the opposition of this limiting *non-I*. Schelling, after him, strives to explain the nature of this second principle, and to account for its relation to the point from which he begins his essay on the unconditioned in knowledge.

In his treatise of 1795, Schelling envisages two solutions to the problem that he inherits from Fichte. They rest on two senses of the *non-* of *non-I*, which imply two irreducibly distinct concepts of the "conditioned." According to a first understanding of the *non-I*, this principle may be opposed to the *I* in the exact sense in which the "negative sentence" (*verneinender Saz*) may be contrasted with the "affirmative sentence" (*bejahender Saz*). Here Schelling proposes a brief but dense account of transcendental logic. "As such," he writes, the affirmative sentence "sets something into" or "posits something in some sphere of reality [*in eine Sphäre der Realität*]."[26] An affirmative predicative judgment, grasped in its Kantian form, appears to illustrate this point well. In the proposition, "The soul is immortal," the soul is posited in "some sphere of reality," being subsumed in the expanse of immortal beings. By contrast, Schelling continues, "the thetic-affirmative sentence [*thetisch-bejahender Saz*] posits something only in the sphere of reality *as such*." To this second type of judgment, there corresponds the primary proposition of pure self-positing, uttered in its exclamatory form: "I am!" This sentence posits the self as belonging to "the sphere of reality *as such*," without, however, defining it in any further manner.

Next, Schelling considers the form and force of "negative sentences." He distinguishes between a negation that merely denies a predication and a negation that denies a predication and at the same time contains an affirmation. First, "the negative sentence merely posits, and does not posit into any *determinate* sphere; but since it does not posit that which it takes away from one sphere into any other, it excludes it from the sphere of reality as such." Schelling provides an example for such a negation, or denial: "God is not real" (*Gott ist nicht wirklich*). This sentence "takes God out of the sphere of reality, without placing him in another." Such a negation simply denies that the predicate (reality) belongs to the subject (God), without asserting any more. To this degree, its logic follows that of Kant's second quality of judgment, which excludes one concept from belonging to the sphere of another. Now, however, Schelling introduces another variety of philosophical proposition. This is "the thetic-negative (otherwise known as infinite) sentence." For it, Schelling proposes the following paradigm: "God is non-real [*Gott ist nicht-wirklich*]." This proposition does more than remove its subject from a certain sphere. "It also posits it in another, which is opposed to it."

Schelling does not pause to explain the nature of the "sphere" he evokes, which would be "opposed" to reality without being, however, nothing. What is clear is that he follows the Kantian doctrine to the degree to which he distinguishes the negative judgment from the infinite: the first

merely denies a certain predication, while the second negates and also posits. In his analysis of the "thetic-negative proposition," however, Schelling
draws on logical principles unknown to the inventor of transcendental
logic. Schelling argues that, in accounting for the varieties of sentences in
transcendental philosophy, one must set aside considerations of a purely
"general" or formal kind. "God is non-real" may appear to be an "infinite
judgment" in the Kantian sense because its predicate is marked by a *non-*.
Yet from this fact one ought not to deduce that any statement containing
a grammatically indefinite predicate exhibits the same logic. "To produce
a thetic-negative sentence," Schelling asserts, "it is not enough arbitrarily
to bind the negation with the predicate." Kant was, in short, mistaken. To
articulate an infinite judgment, it does not suffice to affix a *non-* to the
logical term that is predicated of a subject. More is required: "The *sheer*
positing of the subject in the *I* must already posit it in a sphere opposite to
the predicate." The difference between the "negative" and the "thetic-negative" concerns content as well as form, for it pertains to transcendental
rather than merely general logic.

Examples drawn from the field of geometry illustrate this point:

> For instance, I cannot turn the negative proposition "A circle is not square"
> into a thetic-negative judgment, because the sheer positing of the subject,
> "circle," does not yet posit it in a sphere that as such is opposed to four-sided-
> ness. The circle could just as well be five-sided or many-sided. However, the
> proposition, "a circle is not sweet" is necessarily an infinite judgment, because
> the subject, "circle," through its mere being posited, is already outside of the
> sphere of the sweet, therefore already posited in a sphere exactly opposed to
> the sphere of "sweet." For that reason, the negation in the thetical-negative
> judgment does not lie in the copula but in the predicate, that is, the subject is
> not merely being removed from the sphere of the predicate but is *posited* in a
> sphere that opposes the sphere of the predicate.[27]

That these examples recall those of Maimon's "new logic" can
hardly be doubted. Lest the genealogy of the doctrine of the "thetic-
negative proposition" be lost on his readers, however, Schelling adds a final
remark: "As far as I know, Maimon was up to now the one who put the
greatest emphasis on this differentiation between the infinite judgment,

the affirmative and the negative."[28] What Maimon conceived as a cessa-
tion of determination is what Schelling now apprehends, after Fichte, as
a thesis. The zero of non-determination and the thetic judgment are thus
conjoined. Withdrawing the subject from predicative determination, the
"thetic-negative judgment" posits it in a field "opposed" to that of the
named predicate.

Schelling's development of the post-Kantian doctrine of infinite judgment may seem little more than a detail of transcendental logic. In *On the
I as the Principle of Philosophy*, however, this point plays a major role. The
"thetic-negative" proposition furnishes Schelling with the crucial means
to resolve the problem that he inherits from Fichte's *Doctrine of Knowledge*:
that of the relation between *I* and *non-I* or, in more Schellingian terms, of
the unconditioned principle of philosophy and the conditioned reality that
would seem to limit it. Schelling appeals to the Maimonian doctrine of the
infinite judgment in seeking to resolve a basic question in his transcendental inquiry: how may one affirm, "The *I* is not the *non-I*"? To tell the
unconditioned from the conditioned, Schelling must account for the logic
of such a sentence. That Schelling cannot define the "I" by any affirmative
judgment is evident. An affirmative judgment is predicative in structure;
for the "I" to appear as its logical element would be for it to be determined,
that is, "conditioned," and for it therefore to cease to be itself. Yet Schelling
also cannot seek to state the nature of the unconditioned by the statement
"the *I* is not the *non-I*," when understood as a "negative sentence." For if
that judgment is truly a "negation," then it denies a certain property to the
subject, without accomplishing any more. Such an assertion would then
merely remove the *I* from the field of the conditioned. The problem of the
relation of unconditioned and conditioned would persist.

The solution is to understand the judgment "the *I* is not the *non-I*" as a
"thetic-negative sentence" in the precise sense defined by Schelling, after
Fichte, Maimon, and Kant. "Applied to the relation of *I* and *non-I*," J.-C.
Lemaitre notes, "the limitation of the sphere of the *non-I* by the negation
of the infinite judgment makes it possible to posit this sphere as finite,
without encroaching upon the infinite character of the *I*."[29] Thanks to the
logic of the infinite judgment, Schelling's unconditioned may be discur-
sively related to the conditioned, without being thereby determined by

it. Thus the *non-I* emerges not as the negation or as the antithesis of the *I*, but as its strictly "indefinite" limitation. That "the *I* is not *non-I*" means: "The infinite is non-finite," according to the model of "The circle is non-sweet," and "God is non-real." Recalling Maimon, one might add that, when properly understood, this sentence is synonymous with its apparent contradictory. In transcendental logic, "The *I* is not *non-I*" is equivalent to "The *I* is the *non-I*," or "The unconditioned is the conditioned," for in each case, the statement exhibits the absence, in the subject, of any a priori ground of determination. In its deference to grammar, general logic, of course, views such sentences as punctually opposed; in transcendental logic, however, they illustrate a single pattern. Such propositions all posit the unconditioned in a sphere that is opposed to the "conditioned" and the "non-conditioned" alike. They establish that the beginning point of philosophy is indeterminable by any condition, including its negation. Thus a subject is posited, in opposition both to the non-subjective that is the *non-I* and the conditioned *I* that would be its logical contrary. Nothing less, for Schelling, is meant by the simple exclamation: "I am!"

Schelling's argument is novel, but it is not unprecedented. Only after the Copernican Revolution, as Maimon understood it, and after the submission of both subject and object to a single law of thinking, could the infinite judgment, interpreted in Fichtean terms, come to play such a role. From Fichte's *Doctrine of Knowledge* to Schelling's treatise on the unconditioned, the crucial element in philosophy remains the zero of infinite non-determination. Like the cipher introduced into European arithmetic in the early modern age, this null-point enabled the most diverse of operations. Maimon took it to signify no more than an "absence of a reason for position." From that mere "absence," the most major of metaphysical principles were to be derived. A divinity, conceivable in His utter dissimilarity with respect to His creation; a subjectivity, grasped in its pure self-positing without properties; an unconditioned *I*, reconciled to the conditioned *non-I*, without being reduced or reducible to it — all entered into philosophical discourse insofar as they could be contained by such "inertial" judgments. Following Maimon, Fichte and Schelling both found in Kant's third quality of judgment the glimmerings of the law of thinking that would lead them to the limits of the doctrine of the assertion, where a new theory of reason could be identified and developed. The infinite judgment allowed them to conceive of a subject of which it would be illegitimate to speak by stating "one thing concerning another," or by classing "the sphere of one concept under that of another," as Kant had held. Maimon's zero allowed them to posit an absolute subject, a self irreducible to all "things." The vastly influential friend of Schelling's youth would take a further step. Hegel would soon also seek to provide the final premises lacking to philosophy, transforming its results anew. Reading and rewriting the Kantian and post-Kantian theorists of the indefinite, he would devise a doctrine of knowing in which the very difference between the "general" and the "transcendental" would be overcome, and judgment itself, as a form of thinking, would be undone.

CHAPTER TWELVE

Collapsing Sentences

In 1807, Hegel publishes *The Phenomenology of Spirit*, a book that seeks to retrace the entire passage of the human mind from ignorance to knowledge, or, in the more technical terms of its author, the movement of the Spirit by which "consciousness . . . progresses from the first immediate opposition of itself and the subject matter to absolute knowledge," following the arduous yet exhaustive path that "traverses all the forms of the *relation of consciousness to the object*." The "result" is "the *concept of science*."[1] Five years later, in 1812, Hegel undertakes to exhibit this "result" in its totality in *The Science of Logic*, whose final volume appears in 1816. This was to be Hegel's last major work, and the one in which his system of absolute idealism reached completion. In the introduction to its first edition, Hegel suggests that his treatise constitutes the fulfillment of not only his own philosophical undertaking but also the project announced by Kant. Properly defined, *The Science of Logic*, he writes, is "the system of pure reason."[2]

The reader quickly learns, however, that the "system of pure reason" evoked by Hegel differs substantially from the one envisaged by Kant. The "reason" of the critical philosopher is that of a finite intellect. However "spontaneous" the power of its understanding, it must rely, in cognition, on sensible intuition, with respect to which it is passively affected. Kant's is a reason that runs up against the limits of the "thing in itself," a being withdrawn from all perception, which may be conceived yet never truly "known." Hegel takes this restriction of our cognitive powers to be illegitimate. The "pure reason" of his logic is identifiable with the "realm of pure thought," with respect to which no "matter," whether sensible or intelligible, is external. The activity of thinking is now to be grasped as the principle of what is thought; subject and object, that which is "for itself" and "in itself," will be united. The "realm" of *The Science of Logic*, Hegel asserts, underlining his words, "*is truth unveiled, truth as it is in and for itself. It can therefore be said that this content* [of *The Science of Logic*] *is the exposition of God as he is in his eternal essence before the creation of nature and of a finite spirit.*"[3]

Kant's position is to be surpassed in the transition to a doctrine of knowledge that is infinite in its absolution from all external restrictions, starting with those that the critical philosophy imposed upon the mind. Logic, in its Kantian as well as its pre-Kantian varieties, is therefore to be reconceived. Hegel recalls that, even as he introduced the study of transcendental logic, Kant continued to admit the validity of a "general logic," which he grasped as the knowledge of the forms of utterances, their relations and implications. From the point of view of an "absolute knowing," however, the distinction between the mere shapes of argument and their content is untenable. "Logic has nothing to do with a thought *about* something which stands outside by itself as the base of thought," Hegel writes, "nor does it have to do with forms meant to provide mere *markings* of the truth; rather, the necessary forms of thinking, and its specific determinations, are the content and the ultimate truth itself."[4] To demonstrate this bold claim, Hegel appeals to a new method, which will show how exactly "forms" and "determinations" of the old "art of thinking" illustrate the "vital concrete unity" of the mind.[5] "For the dead bones of logic to be quickened by spirit and become substance and content," Hegel writes, "its *method* must be the one which alone can make it fit to be pure science."[6] It is not enough for general logic to be subordinated to transcendental logic, as Maimon, for one, had proposed. Transcendental logic, defined as a logic of content rather than form, must also be surpassed. A "speculative logic" is now to take the place of these divided fields. It will treat the matter and the shape of thinking in one science.

Hegel remarks that previous philosophers presented the types and categories of reason as a set of heterogeneous forms, to be classified, more or less successfully, in taxonomies of the kind known to "empirical sciences." This resulted in variously haphazard accounts of terms and relations. In his speculative logic, he aims to proceed otherwise. Hegel will grasp the so-called "forms" of reason as the continuously unfolding moments of a single activity of thinking, which engenders its form and its matter in a single progression. The structures of his logic will appear in immanently dialectical development, like the shapes of consciousness and self-consciousness that emerge and vanish along the path from the "immediate opposition of itself and the subject matter to absolute knowledge." In the *Phenomenology of Spirit*, Hegel had stated the principle of this movement: "The true is the Bacchanalian revel in which no member is not drunk; yet because each member collapses as soon as he drops out, the revel is just as much transparent as simple repose."[7] The *Science of Logic* integrates the elements of pure reason into the mobile repose of this sober revelry.

In introducing the second edition of his book in 1831, Hegel pauses to affirm a point that he failed to stress in 1812. Now he makes clear that the elements of traditional logic share a common source in one entity:

> The forms of thought are first set out and stored in human *language*, and one can hardly be reminded often enough nowadays that thought is what differentiates the human being from the beast. In everything that the human being has interiorized, in everything that in some way or other has become for him a representation, in whatever he has made his own, there has language penetrated, and everything that he transforms into language and expresses in it contains a category, whether concealed, mixed, or well defined. So much is logic natural to the human being, is indeed his very *nature*. If we however contrast nature as such, as the realm of the physical, with the realm of the spiritual, then we must say that logic is the supernatural element that permeates all his natural behavior, his ways of sensing, intuiting, desiring, his needs and impulses; and it thereby makes them into something truly human, even though only formally human — makes them into representations and purposes.[8]

Hegel goes on to argue that the logic that defines human nature is detectable in the parts of given grammatical systems, which vary among languages, both in their quantity and in their quality. "It is to the advantage of a language," he writes, "when it possesses a wealth of logical expressions, that is, distinctive expressions specifically set aside for thought determinations."[9] Among such "distinctive expressions," Hegel considers "substantives and verbs" to be especially worthy of note. They "stamp" the categories of thought "into objective form." To this degree, they are more valuable than the minor parts of speech, such as "prepositions and articles." The reader learns that even if they may "pertain to relations based on thought," such particles "play a totally subordinate role, only slightly more independent than that of prefixes and suffices, inflections and the like."[10]

A principle of method is contained in this apparently incidental remark. Parts and particles of speech, in Hegel's *Logic*, are quickly and at times quietly absorbed into the motion of more "distinctive expressions" of thought. The consequences of this fact can be far-reaching, if also difficult to detect. This is nowhere more apparent than in the fate that this book reserves for the form of judgment that, in the Kantian doctrine, distinguishes itself by means of a single, inseparable particle, which is also a prefix: *nicht-*, or *non-*. Readers will recall that the *Critique of Pure Reason* offered a single example for the negative judgment: "The soul is not mortal [*die Seele ist nicht sterblich*]." Kant suggested that this "quality" can be transformed into another by the metamorphosis of a "not" into a "non-," or, in German, by the displacement of the "negative" particle *nicht* from the copula "is" to the predicate *sterblich*. The infinite judgment thus appears, in the First *Critique*, as "The soul is non-mortal [*die Seele ist nichtsterblich*]." In German syntax, the difference between these judgments is subtle. It hinges on the syntagmatic position of the particle *nicht* (or *nicht-*). It may precede the predicate *sterblich*, as a word, so as to deny the attribution of the property of "being mortal": "the soul is not mortal [*die Seele ist nicht sterblich*]." Or it may be attached to the predicate, such that the sentence affirms the property of being "non-mortal": "the soul is non-mortal [*die Seele ist nichtsterblich*]." In speech, the rhythm of enunciation alone distinguishes these possibilities, which the typography of the printed page renders discernible.

In Hegel's logic, almost nothing of this apparently formal difference of grammar remains — at least literally, and in the shape of the "dead bones" of syntactic structure. Yet it would be an error to conclude that the infinite judgment is lacking from Hegel's system, or that its place in it is negligible. The truth is that the third quality of judgment plays a decisive role in the *Science of Logic*, as in Hegel's other works, from his early Jena sketches of a systematic philosophy through to the *Phenomenology of Spirit* and the account of his doctrine that he offers in the 1830 *Encyclopedia of the Philosophical Sciences*. In its passage from critical to speculative logic, however, the infinite judgment undergoes a metamorphosis, from which unprecedented consequences follow. To measure the novelty of Hegel's treatment, one must begin by recalling the architecture of his theory.

Hegel divides the *Science of Logic* into three parts, which seek to trace the unfolding of the concept of science from beginning to end. Part One contains the "doctrine of Being." It opens with the most rudimentary and indistinct of ideas, "Being" and "Nothing." This part sets out the way in which their indeterminate opposition, when grasped as such, leads to becoming, which in turn announces the notions of determinateness (or quality), magnitude (or quantity), and measure. Jean Hyppolite observed that this part and its sequels effectively dismember and rearrange the sections of Kant's First *Critique*. Hegel's "doctrine of Being" corresponds, in Kantian terms, to the Transcendental Aesthetic, furnishing thinking with a "logic of the sensible."[11] For Hegel, this doctrine holds not only for our mind, as did the Transcendental Aesthetic; rather, it constitutes the ground of all knowledge. Hegel presents the "doctrine of essence" in his Part Two. Moving from mere "essence" to "appearance" and "actuality," this portion of his treatise exhibits the shapes by which sensible and intelligible being may be defined. After this radically revised and speculative "Transcendental Analytic," Hegel passes to the concluding volume of his treatise, Part Three: the doctrine of the concept. "It corresponds to the Transcendental Dialectic, the Idea that Kant had considered only as regulative, wanting to recognize as metaphysics only the old dogmatism, the metaphysics of the intelligible world, and not explicitly comprehending the transcendental logic that was in itself already speculative logic."[12] Hegel's "concept" is the "unity into which being and essence return," the ultimate ground of the relation of immediate and mediate, which the *Logic* presupposes from its beginning to its end.[13]

The reader learns that Hegel holds this concept to be the same principle of thinking that Kant uncovered in his *Critique of Pure Reason*. The concept is not a thing belonging to the self in the sense of "the ordinary way of speaking," "as the property of a thing stands related to that thing." According to such an understanding, "I *have* concepts, and I *have* the concept, just as I also have a coat, complexion, and other external properties."

The relation of subject and attribute remains in such cases merely external, binding a substance to a determination of which it might also be deprived. Kant saw that such a representation of the relation of the self to thinking is inadequate. The concept is neither "coat" nor "complexion" and bears a wholly different relationship to the *I*. As Kant intuited, the power of reason and the self are in truth identical. "It is one of the profoundest and truest of insights to be found in the Critique of Reason," Hegel remarks, "that the *unity* which constitutes *the essence of the concept* is recognized to be the *original synthetic* unity *of apperception*, the unity of the '*I think*,' or self-consciousness."[14]

With this insight, Kant attained the beginning point of true "speculation," as Hegel understands it: the identity of object and subject, which is to say, the grounding of reality itself in reason. Yet Kant retreated from the consequences of his discovery and, following a "psychological reflex," "reverted" to a common understanding, according to which cognition is "permanently conditioned" by a thing outside it: "the manifold of intuition."[15] Kant thus took the concepts of the understanding to be "empty" without sensible matter, and he claimed that intuition is "blind" when without thought. In other words, Kant grasped the principle by which he might surpass such a formal opposition between reason and reality, thinking and its thoughts; but he failed to follow it to the consequences that it entailed. Hegel explains: "In the *a priori synthesis* of the concept, Kant did have a higher principle in which it was possible to recognize a duality and therefore what is required for truth; but the material of the senses, the manifoldness of intuition, was too strong for him to be able to wrest himself away from it and turn to a consideration of the concept and the categories *in and for themselves*, and to a speculative form of philosophizing."[16]

This is the "turn" that Hegel proposes in his doctrine of the concept. It leads to the revision of all the logical elements of the critical philosophy, beginning with the form of the judgment, with which Kant identified thinking. For Hegel, judgment constitutes not the synthesis of concepts but a form of partition. From his earliest to his last works, Hegel draws attention, as had Fichte and Hölderlin before him, to the shape of the word in German: "judgment," *Urteil*, for Hegel, spells *Ur-teil* or *Ur-teilung*, "original division" or "original dividing."[17] The *Science of Logic* stresses this point:

"Judgment is the self-diremption of the concept [*die Diremption des Begriffs durch sich selbst*]; therefore, it is by starting from the *unity of the concept* as ground that the judgment is considered in accordance with its *true* objectivity. In this respect, judgment is the *originative division* of an originative unity [*die ursprüngliche Teilung des ursprünglich Einen*]; the German word for judgment, *Urteil*, thus refers to what judgment is in and for itself."[18] The articulation of the judgment is the form that this "division" takes, when projected into language: subject and predicate partition the unity of a single concept. To grasp the judgment, then, is no longer merely to consider it in its constituent parts, as philosophers since Aristotle maintained. Above all, it is, for Hegel, to resolve such terms into the conceptual unity that they compose.

This doctrine dictates a rethinking of the order of the moments of assertion laid out on Kant's Table of Judgments. According to the *Critique of Pure Reason*, any judgment may be considered with respect to four aspects: quantity, quality, the relation that it bears to its condition, and modality. Such divisions express the dimensions of a single logical form. In the *Science of Logic*, Kant's quartet is undone; in its place, Hegel sets four types of judgment, which are ordered in the continuous development of reason. Hegel retains the triadic divisions that Kant had introduced in each title; in logical "quality," Hegel thus distinguishes, as had Kant, among the affirmative, negative and infinite moments. Yet in Hegel's *Logic*, each of the four critical titles acquires a decidedly new shape. What Kant conceived as "Quality" appears as the "judgment of existence" (*das Urteil des Daseins*); "Quantity" becomes "the judgment of reflection" (*das Urteil der Reflexion*); "Relation" is reconceived as "the judgment of necessity" (*das Urteil der Notwendigkeit*); modality emerges as "the judgment of the concept" (*das Urteil des Begriffes*). This series of modifications is more than nominal. It expresses an understanding of the varieties of judgment as the evolving expressions of a concept that engenders what it conceives. As Béatrice Longuenesse observes, "What we now have under the different titles are different types of judgments characterized by their form *and their content*: they correspond respectively to different moments in the progression towards the identity of predicate and subject in judgment, and so to different contents for *both* predicate and subject. Moreover, it appears that these contents are no other than the various stages of determinations of Being and essence laid out in the first part of *The Science of Logic* (the Objective Logic), now internalized within the process of self-division and return to the self-identity of the concept."[19]

In *The Science of Logic*, the first moment of judgment is that of "immediate existence" (*Dasein*), its simplest figure being the assertion. Here the distance separating Hegel's understanding of the judgment from Kant's comes quickly to light. Starting with his 1801 essay, *Faith and Knowledge*, Hegel recalls and reinterprets Kant's theory of the synthesis of concepts. He calls to mind the fundamental question of the *Critique of Pure Reason*: "How are synthetic a priori judgments possible?" Hegel casts this "problem" in new terms, noting: "This problem expresses nothing else but the Idea that subject and predicate of the synthetic judgment are identical in the *a priori* way. That is to say, these heterogeneous elements, the subject which is the particular and in the form of being, and the predicate which is the universal and in the form of thought, are the same and absolutely identical."[20] Subject and predicate are no longer to be understood as formal or syntactic distinctions. Their "heterogeneity," when properly grasped, now reveals itself to be metaphysical. For Hegel, the subject is definable as the "the particular," and "the form of being," while the predicate is "the universal and the form of thought."[21] In the terms of *The Science of Logic*, the subject may be viewed as "the *in-itself*, and the predicate as *determinate existence* in contrast to it. The *subject without the predicate* is the *thing without properties*, the *thing-in-itself*, is in the sphere of appearance, an empty indeterminate ground; it is then the *implicit concept* that receives a difference and a determinateness only in the predicate; the predicate thus constitutes the side of the *determinate existence* of the subject."[22] The "concept" alone, in Hegel's sense, integrates these elements, reconciling singularity and universality in the union of "existence" and "determination."

The affirmative judgment accomplishes such a determination only immediately, that is, imperfectly and therefore unstably. It is "as yet quite *simple*, still not enriched by mediation and also still caught up in the abstract opposition of *abstract singularity* and *abstract universality*."[23] Hegel warns against the path of his predecessors, which consisted in proposing accounts of this judgment so formal as to be algebraic. "This expression must not be put in the form of 'A is B,'" he writes, "for "A and B are totally formless and hence meaningless names, whereas judgment in general, and therefore already the judgment of existence, has determinations of the concept for its extremes."[24] For shorthand, he proposes, instead: *the singular is universal [das Einzelne ist allgemein].*" As examples, he evokes such sentences as "Gaius is learned" and "the rose is red." In both cases, the subject is thought as one with the predicate; an "indeterminate existence" is thereby rendered "determinate" by the attribution of a property. Yet the predicate "contains only *one moment* of the subject's totality, to the exclusion of all others." "The particular in the form of being" and "the universal in the form of thought" are united, yet only imperfectly and in part. "The predicate expresses only *one* of the *many* properties of the rose; it isolates it, whereas in the subject the property is joined with the others; likewise in the dissolution of the thing, the manifold properties that inhere in it *become isolated* in acquiring self-subsistence as *materials.* From this side, then, the proposition of the judgment says: *the universal is singular.*"[25] Despite the identity they would seem to state, in such affirmations the "subject is not at all the one *single* property that its predicate declares."[26]

To grasp that truth, however, is already to depart from the affirmative judgment of existence. It is to conceive of the heterogeneity of subject and predicate and, therefore, to pass over into a second moment of thought. "The positive judgment first attains its truth in the negative judgment: *the singular is not* abstractly *universal.*"[27] Hegel's analysis of the first "quality" of predicative judgment thus leads ineluctably to his exposition of the second. Yet he conceives of "negation" according to a distinctly non-Kantian form. For Kant, as for many of his predecessors, the judgment is a being of at least three independent terms: subject, predicate, and copula. Negation is distinguishable from affirmation by the presence of a negative particle, such as "not," or *nicht.* According to this account, judgment is a composite structure. Grasping the judgment as the "partition" of the higher unity that is the "concept," Hegel can hardly accept this understanding. For him, the relation between the two terms of the judgment is not added, as a third term, to that which it relates. The copula, in his eyes, is not a supplement, nor is the *not* a term added to that which it modifies. Each logical relation, for Hegel, is simultaneous with its *relata.* It is therefore not enough for the negative judgment to be grasped as the affirmation that a singular being is "not universal" (*nicht allgemein*). Exploiting the possibilities of German grammar, in which the same particle can act upon a verb and a noun, denying the copula or rendering a predicate "indefinite," Hegel comments: "The *not* [*nicht*] of the copula must just as equally be attached to the predicate and . . . the latter must be determined as the non-universal [or "the not-universal," *das nicht-Allgemeine*]."[28]

It is worth pausing to consider the stages of this dialectical development. In his account of the first quality of judgment, Hegel argues that the statement "the rose is red" does not merely affirm a certain identity between a particular ("rose") and a form of being ("red"); it also entails a division, suggesting that the rose, being a totality of determinations, is not strictly identical with being red, and, more simply, that the rose "is not red." The first quality of judgment thus gives way to the second. Now Hegel adds, however, that to assert "the rose is not red" is also to say that it is non-red. The sign of the denial of the copula metamorphoses into the sign of the indeterminate "negation" of a predicate. A *not* passes into a *not-* or *non-*. According to this speculative logic, affirmation thereby generates negation, and negation, in turn, entails an "infinite proposition" or "pseudo-negation." From the first of Kant's qualities of judgment, Hegel has, in effect, derived the remaining two.

The movement of this speculative logic, however, does not stop here. The indefinite says more than it would seem. The *non-* must be interpreted. "Like *non-Being* [Nichtsein] itself," Hegel writes, such a "sensuous content" as "the non-red" (*das Nicht-Rote*) or "the non-white" (*das Nicht-Weisse*) demands to be grasped in its positivity. It "ought to be *conceptualized*; ought to shed that indifference and abstract immediacy with which it is affected in the blind immobility of pictorial representation."[29] And just as non-Being, when conceived as such, "becomes *limit*, and by virtue of this limit the *something refers* to an *other* despite itself," so the non-redness that may be attributed to the rose, when grasped in itself, signifies something "essentially positive."[30] "When it is said that, for instance, the rose is *not* red [or is *non-red*: *ist nicht rot*], only the *determinateness* of the predicate is thereby denied and thus separated from the universality which equally attached to it; the universal sphere, *color*, is retained; if the rose is not red, it is nonetheless assumed that it has a color, though another color. From this side of the universal sphere, the judgment is still positive."[31]

Just as the affirmative judgment led to the negative, so the negative, in its suggestion of an indefinite proposition, now leads to a new affirmation. That which is affirmed to be not red is stated to be non-red; in other words, it is positively asserted to possess a color — any color whatsoever, except red. In such sentences, therefore, there "remains a *positive connection* of subject and predicate, as well as the *universal sphere* of the latter."[32] Yet such a "connection" is inadequate to the act of thinking to which it testifies, for "the negative judgment is as little of a true judgment as the positive."[33] The reason for this fact may be simply stated. The affirmative and the negative qualities belong to the form of the judgment; they both constitute partitions (*Ur-teilungen*) of the "concept of science," in which the singular and the universal, while opposed in their content, are still only unstably bound. Reason has yet to follow their contradiction through to its most extreme point, grasping the principle of their ultimate identity and difference. To reconcile the statement to the truth that it announces, a further step is required. A more radical sundering of subject and predicate must be affirmed. Such a rupture alone will testify to the "heterogeneity" of particular and mode of being, thing and universal, and, in exhibiting their opposition, announce a resolution in the "concept of science."

Collapsing sentences are required, and it is precisely such utterances that Hegel finds in the type of assertion his predecessors called the infinite judgment. This is, for him, the third quality of the "judgment of determination." It is "a *nonsensical judgment* [ein widersinniges Urteil]," Hegel maintains. "It ought to be *a judgment*, and hence contains a connection of subject and predicate; but any such connection ought not *at the same time to be* there."[34] Whereas the "negative judgment" could be exemplified by the statement, "The rose is not red" or "The rose is non-red," the infinite judgment, for Hegel, is illustrated by far stranger and indefinitely extended assertions: "Spirit is not [or *non-*] red, yellow, etc., is not [or *non-*] acid, alkali, etc.," or, more simply: "The rose is no elephant [*Die Rose ist kein Elephant*]; the understanding is no table [*Der Verstand ist kein Tisch*], and so on."[35] Such judgments possess the curious status of exhibiting a truth and correctness that is so odd as to incline the philosopher to consider it to be none at all. Hegel explains: "These judgments are *correct* or *true* [*richtig oder wahr*], as it is said, and yet, any such truth notwithstanding, nonsensical and fatuous [*widersinnig und abgeschmackt*]."[36] One sentence later, however, after a pause, Hegel appears to rescind his claims concerning these unusual sentences. Employing the syntactic form of the "infinite judgment" itself, as he defines it, he now declares: " — Or, more to the point, they are *no judgments at all* [*Oder vielmehr sind sie keine Urteile*]."[37]

That such a judgment as "The rose is no elephant" should belong to the exposition of "*truth unveiled, truth as it is in and for itself*" is a striking fact. No less perplexing, however, is the conclusion to which its study leads. Infinite judgments are included in the chapter on judgment in *The Science of Logic*, the reader learns, although, in truth, they are "no judgments at all." As if to dispel the perplexity that his discussion of such sentences might cause, Hegel offers his readers a "more realistic example of the infinite judgment." This illustration is drawn from the domain of not speech but deeds. It is "the *evil* action [*die böse Handlung*]."[38] In a "civil litigation," one person effectively "negates" another's right to possess a certain thing, while admitting that "the same thing would indeed belong to that party if the latter had a right to it. It is only under the title of right that the possession is challenged; in the negative judgment, therefore, the universal sphere, 'right,' is still acknowledged and maintained."[39] By contrast, "*crime* [*das Verbrechen*] is the *infinite judgment* that negates, not only the *particular* right, but the universal sphere, the *right as right*. It has *correctness*, in the sense that it is an effective action, but since it stands in a thoroughly negative fashion with respect to the morality that constitutes its sphere, it is nonsensical."[40]

The depth of Hegel's commitment to this account of the infinite judgment can be measured by its persistence in his books and many courses. The posthumously published *Lectures on the Philosophy of Right* contain an analysis of "evil action" that is close to that of *The Science of Logic*. Crime is defined as the action that "negates not only the particular object of my will, but also the universal or infinite, which is involved in the predicate 'mine,' the very capacity for possessing rights."[41] So, too, in his *Encyclopedia Logic* of 1830, Hegel explains that the "infinite judgment" can be defined as a sentence that "collapses into itself" (*in sich zerfällt*), expressing the "complete incommensurability [*völlige Unangemessenheit*] of subject and predicate." "Examples of the latter are 'spirit is no elephant,' 'a lion is no table,' and so forth"—all "sentences" that are "correct but nonsensical [*richtig aber widersinnig*]."[42] Here again, Hegel also evokes the example of "crime," defined as an action that "does not merely negate, as in the civil juridical dispute, the particular right of someone else," but "negates the right of that person altogether." "Likewise, then, too," Hegel adds, "sickness" is a merely negative judgment; but "death" is an infinite judgment. In the event of decease, exactly as in the third moment of the judgment of existence, "body and soul are divorced from one another [*sich scheiden*], i.e., subject and predicate fall completely outside one [*gänzlich auseinanderfallen*]."[43]

On this point, Hegel's late work is remarkably faithful to his earliest. His *Jena System* of 1804–5 already defines judgment as "the moment of otherness of the determinate concept . . . wherein what is posited as one in it goes asunder and is distinguished on its own account."[44] As in *The Science of Logic*, the affirmative judgment appears as one in which subject and predicate are not only identified but also distinguished, such that the positive statement, when grasped as such, becomes the negative. Employing the symbolism that he would later castigate, Hegel explains: "The immediate display of the judgment B is A" not only unites the subject B and the predicate A; it also distinguishes them, the predicate being "something determinate subsumed under the subject B."[45] The positive judgment, in this way, reveals itself to be negative: "B is A" becomes "B is not A." Here, too, Hegel understands "the negative" as "something with a double sense": "the 'not' [or *non*-] in general, pure nothing or being; or the 'not' [or *non*-] of this determinate A, whereby it is itself a determinate 'not' [or *non*-] which is opposed to A as positive."[46] To be "not A" (*nicht A*) is to be "non-A" (*nicht-A*). "'B is not green; it does not have this color.' By that is meant: α) it has some other determinate color; and β) it has color in general."[47]

Yet for the heterogeneity of predicate and subject to be fully expressed, for the "partition" in thinking to reach its most extreme point, a greater break must be asserted. "The other color, as color in general, must fall away, and with color in general also every other determinate color in general falls away."[48] Now, however, the "negative judgment has become an *infinite* one: 'Feeling does not have a red color'; 'Spirit is not six feet long';

and any nonsense of the same kind."[49] Whereas the negative judgment asserted that the subject "does not have" a given predicate, leaving open the logical space for the related predicate that it does possess, the infinite judgment, more radically, eliminates the very relation of the subject to its properties: "the predicate as such is negated [*negiert*]."[50] Hegel concludes: "An infinite judgment of this sort immediately presents itself as an absurdity because, since the predicate is completely negated, no judgment at all occurs; there is only an empty semblance [*leerer Schein*] of one (a subject and a connection with a predicate having been posited). Yet in that semblance, the judgment collapses [*zerfällt*] and is no more."[51]

A reader familiar with the Kantian doctrine on which Hegel draws in these works would be startled by such examples of "infinite judgments." They are not only striking in themselves, as fragments of "nonsense" and "absurdity," integrated, by dialectical necessity, into the system of speculative logic. They are also puzzling for a more technical reason. Any student of the critical doctrine of logic might observe that Hegel's "infinite judgments," taken strictly, hardly deserve their Kantian name. According to the critical theory, the third quality of judgment is distinguished by two unmistakable syntactic traits: it is, first, affirmative, in its "general" logical form; it contains, second, an "indefinite" predicate, such as "non-mortal." Sentences such as "Spirit is not red, yellow, etc., is not [or *non-*] acid, alkali, etc.," "Spirit is no elephant [*der Geist ist kein Elephant*]," and "The understanding is no table [*Der Verstand ist kein Tisch*]," meet neither of these two minimal logico-grammatical requirements. These sentences all appear to be negative in form, in that the relation of subject to predicate is denied in them. Moreover, there seems no reason to view the predicates in question as indefinite or "infinite." In such sentences, the *non-* of the infinite judgment has become a *not*, if not also a *no* or *no one* (*kein*). From a Kantian perspective, the syntax of such "infinite judgments" is therefore aberrant. Recalling Hegel's own formulation, one might wager that the collapsing sentences of speculative logic are not only "no judgments at all." They are also, more precisely and specifically, if only in the terms of the Kantian doctrine, "no *infinite judgments* at all."

Among the many studies of Hegel and his speculative logic, these details have often gone unnoticed, and when they have been observed in passing, they have occasionally been declared unworthy of attention. One recent commentary on *The Science of Logic* omits from its reconstruction of Hegel's treatise any discussion of infinite judgments whatsoever, on the grounds that the "dialectical movements" of such sentences are "so far-fetched as to be entirely implausible."[52] When scholars have lingered on this appropriation and transformation of transcendental logic, however, the question of Hegel's revision of Kant has also been posed. In an incisive study of Hegel's thought, Hermann Schmitz faced the problem squarely. Defining Kant's infinite judgment as "a negative judgment, in which negation is bound not to the copula, but to the predicate, such that the subject is determined by a negative yet positively expressed predicate," Schmitz wondered "why Hegel would give this logical form that name and, at the same time, completely deviate from its traditional meaning," Hegel's own "definition" of this utterance having "hardly anything to do with it."[53]

There are good reasons to hold that the "infinite judgment" of *The Science of Logic* illustrates a specifically Hegelian conception of infinity. Starting with his early works, Hegel calls to mind several types of the infinite. One among them is, to employ Hegel's preferred term, profoundly "negative." This infinity already appears in the logical portion of his 1801 *Jena System*, where he evokes "the annihilating restlessness of the infinite."[54] Elsewhere he summons a similar notion, stating that in itself, the infinite is "nothing other than the immediate opposition to itself," that is, "absolute contradiction."[55] In his 1802–3 *Faith and Knowledge*, Hegel presents his theory in fuller form, proposing a doctrine of two infinities. The first is "the true infinite," or "absolute Idea"; it is, he explains, the "unity of the universal and particular." The second is the "bad infinite": in other words, "pure identity or negativity." Such a "negative" infinite consists in "the absolute nothing of the finite: $+ A - A = 0$. It is the negative side of the absolute Idea."[56] It is an endless finitude, equivalent to "empty thinking," representable by the operation "$+1-1$."[57] Although it lays claim to "infinity," it is therefore null. Schmitz takes this notion to ground Hegel's curious use of the expression "infinite judgment": "We may infer that the doctrine of the infinite judgment in Hegel was influenced by his early, decisively negative concept of infinity, which later . . . acquired a more positive shape."[58]

This explanation is compelling, but on its own it is also incomplete.

Hegel's logic is conceived not only after Kant; it is also conceived after Kant's first readers. Between the *Critique of Pure Reason*'s third quality of judgment and the speculative logical propositions in which "subject and predicate fall completely outside one another," there are also other infinite judgments, which Hegel himself knew well. They mark out the path that leads from Kant's third quality of judgment to the third moment in Hegel's own analysis of the "judgment of existence." Before Hegel, Maimon, Fichte, and Schelling had, each in his own way, envisaged an "infinite judgment" that is affirmative in syntax and yet devoid of any "indefinite" predicate. As examples, it suffices to recall such sentences as "Virtue is quadrilateral," "Man is free" and "This is beautiful," which, for Maimon and Fichte, illustrate a form of transcendental logic that neither grammar nor "general logic" alone may identify. Maimon, Fichte, and Schelling all grasped the infinite judgment not as a form of syntax, but as a discursive construction that states the non-determinability of a subject by a predicate and its contrary. Each took the infinite judgment to be an assertion exhibiting the "complete incommensurability" of the two terms in the proposition.

Only by restituting Hegel's theory of the infinite judgment to its place in the aftermath of Kant's philosophy can one grasp the real novelties of the account offered in *The Science of Logic*. The most striking among them is the thesis that the infinite judgment is not only the last of the three qualities of the predicative assertion but also the first in which judgment runs up against a limit at which it ceases to be itself, becoming, as Hegel writes, "no judgment" whatsoever. After being concealed in the affirmation, after beginning to be discernible in the negation, the difference between "singular" and "universal" becomes, in Hegel's infinite judgment, finally explicit. "Being" and "determination," which are united by the copula while being posited in their utter heterogeneity, pull the statement apart. The "partition" that defines the judgment now reaches a point of maximal intensity, which is resolvable only by the "concept of science" that speculative logic takes as its inception and end.

Yet there is more. Throughout his works, Hegel integrates into his theory of the infinite judgment an idea proposed by Schelling in *On the I as Principle of Philosophy*. In the excursus on transcendental logic contained in that early essay, Schelling argues that the infinite judgment is not only, as Kant held, a third variety of assertion, distinct from the two other qualities. Schelling writes that it can also be viewed as a variety of "negation," to which there corresponds a special "affirmation." Schelling's position is that the infinite judgment is best grasped as the "thetic-negative sentence," which is opposed, in its form, to the "thetic-positive sentence." Whereas the infinite judgment "removes" its subject from a logical sphere, positing it "in another," its correlated affirmative sentence, the thetic-positive judgment, "posits" its subject "only in the sphere of reality *as such.*" Schelling thereby suggests that to an infinite judgment such as "God is non-real," there corresponds a judgment such as "God *is,*" which merely posits divinity "as such." Hegel systematically appropriates this argument, while deriving from it new consequences.

In his works of logic, Hegel writes regularly of the "negatively infinite [*negativ-unendliche*] judgment," a phrase that clearly implies that there also exists a "positively infinite judgment." *The Science of Logic* presents an explicit, if abbreviated, argument to this effect. In the dense chapter of this work dedicated to the infinite judgment, Hegel passes from the expression of the "negatively infinite" to the utterance of the "positively infinite." He begins by showing how, in the correct nonsense of the "negatively infinite judgment," subject and predicate fall apart: to assert "Spirit is no elephant" is to state that the "thing" in question, Spirit, completely lacks the determination of "being an elephant." In other words, such a judgment asserts the "singular" to be no "universal." One may add that the reciprocal is also true: in absolutely denying the attribution of the predicate to the subject, this judgment also isolates the "determination," or "universal" property. Separating the universal, "elephant," from anything singular, such a sentence, in other words, abstractly asserts that the "universal" is no "singular." But these facts, Hegel reasons, can be dialectically converted into their contraries. In the collapse of subject and predicate, "the singular is singular," affirmatively, and "the universal is universal."[59] These, then, are "positively infinite judgments [*positiv-unendliche Urteilen*]." Between the negative and the positive varieties of infinite assertions, a symmetry may be observed. In the negatively infinite judgment, the "difference" between logical elements "is, so to speak, too great for it still to remain a judgment; subject and predicate have no positive connection whatsoever to each other; in the positively infinite judgment on the contrary, only identity is present, and because of this total lack of difference, there is no longer a judgment."[60]

The 1831 *Lectures on Logic* amplify this doctrine. "Immediate qualitative judgment" begins with "the first, *positive* judgment." It consists in the assertion that "The singular is something universal." Examples include the judgments, "All men are mortal" or "The rose is red." "But if I say, 'The singular is *not* something general or universal, but rather is something particular,' that may also be correct. Thus we arrive at a *negative* qualitative *judgment*." Negation, however, still preserves the link between the two expressions that it binds. "The rose is not red" means "that the rose has positively some particular color or other, but that its color is not red. Thus I have negated one determinate color, but I have left in place the universality which here is called 'color' . . . We still have an implicit reference by the subject to some other particular predicate."[61] It is this "reference" that is at last exhausted in the movement by which the negation passes over into infinity. Hegel once again evokes his paradigmatic proposition: "Spirit is no elephant." He comments: "What is said here fails to make reference to spirit, the subject, whether in the particular or universal character of what spirit is. For spirit does not belong to the genus to which elephants belong, since it is no animal at all." After such a sundering of the connection between subject and predicate, "what remains is only the singular thing's empty reference to itself as identical with itself." The "negatively infinite" sentence thus becomes affirmative: "Spirit is only spirit, in its perfect singularity." Vacuity is the hallmark of the "positively infinite judgment." "'The singular is singular' is a judgment of empty identity. But such a judgment as a judgment is as nonsensical as the [negative] infinite judgment, which is the judgment of the bad infinite."[62]

In drawing out the logical consequences of the collapsing sentence, Hegel thus places the infinite judgment into relation with the fundamental — and fundamentally obscure — propositional form commonly known as the "tautology." This is the statement that, as its name would have it, merely "says the same." In the history of philosophy, it finds its most famous important illustration in the "principle of identity," which dictates that, whatever the nature of a thing may be, it is itself and, therefore, cannot both be one thing and not that thing. In the preface to the second edition of *The Science of Logic*, Hegel alludes to this principle in passing, as the supreme example of the "merely formal categories" by which "school logic and school metaphysics" reason. In their inert exclusion of all thought content, such forms show themselves to be "stamped as finite" and "unfit to hold the truth, which is itself infinite."[63] "The simple basic determination or common form of the collection of such forms," Hegel asserts, "is *identity* which, in the logic of this collection, is asserted as the law of identity, as A=A, and as the principle of contradiction. So much has healthy common sense lost respect for this school which still holds on to such laws of truth and still busies itself with them, that it ridicules the school and regards as insufferable anyone who believes that in following such laws one actually says anything at all: the plant is a — plant; science is — science; *and so on in infinitum.*"[64]

Yet several volumes later in the *Logic*, Hegel pauses to treat such "ridiculous" sentences with considerable attention, if not seriousness. After recalling the just derision with which "healthy common sense" views such sentences as "the plant is — a plant" and "science is — science," Hegel lingers on such propositions as "Spirit is — spirit" and "Elephant is — elephant." He grasps them as two positively infinite judgments, derivable, by dialectical analysis, from a single negatively infinite judgment: "Spirit is no elephant." Hegel thereby recasts Fichte's and Schelling's "thetic" and "thetic-positive" judgments, making them into corollaries of the "infinite negative judgment." According to Hegel's doctrine, the statements "Spirit is spirit," and "Elephant is elephant," on the one hand, and "Spirit is no elephant," on the other, present a single truth in two correlated forms. The two first propositions state two sterile identities. In them, judgment has "collapsed in itself," as *Encyclopedia Logic* has it; of what was a predicative assertion, all that remains is the "the empty *identical* relation: the individual is the individual."[65] By contrast, the third proposition, "Spirit is no elephant," asserts a principle of double negation. It states that the individual is "not other" than itself. All three propositions are "infinite" in the sense of the "bad infinite." They express either utter sameness or absolute opposition; but each time, what they assert is lacking in "determination." Their content, therefore, is void. Yet Hegel's dialectical method is to render such nullity productive. In the concluding volume of the *Logic*, the emptiness of such sentences announces the overcoming of judgment itself as a form of thought.

In *The Phenomenology of Spirit*, Hegel had announced such a development, yet in terms so dense as to be almost unintelligible. On its voyage of self-discovery in that book, Spirit passed through the many stations of finite judgment. After beginning in crude consciousness, believing its sole certainty to lie in sensible appearances opposed to it, after progressing to the point at which it understands that the truth of such appearances lies in itself and its own knowing, Spirit, in the second section of the *Phenomenology*, enters the domain of self-consciousness, "the native realm of truth." It then grasps itself as "reason" (*Vernunft*), "certain that it is itself reality, or that everything actual is none other than itself."[66] It becomes, in short, "idealist." Yet its self-understanding remains abstract, and still it continues to search for itself. "Reason," Hegel recounts, "wants to find and to have itself as existent object, as an object that is actually and sensuously present."[67] To this end, it turns to the study of physical nature, becoming "observational."

First reason strives to find its reality in organic life. Frustrated in its initial pursuits, it sets out to find itself in the inorganic. Unsatisfied again, it devises a doctrine of teleology, which is to unify the organic and the inorganic in the harmony of a purposeful conjunction. Failing in each of these three endeavors, reason begins anew. Now it aims to grasp hold of its essence by attending to its own cognitive activity and the various "laws of pure thought." Psychology, however, proves infertile. In a final observational adventure, reason dedicates itself to the new sciences of physiognomy and phrenology, following Franz Joseph Gall and Johann Kasper Lavater. In its last effort, reason searches for its own nature in the lifeless materiality of the skull.[68] "This final stage of Reason in its observational role," Hegel remarks, "is its worst; and that is why its reversal becomes a necessity."[69] At the pinnacle of its empirical endeavors and the nadir of its self-loss in allegedly positive science, "Reason takes itself to be *all thinghood*, even *purely objective* thinghood itself."[70]

Spirit, espousing Gall's doctrines with unprecedented ferocity, now takes a memorable step: it grasps itself to be of "the same kind of being that a *bone is.*" "When in other respects it is said of Spirit that it *is*, that it has *being*, is a *Thing*, a single, separate *reality*, this is not *intended* to mean that it is something we can see or take in our hands or touch, and so on, but that is what is *said*; and what *really* is said is expressed by saying that the *being of Spirit is a bone*."[71] Momentarily convinced that it has at last discovered itself in nature, Spirit utters one of the strangest sentences in the *Phenomenology*: "This consciousness, in its result, enunciates as a proposition that of which it is the unconscious certainty — the proposition that is implicit in the notion of reason. This proposition is the *infinite judgment* that the self is a Thing, a judgment that suspends itself [*sich selbst aufhebt*]."[72]

In the haste of its motion toward the absolute, Hegel's book hardly lingers on this judgment. Nor does it pause to define its specific "infinity." Viewed from a critical perspective, Spirit's words seem even more removed from Kant's third quality of judgment than the sentence "Spirit is no elephant." That assertion, at least, contains the word "no," evoking a negation of some kind. The sentence, "The self is a Thing" appears, by contrast, wholly positive. Yet the development of the theory of the infinite judgment from the early post-Kantians through to *The Science of Logic* affords a means to grasp the structure of this utterance and the reasons for its qualification as "infinite." Judging that "the self is a Thing," "Observing Reason" unites two terms that, in being "absolutely incommensurable," cannot but fall apart. The sentence collapses, or, as Hegel's own commentary specifies: it "suspends itself." Immediately identifying the principle of thinking with the materiality of a bone, this judgment expresses Spirit's most extreme self-alienation in observation. It is false as well as absurd, when grasped as a predicative assertion. Yet in the dialectical unfolding of Spirit's developing discourse about itself, it is also more. The sentence "The self is a Thing" is true, because it expresses Spirit's alienated self-understanding in observation. At the same time, it announces the union of its "being" (*das Sein*) with what is "its own" (*das Seinige*).[73]

Like every "finite shape of consciousness" in the *Phenomenology*, Observing Reason says more than it knows. It speaks a truth that eludes it, which it will, however, grasp in reaching its final form in "Absolute Knowing." At the end of Hegel's book, Spirit recalls the words it once uttered, apprehending the sense that they contained. The narrating philosopher now explains: "We saw Observing Reason at its peak express its specific character in the infinite judgment that the *being of the 'I' is a Thing*, and, moreover, a sensuous immediate Thing."[74] Hegel comments: "That judgment, taken just as it stands, is non-spiritual, or rather is the non-spiritual itself." Such an assertion is the most extreme instantiation of the attempt to grasp the *I* or "self" as a kind of thing — be it *cogitans* or *extensa*, organic or inorganic, soul or body. The thesis that "the self is a Thing" thereby expresses the simultaneous truth and falsity of every effort to define the thinking self by means of the duality of subject and predicate, or, in other words, as "thing" and as "determination." Its "non-spiritual" sense is that of judgment as a finite discursive means of thought.

At the conclusion of *The Phenomenology of Spirit*, "Absolute Knowing" frees itself of this means, beginning with the "infinite judgment" uttered by Observing Reason — not by denying it, to be sure, but by affirming it in its dialectical reversal. Judgment now passes into the concept of science. Recalling the predicative proposition that it once uttered, consciousness twists it back upon itself. "I" and "Thing," subject and predicate, "thing-in-itself" and "implicit concept," pass into each other in the utterance of a new infinite judgment, the inverse of the old: "*The Thing is I.*"[75] Hegel comments: "In this infinite judgment, the Thing is superseded; in itself it is nothing; it has meaning only in the relation, only *through the 'I'* and its *connection* with it."[76] The movement of this rewriting is that of the "speculative proposition," which Hegel most famously presents in the preface to the *Phenomenology*. There he warns against confusing "the speculative with the ratiocinative methods" and believing that in philosophy, "the usual subject-predicate relation obtains," together with the "usual attitude towards knowing" that that relation articulates.[77] Such an "attitude" belongs to "representational" or "picture-thinking" (*vorstellendes Denken*), for which "the self is a *Subject* to which the content is related as Accident and Predicate."[78] "Speculative thinking" (*begreifendes Denken*) "behaves in a different way." It conceives of a self that is "not a passive Subject inertly supporting the Accidents" but "the self-moving Notion that takes its determinations back into itself." In that "self-motion," "the passive Subject perishes"; its properties cease to be external determinations abstractly opposed to it. The "Predicate becomes the Substance," even as "the Subject passes over into the Predicate," as it is negated and preserved in being "suspended" or "sublated" (*aufgehoben*).[79]

To exemplify the movement of thinking beyond predicative assertion, *The Phenomenology of Spirit* gives a first example: "God is Being [*Gott ist das Sein*]." "Being," in this sentence, appears to occupy the position of the predicate, in distinction to "God," the subject. Thinking and grammar, however, now diverge. It suffices to consider the content of the statement to grasp that "Being," in this judgment, is no "determination," even as "God" is no thing. "The Predicate is 'Being'; it has the significance of something substantial in which the Subject is dissolved. 'Being' is here meant to be not a Predicate, but rather the essence."[80] Striving to pass from subject to predicate, according to the movement demanded by the statement, the mind finds that the formal distinctions of representation give way. Searching for "God" at the start of the sentence, reason comes up against its "dissolution" in "Being"; it must register "the loss of the Subject" in the traditional sense. Conversely, since "the Predicate itself has been expressed as a Subject," the place of the predicate is now also lacking. So, too, Hegel reasons, "when one says: 'the *actual* is the *universal*,' the actual as subject disappears in its predicate. The universal is not meant to have merely the significance of the predicate, as if the proposition asserted only that the actual is universal; on the contrary, the universal is meant to express the essence of the actual."[81] Finite reason loses its bearings. In its syntax, the sentence is a predicative assertion; in its content, however, it has transgressed the form of thought articulated by the parts of grammar. Hegel concludes: "The general nature of the judgment or proposition, which involves the distinction of Subject and Predicate, is destroyed [*zerstört*]." The grammatical subject and predicate survive. Their difference, however, is now grasped as a unity in the concept. "The form of the proposition is the appearance of the determinate sense, but that the predicate expresses the Substance, and the Subject itself falls away into the universal, this is the *unity*."[82]

On the surface, the logic of such speculative propositions seems distant from that of the infinite judgments of the *Phenomenology* and *Logic*. The two types of assertions may even appear to be systematically opposed. Their content is contrasted. The speculative propositions proposed in the *Phenomenology* bear on God in His Being and the actual in its universality.

The infinite judgments of the *Phenomenology* and *Logic* evoke subjectivity and the skull's bones, lions and tables, Spirit and the elephant that it is not. Speculative propositions would seem to ascend to the heights of sublimity, defining the supreme essence in which essence and existence coincide. Infinite judgments, by contrast, attract the scorn of "healthy common sense." One may go still further, for their dialectical movements also appear to be opposed. In the speculative proposition, the subject is "dissolved" into the predicate, even as the predicate itself, in dialectical reversal, becomes the subject. As each logical element loses itself in its other, the abstract and immediate "partitioning" of the judgment is at last overcome. In the infinite judgment, subject and predicate, being "completely incommensurate," simply fall apart. They state not a truth of theology but the emptiest tautology, or a judgment that is none at all: "Spirit is Spirit"; "Elephant is elephant"; that is, "A is A," or, to rewrite that infinitely positive judgment in its infinitely negative form, "A thing is no thing other than itself." Yet in the collapse that such abstractly formal constructions articulate, a speculative resolution is also anticipated. In its nonsensical correctness and absurdity, the infinite judgment testifies to the dissolution of representational thinking that the concept alone achieves. It is the inverted image of the speculative proposition, which it announces.

In his *Lectures on Aesthetics*, Hegel presents the many shapes by which art, since its known beginnings, has reconciled two apparently opposed principles: reason and sensible matter, or "the infinite freedom of conceptual thinking" and the "finite reality of nature."[83] It is well known that, for Hegel, the mediation that art embodies is incomplete. Philosophy and, later, "science" succeed in accomplishing what art only promised to achieve. Less familiar is the shape in which the properly "aesthetic" reconciliation of thought and matter reaches its conclusion. The end, for Hegel, is dissolution: comedy on stage, accompanied by "the laughter in which the characters dissolve everything, including themselves."[84] In the *Aesthetics*, as in the *Phenomenology*, art fulfills itself in disintegrating into irony, even as it reaches "the limit of substance," in Werner Hamacher's words, "and hence the dissolution of its own principle of the production and presentation of something enduring in itself."[85] Judgment, in *The Science of Logic*, draws to its close in a like unraveling. Its end lies in neither synthesis nor positing, as the post-Kantians had claimed, but in an absolute "analysis," in the sense of the old Greek word: a loosening up of traditional logical form.

The section of *The Science of Logic* devoted to the "judgment of existence" sets out the dialectic of this dissolution in speech and thought. The predicative statement appears in it as the first form of discursive knowledge, which is at once determinate and traversed by a tension that it cannot, on its own, resolve: that of the asymmetry of subject and predicate, singular and universal. This opposition is overcome only when the partition of the predicative judgment is intensified to the point at which, in twin forms of stated infinity, it "loosens up" into logical vacuity. From the simple affirmation, Hegel's *Logic* passes to the negation, from the "is," it thus journeys to the "is not," the "is not-" and the "is non-," before reaching a threshold at which the sentence, collapsing, speculatively falls apart. As judgment vanishes in becoming "no judgment," a thinking beyond any predicative assertion makes itself heard. That this thinking should be that of the "concept of science" was, of course, to be expected. More remarkable is that this concept is announced in nonsense: that from which the small particle *non-* itself has vanished, to be sure, but whose movements unfold, step by step, according to an argument that retrieves and reworks the post-Kantian transcendental logic of the infinite proposition. Just as Hegel's art resolves itself into philosophy by dissolving itself to the peals of laughter, so his science starts to prove itself adequate to *"truth unveiled, truth as it is in and for itself"* in becoming a doctrine of valid absurdities. The *"exposition of God as he is in his eternal essence"* begins to end in self-suspending sentences.

CHAPTER THIRTEEN

The Springboard Principle

Hegel demanded that thinking become a system, that this system be complete, and that, in its encyclopedic totality, it comprehend all science. Each of these imperatives was to be contested in multiple ways, both during the period in which Hegel wrote and taught and following his death in 1831. The disparate texts known all too summarily as the "fragments" of the Romantics, from the diverse aphorisms of the *Athenaeum* to the variously partial pieces that succeed them, suggest that, to grasp its object, thinking must forsake the ambition to issue in a system.[1] Their indications were to be developed in new ways by the great nineteenth-century anti-philosophers, from Kierkegaard to Nietzsche. Yet it was not only Hegel's notion of philosophy that later writers would refuse. In the second half of the nineteenth century, the validity of the ideal of "science" itself, as Hegel conceived it, would also be profoundly shaken. The Hegelian philosophy of nature, in particular, being "dominated by a vigorous anti-mathematicism" and methodically opposed to Newtonian physics, proved difficult to maintain in the face of the progress of the sciences.[2] As discoveries continued to be made in the empirical study of nature, from biology and chemistry to physiology and physics, cognition and the question of the conditions of its possibility seemed increasingly "absorbed" by positive sciences, in their indefinite yet undeniable plurality.[3] When defined as a system of cognition, philosophy appeared to many to be obsolete.

Precisely then, a new and resolutely anti-dialectical note was sounded: "Back to Kant!" These words were first and most famously spoken by Eduard Zeller in his inaugural lecture at the University of Heidelberg in 1862.

Otto Liebmann appropriated them in his 1865 book on Kant's "epigones."[4] Yet the new road backward would be traveled only later, in the years joining the nineteenth century to the twentieth. Hermann Cohen, professor of philosophy at the University of Marburg, would clear the way to a new critical philosophy. From his first works to his last, he argued for a return, after Hegel, to Kant; but he did not conceal the fact that the Kant to whom he would lead his readers would not be the thinker of the late eighteenth century. More than once, he declared that the present can and must understand Kant "better than he understood himself."[5] Cohen's was to be the philosophy of an explicitly reconstructed Kant.

Cohen's avowed point of orientation was to be a phenomenon to which Hegelianism, by the last quarter of the nineteenth century, seemed manifestly inadequate: the "fact of science" (*das Faktum der Wissenschaft*). The equivocations of this phrase deserve to be dispelled. By this "fact," Cohen evokes not a fixed body of positive knowledge in the natural sciences but the emergence and development of cognition, the "becoming and unfolding of science in the limits of pre-given problems."[6] Cohen's erstwhile student, colleague, and successor in neo-Kantianism, Paul Natorp, would ably define the meaning of this "becoming and unfolding" in his 1910 study, *The Logical Foundations of the Exact Sciences*. In science, Natorp writes, "progress, method is everything, or, to use a Latinate word: *process*. The *factum* of science is therefore to be understood only as a *fieri*."[7] For the "Marburg School" that Cohen founded, the "factuality" of science is its "happening," its emergence and development.

Cohen argues that in the elaboration of his transcendental philosophy, Kant was above all concerned with the establishment of the conditions of this *fieri*. Writing almost a century after the publication of the *Critique of Pure Reason*, Cohen begins by explaining that Kant must be understood in his historical setting. In his first major work, *Kant's Theory of Experience* (1871), Cohen argues that Kant departed from the point to which Hume's skepticism had led: the recognition of the empirical foundation of the science of nature. Concluding that "the connection between cause and effect" is the result of "the merely self-repeating changes of perceptions," Hume "dissolved" a principle of natural necessity in "the habits of experience." "Kant starts with exactly this thought. With the acknowledgment of one member of this thought and the opposition to the other, the *Critique* begins. 'That all our cognition *begins* with experience, there can be no doubt.... Yet even if all our cognition *arises* with experience, it does not at all follow that all our cognition also *originates from* experience.' This is the first sentence of the *Critique*. In this sentence experience is proposed as a riddle. The solution of this puzzle is the content of Kantian philosophy. *Kant has discovered a new concept of experience*."[8] For Kant's predecessors, "experience" is immediately identifiable with sensation; it is "given" (*gegeben*), as a "prolix series of perceptions," with respect to which the mind is only passive.[9] To this dogmatic doctrine of "givenness," Cohen's Kant counters: "The object is given only because it is intuited."[10] The "Copernican Revolution" consists in the principle that the necessary and universal character of our cognition derives from the fact that human reason "produces" its own experience. As Kant wrote in the First *Critique*: "We can cognize of things a priori only what we ourselves have put into them."[11]

With Kant, the term "experience" acquires, therefore, a new sense. Cohen explains: "Experience itself becomes a concept that we have to construct [*construiren*] in pure intuition and pure thought. The formal conditions of its possibility, space, time and synthetic unity, count henceforth as a priori, because with them we *construct* experience, because they are the formal constituents of experience."[12] As Alan W. Richardson observes, Cohen's "experience" "becomes, in essence, a word meaning empirical knowledge, knowledge that is expressed in the synthetic unity of judgments. The a priori is not knowledge independent of experience but knowledge that expresses the conditions of experience."[13] Such an understanding of Kant's achievement constitutes a major innovation, which implies a new definition of the structure of the a priori. As Cassirer, Cohen's student and successor, would explain in *Substance and Function*, "from this point of view, the strictly limited meaning of the 'a priori' is clearly evident. Only those ultimate logical invariants can be called a priori which lie at the basis of any determination of a connection according to natural law. A cognition is called a priori not in any sense as if it were *prior* to experience but because and insofar as it is contained as a necessary premise in every valid judgment concerning facts."[14] Proposing his "concept of experience," Cohen's Kant therefore lays the bases for the field of knowledge of modern science. "An object apprehended in experience is grasped according to the mathematical laws of physics, and the objects of physics, in their totality, constitute *experience*."[15] In first presenting "experience" in its a priori structures, the *Critique of Pure Reason* becomes the inaugural account of the "fact of science."

By 1902, however, Cohen judges "critique" to be inadequate to its aims. Having reconstructed the parts of the Kantian system in three brilliant works, *Kant's Theory of Experience* (1871), *Kant's Grounding of Ethics* (1873), and *Kant's Grounding of Aesthetics* (1899), Cohen sets out on an original project: a *Logic of Pure Cognition*, as he titles the Part One of his "System of Philosophy." Introducing his work, Cohen writes: "Even *critique* and the critique of knowledge are not incontrovertible. Kant could and needed to draw up the critique, because he presupposed logic as a doctrine of pure sensibility."[16] That presupposition, however, was "dogmatic," or unfounded. Kant began his account of "pure sensibility" with the evocation of a thing called "intuition," whose origin and structure he failed to render intelligible. "*An intuition was presupposed for thinking*," such that the mind seemed to depend on something the Kantian theory could not explain. Thinking then appeared to have "its inception in a thing *external* to itself. Herein," Cohen writes, not without severity, "lies the weakness of Kant's foundation. Herein lies the ground of the decadence that immediately made itself felt in his school."[17] It is this "weakness" that Cohen strives to remedy. Holding fast to the Kantian understanding of "critique" as the transcendental inquiry into the conditions of cognition, Cohen departs from the *Critique of Pure Reason*. He aims to resolve its contradictions by providing the system of cognition with the foundation that its first formulation lacked. Like Maimon and Hegel before him, albeit in a new manner, Cohen sets out to derive sensible "intuition" from the pure activity of thinking, absolving reason of its dependence on an unexplained "given." He resolves, in other words, to eliminate the Transcendental Aesthetic. "Critique" is to become a "logic" unimagined by the first architect of the critical philosophy. "Here," Cohen writes, in his introduction, "we begin again. That means that we place ourselves again on the ground of the principles of mathematical natural science. They must be indicated anew as pure cognition. They must be discovered anew in connection to logical reason."[18]

In the passage from the *Critique of Pure Reason* to the *Logic of Pure*

Cognition, the word "pure" alone remains. It is a crucial term for Cohen. "Exaggerating," Wolfgang Marx has remarked, "one may say that the making intelligible of the purity of thought was Hermann Cohen's sole subject."[19] Helmut Holzhey observes that, for Cohen, "the three basic orientations of consciousness, that is, thinking (or knowledge), will and feeling represent, in their 'purity,' the members of the philosophical system."[20] In each case, to be "pure" is, first of all, to be unadulterated; it is, second, to be, in such freedom from anything other than itself, a condition of possibility, or "origin." By definition, "pure cognition" is for Cohen, as it was for Kant, non-empirical. For the neo-Kantian, moreover, pure cognition is, as Andrea Poma writes, "cognition that has its origin solely in thinking; thinking is therefore 'pure' not only insofar as it 'has no origin outside itself,' but also insofar as it is the origin of cognition."[21] "Insofar as we are placing ourselves on the historical ground of critique," Cohen asserts, introducing his bold project, "we decline to allow ourselves to consider logic as a doctrine of sensibility. *We begin with thinking.* Pure thinking may have no origin outside itself, if its purity is to remain unlimited and unsullied. Pure thinking, in itself and only from itself, must produce pure cognition. Therefore, the theory of thought must become the theory of cognition. *Here we aim to construct the logic of this doctrine of thinking, which is in itself the doctrine of cognition.*"[22]

Cohen's aim in his *Logic of Pure Cognition* is in this sense also that of Kant's First *Critique*: to uncover the conditions of possibility of a priori synthetic judgments, such as those familiar to modern mathematical physics. Yet whereas Kant set out to accomplish his task by presupposing a double source of knowledge in intuition and concept, or sensibility and understanding, Cohen proposes a more ambitious task: to derive scientific knowledge from the laws of the concept alone. A new "logic" is to account for the existence of all sensible content. In its form, his project recalls those of Kant's earlier successors, such as Hegel. For this reason, Cohen takes pains to distinguish his aims from those of the "Romantic" idealists who derived reality from reason. Like such philosophers, Cohen refuses to grant the irreducible "factuality" of sensibility, yet unlike them, he admits one fundamental datum: the "fact of science." Defining "thinking" as a "thinking of cognition," and, more exactly, as the pure cognition grounding the concept of experience in modern science, he concludes that the theory of logic is in essence identical with "the thinking of science."[23] Such a "thinking," for Cohen, founds the truth of scientific propositions.

To guarantee the necessity and universality of such propositions, "thought," for Cohen, must be free of psychology. "Thinking" cannot be reducible to consciousness, for on its own consciousness affords no grounds to distinguish truth from falsity. Cohen is well aware of the challenge that his concept must then meet. He confronts the question directly. "Is there a means and a way to define the specificity of thinking, that of the thinking of cognition, without coming into contact with the interests and tasks of psychology, let alone entering into conflict with them?"[24] In identifying thinking with judgment, Kant suggested a response: thinking is "synthesis," more exactly, the "synthesis of a manifold." Yet Cohen cannot accept this answer. The Kantian "manifold" is that of sensible intuition, and it is precisely of this "given" that the *Logic of Pure Cognition* seeks to purify the mind. After Kant and in distinction to him, Cohen thus proposes a new definition of the unifying act of reason: "Thinking is the synthesis of unity [*Einheit*]."[25] Synthesis lies not in the "composition" (*Zusammensetzung*) of a given multiplicity but in the "unity" of "separation and unification."[26]

To represent this act of pure synthesis, Cohen suggests a basic "figure," on which he draws throughout his *Logic*. Thinking is "generating" (*Erzeugung*), in the sense in which, "in mathematical as in philosophical literature, already in antiquity, as in the modern age, and not only in scientific discourse, 'generating' gives figural expression to the creative sovereignty of thinking."[27] Cohen adds an important qualification: the "generating" that is thinking is absolutely immanent to its activity, in that it issues in no product that might be opposed to it. In cognition, therefore, *"The generating is the generation," "The producing is the product"* (*Die Erzeugung ist das Erzeugnis*).[28] This is the principle of the *factum scientiae* grasped as a *fieri*. Cohen explains: "In thinking, it is not a matter of creating a thought, insofar as the thought may be viewed as a finished and ready-made thing; rather, thinking itself is the aim and object of its activity. This activity does not vanish in the thing; it does not leave itself. If it reaches its end, it is finished, and ceases to be a problem. The activity itself is the thought, and the thought is nothing outside thinking."[29]

To define this activity, Cohen turns to the forms of assertion by which Kant, drawing on the logical tradition, distinguished the varieties of judgment. Cohen begins not with the three quantities of propositions, as had Kant in his Table of Judgments, but with the three qualities, from which Hegel had also started. In his founding presentation of transcendental logic, Kant distinguished among affirmative, negative, and infinite statements. It is unsurprising that Cohen does likewise. More striking is the fact that in the *Logic of Pure Cognition*, these qualities appear not as three possibilities of predicative assertion but as the first three "laws of thinking" (*Denkgesetze*). What is most innovative, however, is a further point. It concerns the first among their number. This is a judgment that assures nothing less than the possibility of cognition in general. This first judgment is not, as a reader of Kant might have expected, affirmative in form; nor is it, as a Hegelian could have anticipated, negative. In this *Logic of Pure Cognition*, the ceaseless "generating" that is "thinking" begins, rather, with the infinite judgment — more exactly, with the proposition that Cohen baptizes "the judgment of origin" (*das Urteil des Ursprungs*). "*Logic*," he declares, "*must become logic of the origin*. For the origin is not only the necessary beginning of thinking; rather, it must confirm itself as the driving principle in all progress. *All pure cognitions must be modifications of the principle of origin.*"[30]

The "judgment of origin" furnishes thinking with the beginning of logic, while also constituting the point from which metaphysics must depart. As such, this judgment constitutes a principle more fundamental than those known to earlier accounts of the varieties of statement-making sentences. These accounts, from Aristotle to the nineteenth century, begin as a rule with the affirmative predicative assertion, formalizable as "*A is B.*" Such a synthesis presupposes that the subject and the attribute are given to reason. In the "principle of origin," however, Cohen places himself "on the ground" of logic; he seeks to identify the source from which both such terms emerge. It is an axiom of his *Logic* that, to be "pure," thinking must refrain from admitting any elements whose genesis it cannot reconstruct. Positively stated, "thinking must take as given only that which it itself can find."[31] Cohen's *Logic* cannot, for this reason, begin with a discursive representation such "*A is B.*" It must first confront the question of the "origin of content." "If *A* be taken as the sign of the simplest content,"

Cohen writes, "then first it must be asked: *Whence this A?*"[32] This question precedes every statement. Cohen reasons that such a query was, in essence, also Socrates' question: "What is?" (τί ἐστι;).[33] The question bears, in each case, on a strictly indefinite subject. For this reason, Cohen argues, the letter *A* is inadequate to its expression, "for *A* already designates a determinate value, whose determinacy closes off the value of any questions as to its provenance." Mathematics furnishes a more appropriate sign of the object of the primordial question in philosophy. It is the algebraic *x*. "This sign means not indeterminateness [*Unbestimmtheit*] but, rather, determinability [*Bestimmbarkeit*]. It is thus equivalent to the true sense of the given. For *x* already contains within it the question of where it is from, wherein it springs. *X* is thus the right symbol, in logic, for an element of pure thought."[34]

To ask after this algebraic cipher is to pose the question of the origin. If one believes Cohen, thinking, in antiquity, began with precisely this activity. "The science of the Greeks started with it, as did philosophy, according to tradition." Hence Thales and his fabled doctrine of the principle of all things: "Water appears as the origin of things. And so in this origin the abstraction of matter emerges."[35] Such an origin conditions the "principle" (*Prinzip*) of thinking, which in turn conditions all cognition. Analogously, Cohen continues, the modern thinkers attempted to locate the "principle" of thinking in self-consciousness. From antiquity to the modern age, a single rule may be discerned: "*Thinking is thinking of the origin.*"[36] This genitive construction expresses the "entire complexity of the relation of thinking and origin," Helmut Holzhey notes. "The genitive states first that the origin (of all thought content or all cognition) lies in thinking (origin 'is' thinking); it also states that thinking allows for emergence and generates (thinking 'is' origin). In the first reading, the genitive responds to the question, 'What is the origin?' In the second . . . it responds to the question 'What is thinking?' The answer to the first question is: 'not intuition, not intuition and thought, etc., but rather thinking (alone).' The answer to the second question is: not representation, union, etc., but rather 'generating,' productive activity, in other words, 'origin.'"[37]

Kant's Theory of Experience announces the importance that Cohen will grant to the judgment of origin in his own philosophy, and the way in which he will relate it to an obscure point in Kant's theory of transcendental logic. In his early reconstruction of the critical philosophy, Cohen does not hesitate to attribute to Kant a striking claim: thinking "begins" with the infinite judgment. "If ever logical activity is to have and determine a methodical beginning," he writes, referring to Kant's foundation of the fact of science, "it must be defined in origin. *Methodical beginning is origin.* Infinite judgment is the judgment of origin."[38] Yet it is only in the *Logic of Pure Cognition* that Cohen draws out the full consequences of this affirmation. Now the reader learns that the origin that is at issue in the infinite judgment is not that belonging to anything in particular. It is not the origin of some thing but the origin of "the Something" (*das Etwas*) in general, in its distinction from "the Nothing," or "nothingness" (*das Nichts*). In defiance of Parmenides, Cohen thereby affirms, with Kant and Hegel, that "the Nothing" can become the object of thinking. It must, indeed, be conceived, in order for the Something to be defined. Cohen does not ask, as had Leibniz, "Why is there something rather than nothing?" The neo-Kantian's question instead concerns the "leap" lodged in the German "origin," or *Ur-sprung*. From where, he wonders, does the Something spring?

Cohen begins by identifying a representation that would be inadequate. The "path" (*Weg*) from the Nothing to Being, he writes, cannot be "direct" (*gerade*), on account of two implacable metaphysical necessities. First, Being cannot derive from Being: "There is no searching for the origin of the Something in the Something itself." But so, too, it would seem, the origin cannot lie in the Nothing, the "old dictum" "warning us," as he notes, "that *ex nihilo nil fit*," "nothing comes from nothing." To this, however, Cohen adds, almost in passing: "perhaps" something can come "*ab nihilo*," "off Nothing."[39] The reader learns that the path from the Nothing to the Something is not only not rectilinear; more exactly, it is curved, or crooked, admitting a "detour" (*Umweg*). Following the irregular motion of this path, thinking sets out on an "adventure" (*Abenteuer*), which brings it before the Nothing, before delivering it at last to the Something. "This adventure of thinking," Cohen writes, "presents *the Nothing. On the detour of the Nothing, the judgment of origin presents the Something.*"[40] Searching for the origin of the Something, thinking has no choice, therefore, but to tarry with the Nothing, at least for a moment. Yet Cohen hastens to add that the Nothing that thinking encounters is not any "nullity" whatsoever. In particular, it is not an "unthing" (*Unding*), or sheer impossibility. The Nothing that thinking runs up against in its primordial adventure "is, rather, the spawn of the deepest logical perplexity, which, in conceiving of being, does not let itself be discouraged and despair."[41] It is a non-Something.

In his *Logic* as elsewhere, Cohen avails himself of a grammatical distinction to illustrate the philosophical opposition that he strives to posit. He argues that, in grasping the origin of Being, thinking encounters a non-Being to which the ancient Greek particle *mē*, rather than *ou*, is adequate.[42] The distinction between these two words is far from easy to define. Each is translatable by the German *nicht* and the English "not" or "non-." One classical exposition presents *ou* as the word employed in "the indicative and optative and all independent sentences, except wishes," *mē*, being used, by contrast, "with the subjunctive and imperative in all constructions."[43] Cohen places considerable doctrinal weight on this grammatical difference. He also supposes that it may become the object of a judgment in translation. Tacitly, Cohen presupposes the existence of a meta-language, such as that of a commentary, in which he may say yes to *mē*, the particle of modal or "qualified" negation, and no to *ou*, the term of indicative predicative denial. Only in such an idiom may he specify that the Nothing from which thinking springs is "relative," rather than absolute; or, as he at times suggests, that the Nothing of thinking is "privative" rather than "negative." "Being itself must receive its origin through non-Being [*Das Sein selbst soll durch das Nichtsein seinen Ursprung empfangen*]," he may then maintain. "Non-Being is no correlative concept to Being; rather, the relative Nothing designates the springboard [*Schwungbrett*], from which the leap can be made, by virtue of continuity."[44] A deviation through a foreign tongue allows the philosopher to define the detour by which thinking generates its thought. The circumnavigation in speech enables the theory of the primal leap: thinking springs "off nothing," and sets out from its non-Being toward the non-Nothing that is the Something.

In expounding the doctrine of this recoiling, Cohen recalls the transcendental logic of the infinite judgment and reconceives of it at once.

Kant and his followers treated the third quality of propositions above all as a variety of predication. For the author of the *Critique*, the statement "the soul is non-mortal" defines the soul with respect to a property, "mortality," positing it as a "thing." Despite the differences that separate them, Maimon, Fichte, and Schelling also understand the infinite judgment as articulating some manner of predicative determination, albeit at the edge of such discursive forms. Even Hegel, who grasps the infinite judgment as a collapsing sentence, deems it, in its absurdity, the last of predicative assertions, and the first in which the judgment gives way to "the Concept." Cohen knows his predecessors well, and he judges their treatments to be inadequate. He condemns Hegel, in particular, for having first initiated the discussion of the infinite judgment in a "tone" of jesting and mockery. In his 1874 *Logic: Three Books on Thinking, Investigation, and Cognition*, Hermann Lotze followed suit. Viewing the infinite judgment as little more than an expression of "arbitrariness and lunacy," both philosophers mistook its true significance, obstructing the way for their successors. Cohen observes that as a result of their unfounded contempt, the infinite judgment fell into "ill repute" for "the entire previous century."[45]

The *Logic of Pure Cognition* proposes an account of the infinite judgment that is fundamentally novel. In Cohen's theory, this judgment neither binds nor separates two thought terms. The operations of conjunction and disjunction presuppose the determinable content that they articulate, and it is precisely this that Cohen's first law of thinking "generates." Placing himself "on the ground" of critical philosophy, "beginning with thinking," and with thinking alone, Cohen departs from a point that is prior to the synthesis and opposition of concepts. This is a point of logical and metaphysical inception. Here no determinacy is posited, and none is to be reached, as in Hegel's dialectical development, after a movement of contradiction. Before the affirmation of a *yes* and the negation of a *no*, thinking, for Cohen, begins in a *non-*. Or, as he would specify, it emerges in a *mē*. The "non-" of the infinite judgment, for him, is not a sign of the absence of a ground of predicative determination, as it was for Maimon; nor is it the marker of the incommensurability of the parts of the judgment, as it was for Hegel. For Cohen, the *non-* announces the leap from nullity toward a determinable x. The logical syntax of his infinite judgment states this inception: thinking begins by affirming not "*A is B*," or "*A is not B*," but "*A is non-B*," where "non-B," before signifying any particular content, names "non-nothing."[46] From this "springing" off nothing, something comes to be: in the "pure" act by which the infinite is limited by thought, a finite content is "generated." Without ever leaving itself, reason produces a Something from the Nothing, availing itself solely of naming by *non-*.

To do so, however, reason must also hold fast to one fundamental law. This is "continuity" (*Kontinuität*), the crucial "compass" that thinking requires in journeying on the "adventurous way towards the discovery of the origin."[47] The *Logic of Pure Cognition* defines continuity as a "law of thinking" that is strictly "*independent of sensation*, for which there is only discreteness, if not only the unity of the heap."[48] Thinking alone "generates *unity* and the *connection of unities*," being itself "*conditioned by connection*. And since thinking is the generating of the origin, so is the origin conditioned by connection. No frightful image of the Nothing interrupts this continuity of the original unities to be generated. Nowhere may the abyss yawn. Everywhere, the Nothing presents the true transition; for it is the *turning away of the Something* [*die Abkehr des Etwas*], *as a given*, whether it be in sensation or elsewhere. This turning away alone leads through to the origin."[49] It is by virtue of such continuity that the Nothing may be grasped as not an "unthing" but the point from which the "adventure" of thinking begins. "Springing off" the Nothing by means of the *non-*, thinking recoils from the absence from which, in its purity, it begins; it accomplishes a "turning away of the turning away" (*Abkhehr der Abkehr*) from which it starts, or a "turning back of the turning way" (*Umkehr der Abkehr*), as Jakob Gordin remarks in his *Investigations into the Theory of the Infinite Judgment*.[50] Cohen assures his readers that nowhere along the course of this long "turning" will thinking run the risk of being interrupted; "nowhere may the abyss yawn," once the principle of continuity has been established. From the Nothing, thinking "generates" the beings determinable by science — albeit always on a single condition: "The Nothing must correspond to *mē*. Thus the detour will be justified as the direct way."[51]

The principle of this springboard echoes throughout Cohen's system of philosophy. After proposing his first systematic rereading of Kant in 1871, Cohen returns to the question of the productivity of pure thinking in his 1883 study, *The Principle of the Infinitesimal Method and Its History: A Contribution to the Foundations of the Critique of Cognition.* Here Cohen credits Newton and Leibniz with having developed a new technique in the calculation of quantities and with having thus initiated a metaphysics of the infinite grounded in the law of continuity. In the invention of differential and integral calculus, the early modern thinkers would have demonstrated that the infinite can be rigorously defined as the source of the finite — if, that is, one presupposes the principle of continuity. "*Continuity becomes the higher concept, from which the infinite is to be derived.* With this change, however, the change in the *correlation* of the concepts concerning the distinction between being and thought, which is more important from the systematic point of view, was also given. Now a question could be raised: to what degree the infinite, although it itself does not exist, nonetheless and precisely for this reason, has validity in nature. For now the *being* of the infinite rests on the *thought* of continuity. Continuity is now a principle, as idea and as law, both of reason and of nature."[52] Defining the operations of integration and differentiation, Leibniz and Newton would have discovered a means to relate finite quantities to quantities infinitely less than any given value, passing, by thinking, from "something" to "nothing." Conversely, the early modern thinkers would have shown how infinitely small quantities, "summed" in thought, produce finite values. Cohen takes the "infinitesimal method" to be the crucial tool of modern science, the enduring testament of "the sovereign power of thinking over being," as Natorp would later write, "a power to which no limit can be opposed."[53]

In his *Logic* of 1902, Cohen leaves no doubt as to the relation of the "infinitesimal method" to his own doctrine of pure cognition. Introducing the "judgments of mathematics" in this book, he recalls how Leibniz located the true "Archimedean point" of cognition in the infinite — not, to be sure, in the infinitely large of "metaphysico-theological speculation" but in the infinitely small, which subsequently became "the central point of all mathematics." "The first methodic step that we must recognize in mathematics is the one by which it *achieves the generation of the infinitesimal number. Leibniz* and *Newton* both made this discovery." Newton termed this generation "Fluxion," "presupposition and basis of the *Fluente*."[54] By contrast, "Leibniz designates the new concept by dx. This dx, however, is the *origin* of *x*, with which analysis reckons, and which is the representative of the finite. This definition therefore seizes hold of the judgment of origin, in order to define the infinitely small. And the infinitesimal, like the fluxion, is the great *example* of the fundamental meaning of the judgment of origin."[55] Cohen taxes Kant with not having drawn the consequences that the infinitesimal method entailed. The method of the integral and differential calculus constitutes a "triumph of pure thinking," but the founder of critical philosophy did not admit it; more exactly, he did so only in part, in his brief but significant disquisition on the "Anticipations of Perception."[56] "Had the infinitesimal principle obtained the place it deserved in criticism," however, "sensibility would no longer have preceded thought; pure thought would not have been overshadowed in its autonomy."[57] The *Logic of Pure Cognition* might already have been devised.

That the "judgment of origin" determines a metaphysics as well as a theory of thinking was not lost on Cohen's most perspicacious contemporaries. In *Plato's Logic of Being*, which appeared in 1909, published in a series of "Philosophical Contributions" directed by Cohen and Natorp, Nicolai Hartmann lingered on the ways in which the theory of non-Being (*mē on*) developed in the *Sophist* had found a new echo in the neo-Kantian's doctrine of the infinite judgment. Having reconstructed Plato's account of "existing non-Being [*seiendes Nichtsein*] as the principle of the synthetic," Hartmann commented: "We have reached the exact sense of Cohen's 'judgment of origin' ... 'Origin' in the sense of generation must be that which is presupposed by all content, which it first renders possible. Considered in relation to determinate thought content, it must, therefore, signify a '*problem*'; and, in relation to Being, it must signify a *non-Being*. Insofar as it necessarily leads towards a being, and insofar as it necessarily leads to a solution, the origin, at the same time, is the principle of necessary original connection — that is, continuity. The Cohenian '*origin*' from the 'Nothing' is the steering back of Kant's '*synthetic unity*' towards Plato's *non-Being* (*mē on*)."[58]

Further from the Marburg School, Franz Rosenzweig would comment in 1921 on the new metaphysics that Cohen had drawn from mathematics. Millennia after Plato, after "a two thousand year movement completed its course," Cohen became the first to grasp "science" itself as the infinitesimal method, insisting upon the "perpetual derivation from a 'something' —and never more than a something, an anything—from the Nothing, and not from the empty Nothing in general, but always from 'its' Nothing, belonging precisely to this something: mathematics." He explains:

> Only Hermann Cohen discovered in mathematics an organon of thinking, precisely because mathematics does not produce its elements out of the empty Nothing of the one and universal zero, but out of the Nothing of the differential, a definite Nothing in each case related to the element it was seeking. The differential combines in itself the properties of the Nothing and of the Something; it is a Nothing that refers to a Something, to its Something, and at the same time a Something that still slumbers in the womb of the Nothing. It is, on the one hand, the quantity that is dissolved in that which is without quantity, and then, on the other hand, it has, as 'infinitesimal,' and by this right, all the properties of the finite quantity, with only one exception: precisely this property of the quantity. It is in this way that it draws its strength that founds reality, at one time from the powerful negation with which it breaks the womb of the Nothing, and yet then equally at another time from the calm affirmation of all that borders on the Nothing, to which it remains, in spite of all, itself bound as infinitesimal. It thus determines two paths that go from the Nothing to the Something, the path of the affirmation of that which is not Nothing, and the path of the negation of the Nothing.[59]

Cohen himself suggests that this metaphysics has its roots in physics, and, more exactly, that with which modern mathematical science begins. Mechanics is his preferred example. He asserts that, conceiving of rest and motion as absolutely opposing states, ancient physics reasoned in terms of "negation." Faced with the flying arrow that, in each moment, is immobile, Zeno concluded, correctly but in excessive haste: "The arrow does not move." In this judgment, the "not" is a particle of unqualified indicative denial; it translates the "absolute" *ou*. If one believes Cohen, the moderns, instead, reason with *mē*. Galileo sees that rest is merely the inception of movement. Even as the geometric line "springs" off the point, which is "non-extended," so motion originates in the "relative Nothing" that is "non-motion." "To the Greeks rest was merely the negation of motion," Bergman writes, rendering Cohen's position, "whereas for modern physics rest is not the negation of motion but the zero-point of motion, so that it is possible to think of rest also as a kind of motion and subsume both under one law. Rest is the 'beginning' of motion. . . . The judgment 'the arrow is not flying at one instant' was for Zeno a *negative* judgment, whereas it was for Galileo an *infinite* judgment that determined a continuous transition from motion to non-motion and *vice versa*."[60] "This origin does not hold only for the beginning of motion," Cohen specifies; "rather, *its every progress must always emerge from the same origin*."[61] Physical movement as such — in being and becoming — is subject to the principle of origination. And ever since Galileo "transformed the problem of Being into the problem of movement," thinking has had no other object. "The identity of thought and being could be designated as the *identity of thought and movement*."[62]

The judgment of origin is the foundation stone in the system of pure cognition. It furnishes its inventor with a means to approach the most varied of subjects from a new perspective. Six years after publishing his *Logic of Pure Cognition*, Cohen turns to the springboard principle to define the correct interpretation of the biblical description of God. To this end, he draws, as had Maimon before him, on the first book of Maimonides's *Guide of the Perplexed*. In an important essay, "Maimonides' Ethics," Cohen lingers on the very passage of the Judaeo-Arabic author that attracted Maimon's attention. Here Maimonides teaches that all the divine attributes of Hebrew Scripture are best understood as either attributes of divine action or as "negative attributes." When an attribute refers to divine essence, rather than action, it "signifies," Maimonides asserts, "the negation of the privation of the attribute in question." Without ever mentioning the post-Kantian Jewish philosopher who preceded him in commenting on the *Guide*, Cohen observes: "Here we have reached a point at which I pursue a basic idea of my own systematic logic."[63] Like Maimon, Cohen understands Maimonides's "negation of a privation" to illustrate the reasoning articulated in the form of the infinite judgment. The terms by which Cohen understands this judgment, however, are those of his doctrine of origin.

Cohen offers several examples. He argues that to state that "God is wise" is to express a wish to define the divine essence. Yet the "problem of the knowledge of God ought not be that of divine essence, but his meaning as an ethical model. On the other hand, if I say, 'God is non-ignorant' [or 'not ignorant', *nicht unwissend*], the judgment reaches its ground and the *origin* of this attribute; I affirm at once the *self-consciousness* and *providence* of God." So, too, the statement that God is "omnipotent" must be understood to mean: "He is 'non-powerless' [or 'not powerless,' *nicht unmächtig*]. This means that his existence suffices for bringing things other than himself to emergence. The attribute 'non-powerless' is the *origin* of beings other than him, while the attribute of *omnipotence* is absolutely inadequate to this meaning."[64] In other words, "the designation of the negative as *the negation of its privative*" signifies "the *infinite judgment as the judgment of origin*."[65]

The consonance and contrast between Maimon and Cohen is striking. For Maimon, the infinite judgment asserts the absence of a ground of determination in the subject, effecting the equivalent of an arithmetical zero in logic. That "God is non-powerless," in this sense, means that God is disjoined both from the predicate "powerful" and from its contrary, "powerless." For this reason, Maimon might add that the logical content of the sentence "God is non-powerless" is equivalent to that of its contrary: "God is powerless." In the absence of an a priori ground of determinability, subject and predicate remain absolutely disjoined, or, in Hegel's phrase, they "fall apart." For Cohen, by contrast, the infinite judgment asserts the pure "generation" of a thought content by the indefinite limitation of a predicate. Just as rest, grasped as "non-movement," is the source from which movement may be conceived, and just as the point, understood as "non-extended," is the source from which the line may be drawn out, so "non-powerless," in this sense, is the origin of all representable degrees of power. The judgment of origin sets zero and a range of finite values in a single thought continuity.

In his last major work, *Religion of Reason out of the Sources of Judaism* (1919), Cohen takes a further step. He argues that, correctly understood, the principle of origin offers the key to the understanding of what has long seemed, in religion, most foreign to reason: the doctrine of creation. Maimonides remains his crucial guide. It was he, the reader learns, who "corrected the expression 'negative attribute,'" by drawing on an ancient but little understood "variety of judgment": the seeming "play of the wit" that was once exploited, as "a hairsplitting distinction," by the lawyers, rhetoricians and sophists of antiquity who exploited an "intermediary concept between affirmation and negation." Maimonides recovered the judgment of privation, for which the "Greek language," Cohen adds, reserved a special "particle," *mē*, which distinguished it from mere negation. Later, in the passage of Greek to Latin, that particle would be "darkened" into the Roman *non*; then privation and negation would no longer clearly be told apart.[66] Yet Maimonides, after a long period of obscurity, dispelled this logical confusion. He became "a classic of rationalism in the monotheistic tradition most decisively, perhaps, through his interpretation of the crucial problem of negative attributes. He elucidates the traditional problem of negative attributes through the *connection of negation and privation*. It is not the positive attributes that are negated but those of privation."[67]

Cohen proposes an example to illustrate the philosophical teachings of Maimonides. It is an odd sentence: "God is non-inert [or "not inert," *nicht träge*]." This statement would seem to do no more than to deny inertness of God. Cohen, however, adds: "The deeper meaning of this figure lies not only in the warding off and exclusion of inertness from God but in basing this exclusion on a new and genuine positivity [*Positivität*] and, hence, entirely rooting out negation. This new positivity has been discovered and determined in the concept of the *principle of origin*, which has been distinguished as a category in my *Logic of Pure Cognition*."[68] Properly understood, in other words, "God is non-inert" means: God "is the *origin of activity*," even as inertia itself is, after Galileo, the origin of motion.[69] The Scriptural doctrine of creation thus shows its hidden rationality. "In this logic, the religion of creation itself has become reason. That God is non-inert means: God is the primal ground of activity; God is the Creator. His being cannot be determined except through this immanence of creation in its *uniqueness*. Creation is not a heterogeneous concept in — or in addition to — his Being but, rather, his Being as uniqueness means precisely this: that becoming is conceived together with him, proceeds out of him, and must be derived from his concept."[70] Émile Bréhier long ago drew the conclusion to which this argument leads. "To conceive of God is precisely to conceive of Being beyond experience and as the origin of experience."[71]

The "new and genuine positivity" of the origin matters also for ethics. After Kant, but also Fichte, Cohen strives in the second part of his "system of philosophy," *Ethics of the Pure Will* (1904), to account for the principle of the moral subject, both in its self-determination and in relation to other selves. He recalls that in his *Doctrine of Science*, Fichte posited the *I*, grasped as a self-consciousness, in relation to the *non-I*. Cohen alleges that this *non-I* is radically indistinct. Indeterminate with respect to the difference between human and non-human, it "is the thing, the object as such; every objectivity whatsoever."[72] Such a stark opposition, however, leaves a fundamental question in ethics unanswered: *"What does the opposition of I and non-I mean for the theory of morals?"*[73] Seeking to define the exact relation in which *I* and *non-I* stand for ethics, Cohen evokes the "first law of thinking" of his *Logic*, declaring: "It is a question of an *infinite judgment*. This, however, is a judgment of *origin*." "In the detour through the Nothing, a new Something" is now to be found. Cohen locates the origin of the *I* in the *non-I*, grasped not as an indeterminate "correlate of thing and matter," but, according to the "Greek particle *mē*," as the springboard from which the *I* comes to be.[74] He proceeds to argue that such a *non-I* is not identifiable with human beings as a "plurality" (*Mehrheit*); the *non-I* is, in each case, a "second human being," that is, the "neighbor" (*Nebenmensch*). More precisely, he is "the Other" (*der Anderer*). But "the Other is not an Other; he stands in a precise correlation, better, in a relation of continuity to the *I*. The Other, the alter ego, is the origin of the I."[75]

Amos Funkenstein has argued persuasively that the progress of reason itself, for Cohen, also exhibits this logic of origin. The "principle of the infinitesimal method," while itself an historical invention, is a key to the unfolding of knowledge. In the development of science, two sensible phenomena seem initially to be "facts," when grasped in their apparent opposition; as their relation becomes the object of cognition, they become "problems." The negativity that opposes them is then "qualified." Thinking rises to a further stage, at which "only a richer structure than a mere contradiction can link them: non-*P* is converted into a genuine non-*P*, say rest as the negation of motion into the genuine privation of motion — the instantaneous motion, the 'beginning' of motion. The reason for both *P* and non-*P* is now expressed in the generating principle of both *P* and non-*P*, of affirmation and privation, as constituting correlative elements of a continuum."[76] As the empirical becomes the object of cognition, thinking grasps an opposition as nothing but the result of a process of "generation." Knowledge purifies itself, as contradiction is resolved into logical continuity. Even as *P* and *non-P* come to be linked by the principle of continuity, what once seemed a mere "given" (*Gegebene*) appears in a new light. It becomes a "task" (*Aufgabe*) for thinking. Following Kant, Cohen maintains this task is infinite, being susceptible only to an endless approximation. In science, as in philosophy, "no system is closed. New tasks grow out of new solutions. But the new tasks must also grow into old solutions. The system demands this, too."[77] Properly grasped, the *factum* of science remains in each case a *fieri*.

Cohen's use of the "principle of the infinitesimal method" to found his system of philosophy raises several questions. The most obvious today concern the idea of the "infinitesimal" itself. Early readers of Cohen's study of the history of the calculus observed that it bears crucially on the idea of the "infinitesimal" quantity, which appears in it as the proof of the modern mathematical domination of the infinite. Yet by the end of the nineteenth century, the idea of the infinitesimal had become obsolete. As Bertrand Russell wrote in his 1901 *Principles of Mathematics*, proposing a discussion of Cohen's book that was both sensitive to its "historical excellence" and unsparing of its "very important mathematical errors," the modern definition of the differential and integral calculus "nowhere involves the infinitesimal," a "mathematically useless" idea.[78] "It is the doctrine of limits that underlies the calculus, and not any pretended use of the infinitesimal."[79] "The limit does not belong to the series which it limits; and in the definition of the derivative and the definite integral calculus we have merely another instance of this fact. The so-called infinitesimal calculus, therefore, has nothing to do with the infinitesimal, and has only indirectly to do with the infinite — its connection with the infinite being that it involves limits, and only infinite series of limits."[80] John Grier Hibben, one of the early reviewers of Cohen's *Logic*, drew a severe consequence from these facts: "The infinitesimal as the *Ursprung* of all reality is a conception which has no place in modern mathematics. But this conception is the foundation of the so-called system of pure thought. That system, therefore, cannot stand."[81]

However one understands its models in early modern mathematics, the principle of the origin possesses a logical status in Cohen's system of philosophy that is also questionable in itself. "At the ground" of logic, it supports the categories and concepts of cognition. Yet as a principle, it

THE SPRINGBOARD PRINCIPLE

would also seem to elude the process of generation that it enables. Funken-stein has pointed out that the origin may not "itself be a category — let alone a concept. If it were a concept or even a concept of concepts, it would lead us straight into the paradoxes of self-reference, and invite its own abrogation. For if the principle of origin is a concept, we may just as well ask for *its* beginning. Does the concept of continuity between concepts emerge out of its opposite, the concept of discontinuity, and can both be linked by a different continuity?"[82] Although he never confronts such paradoxes directly, Cohen effectively avoids them by a single decision. He withdraws the principle of origin from that which it conditions, making of the *Ursprung* an ultimate ground. Yet this abstraction comes at a price. Even as he purifies thinking of the sensible "datum," Cohen must admit a new "given," which is at least as enigmatic as the intuition from which Kant began his Transcendental Aesthetic. Cohen implicitly stipulates that, to ground cognition, there must be an "origin." His system bespeaks an immemorial beginning: an inception that precedes even pure cognition, remaining essentially unfathomable by it.

Such an inception may well be named, but it can scarcely be conceived. Its unmarked logical position in Cohen's system, however, is discernible. Its place is that of "the Nothing" and its equivocations. According to the springboard principle, thinking, in its origin, leaps toward the Something from the Nothing — but solely, as Cohen always adds, on one condition: that the Nothing that is at issue be "relative." Yet what exactly is such a thing? "Nothing" would seem, by definition, to be lacking in all properties, for, once qualified and positively defined, it becomes "something." Yet in several ways and formulations, Cohen insists that the Nothing from which thinking departs be qualified. It must be specified — and therefore more, and also less, than simply "nothing." Only then can thinking avoid the sterility of the *ex nihilo*, acceding to the productivity of a recoiling motion *ab nihilo*. To be "veritable," the origin must begin in a Nothing that is only "apparent": "The Something must be led out of the apparent Nothing [*scheinbaren Nichts*], to receive a veritable origin [*wahrhaftigen Ursprung*]."[83] In the logic of the origin, the Nothing must therefore be represented as "a station on the way" toward the Something, its "relative" negativity being the "operational means" (*Operationsmittel*) of generation.[84] "For the discovery of the origin, we need the Nothing," Cohen writes, adding: "at least as a means. It was no absolute Nothing, but rather a relative one, directed towards a determinate way of discovery. It was an *Original-Something* [*Ursprungs-Etwas*]."[85]

Systematically, Cohen distinguishes the "Original-Something," in this sense, from the "absolute Nothing" of pure contradiction. He calls the "Original-Something" the "Original-Nothing" (*Ursprungs-Nichts*), an expression by which the Nothing is literally qualified as a particular variety of non-Being. In his *Logic*, Cohen presents "Absolute Nothing," by contrast, as the Nothing of logical "negation" (*Verneinung*). He assigns to this type of statement a markedly affirmative function in his doctrine. He presents negation as the crucial means for the "securing of identity." "Between an *A* and a non-identical *A*, there is no reconciliation for thinking. This must be annihilated in the Nothing, or rather the Not, such that a judgment becomes achievable in its content."[86] Such a "Nothing" is, therefore, but the confirmation of identity. The law that states that "A cannot be A and be non-A at once" is the same supreme law that affirms that "A is A," and "non-A is non-A." In guaranteeing self-identity by forbidding its infraction, this Nothing, Cohen writes, "is therefore of an entirely different kind [*von einem ganz anderer Art*] than the Nothing that is the source of the Something."[87]

Such terms raise problems of an almost intractable philosophical difficulty. They were never as acutely evoked as in an article on Cohen's *Logic* that Natorp drafted but dared, in deference to his teacher, not publish. Commenting on Cohen's claim that "the origin of the Something" lies in "the Nothing," Natorp remarks: "Here everyone will stop short. Cohen himself stops short: 'The old dictum warns us: Nothing comes from nothing (*ex nihilo*). Perhaps, however, *off* nothing (*ab nihilo*).'" In his remarks, Natorp seeks to reconstruct the reasoning that supports these terse pronouncements. Beyond the Nothing from which nothing comes, for Cohen, "there is to be, then, a non-real Nothing. It is called an 'apparent Nothing,' the 'so-called Nothing,' which is not to be understood as such (but then why it is it so-called?), the 'relative Nothing,' indeed, the Origin-Something." In bewilderment, Natorp poses the crucial question: "What is this Nothing, which is rather a Something — and yet which ought not to be a Something, so that Something can first proceed from it?"[88] Cohen suggests, in effect, the most perplexing of logical and metaphysical theses: that there exists, first, a set of "kinds" of Nothings, and that, second, not every Nothing belongs to it, since there is at least one Nothing that is "of an entirely different kind" from another. Thus Cohen argues both that the origin of the Something is in the Nothing, and that such a Nothing — grasped also as an "Origin-Nothing" or "Origin-Something" — is not the "Nothing" of negation.

In his article, and later in his *Logical Foundations of the Exact Sciences*, Natorp proposes two resolutions to this Cohenian predicament. The first would be to understand the "Original-Nothing" as shorthand for an axiom: there must be an absolutely "first principle of thinking." For Natorp, Cohen would then argue, following Plato, that "one must go back behind *every* determinate positing of an *A*," to reach a "presuppositionless inception (origin)" — that is, the "original law of thinking itself (*autos ho logos*)."[89] Natorp foresees, however, that such a solution would fail to satisfy the author of the *Logic of Pure Cognition*. Cohen strives in his logic of the origin to account for "something more determinate" than the first law of thinking: namely, its "first particular formation" in the generation of the Something. Natorp's second solution is to treat the positing of an "Original-Nothing" as condensing a different axiom: that "every positing of a determinate content (A) be related to the *point in thought* [*Denkpunkt*] *that is not yet posited*." This is the solution that Natorp himself appears to affirm. The Nothing would then constitute "the precise qualitative counterpart to the zero in quantity, which is also not absolutely nothing (although *not yet a quantity*)," and with respect to which all positive and negative quantities may be reckoned. "A Something is, therefore, to be posited in thinking in an original fashion, in relation to its thought non-being (non-being posited), and this means: It is originally posited."[90] Yet Cohen, as Natorp well knows, must argue that, "in this qualitative null-positing [*Nullsetzung*]," "not absolutely nothing is posited." For there is a "direction" to be indicated: "The *direction* towards the Something, just as in zero, the direction of $\pm$ is to be thought, without a determinate value's being posited in one direction or the other."[91]

The truth is that the confusion of nothings is ineradicable in Cohen's *Logic*. It follows from the force with which the philosopher sets out to respond to two fundamental imperatives. The first is that thinking, "at the ground of logic," begin from nothing. The second is that, in so doing, thinking lead to something. In striving to remain faithful to these commands, Cohen pays homage to both, before betraying the first to fulfill the second. The *Logic of Pure Cognition* thus summons a sovereign principle and strips it of its absoluteness at once. The logico-metaphysical act can be simply stated. Even as the treatise calls to mind Nothing, in its difference from the Something, it surreptitiously transforms Nothing into *a* Nothing: the "Nothing-Something." Or, to put matters differently, to avoid confronting a "Nothing" that would be merely nothing and that would therefore be lacking all "relativity," Cohen disguises the "Something" as a "Nothing-Something," presenting the former as that which was once generated by the latter. Reaching methodically beyond the "given," the neo-Kantian philosophy appears to depose ontology in its historical role as "first philosophy"; in its place, it seems to found a new "me-ontology," "otherwise than being."[92] Yet the destitution, for this reason, is only apparent. In Cohen's system, the Something must always be slumbering "in the womb of the Nothing," as Rosenzweig saw, for without that "slumber" and without that "womb," thinking would be sterile: Nothing would come of Nothing, and science would be groundless.

Precisely to secure the origin, Cohen must therefore begin before it. The real but unavowed point from which he sets forth is no "pure" inception. Before thinking ventures out on its adventure, journeying toward the beginning of cognition, an unthinkable act of division and distinction has already occurred. "The" Nothing has been partitioned, and one nullity, qualified and relativized, has been distinguished from another, such that it can be represented as such. The fact of science is to stand on this specified — if not specious — foundation. In this sense, too, the "null-positing" of Cohen's logic of the origin recalls that of the "quantitative" nothing of arithmetic. Prior to "the Something" and its algebraic symbol as a "determinable x," another cipher is required. Zero is demanded; yet it must lend itself to serving two functions, which are not only distinct but also incommensurable. This cipher must signify pure "Nothing"; but it must also mark the place between the minus and the plus of quantities, representing "the direction of $\pm$" and so becoming a "station" on the line leading to the calculable realities of modern science.[93] Zero must be, in Natorp's terms, "not a quantity" and also "not *yet* a quantity." In short, "not" must mean "not yet." Only then can thinking depart on its odyssey in pure logic, renouncing the evidence of the Something for the obscurity of the Nothing, in tacit certainty of being guided along by the "secure star" of continuity.[94] The path of thinking is that of a voyage solely if it can be traveled back.

In this adventure in logic and metaphysics, thought is anticipated by language and by languages. The equivocations of the Nothing are mirrored in those of its spoken signs, and the most perilous of reflections lie on the surface of the simplest of German particles. Everything starts, in one sense, with the glossing of a single word: *nicht*, translatable as "not" or "non-." Even as the *Logic of Pure Cognition* sets forth its principles of epistemology and metaphysics, it continues also to issue this minimal grammatical demand: that *nicht* not be univocal, that "not" and "non-" not be synonymous. Negation and privation, contradiction and origin, Cohen stipulates, must not be confused, even — or especially — where speech suggests that they are one. Positively stated, there must be two *nots*, or a "not" and a "non- ," as in the contrasting words that Cohen summons from the grammars of ancient Greek: *ou* and *mē*. Yet Cohen also requires that these old words partake of some common "negativity," in language and in thought; otherwise one cannot be the species of the other, the "relative" or "qualified" determination of what might also be taken to be absolute. Inevitably, although unwillingly and perhaps unwitting, Cohen therefore presupposes the very possibility that he most insistently seeks to exclude: that of a commonality among "Nothings," a secret synonymy of "not" and "non-." How might one define it? Whatever could bind one zero to another? The unity of one non-Being and another — supposing, as Cohen does, that non-Beings are in truth only two in number — seems a "problem" no less intractable than the origin.

One may go further. It may be that these problems are entwined. The *not* and the *non-*, in their grammatical discernibility and indiscernibility, also bear witness to a source from which cognition springs. One may call this source the grammatical capacity, or the faculty of speech. Were there no languages, were it not possible to speak by means of "not" and "non-," and to distinguish these two operations, grasping them as the species of a genus of "negation," the source of thought, as Cohen presents it, would be unreachable because inconceivable. Before bearing on the varieties of sentences, logic draws on a *logos* that is articulated in grammar and in grammars. Such words and word-parts as *ou* and *mē*, *nicht* and *nicht-*, "not," "not-" and "non-," furnish a hidden point of inception for the theory of the Cohenian "origin." Their equivocations are also fertile for thinking, albeit in a manner distinct from the "generating" that, in Cohen's system, characterizes the progressive unfolding of scientific knowledge. One might wager that the first productivity is older than the second; yet any simple order of precedence, in this field, would be difficult to maintain. The facts of grammars become audible in being conceived; they are perceptible only by means of constructions, which articulate some knowledge. At one with thinking, while being distinct from it, older than reflection, but expressible solely by means of it, the fact of language and languages is implicit in the "fact of science," in which it comes to light.[95] To have rendered this interlacing discernible, in its productivity and in its perils, is not the least of the achievements of Cohen's *Logic*, the first and last to make of the infinite judgment the springing start of thought.

CHAPTER FOURTEEN

After the Judgment

From Aristotle to Kant and from Hegel to Cohen, language becomes the object of logic on a single condition: that it be either true or false. Speech that is expressive without laying claim to correspond with any ascertainable reality, that signifies without denoting what there is, or that sways its listener but does no more, is therefore traditionally excluded from the domain of logic. Aristotle assigns such language to the domains of "poetics and rhetoric."[1] Yet, with Aristotle, philosophy does more than accord a privilege to true speech. It also resolves to find it in a single syntactic pattern. *On Interpretation* teaches that the first place of truth is the assertion. This thesis was often to remain unquestioned in philosophy, but it is contestable. What of the truth of naming, of the exclamation, and of the question? In becoming the doctrine of "apophantic" sentences, classical philosophical logic effectively avoids such questions, or presupposes that they may be easily answered. Since, moreover, Aristotle defines "statement-making sentences" as "stating one thing concerning another," specifying the relation between substances and their properties, the varieties of attribution are what have most attracted philosophical attention. Such concepts as subject and predicate, the operations of conjunction, disjunction, and implication, the quantities by which terms are called singular, particular, or universal, copulae such as "is," "applies" and "belongs to," fall within the domain of this "term logic," as it is often called today. So, too, do the relations of implication and inference that hold between the sentences that individual terms compose.

The discussion of infinite names and indefinite particles also belongs to this delimited field of inquiry. In the history of philosophy, such words and word-fragments as *non-* and *not* become problems in themselves above all within the investigation into the truth and types of predicative statements. Neither Aristotle nor his late antique commentators, neither the medieval theorists of the universal nor the early modern thinkers of the "supertranscendental" properties, set out to reason the meanings of such words as *ou*, *ghayr*, or *non* as such, considering all their known uses in languages; nor did they aim to define such variously "negative" syntactic elements in some artificial logical idiom that they would construct and regiment. The philosophers started, rather, with a syntactic form that their languages furnished them. They began with the "statement-making sentence" and proceeded to investigate its forms and characteristics. Orienting their reflections with respect to the predicative assertion, they parsed the various ways in which a property may be stated of a subject, according to a set of categories, from substance and accident to quantity, quality, and relation, and many more. When examining such words as "not" and "non-," these thinkers therefore restricted their inquiries, as a rule, to the study of assertions and denials. In the same way, albeit in different terms and for new systematic purposes, Kant and the post-Kantians, from Maimon to Cohen, aimed in their transcendental logics to set out the ways in which types of judgment, in their content and their form, define the nature of pure reason. They considered the functions of "not" and "non-" above all as they pertain to the varieties of predicative determination. When they encountered infinite naming, it was in the shadow of the doctrine of predication.

All this changed in the twentieth century. The age in which Antonin Artaud issued the imperative "to have done with the judgment of God" was also the one in which philosophers sought, in often opposing ways, to "have done" with the form of the predicative judgment. The belonging of properties, the determination of subjects, the operations of synthesis and opposition, assertion and denial, were all to be reconceived. Despite their diversity, however, the most innovative undertakings of the first half of the twentieth century would accord in insisting on a single theoretical necessity: that the "statement-making sentence" be deposed of its sovereign status. The predicative assertion would be variously relativized and reinterpreted, dismantled and subordinated to more fundamental forms of discourse. Within a few years of the period in which Cohen began his system of philosophy, seeking to found logic and metaphysics on the "judgment of origin," the accepted grounds of such a transcendental inquiry into the laws of thinking would begin to give way. The self-evidence of judgment as the model of true speech and thought would be profoundly and irrevocably shaken.

This shift may be attributed to several currents in philosophy. The first can be dated to the last quarter of the nineteenth century. It is then that philosophers begin to loosen logic, as an art of reasoning, from "natural language," understood as a system defined by rules that are unconsciously acquired by speakers. The relations of logic, of course, had long been articulated in a symbolic notation, which could be apparently foreign to that of ordinary speech. Aiming to clarify the relations between the terms of the statement, Aristotle already employed individual Greek letters in place of definite subjects and predicates. Presenting the first two of his syllogistic figures, which would be known to the tradition as *Barbara* and *Celarent*, he explained: "If *A* is predicated of every *B*, and *B* of every *C*, then *A* must be predicated of every *C*.... Similarly, also, if *A* is predicated of no *B*, and *B* is predicated of every *C*, then it is necessary that *A* will belong to no *B*."[2] Alexander of Aphrodisias commented on the reasons for this expedient: "Just as a geometer will construct a diagram for the sake of clarity in his exposition," a logician will use alphabetic signs in place of words.[3] Schematic representation was to have a long history in philosophical logic. As examples, it suffices to think of the classical use of the square of opposition, which rests on the substitution of sentences by single letters, or Ramon Lull's project for a "combinatory art" of thinking, or, still later, Leibniz's ambitious "universal characteristic."

At the end of the nineteenth century, however, a different step is taken. Frege, Peano, and Peirce lay the foundations for new symbolic notations in mathematics. They are not only "formal," as was traditional logic. They aim, rather, to be "formalistic," constituting a code of writing in which the sense of every expression is determinable on the basis of its form.[4] The principal element in these new notations is not the term or concept but the proposition, taken as a unity and inserted in a chain of implication. Whereas Scholastic logic considered terms in their relations, such that they compose statements, linked among themselves in a syllogism, mathematical logic, beginning with Frege, bears on the implications of propositions, containing "bound variables," functions and connectives or operators. Quantity is reconceived. Aristotelian logic had distinguished "universal" and "particular" propositions according to the differing nature of their subjects: in the assertions "All men are mortal" and "Some men are mortal," it had been taught, the predicate remains the same, while the two subjects differ, "all men" being universal, "some men" "particular."[5] In the logics that develop from Frege and Peirce's inventions, the unity of those old subjects is broken. Concept and quantity are rigorously distinguished.[6] In the customary modern logical analysis of statements such as "All men are mortal" and "Some men are mortal," the concept "man" will be considered to be invariant; quantity alone will be thought to differ. "All men are mortal" will be written as the stipulation that "If x is a man, $f(x)$, for all values of x," where f denotes the function "being mortal." "Some men are mortal" will be represented according to a similar form: "There is at least one x, such that, if x is a man, $f(x)$." In each case, the meaning of the variable (x) is "bound" to a certain quantity, which every proposition must first define. The algebraic x of such logic holds solely for "as much" of it as there is.[7]

A great novelty is contained in the quantificational structure of such notations. In Frege's algebra of thinking, as in Peirce's roughly contemporaneous "existential graphs," the distinction between subject and predicate is dissolved. As early as 1879, publishing his epoch-making *Begriffsschrift*, or *Conceptual Notation: A Formula Language of Pure Thought*, Frege draws this line of demarcation between the syntax of his symbolism and a language such as German. Presenting his "concept-script" to the public, Frege recalls that, "in my first draft of a formal language, I was misled by the example of language into forming judgments by combining subject and predicate. I soon became convinced, however, that this was an obstacle to my special goal and led only to useless prolixity."[8] Now he resolves to distinguish his "formula language" from ordinary speech in this respect. "Up till now," he writes, "logic has always confined itself too closely to language and grammar." Their ways are to be distinguished: "A distinction between *subject and predicate* does *not occur* in my way of representing a judgment."[9] In releasing "pure thought" from its longstanding "confinement" by language, Frege accords special importance to this seeming detail: "In particular, I believe that the replacement of the concepts *subject* and *predicate* by *argument* and *function* will prove itself in the long run."[10] In later writings, Frege restates his thesis more forcefully. "We can see that the grammatical categories of subject and predicate can have no significance for logic," he writes in his 1897 *Logic*, adding, a few pages later: "We shall completely avoid the expressions 'subject' and 'predicate,' of which logicians are so fond."[11] In his 1891 "Comments on Sense and Reference," he goes even further: "It would be best to banish the words 'subject' and 'predicate' from logic altogether."[12]

The consequences of this decision are philosophical as well as technical. In 1879, Frege already draws out the first among them. Differences of grammar will now not be viewed as being pertinent to logic, except where their variation entails a distinction among the consequences derivable from propositions. The opposition between active and passive voice, for example, while crucial to the traditional analysis of languages, is of no importance to this new logic. From the "two propositions, 'At Platea the Greeks defeated the Persians,' and 'At Platea the Persians were defeated by the Greeks,'" the same facts are deducible; the two propositions may therefore be taken to be synonymous.[13]

In the old logic, the presence or absence of a sign of "negation" (*Verneinung*) marked the difference between two qualities of judgments: the affirmative and the negative. In the conceptual notation that Frege introduces, there is no place for such distinctions. "In an indirect proof we say, 'Suppose that the line segments AB and CD were not equal.' Here the content — that line segments AB and CD are not equal — contains a negation." "Judgment," however, is distinct from such "content," being no more than the assertion that a given content is true. "Negation," consequently, emerges as "a characteristic of the *assertible content* [*beurtheilbarer Inhalt*]," rather than of judgment, which is invariant. Frege states this thesis more than once. Judgment is but "assertion," the stating that a certain proposition is true.[14] Similarly, Frege avows, "the distinction of categorical, hypothetical and disjunctive judgments appears to me to have solely a grammatical significance."[15] In systematically setting the quantificational syntax of his "formula language" in place of the predicative syntax of natural language, Frege departs decisively from Aristotle. His *Conceptual Notation* becomes "the antithesis of *On Interpretation*," in Claude Imbert's words, "and the first alternative that put an end to the absoluteness of natural language."[16]

Yet even as he proposes the notation that he has "constructed in imitation of arithmetic," Frege remains faithful to one principle that is central to the Kantian tradition. After the "banishment" of subject and predicate, logic continues to be, in his eyes, a doctrine of judgment. His "perfect symbolic language [*vollkommene Zeichensprache*]" is crafted to enable the unequivocal recording of "assertions," which are to appear in distinction from "assertible" contents. To tell these two logical entities apart, Frege employs a special symbol. He calls it the "judgment stroke" (*Urteilsstrich*), or "assertion stroke," as it is better known today. It is to be written, before a propositional content, as $\vdash$. The horizontal line signifies that the successive content has been combined into a unity; the vertical line indicates that it has been asserted. The *Begriffsschrift* opens by specifying the meaning and function of this sign. Whenever the "assertion stroke" is lacking before a proposition, the reader learns, some content of judgment has been entertained, but not asserted, as when one seeks to "derive some conclusions from it and to test the correctness of the thought."[17] In 1906, long after the publication of his *Conceptual Notation*, having renounced much of its detail and forsworn parts of his mature work, Frege continues to insist upon the necessity of this symbol in logic. In a posthumously published fragment, "What May I Regard as the Results of My Work?" he writes, "It is almost all the *Conceptual Notation*," before adding, a few lines later, after a pause: "Strictly I should have begun by mentioning the judgment-stroke, the dissociation of assertoric force from the predicate...."[18]

Frege's assertion sign was long taken as a troublesome element in his notation. In 1895, Peano reviewed Frege's *Basic Laws of Arithmetic*, which also employed this sign, and remarked: "I fail to see the purpose of such conventions, which have nothing corresponding to them in my *Formulaire*."[19] In his 1921 *Tractatus Logico-Philosophicus*, Wittgenstein went further, singling out the "assertion stroke" as the symptom of theoretical confusion. "Frege's assertion sign $\vdash$," he wrote, in an extended parenthetical remark, "is logically altogether meaningless; in Frege (and Russell) it only shows that these authors hold as true the propositions marked in this way. $\vdash$ belongs therefore to the propositions no more than does the

number of the proposition. A proposition cannot possibly assert of itself that it is true."[20] Wittgenstein's note is of more than incidental significance to his *Tractatus*. Pronouncing the assertion sign to be "absolutely meaningless," Wittgenstein rejects the transcendental inheritance that Frege implicitly retains. In place of "judgments," Wittgenstein sets logical entities of another nature: "propositions" or "sentences" (*Sätze*). In their "totality," they "compose language" (*Sprache*).[21] This is a "language" that, to paraphrase Wittgenstein, "takes care of itself"; its validity cannot be assured by symbols such as those meant to distinguish "assertible" content from "assertions."[22] The "judging" of propositions appears as philosophically illegitimate. In the sharply delimited world of the *Tractatus*, there is no one left to make assertions. "The thinking, representing subject does not exist."[23] This is but one consequence of Wittgenstein's "fundamental thought" that "logical constants do not represent."[24] "That which mirrors itself in language, language cannot present [*Was sich in der Sprache spiegelt, kann sie nicht darstellen*]."[25]

The path on which Wittgenstein set out from Frege's "formula language" was unique. Yet in the same years in which he worked on his *Tractatus* and the projects that followed it, others aimed to develop philosophy by means of mathematical logic. They, too, would insist on the distance between the syntax of formalistic notations and the grammar of natural languages.[26] Various possibilities were to be explored. One was that of precisely regimented symbolic notations in mathematics, which promised unexpected resolutions to problems long viewed as crucial and intractable. Hilbert's program of a logical foundation of mathematics constitutes one example. Tarski furnishes another in a famous essay in which he contrasts the syntax of natural languages with that of artificially constructed "formalized languages." In his 1931 work, "The Concept of Truth in Formalized Languages," Tarski seeks to demonstrate that it is possible to offer a "materially adequate and formally correct definition of the term 'true sentence.'" Yet he holds that to do so, one must set "colloquial language" — that is, natural language — aside.[27] "With respect to this language," Tarski warns his readers at the outset of his essay, it is strictly speaking impossible to provide a definition of truth. The possibility of even "the consistent use of this concept in conformity with the laws of logic" appears to be excluded.[28]

Russell, the first to hail Frege's advances in the philosophy of mathematics, embarked upon a different path in philosophy. In his 1914 lecture, "Logic as the Essence of Philosophy," he drew a sharp line between the "old" and "ordinary" logic and Frege's, known as "logistic or mathematical logic."[29] Conceding that "mathematical logic is not *directly* of philosophical importance, except in its first beginnings," Russell maintains there that "logistic" may nonetheless be a model to philosophy. In itself, it suffices to dispel old errors and to announce a bright future. The fact that modern logic accords no special importance to the relation of subject and predicate appears to Russell to be one of its major advantages. "The belief or unconscious conviction that all propositions are of the subject-predicate form — in other words that every fact consists in some thing having some quality — has rendered most philosophers incapable of giving any account of the world of science and daily life."[30] Attention to the syntax of the "new logic," Russell promises, will lead to conclusive "results," "which must command the assent of all those who are competent to form an opinion." Hence his conclusion: "The old logic put thought in fetters, while the new logic gives it wings."[31] Russell takes Frege's quantificational notation to provide a new ideal of clarity and exactitude, which will guide philosophy toward the solution of its old "problems."

Carnap derived the formal dimension of his positivist project from this vision. In a programmatic statement on the emergence of mathematical "logistic" published in 1930–1931, he writes: "The creation of a new and efficient instrument in the place of the old and useless one took a long time."[32] Once available, "logistic," the reader learns, supplants more than old logic; the entire history of philosophy of which the logic was one branch now shows itself to be obsolete. "Before the inexorable judgment of the new logic, all philosophy in the old sense, whether it is connected with Plato, Thomas Aquinas, Kant, Schelling, or Hegel, or whether it constructs a new 'metaphysic of Being' or a 'philosophy of spirit,' proves itself to be not merely materially false, as earlier critics maintained, but logically untenable and therefore meaningless."[33] Emancipated from the constraints of natural language, the new logic is to become the crucial instrument of a unified field of knowledge, purged of the illusions spawned by an inadequate analysis of the idiom of empirical science. "With the aid of the rigorous methods

of the new logic, we can treat science to a thoroughgoing process of decontamination [*eine gründliche Reinigung der Wissenschaft*]. Every sentence of science must be proved to be meaningful by logical analysis."[34]

In the same years in which some philosophers looked to modern logic as to the source of a philosophy "uncontaminated" by natural language, a different current in twentieth-century thought, however, was also underway. It led not beyond the predicative assertion of the tradition, toward a logical syntax of a more supple and powerful form, but, so to speak, beneath it, bringing to light a prelogical foundation of which thinking had lost sight. "Phenomenology" was its watchword, "Back to things themselves!" its battle cry. It dates to the first years of the century, when Husserl developed his new "method and attitude" in philosophy. Husserl aimed, as did the neo-Kantians, to "clarify the essence of knowledge and known objectivity," conceding nothing to psychology.[35] Yet Husserl's point of departure was one that no member of the School of Marburg would grant. His philosophical project was to begin with the "absolute givenness" of experience in consciousness.[36] By a description of the "natural attitude" of the mind in its intuitions, Husserl's phenomenology sought to secure the foundations of cognition. Logic was then to appear in a new light. In becoming the doctrine of "pure intuitions," phenomenology aimed to reach the ground of all "matters of fact," before their predicative determinations. "Any possible object — logically speaking, 'any subject of possible true predications,'" Husserl explains in his 1913 *Ideas Pertaining to a Pure Phenomenology*, "has, prior to all predicative thinking, precisely *its* modes of becoming the object of an objectivating, an intuiting regard which perhaps reaches it in its 'personal selfhood,' which 'seizes upon' it."[37] It is these "modes" that Husserl set out to define.

"Negation" (*Negation*) constitutes a telling illustration of this principle. Husserl argues that, as a judgment, negation is phenomenologically derivable from "intentive mental processes": "perceiving or some other simply positing objectivating."[38] "Every denial [*Verneinung*] is a denial of something," he explains, "and this something refers us back to some belief-modality or other." In its intentional structure, negation may therefore be defined as "the 'modification' of some 'position' or other'; that does not signify an affirmation but instead a 'positing' in the extended sense of some belief-modality or other." Negation effects the "'*crossing out*' [*Durchstreichung*] of the corresponding posited characteristic," and "its specific correlate is the cancellation-characteristic, the characteristic of '*not*' or '*non-*' [*nicht*]. The line of negation goes through something positional, more concretely stated, through a '*positum*' and, more particularly, by virtue of the cancellation of specific *positum-characteristic*, i.e., of its being-modality."[39] In *Experience and Judgment* (1939), Husserl refines this thesis. The "negation" familiar to the tradition now appears as rooted in a "modification of consciousness," in which such phenomena as disappointment, frustration, and repression all play roles. Before the logical denial of the attribute, there lies, therefore, an "original negation," a "crossing out" that affects the mind's horizons of expectation. "It is thus shown," Husserl concludes, "that *negation is not first of all a matter of predicative judgment, but, rather, that in its original shape it is present in the pre-predicative sphere of receptive experience.*"[40]

The early Heidegger would follow in Husserl's steps, seeking to derive the possibility of predicative determinations from pre-predicative experience. Yet Heidegger's confrontation with traditional logic was to be unprecedentedly radical and far-reaching. It emerges slowly in his work. His 1914 dissertation, *The Theory of Judgment in Psychologism*, sets itself the task of defining the object of philosophical — that is, non-formalized — logic. On the first page of the introduction to his study, Heidegger situates his project with respect to the conflict between the psychological and the transcendental readings of the *Critique of Pure Reason*. Heidegger pledges unwavering allegiance to the Marburgers: "Today," he writes, the dispute "may be considered to have been resolved by the transcendental-logical understanding that has been represented since the 1870s by Hermann Cohen and his school."[41] Yet Heidegger also credits Husserl with having "broken the psychological spell," "clarifying logic and its tasks."[42] In this period, Heidegger declares that logic is "the field that most interests me."[43]

Little more than a decade later, he announces a decidedly different project. Posing "the question of the sense of Being" in *Being and Time*, he judges the discipline of logic to be inadequate to the question that it involves. Unable to clarify the "is" that links subject and predicate, logic cannot explain itself. "We always move within an antecedent understanding of Being," we read in the introduction to this book, which appears in 1927. "We do not *know* what Being means. But already when we ask: 'What is 'Being,' we keep within an understanding of the 'is,' although we are unable to fix conceptually what 'is' signifies. But this average understanding of Being is still a fact."[44] Heidegger strives to bring this phenomenological "fact" of this understanding to light through an analysis of the hermeneutic structure of Dasein, the being that we are. "Traditional logic [*überlieferte Logik*]," he states in his 1928 course, *The Metaphysical Foundations of Logic*, must therefore be submitted to a "critical deconstruction" (*kritischer Abbau*).[45]

Being and Time constitutes the classic statement of this program. Heidegger aims to show in the "existential analytic" of this book that an apophantic statement of the form "*S is P*" has its transcendental condition of possibility in a structure of "understanding" (*Verstehen*). More exactly, such a statement draws its possibility from Dasein's non-thematic or "pre-ontological" understanding of Being as its own being-possible. Heidegger's argument may be simply stated. To grasp a thing as possessing a property, according to the syntax of predicative judgment, Dasein must have grasped its Being in the modality of "circumspective introspection," having interpreted itself. To state, "S is P," it must have grasped "S *as* P"; "S" must be given to it, within the "world" in which it always already grasps itself. "Thus assertion [*Aussage*]," Heidegger writes, "cannot disown its ontological provenance in an interpretation that understands. The primordial 'as' of an interpretation (*hermeneía*) that understands circumspectively we call the 'existential-*hermeneutical* 'as' in distinction from the '*apophantical*' 'as' of the assertion."[46] Frege had sought to "banish" the copula from logic. Heidegger, for his part, insists on it. He takes it as the witness to a truth that logic cannot define but must nonetheless presuppose. Before a subject can be linked to a predicate by a copula, the "is" of the judgment must be revealed. That "revealing," however, is more "original" than the correspondence of judgment and what it is judged, being its hidden but fundamental condition. "To say that an assertion '*is true*' signifies that it uncovers the entity as it is in itself. Such an assertion asserts, points out, 'lets' the entity 'be seen' (*apóphansis*) in its uncoveredness. The *being-true* (*truth*) of the assertion must be understood as *being-uncovering*. Thus truth has by no means the structure of an agreement between knowing and the object in the sense of a likening of one entity (the subject) to another (the Object)."[47]

This principle would be crucial in Heidegger's subsequent project. "Logic must be put in quotation marks," we read in his 1935 *Introduction to Metaphysics*. "This is not because we mean to speak against 'the logical' (in the sense of the correctly thought). We are searching, in the service of thinking, to attain that which determines the essence of thinking, *aletheia* and *physis*, being as unconcealment, which was lost precisely through 'logic.'"[48] Heidegger holds that, to perceive the pre-logical dimension of speech, the traditional and the modern disciplines of language study must be set aside. *Logos* is to be understood, in a sense both novel and archaic, as *legein*, where this Greek verb means first of all neither "speaking" nor "relating" but "laying" and "gathering," and, more properly, "the laying-down and laying before which gathers itself and others."[49] For this "gathering" to become perceptible in speech, language itself must be "freed" from grammar and logic. Heidegger acknowledges that, to be completed, such a task requires nothing less than a transformation in the concept of reason known since antiquity. "'Subject' and 'predicate' are inappropriate terms of metaphysics, which very early on in the form of Occidental 'logic' and 'grammar' seized control of the interpretation of language," he writes in his 1946 "Letter on Humanism." "We today can only begin to descry what is concealed in that occurrence. The liberation of language from grammar into a more original essential framework is reserved for thought and poetic creation."[50]

This "liberation" demands an overcoming of the theory of "the subject-predicate relation" as well as the strictures of "mathematical logic," or "logistics."[51] In his later works, Heidegger also rejects the modern field of inquiry that claims to constitute a science of natural languages. Linguistics seems to him to rest on an unreflective and "metaphysical" grasp of speech as a means of communication. "Meta-linguistics is the metaphysics of the thorough technification of all languages into a functioning, inter-planetary instrument of information," Heidegger writes in *On the Way to Language*, from 1959, before concluding: "Meta-language and Sputnik, meta-linguistics and rocket technology are the same."[52] Heidegger seeks his "more essential framework" for language in the work of poets, such as Hölderlin, Rilke, Trakl, and George, and in fragments of Greek philosophical prose from the age before Socrates. In his last period, Heidegger also searches for such a "framework" in German syntax. Heidegger relies crucially on the impersonal grammar of an expletive "It" or "There," which, in standing for no subject, poses a barrier to all predication. *Time and Being,* published in 1962, contains a program for a philosophical discourse that will reject every judgment of the form, "*S is P,*" setting a statement of existence in its place. "We do not say, Being is, Time is, but rather: There is Being and there is time [or 'It gives Being and it gives time,' *Es gibt Sein und es gibt Zeit*]." Heidegger explains: "So far we have only changed our linguistic usage with such phrases. Instead of 'It is,' we say 'There is,' or 'It gives.' To go back beyond the linguistic expression, we must show how this 'It gives' can be experienced and glimpsed. The appropriate way to get there is to explain what is given in the 'It gives,' what Being means, which—It gives; what 'time' means, which—It gives. Accordingly, we try to look ahead to the It which—gives Being and time."[53]

The contrast between Heidegger's project to "liberate" thinking from the bonds of grammar and logic and the post-Fregean programs to free philosophy from the "fetters" of natural languages and predicative logic is sharp. It is not surprising that it became visible long before Heidegger's late reflections on the "It which—gives Being and time." In the early 1930s, Heidegger and Carnap entered into an exchange that clearly marked out the differences separating their critiques of "philosophical logic." In April 1929, Heidegger had participated in a public disputation in Davos with Ernst Cassirer, then generally recognized as the leading figure of the School of Marburg. The question debated was that of the correct interpretation of Kant. Against the neo-Kantian reading of the *Critique of Pure Reason* as the foundation of the theory of scientific "experience," Heidegger defended the account of the *Critique* that he had given in his 1929 monograph, *Kant and the Problem of Metaphysics.* Heidegger proposed the following summary of his own argument: "Kant searches for a theory of Being in general, without taking into account any objects that would be given, without taking into account any determinate circle of beings (either psychic or physical). He searches for a general ontology, which lies before an ontology of nature as the object of natural science and before the ontology of nature as the object of psychology."[54]

In the audience, which included many of the thinkers who would most profoundly mark philosophy after the war, Carnap was present. At the disputation, he seems to have been favorably impressed by Heidegger as well as Cassirer.[55] By the following year, however, his position had changed. In a paper published in 1932, "The Elimination of Metaphysics through the Logical Analysis of Language," Carnap advanced a simple thesis: Fregean logic furnishes an incontrovertible means to invalidate traditional metaphysics, of which Heidegger's project is but the most recent prominent example. "The development of *modern logic*," Carnap wrote, "has made it possible to give a new and sharper answer to the question of the validity and justification of metaphysics."[56] "Logical analysis" demonstrates that the statements of metaphysics are, by virtue of their form, "entirely meaningless," or spurious. As examples of "metaphysical pseudo-statements of a kind where the violation of logical syntax is especially obvious," Carnap offered his readers "a few sentences from the metaphysical school that at present exerts the strongest influence in Germany." Heidegger, named in a footnote, was their author.[57]

The text from which Carnap drew "a few sentences" was Heidegger's 1929 inaugural discourse at the University of Freiburg, "What Is Metaphysics?" The egregious utterances, however, concerned neither substance nor Being. Carnap's critical remarks all bore, instead, on words for nothing and negation. In metaphysics, Heidegger had declared, "what is to be investigated is Being only — and *nothing* else; Being alone and further — Nothing; solely Being, and beyond Being — Nothing. What about this Nothing? *Does the Nothing exist* only because the *not* [or *non-*: das Nicht], *that is, negation* [die Verneinung], *exists*? Or is it the other way around? *Does negation and the not* [or *non-*] exist only because the Nothing exists?" The grammar of that questioning is novel, but its phenomenological inheritance can hardly be doubted. Heidegger asks about the relation between a logical content and the pre-predicative "processes" that, in Husserlian terms, surround and condition it. Heidegger quickly answers the question that he poses: logical negation and its expressions are derivable from the field of experience. Anxiety, defined as the phenomenological attestation of the Nothing, emerges as the origin of the "negation" that plays a role in the theory of the statement. In his polemical essay, Carnap quoted Heidegger's own conclusions in an abbreviated form: "We assert: *The Nothing is prior to the* not [or *non-*] and negation [*Das Nichts ist ursprünglicher als das Nicht und die Verneinung*]. . . . Where do we seek the Nothing? How did we find the Nothing? . . . We know the Nothing. . . . *Anxiety reveals the Nothing*. . . . That for which and because of which we were anxious was 'really' — nothing. Indeed: the Nothing itself — as such — was present. . . . *What about this Nothing? — The Nothing itself nihilates* [Das Nichts selbst nichtet]."[58]

To invalidate such claims, Carnap, empiricist as well as logician, might have advanced a simple argument. He could have reasoned that since, by definition, no being corresponds to "the Nothing" evoked by Heidegger, a discourse about it must be unverifiable. Another possibility would have been for Carnap to contest the meaning of Heidegger's neologism, "nihilates" (*nichtet*), in his concluding thesis: "The Nothing itself nihilates." As Michael Friedman has noted, however, for Carnap "the main problem is rather a violation of the logical form of the concept of nothing. Heidegger uses the concept both as a substantive and as a verb, whereas modern logic has shown that it is neither. The logical concept of the nothing is constituted solely by existential quantification and negation."[59] Transcribing Heidegger's German sentences into modern symbolic logic, Carnap explains that "nothing," in natural language, means no more than that "there is none," that is, that the extension of a given concept is null; more formally, it is representable as the negation of the quantifier for a bound variable ($\sim\exists$). From this fact of notation, Carnap derives his conclusion that Heidegger's statements, being formulated in an illogical syntax, are "pseudo-statements." On one point alone does the positivist concur with the metaphysician. Heidegger stated: "No rigor of a science can attain the seriousness of metaphysics. Philosophy can never be measured by the standard of the idea of science." Carnap, for his part, observes: "We thus find a good confirmation for our thesis; a metaphysician here arrives himself at the statement that his questions and answers are not consistent with logic and the scientific mode of thinking."[60]

That Heidegger took Carnap's criticism to be noteworthy can be inferred from the fact that he responded to it twice. In his 1935 lecture course, *Introduction to Metaphysics*, Heidegger cites the title of Carnap's article and the journal in which it appeared as witnesses to "the most extreme flattening out and uprooting of the traditional theory of

judgment . . . under the semblance of mathematical science." "Here,"
Heidegger states, naming Carnap's essay, but not its author,

> the last consequences of a thinking are brought to a conclusion. It is a thinking
> that began with Descartes, for whom truth is no longer disclosedness of what
> is and consequently the insertion and grounding of Dasein in the disclosed
> being, but, rather, [truth is] diverted into certainty — into the mere securing
> of thought, and in fact the securing of mathematical thought against all that
> is not thinkable by it. The conception of truth as the securing of thought led
> to the definitive profaning [*Engötterung*] of the world. The supposed "phil-
> osophical" tendency of mathematical-physical positivism wishes to supply
> the grounding of this position. It is no accident that this kind of "philosophy"
> wishes to supply the foundations of modern physics, in which all relations to
> nature are in fact destroyed. It is also no accident that this kind of "philoso-
> phy" stands in inner and outer connection with Russian communism. And it is
> no accident, furthermore, that this kind of thinking is celebrating its triumph
> in America. All this is only the ultimate consequence of an apparently merely
> grammatical affair, according to which Being is conceived through the "is,"
> and the "is" is interpreted in accordance with the conception of the proposi-
> tion and thought.[61]

Heidegger advanced a like claim in the postscript that he later added
to his inaugural Freiburg lecture. "Logistic," he stated in 1943, is but the
"conclusive degeneration" (*folgerichtige Ausartung*) of traditional logic.[62]

It would be difficult to deny that the exchange between Heidegger and
Carnap bears the marks of its immediate historical circumstances and,
more exactly, the opposing political positions that Heidegger and Carnap
adopted with respect to them. Yet Michael Friedman has argued persuasively that the debate also announces what would become the "twentieth century-opposition between 'analytic' and 'continental' philosophical
traditions," an opposition that is partly derivable, like the Davos dispute
itself, from the "systematic cracks" in the Kantian architectonic.[63] It is
not surprising, therefore, that the controversy has become the object of
many critical commentaries. Yet there is one aspect of the debate that has
perhaps not received the attention it deserves. Between the thesis that
the "not" (or "non-") is derivable from "the Nothing" and the thesis that

"nothing" is no more than the denial of the existential quantifier, an equivocal element of signification is lost from view. This element is the word and word-part *nicht*, insofar as it can also mean "non-" as well as "not." Heidegger asks: "*Does the Nothing exist* only because the *"nicht," that is, negation exists? Or is it in the other way around? Does negation and the "nicht" exist* only because the Nothing exists?" In Heidegger's usage, the sense of *nicht* is unequivocal. The particle, for him, abbreviates the meaning of the "is not" (*ist nicht*) of the negative judgment. Only for this reason can it appear as shorthand for "negation."

Another *nicht*, however, is thereby silently effaced: that of the "is not-" or "is non-." Heidegger, who devoted his doctoral thesis to the logic of the judgment and his habilitation thesis to a fourteenth-century treatise of speculative grammar attributed to Duns Scotus, knew the "not-" or "non-" of infinite naming well. In his 1916 dissertation, *Duns Scotus's Doctrine of Categories and Meaning*, Heidegger explained to his readers, by way of commentary on his source, that the term "non-" or "not" (*nicht*) must not always be taken as an "is not" (*ist nicht*), because there also exists a "not" (*nicht*) distinct from the "not" of "negation." "'Non-man' [or *not-man, Nicht-Mensch*]," Heidegger specifies, expounding the Scholastic doctrine in modern terms, "can certainly be said of a donkey, that is, an existing object. But negation, insofar as it is purely grasped as negation, is a being only in the mind, that is, through a subjective positing of thought; negation has no *objective* consistency in the contradictorily opposing proposition. The non-white [or not-white, *Nicht-Weiß*], insofar as it is opposed to the white, is not somehow black; rather, its meaning encompasses every being and non-being, excluding the white."[64] Readers familiar with the history of the theory of infinite names would easily grant this interpretation. Heidegger, they might wager, was rarely more Boethian.

That Heidegger knew Kant's doctrine of the infinite judgment can hardly be doubted. Heidegger was the author of an incisive reading of the First *Critique*, which showed extraordinary attention to the details of the Kantian text in its two editions. Heidegger was also familiar with Cohen's system of pure cognition, in which the "relative Nothing" signified by *non-* plays a fundamental role. In his book on Kant, Heidegger argued forcefully and clearly against Cohen's and Natorp's interpretations. Without ever mentioning Hermann Cohen's name, Heidegger asserted more than once that, as he wrote, Kant never meant to conceive of a "logic of pure cognition." Minimizing the doctrine of the qualities of judgment, Heidegger warned also against making of the "the idea of transcendental logic" a new "absolute"; this, he maintained, would be to produce an "unconcept" (*ein Unbegriff*).[65] Yet after these tacitly anti-Cohenian pronouncements, Heidegger, beginning his professorship at the University of Freiburg, proceeds as if the *non-* of the indefinite were itself nothing. He treats the word-part *nicht* as univocal, its sense constant in its every position in the sentence. Carnap, concentrating on the syntactic conditions in which the term "nothing" may be "legitimately" employed, does not pause to consider this particular point. In 1929, the possibility of a grammatical fissure in the monumental edifice of "negation" interests neither philosopher.

Each has his reasons. Heidegger aims to lead the "not" of the denial back to its source in a phenomenological given: the experience of anxiety (*Angst*), in which "all things sink into indifference" and, in their receding, "turn toward us," the receding of beings as a whole closing in on us and oppressing us. It is this fundamental "mood" or "attunement" (*Stimmung*) that most interests the existential Heidegger. "We 'hover' in anxiety," he comments. "More precisely, anxiety leaves us hanging because it induces the slipping away of beings as a whole. This implies that we ourselves — we men who are in being — in the midst of beings slip away from ourselves. . . . In the altogether unsettling experience of this hovering where there is nothing to hold onto, pure Dasein is all that is still there." In such a state, Dasein is there, but without words to speak: "Anxiety robs us of speech [*verschlägt uns das Wort*]."[66] The experience is one of muteness, if not silence. Grammatical distinctions would be out of place.

Carnap, by contrast, aims to carry out a "logical analysis" of metaphysics in a natural language. That such an analysis has its axioms becomes quickly evident. Carnap explicitly presupposes the existence of a "logically correct language," identifiable with a single notation, which he draws from Frege and Russell. His argument, however, also rests on a further claim: that ordinary and philosophical speech may be translated, without any significant loss of "meaning," into this notation. Both theses are contestable, although Carnap does not defend them. For his purposes, what is essential is that the subject of Heidegger's statements possesses a meaning that may be properly rendered by a symbol of modern "logistics." Carnap finds this symbol in the negated existential quantifier. Rushing past the question raised by Heidegger of the difference between "Nothing" (*Nichts*) and "not" (*nicht*), Carnap leaps over the difference between one grammatical *nicht* and another, that is, between "not" and "not-" (or "non-"). Even as the word "not" and "Nothing," for Heidegger, are both grounded in a single existential phenomenon, so, for Carnap, the idea of "nothing" is therefore resolvable into one symbol of modern formalized logic. And just as experience, for Heidegger, "robs us of speech," so an unequivocal notation, for Carnap, takes the place of "our language" and its many "faults." Beneath the judgment or beyond it, before the old logic or after it, there is, in either case, no time for philosophers to tarry with a particle.

This was but a consequence of the setting aside of the predicative judgment. In the "philosophical logic" of the tradition, from Aristotle to Kant and his successors, the central question remained that of the various patterns by which properties might be affirmed and negated of subjects. In such a logic, the problem of *non-* might well be treated only occasionally, or in passing; but it could never entirely be avoided. By the first quarter of the twentieth century, however, the conditions for the reflection on the nature of speech had undergone a fundamental change. Heidegger and Carnap bear witness to this mutation in their tacit concordance on this point: philosophy need not bother with a detail of grammar such as the possibility of affixing *non-* to a word. The reasons for the philosophers' decisions, of course, are fundamentally distinct. Heidegger sets aside the classical theory of the *logos* because he aims to root thinking in the phenomenology of pre-predicative experience; Carnap, by contrast, dismisses the "old logic" and its distinctions because he admits only those operations of reason that may be notated in the logico-mathematical script that he adapts from Frege. In both cases, however, philosophy renders itself insensitive to one grammatical fact. In the existential "de-struction" of traditional logic, as in its scientistic "overcoming," the same particle goes unnoticed. With its vanishing, the questions that it raises are also lost from view. *Non-* was never again to regain the position in philosophy that it formerly possessed. It persisted, however, in language and in languages, and thinkers would, therefore, encounter its force again. After the attempt to reach beneath the rigidified form of the statement and to leap beyond its imperfections, after the programs to forsake grammar for a modern calculus of thinking, or a new poetry of thought, the sense and nonsense of the particle of indefiniteness would continue, from time to time, to sound. Then it would demand, once again, to be transcribed anew.

CHAPTER FIFTEEN

A Persistent Particle

Today, almost a century has passed since Heidegger and Carnap's metaphysical and logical disputation about "nothing," "the Nothing" and the meanings of "negation." Yet whether one looks to projects that understand themselves as following after Heidegger's inquiry into the forgetting of the "truth of Being" or to those that have shared Carnap's aim to be guided by the model of modern "logistics," one fact seems certain: in philosophy, the many questions raised by the particle *non-*, once absorbed in the theories of predicable terms, transcendental and supertranscendental properties, and the infinite judgment, seem to have retreated from view. Today, the problem of "term negation," like "term logic" itself, would appear to belong solely to the history of philosophy.[1] It seems that, with the waning of the classical theories of the assertion, the questions raised by the indefinite have fallen, for the most part, into oblivion.

It is striking that, before the field of academic philosophy found itself divided by opposing attempts to overcome the neo-Kantian project proposed by Cohen, the logicians of the nineteenth century suggested that non-words belonged to those features of traditional thought that a rigorous theory of cognition ought to set aside. In one sense, it is not surprising that mathematical logicians should have shown little interest in the class of "indefinite" expressions discussed by Aristotle and his successors. The passage from the "denial" of a single term, such as "non-man," to the "denial" of a single predicate, such as "is not a man," is justified by the grammar of certain languages, yet it does not necessarily follow that logic must account for it. Logic might well profit by renouncing any claims to explain such facts of natural language. As early as 1840, Friedrich Adolf Trendelenburg,

drawing attention to the equivocal signs of negation, privation, and affirmation among words in natural languages, observed in his *Logical Investigations* that "whether a concept that is a predicate in a judgment is positive
or negative should not be judged by the form of the word alone. The difference is of a material nature and should be derived solely from the content
of the concept."[2] Soon thereafter, one of the major architects of the modern
algebra of the concept, George Boole, proposed an admirably clear account
of the one function that an "indefinite" term might play in formal logic. In
his 1854 *Investigation into the Laws of Thought*, he argued that to each name
signifying a class of objects in the "whole Universe" of things, there corresponds a second name, which signifies the rest: "If x represent any class
of objects, then will $1 - x$ represent the contrary or supplementary class of
objects, i.e., the class including all objects which are not comprehended in
the class x."[3]

Boole illustrated this formal proposition by means of the ancient example. "For greater distinctness of conception," he explained, "let x represent
the class *men*, and let us express, according to the last Proposition, the
Universe by 1; now if from the conception of the Universe, as consisting
of 'men' and 'not-men,' we exclude the conception of 'men,' the resulting
conception is that of the contrary class, 'not-men.' Hence the class 'not-
men' will be represented by $1 - x$. And, in general, whatever class of objects
is represented by the symbol x, the contrary class will be expressed by
$1 - x$."[4] As Frege's early reader Ernst Schröder remarked, such a principle
effectively relieves the thinking mind of the daunting task of defining
"indefinite" notions. Instead of seeking to combine "triangle, melancholy
and sulfuric acid into the concept *non-man*, for instance," the logician can
take "non-man" as the sign of all things that are not man.[5] A name such as
non-x will then be said to signify the class that is "complementary" to x,
where x and *non-x* together compose the "whole Universe." Of terms such
as "non-man," no more, in the domain of logic, would need to be said.[6]

Philosophers, however, would run up against the power of the *non-* long
after this strictly technical solution, even as they would encounter the
effects of "indefinite negation" after Heidegger and Carnap each deemed
it unworthy of consideration. Such encounters would be diverse, yet one
constant among them may be discerned: as a rule, *non-* would no longer be

grasped within the limits of the predicative judgment. Diverse examples might be evoked, each of which bears witness to the role played by the particle beyond the limits of the classical theory of the statement-making sentence. An entire book might be written on the uncharted adventures of the particle *non-* in the thought of the second half of the twentieth century. Yet a few indications concerning some of these developments may also briefly be proposed.

Against Hegel, albeit in his idiom, Adorno would develop his "negative dialectics," in which a new non-concept would become an "absolute": the "non-identical," loosened from its relation of contrariety with respect to the "identical."[7] "Dialectics is the consistent consciousness of non-identity," Adorno would write in his 1966 *Negative Dialectics.*[8] "The non-identical is not be obtained directly, as something positive on its part, nor is it obtainable by a negation of the negative."[9] It is recoverable solely in the *non-* that marks the failure of correspondence between a thought object and its concept: "What is indissoluble in any previous thought context transcends its seclusion in its own, as non-identical. It communicates with that from which it was separated by the concept. It is opaque only for identity's claim to be total; it resists the pressure of that claim. But as such it seeks to be audible. Whatever part of non-identity defies definition in its concept goes beyond its individual existence; it is only in polarity with the concept, in staring at the concept, that it will contract into that existence. The inside of non-identity is its relation to what is not, and which its managed, frozen self-identity withholds from it."[10] Rarely was greater weight accorded to the power of the *non-* in dialectics.

In the same years, albeit from an entirely different perspective, John Searle would concentrate with new intensity on the equivocations of saying "not" and "non-." Developing J. L. Austin's theory of "speech acts," which do not state "one thing concerning another," but bring about certain events by the fact of their utterance, Searle's 1969 *Speech Acts* introduced a distinction between what he called "illocutionary negation" and "propositional negation." It rests on the shifting syntactic place of the logico-grammatical operator commonly expressed in modern English by the word "not." "The sentence, 'I promise to come,'" Searle thus observed, "has two negations: 'I do not promise to come' and 'I promise not to come.' The former is an illocutionary negation, the latter a propositional negation."[11] One might paraphrase that distinction by evoking the difference between "negation" and "infinitation," that is, *not* and *non-*. To the statement "I promise," one could then reason, there correspond two opposing others, which are its negation, in the classical sense, and its "indefinite" distortion: "I do not promise," and "I promise to not-," or "I promise to non-."

After Nietzsche, but also after Cohen and Heidegger, Deleuze would propose a new project in metaphysics, also articulable by these particles of "negation." In his 1968 book *Difference and Repetition*, Deleuze argued against Hegel's integration of every "not" and "non-" into a single doctrine of dialectical "negativity." "There is a non-Being [*Il y a un non-être*]," Deleuze wrote, "and yet it is not negative or of negation. There is a non-Being that is in no way the Being of the negative, but the Being of the problematic. This (non) being, this ?-Being, has as its symbol o/o. Here zero designates only difference and its repetition."[12] Against the "not" of dialectical logic, Deleuze set the "not" or "non-" (*non*) of "the problematic," to which the question mark and an indefinable division of zero by zero alone are adequate. Grammar furnished him with an example of the force of such a non-negative "*non-*." In French, the particle *ne* is generally coordinated with a second particle, such as *pas*, *rien*, or *jamais*, to express a negation; but there also exists a *ne* that is purely "contrastive" and that, employed without any other particle, affirms a difference, as in statements of comparison, such as *L'âme de saint François était plus belle que n'est la mienne*, "The soul of St Francis was more beautiful than mine is," a phrase that in French literally reads: "The soul of St Francis was more beautiful than mine is not."[13] "In the so-called expletive *ne*, which grammarians have so much difficulty in interpreting," Deleuze remarks, "one encounters the (non)-Being which corresponds to the form of a problematic field, although the modalities of the proposition tend to assimilate it to a negative non-Being; it is always in relation to questions developed as problems that an expletive *ne* appears in the proposition, as the witness to an extra-propositional grammatical instance."[14] Deleuze's differentiation of the affirmative "not" or "non-" from the "not" of "negativity" might be read as a retrieval of the classical distinction between the varieties of opposition, although Deleuze himself does not link his discussion to traditional doctrines of the logical indefinite.

Giorgio Agamben would also turn implicitly to the particle of indeterminate negation in his project to render the classical categories of
metaphysics "inoperative." His recurrent point of reference would be the
Aristotelian doctrine of potentiality (*dynamis*), which also attracted Heidegger's attention in his 1931 lecture course. Arguing against the Megarians,
who admitted Being and non-Being and denied any state between them,
Aristotle maintained that those who possess a skill or knowledge retain it
even when they do not make use of it. Such capacities remain, then, "potential." Aristotle defended his thesis by means of a principle that involves
expressions of an indefinite variety. By nature, the potentiality "to do [or
be]," he argued, entails the potentiality "not-to do [or be]." If the architect
is "able to build," Aristotle reasons, he is also "able to not-build [or to non-
build]"; if the musician possesses the ability "to play the cythera," he is also
capable "to not-play [or non-play]" it. From this perspective, "not-doing"
and "not-being" — or "non-doing" and "non-being" — acquire a new force
in metaphysics. They alone preserve the autonomy of potentiality. Without
them, every capacity to do (or be) would have become actual, and *dynamis*
as such would not persist. Aristotle argues, for this reason, that "all potentiality is impotentiality [*adynamia*]."[15] Heidegger had translated: "All force
[*Kraft*] is unforce [*Unkraft*] with respect to the same and according to the
same."[16] For Agamben, after Deleuze as well as Heidegger, Bartleby would
be the most eloquent prophet of this indeterminate potentiality. Melville's
hapless scrivener insists above all on this point: "I would prefer not to ..."
His obstinate inclination "not to ..." opens onto the infinite class of his
unnamed non-preferences.[17]

Twentieth-century developments in the thinking of the *non-* have also
benefited from the invention of one theory and practice distinct from
philosophy, which is psychoanalysis. Freud discovered an entire conti-
nent of indeterminately negative phenomena, derivable from a thing he
called by an indefinite name: "the unconscious" (*das Unbewußte*). In his
account of the "uncanny" or *unheimlich*, which is "somehow a subspecies"
of the *heimlich* to which it is opposed, in his theory of "primal words"
that designate contraries without distinction, in his doctrine of "negation"
(*Verneinung*), which he placed in relation to the "function of judgment" and
repression, to cite only three major examples, Freud was concerned with

the peculiar force of the *not* and *non-*, which defies the classical theories of "negation."

After Freud, and in persistent, if shifting relation to the linguistics of Saussure and Jakobson, Lacan would exploit the many possibilities of indeterminate "negations." One might draw up a catalogue of the modes of nay-saying, not saying and non-saying that became audible in his "return to Freud," from his early seminars through to his last invocations of *mi-dire*, a discourse translatable as "half-speaking," in which one may also perceive a "non-speaking," *mi-* evoking the Greek particle *mē*. Lacan would linger on the "expletive" *ne* that also attracted Deleuze's attention; exploit the homophony that, in French, binds *non*, "no," to *nom*, "name"; gloss the variously negative prefixes of words, from the French *non-* and *in-* to the German *Un-* and *Ver-*; forge new indefinite expressions, perhaps the most crucial being the *pas-tout*, "not-all" or "not-whole"; and evoke the Scholastic squares of logical opposition, as well as the Fregean and Russellian notations of negation, in his exploration of the unimagined "logic" of sexual difference. Such deflected negations accompanied him on the way to his final existential proposition: *y a de l'Un*, "there is (something of) the One" or "there is (some of) One."[18] Keeping in mind the ambiguous Germanic prefix that Lacan knew well, one might also detect in that strange proposition a positing of the indefinite: "there is (some of the) *un-*."

Such a summary, however, would be incomplete were it not also to accord a special place for a new field of knowledge, which bears on what was, for centuries, one of the principal objects of philosophical inquiry: natural languages. In the years in which logic announced its first "formula languages," purified of the ambiguities of grammar, linguistics embarked on its search for the empirical properties of speech. Language would become the object of linguistics not in its truth or falsity, but in its own invariant characteristics: "in and for itself," as Saussure stated in his 1906–11 *Course*.[19] During the twentieth century, the aim and methods of linguistics, of course, would change. Saussure had identified the object of linguistics as *langue*, a given idiom. Noam Chomsky would later take it to be of the order of what in French is called *langage*, "language with a capital L," an entity to which he would give the name "grammar."[20] One might define this designation as shorthand for the properties common to observed languages, such that they are exhibited in the faculty of speech. This faculty has the striking feature of "functioning without knowing itself," in Jakobson's words, in the sense that speakers need not be aware of the constraints that define a language to follow them.[21] Linguists have at times also wagered that speakers cannot be aware of them. Grammatical rules may be too abstract to be audible, even if their consequences are perceptible. Their magnitude may also defy enumeration.[22] What is certain is that the faculty of speech stands in a relation of unsettling intimacy with reason. Distinct from thinking, it accompanies it, remaining largely unobserved.

In studying the grammatical capacity, linguists have also encountered indefinite expressions, casting new light on the force and structure of infinite naming. Aristotle himself hardly asked about the meaning of the indefinite word in itself, his interest bearing above all on the logic of predicative statements. That there could be a name such as "non-man," that "non-heals" could be treated as a single verb, seem to have struck Aristotle as self-evident facts. He presupposed the grammatical admissibility of these expressions, without pausing to define who, or what, such a being as a "non-man" might be. His successors followed him in this respect. Only relatively rarely did they raise the question of the meaning of a term such as "non-white" or "non-just," "non-mortal," "non-elephantine," an "non-extended," on its own. It may be recalled that among the ancient interpreters of Aristotle, two schools of interpretation, however, may be discerned. There is that of Ammonius and Boethius, according to which an act of *infinitatio* sets a thing in the "infinite" logical space outside the given name. In this sense, the word "non-man," as Boethius explains, can signify a dead man, stone, or log of wood. There is also the school of Al-Farabi and Avicenna, which holds that the "imported irregularity" of the ancients is a privative expression. "Non-seeing," in this sense, means "blind." It is more difficult to extract corresponding semantic principles from the modern thinkers, since their treatments are less of names and verbs than of the infinite judgment as a logico-syntactic unity. Certain extrapolations may nonetheless be made. When he writes that the judgment "the soul is non-mortal" leaves the soul "infinitely open" for further determination, Kant sides with Boethius. Arguing that the "non-" is the "operational means" of generation, Cohen, instead, advances an unprecedented claim:

that *non-* evokes the law of continuity. "Non-red" denotes a color distinct from red, within a single spectrum. "Non-moving" signifies an evanescent point in the range of movement: the infinitesimally mobile "origin."

Linguistic research suggests that the senses of indefinite names are unrulier than any single traditional philosophical account admits. From the English language alone, one may adduce ample evidence of this circumstance. That the affixation of a *non-* to a word has long been possible in English can be gleaned from the fact that one of the first "indefinite" expressions is to be found in Chaucer, who put a non-word in the mouth of Philosophy. In Book Three of Boethius's *Consolation*, the sagacious lady offers the dejected and incarcerated narrator lessons in the fickle ways of fortune. To place happiness in the contingent, she teaches, is necessarily to expose oneself to misery; sooner or later, "powerlessness will steal in and make wretchedness." In translation, Chaucer renders this "powerlessness" (*impotentia*) by *noun-power*.[23] Such an expression appears to confirm the theory of the Arabic readers of Aristotle. "Non-power" is not "anything in the universe except power"; it is the absence of power where it could also be present. It seems, in other words, to signify a privation. Yet such logico-metaphysical terms simplify the realities of speech, for in languages, privation admits of several varieties. "Non-seeing" may mean "blind," but the senses of the two expressions are also distinct. The Boethian doctrine of spoken infinity is in this regard instructive. "Blind" signifies the simple absence of the faculty of sight, where it can be expected to be present. "Non-seeing," while designating a privation, signifies more. Perhaps it is for this reason that in contemporary English usage, such a term as "non-seeing" is often preferred to "blind," just as "non-hearing" can be taken to be more extensive than "deaf." Even where its sense would appear to be "privative," *non-* signifies a positivity beyond lack.

Yet the affix can also function in ways distinct from any logical doctrine. In a lexicographic study published in 1971, John Algeo was perhaps the first to observe that in many cases, English *non-* conjures up a thing possessing the value, but not the "surface characteristics, or identity," of what is signified by the supplemented word.[24] This is a *non-* distinct from the exclusive *non-* of Ammonius and Boethius, as well as from the privative *non-* of Al-Farabi. Algeo baptizes it "dissimulative *non.*" "The earliest instance of dissimulative *non* that I have recorded," he notes, "is *nonprofit* 'profit not subject to taxation because of the privileged status of the investment that produces it,' from Jessica Mitford's 1963 *American Way of Death*."[25] Here *non-* is a linguistic means of neither banishment nor deprivation. One may add that it is also not the operator of a continuous approximation, as it was for Cohen. In its "dissimulative" function, the particle is the agent of a disguise, which dresses up its referent favorably. "Thus *nonacting* with dissimulative *non* denotes a style of acting that is so restrained and realistic as to appear not to be acting at all; the appearance, however, is deceptive, for such nonacting requires a high degree of acting skill. . . . A dissimulative *nonwatch* is a fashionable and perhaps costly time piece worn somewhere other than on the wrist — thus, at first glance, appearing not to be a watch."[26] This *non-* has yet to leave our language. As a more recent example, one may evoke the "non-governmental organization": an organization that may effectively "govern," without, however, being subject to the restrictions imposed on State governments.

Such expressions can tend toward a further meaning, whose force is stronger. In addition to the *nons* of exclusion, privation, and dissimulation, there exists a *non-* of deprecation. Algeo argues that its proliferation in English is a recent phenomenon, datable to the years following 1960. Yet, he also argues, it may have long been implicit among the senses of the particle of privation. Milton furnishes an illuminating example. In his divorce tractate, the poet and theologian considers the question of whether God could dispense his subjects from the law that he decrees. He entertains an answer suggested by Andrew Rivet: God may do so, albeit "by some way to us unknown." Dismissing the hypothesis, Milton writes: "Rivetus may pardon us, if we cannot bee contented with his non-solution, to remain in such a peck of incertainties and doubts so dangerous and gastly to the fundamentals of our faith."[27] "The *non* here is privative," Algeo observes, "because the problem of how God dispenses has not been resolved, but there is a pejorative overtone to the word."[28]

The particle of pejoration, however, does not only recall the privative *non-*. It also evokes a dissimulative activity, according to a linguistic pattern that is well attested today. As early as 1970, Clarence L. Barnhart noted in a report on "New English" published in *American Speech*:

The extended meaning of *non-*, which appears with increasing frequency, indicates not so much the opposite or reversal of something as rather that something is not true, real, or worthy of the name. In this use, *non-* is prefixed to a noun and often carries such connotations as "sham, pretended, pseudo-, mock, fraudulent." In its original use non- is part of yes-or-no classification: a statement is either *sense* or nonsense; but in the new use *non-* makes a comment or a criticism. For example, a *nonbook* pretends to be a book; a *nonpolicy* is a vacuum where a policy should be. Apparently the first popular term in which *non-* bore this meaning was *nonbook*, used by *Time* magazine and defined as "a book published in order to be purchased rather than to be read." Some typical derivatives are *nonevent* (an event taking place only in order to be reported in the newspapers), *noncandidate* (a candidate who refuses to admit his candidacy), *nondebate, nonhappening, nonissue, nonstory,* and *noninformation.*[29]

The logic of contrariety implied by such nouns is worth pondering. What exactly is the relation between "issue" and "non-issue," "policy" and "non-policy"? To claim that the "non-candidate" is absolutely excluded from the semantic field of "candidate" would be not only imprecise but also false. It would be no less inadequate to argue that "non-candidate" signifies a privation in any classical sense. The privative *non-* can be one of description, but the pejorative *non-* evoked by Barnhart is more. It is a *non-* of denunciation by unmasking. Carrying "such connotations as 'sham, pretended, pseudo, mock, fraudulent,'" this *non-* does not effect a dissimulation; quite to the contrary, it exposes it. Each time, the particle concerns the relation that a thing bears to the limits of the concept to which it is linked. But the logical operations that the particle effects are incompatible among themselves. The *non-* of dissimulation removes the designated thing from the field signified by a noun, placing it outside it; thus the "non-profit," which, according to Algeo's commentary, subtracts a certain variety of profit from the field of legitimate taxation. The *non-* identified by Barnhart does this and more. Removing the designated thing from the field signified by a noun, it does not place it elsewhere; rather, it insists upon its failure to correspond to its definition. While the "non-profit," therefore, is something other than regular profit, being fiscally advantageous with respect to it, the "non-event" is an event, although one inadequate to the concept that it aims to instantiate. The "non-event" is precisely that species of event in which whatever was expected to occur did not come to pass. It is an event that is none.

It would not be difficult to multiply the examples of this variety of *non-*. Each time, they defy traditional philosophical accounts of infinite naming. Consider, as a next example, the "non-starter," as it is employed in contemporary English. It is not "anything in the universe, except a starter"; nor is it the mere "privation" of a starter. It is also not a "starter" that appears not to initiate a process, before revealing itself to be a beginning of a better sort than was anticipated. The "non-starter" is the starter that failed. Its *non-* is that of "non-event." In such cases, the *non-* is one of deflation. From the name of something, it engenders a new nothing. Yet this "nothing" is no lack; it cannot be defined, like a privation, as a presence that is missing. Its nullity possesses an intensity that is all its own. So, too, the "non-happening," whose failure to occur distinguishes it from being merely "no happening." As a final example, one may cite a vernacular word of curiously philosophical antecedence: the "non-entity." Not everything that is not an entity may be called a "non-entity"; from this one may infer that the "non-entity" denotes a thing more definite than the "entity." Despite appearances, "entities" and "non-entities" are not contrary classes, in Boole's terms; they are in no sense "complimentary." To be a "non-entity" is to be intensely less than any "entity"; it is to be unworthy of this technical and now antiquated name of Being. The *non-* of "non-entity," like that of the "non-starter," points to the undoing of the concept to which it is affixed. It may therefore be viewed as an "operational means," in Cohen's terms. This *non-*, however, constitutes a new zero in the "algebra of thought." Far from being the inception from which something will be generated, it is an end, from which nothing more may come: the seal of ruin, rather than exclusion or privation, dissimulation or generation.

One may draw a consequence from such variously indefinite words. Caught between conflicting senses, suspended between the various and varying suggestions of exclusion, privation, dissimulation, and deflation, the particle of indefinite negation in natural languages is radically homonymous. Like every grammatical datum, it is empirical and contingent in the sense that, while attested in space and time and submitted to the constraints that define individual languages, it could always be otherwise than it is, or not be at all. It may hold a promise for thinking precisely for this reason. A fact of grammar can become, in itself, a provocation for thought. Philosophy's repeated encounters with "not" and "non-" are instructive in this regard. From Aristotle to his medieval commentators, from the early modern thinkers to Kant and his numerous successors, thinkers run up against a single possibility of speech. In various systems and multiple languages, this possibility remains, in different ways, an incitement to reflection. Yet it has long remained concealed from sight. Being concerned with *logos*, in its generality, rather than with languages, in their indefinite plurality, philosophy has rarely lingered on the speaking that precedes and exceeds it. Even Aristotle, who devoted such attention to the meanings lodged in the alpha of privation, did not pause to consider the senses of *non-*. Those who came after him dwelt at greater length on the particle that he summoned. Yet in focusing on the more obviously consequential questions of contrariety and contradiction, and, later, the subordination of concepts, they kept the grammatical detail in a rigidly logical frame. Now, after the passing of the doctrine in which the *non-* had its modest place, after some have set off for artificial symbolisms in place of "colloquial language," and after others have judged the empirical features of speech too minimal to contribute to metaphysics or the furthering of its endless deconstruction, a new possibility may be envisaged. Facts of grammar can become a spur for thought.

One is tempted to begin again at the beginning. There is something in the voice, one might then reason, whose obscurity demands attention. Separable or inseparable from the word on which it bears, word or a word-fragment, one with the "not" of predicative negation or distinct from it, this thing of speech persists across languages, despite their diversity, and it persists in its equivocations. The ambiguities of *non-* mark more than the doctrine of negation, contrariety and contradiction, and they are not restricted to the books of the history of philosophy. Whenever thinking encounters "non-being" or "non-art," the "non-event" or a "non-person," the question of infinite naming arises anew. Faced with such expressions, confronted by the problem of their shared opacity, one could investigate their sense and nonsense. "Non-being" itself, at the horizon of metaphysics, might be sounded in each of the variations played out by its enigmatic *non-*: as "anything but being," as "absence of being," as "being that, at first glance, does not appear to be being," although it is. "Non-being" might be heard — according to a glossing that would be the most extreme and the most colloquial of this set — as "non-being" after the manner of the "non-event": being, in other words, in its failure, and in its utter failing. Such distinctions, of course, would be only preliminary, for among languages, no rule of reason forbids these senses from being confused and superposed. One *non-* may give way to another, according to movements of which speakers need not be aware. The possibilities of non-being and non-beings are as varied as the masks of the "non-man" whom Aristotle summoned long ago.

It may be time to revisit the forgotten ground of that first act of conjuration, in which non-man and non-being, joined in indefiniteness, first came to light. After the twentieth century and its various deposings of the predicative judgment, after multiple rejections of the path of inquiry in which *non-* had a constant, if minor, place, it is worth pausing again to consider the point from which Aristotle departed. There is more in the voice than has yet been discerned. Thinking can learn from listening to the indefinite sayings of languages, not to define their constraints, after the fashion of linguistics, or to discipline their ambiguities by a notation devised "in the image of arithmetic," but to gather from their unruly multitude some keys to the dim workings of our speaking reason. Philology, which bears on parts of languages, in partial attestations, will prove itself a precious method in such an investigation. In fragments of discourse, in words, declined, case by case, according to grammars that are still to be uncovered, an unfamiliar logic and illogic will make itself more audible. It will be our own. The task of thinking with languages, and not only in them, and against them, may still be at its inception.

CHAPTER SIXTEEN

Callings

Few would doubt that a patient practice of reconstruction is required to understand the doctrines of the philosophers. Propositions must be extracted from discourses and, once interpreted, they must be restituted to the arguments in which they play parts. Yet there is also a textual dimension of exposition that exegesis alone cannot register. To perceive it, one must attend to what is said without ever being distinctly stated: suggestions that, while unexpressed as such, are legible on the surface of the text. Such a mute indication may be discerned in the long tradition of investigations into the possibilities of infinite naming. Its place is identifiable: it lies in examples. Seeking to define the force and function of the "not-" and "non-," philosophers, beginning with Aristotle, devise unfamiliar words and phrases as illustrations of their arguments. To be properly understood, such expressions must, of course, be related to the statements that they clarify. Yet they also deserve to be heard in another sense. Their strangeness, demanding attention in itself, is telling.

In the inquiry that stretches from Aristotle to the Scholastics, from Kant to Fichte, Hegel, and Hermann Cohen, the examples suggest a single possibility. No thinker explicitly asserts it; yet it remains obstinately audible from text to text. This possibility may be simply stated: the "infinity" of non-'s sense is our own. Before pertaining to any element of physics or metaphysics, the "indefinite" testifies to those speaking subjects who speak insistently of themselves. In its translations and equivocations, the *non-* points to our own loquacious nature, of which multiple and conflicting interpretations may and must be proposed. No philosophical paradigm, in this sense, is more significant than the first, from which Aristotle and his successors depart. The first example is "non-man" (*ouk anthrōpos*, or *non homo*). Can that fact be inconsequential? One may recall that, as if to ward off any doubt as to the field to which that expression applies, Aristotle furnishes two examples of verbs of a similar logical structure. Both such predicates concern a precariously physiological existence: "non-ails" (*ou kamnei*) and "non-heals" (*oukh' hygainei*).

After these first nominal and verbal illustrations of the forms of indefinite speech, later thinkers forge new examples. They also insistently, if implicitly, evoke human possibilities of non-being, inexistence, and privation. Early on, commentators mark out the various meanings of the indefinite. They distinguish between "not being" a property and "lacking" it, that is, between being "non-seeing" and being "blind"; extending their analyses, they warn against the confusion of the senses of "not being just," "being non-just," and "being unjust." They thereby also begin to untangle the possible meanings of Aristotle's inaugural expression. "Non-man" might be one of many creatures, real and mythological, dead and living, possible and impossible; "non-man" includes within the span of its virtual reference fabled half-men, like the centaur, the satyr, and the Cyclops, as well as once real but now departed men, such as the deceased sovereign whose image would be printed on coins. The antique and early medieval commentators on Aristotle's logic refined the distinctions of these possibilities. Later, the late Scholastic thinkers of the end of the Middle Ages and the early modern period carry them to new limits. In their doctrines of such transcendental and supertranscendental terms as being "thinkable," "loveable," "willable," and "unintelligible," they conceive of the set of indefinite predicable properties that belong to the ideas represented by our mind.

Transforming the classical question, passing from the old teaching of indefinite subjects and predicates to his transcendental theory of the third quality of judgment, Kant orients his system of critical philosophy with respect to a logical paradigm unknown to Aristotle and his followers. The Kantian example is also telling in itself, although neither its inventor nor his successors, being concerned with questions of transcendental structure and consequence, pause to consider its detail. The critical example clearly suggests that Kant tacitly shared Aristotle's intuition. After propositions bearing on "non-man" and the forms of his "non-justness," after such formulations as "non-man walks," "Zayid is non-seeing," and "the loveable is non-intelligible," Kant found his paradigm in a single proposition: "The soul is non-mortal." We are the subjects of the infinite judgment. The limited and endless expanse of its syntax is that which we ourselves inhabit.

In their variously transcendental logics, the post-Kantians appear to have retained Kant's view in this respect. Schelling's first philosophy, on this question, is clear. In the exposition of the doctrine according to which "The *I* is not *non-I*," it is subjectivity, Schelling's absolute "principle of philosophy," which is to be somehow affirmed without being represented as "conditioned." Similarly, in Hegel's speculatively collapsing sentences, "Spirit is no elephant," and "Spirit is no table," what is to be apprehended is the structure by which particular and universal, reconciled in their difference, define our own mind, which being the only one of its kind, is also divine. Cohen presents his theory of the leap from the Nothing to the Something as the epistemological and metaphysical foundation of the "fact of science." Yet he thereby also provides an account of the structure of human reason, the "logic of pure cognition" being, as he argues, the retrieval and purification of Kant's critical project. The Cohenian infinite judgment becomes a means to exhibit human reason in its purest and most intensely "original" activity.

In bearing on "non-man," the soul, Spirit, and our mind, the doctrine of infinite naming silently spirals back, time and again, on those who propose it. It points to our speaking nature. This is a nature that, several millennia after Aristotle's definition of man as "the speaking animal," has still not received the attention it demands. The truth is that we are confronted with the question of Being and non-Being not in understanding, as Heidegger argued in *Being and Time*, but in naming. The point is worth stressing, for the difference between these two positions is not trivial. Acts of speech can exceed and fall short of understanding, although, once committed, they are, like any texts, belatedly susceptible to elucidation by analysis and commentary. The saying reaches further than the said. Speaking before understanding, speaking in misunderstanding, speaking without understanding, we can name what we fail to know. We thereby give ourselves a means to record and measure, after the fact, what we will not have grasped. "Non-man" furnishes an exemplary illustration of this fact. Aristotle employs the term *ouk anthrōpos* and begins to draw out the consequences that it suggests without defining the word's senses or the conditions of its uses. Aristotle was, in this respect, like any subject. Speaking without thinking, speaking in not yet thinking, we, too, do not cease to avail ourselves of the faculty of language, which "functions without knowing itself," which is to say, without our knowing it. We thus evoke such things as "non-violence" and "non-art," "the unconscious," "the unintelligible," and "the inhuman," and do not wonder at the power of *non-*, *un-*, or *in-*.

But "non-man" is too uncanny to be avoided. It calls out for commentary. Ought one to consider "non-man" to be a variety of "negation," the designation of some infinite logical expanse, or the infinitesimal origin from which "man" springs? The philosophical accounts of infinite naming would suggest all these possibilities. Each would be worth investigating in itself. Yet each reflects a restricted grasp of the twists and turns of speech. One might turn to the grammar of natural languages for greater assistance. Recalling the senses of the *non-* in English, one could also gloss the classical paradigm of the "indefinite" according to each of the varieties of word-types that *non-* has been known to forge. Could one define "non-man" according to the grammatical *non-* of privation? This would be a man who is lacking: an absent or, perhaps, a "missing" person. Boethius may have had such a being dimly in mind when, in passing, he alluded to the fact that *non-homo* might denote what was, but is no more, a man.

Could one envisage "non-man" according to the *non-* of "dissimulation"? That would be a man who appears not to be one — for better or for worse. There would be the non-man graspable as a "super-man" or an "over-man," an *Übermensch*, who either once was or is still to come. There would also be a non-man conceivable according to the *non-* of deflation and deprecation. This would be a ruined man, or the ruining of "man" as such. It might be an *Unmensch*, beast or brute, or such a man as the one concerning whom Primo Levi, at the threshold of his first book, defied his readers to decide "whether this is a man." Such beings would be the most troubling figures in this first set of glosses. Non-man could be an individual perilously close to man: a failed or ruined man, who, by misfortune or by fault, has somehow proved himself to be unworthy of his own name. Between term and *infinitatio*, "man" and "non-man," the logical passage, then, would be legitimate; but it would also be lamentable. There would remain the difficult question of the mutations that are left open to a non-man. Some might grant that a ruined being could regain the nature that he once possessed. They might even expressly demand as much, by that familiar, if opaquely menacing, imperative: "Be a man!" That injunction resounds from language to language, according to a multitude of grammars, as if indicating, each time anew, the real threat that "non-man" poses to man. Yet one might also maintain that from "non-man" to man, the path back is obstructed. Being non-man may be irremediable.

Although multiple, conflicting and arresting, such possibilities have hardly come into focus in the philosophical investigations into infinite naming. Only rarely, and as if unaware of themselves, have philosophers drawn close to a troubling possibility of logical determination, which none, however, has dared to state. It is the possibility that "non-man" names not the "contrary" or "complimentary" class of man, as Boole and others naïvely assumed, but a shadow that belongs to man and to him alone. Were this to be the case, the indefinite state of being "non-man" would pertain solely to "man." The obscure power of the "non-" would inhere in the very essence to which it is tied. Some non-being would "be" enclosed in it, however monstrous the logic of that implication — and that "being" — would appear from any classical perspective.

The inquiry into the *non-* inaugurated by Aristotle led to discoveries and inventions. It drew attention to the perplexing power to speak "indefinitely," positing indeterminately, merely by adding a single morpheme to noun and verb. In its incompletion, it provoked repeated commentaries, revisions, and interpretation. It contributed to the elaboration of the notions of contradiction and contrariety, the distinction of negation and privation, the emergence of the concepts of the transcendental "thing," the supertranscendental, the object in general, and the critical and post-critical theories of the conditions and limits of judgment. Implicitly but audibly, it bound the force of the indefinite to our speaking being, which is *unnameable*, in every sense. Yet this tradition in philosphy is also insufficient, for it fails to confront the crucial question that it raises. Some "No One" remains, in it, systematically evoked and rigorously avoided. Today, the non-subject once summoned by Aristotle, therefore, calls out for study.

Who — or what — is he, or she, or it? Even the grammar of such a question is uncertain. Responding to it will require stepping outside the domain of thinking in which such a thing as "non-man" has been conjured up and spirited away. After this exploration of the philosophies of infinite naming, it will therefore be necessary to turn to other fields. A new task will be proposed, which belongs to the next part of the investigation that begins with this book. In literature and law, in anthropology and mythology, psychoanalysis and linguistics, non-man has also been sighted. *Outis* — "No One," "Not-one," "No Man," and "Non-man" — has visited all these domains. "His" ways have been charted in fables and in fictions, in customs and in gestures, in symptoms and in deeds. Now No One's masks demand to be examined, one by one, in their disquieting force and functions. It is our voice that sounds, each time, through them.

Notes

CHAPTER ONE: A GUEST'S GIFT

1. Homer, *Odyssey* 9.364–368; English in *The Odyssey of Homer*, trans. Richmond Lattimore (New York: Harper Perennial, 1963), p. 146.

2. See Seth Benardete, *The Bow and the Lyre: A Platonic Reading of the Odyssey* (New York: Rowman & Littlefield, 1997), p. 76.

3. Homer, *Odyssey* 9.403–406; *The Odyssey of Homer*, p. 147.

4. The pun has been much commented on. See, among others, William Bedell Stanford, *Ambiguity in Greek Literature* (London and New York: Johnson Reprint Corp., 1972), pp. 104–106; Michael Simpson, "*Odyssey* 9: Symmetry and Paradox in Outis," *The Classical Journal* 68. 1 (1972), pp. 22–25; E. Dimrock, "The Name of Odysseus," *The Hudson Review* 9. 1 (1956), pp. 52–70; Seth L. Schein, "Odysseus and Polyphemus in the *Odyssey*," *Greek, Roman and Byzantine Studies* 11. 2 (1970), pp. 73–83; Norman Austin, "Name Magic in the *Odyssey*," *California Studies in Classical Antiquity* 5 (1972), pp. 1–19; John Peradotto, *Man in the Middle Voice: Name and Narration in the Odyssey* (Princeton: Princeton University Press, 1990).

5. Homer, *Odyssey* 9.408; *The Odyssey of Homer*, p. 147.

6. See Konrat Ziegler, "Odysseus — Utuse — Utis," *Gymnasium* 69 (1962), pp. 396–98; Jürgen Wöhrmann, "Noch enimal: Utis — Odysseus," *Gymnasium* 70. 6 (1963), p. 549; and, against the hypothesis, Alfred Heubeck and Arie Hoekstra, *A Commentary on Homer's Odyssey*, vol. 2, *Books IX–XVI* (Oxford: Clarendon Press, 1989), p. 33.

CHAPTER TWO: IN THE VOICE

1. Aristotle, *De interpretatione* I, 16a4. For the Greek text, see Hermann Weidemann, *Aristoteles, De Interpretatione* (Berlin and Boston: De Gruyter, 2014). For an English translation, see J. L. Ackrill, *De interpretatione*, in Aristotle, *The Complete Works: The Revised Oxford Translation*, ed. Jonathan Barnes (Princeton: Princeton University Press, 1984), vol. 1, pp. 2–18.

2. Aristotle, *De interpretatione* I, 16a2–3.

3. *Ibid.*

4. *Ibid.*, 16a13.

5. *Ibid.*, II, 16b26–16b28.

6. *Ibid.*, IV, 17a1–17a4.

7. *Ibid.*, V, 17a5–6.

8. *Ibid.*, VI, 17a25–27.

9. See Jan Łukasiewicz, *Aristotle's Syllogistic from the Point of View of Modern Formal Logic* (2nd ed., Oxford: Clarendon Press, 1957), pp. 1–2. This is why a strictly Aristotelian syllogism, unlike its familiar Scholastic representation, cannot include a minor such as "Socrates is a man."

10. In its details, this matter is more complex than this summary suggests. For a fuller treatment, see Jonathan Barnes, *Truth, Etc.: Six Lectures on Ancient Logic* (Oxford: Clarendon Press, 2007), pp. 154–67.

11. See Aristotle, *Prior Analytics* I, 27, 43a37–40; *Posterior Analytics* I, 19–22, 81b10–84b3.

12. Aristotle, *Posterior Analytics* II, 16, 98 b 5–10.

13. See Łukasiewicz, *Aristotle's Syllogistic*, p. 2.

14. *Ibid.*, p. 3.

15. *Ibid.*, p. 7.

16. *Ibid.*

17. Aristotle, *De interpretatione* XII, 21b9–10.

18. Aristotle, *Metaphysics* V, 1017a27–30.

19. See Barnes's analysis in *Truth, Etc.*, pp. 106–13.

20. Aristotle, *De interpretatione* II, 16a19–22.

21. *Ibid.*, 16a19–26.

22. On ancient notions of the letter, see, for example, the texts collected in Martin Irvine, *The Making of Textual Culture: "Grammatica" and Literary Theory 350–1100* (Cambridge: Cambridge University Press, 1994), pp. 97–103.

23. Aristotle, *De interpretatione* III, 16b6–7.

24. *Ibid.*, II, 16a30–31.

25. *Ibid.*, II, 16a29.

26. *Ibid.*, III, 16b11–15.

27. The point is noted by Łukasiewicz, who adds that in the syllogistic, terms without reference, such as "chimera," are also tacitly excluded: see *Aristotle's Syllogistic*, p. 72.

CHAPTER THREE: SQUARE NECESSITIES

1. Aristotle, *De interpretatione* VI, 17a32–34.

2. *Ibid.*, VIII, 18a28.

3. *Ibid.*, 18a29.

4. Apuleius, *Peri hermeneias* V, in David Londey and Carmen Johansen, *The Logic of Apuleius: Including a Complete Latin Text and English Translation of the Peri Hermeneias of Apuleius of Madaura* (Leiden: E. J. Brill, 1987), pp. 86–87.

5. *Ibid.*, p. 111.

6. For a treatment of the square in the logical tradition, see *ibid.*, pp. 108–12.

7. On the consequences of this fact, see Terence Parsons, "The Traditional Square of Opposition — A Biography," *Acta Analytica* 18 (1997), pp. 23–49, esp. 30–32. Cf. Lawrence R. Horn, *A Natural History of Negation* (1989, reissue ed. Stanford: CSLI, 2001), pp. 25–30 and, more extensively, pp. 252–67.

8. This last principle has been contested. See David H. Sanford, "Contraries and Sub-contraries," *Nous* 2.1 (1968), pp. 95–96. Cf. Lloyd Humberstone, "Note on Contraries and Subcontraries," *Nous* 37. 4 (2003), pp. 690–705.

9. Aristotle, *De interpretatione* X, 19b5–8.

10. *Ibid.*, 19b8–11.

11. *Ibid.*, 19b12.

12. Aristotle, *Prior Analytics* I, 46, 51b5–7.

13. *Ibid.*, 51b7–8.

14. On Aristotle's "two negations," see Horn, *A Natural History of Negation*, pp. 14–18. Cf. George Englebretson, "The Square of Opposition," *Notre Dame Journal of Formal Logic* 17. 4 (1976), pp. 531–41.

15. Aristotle, *Prior Analytics* I, 46, 51b42–52a4.

16. Horn, *A Natural History of Negation*, p. 17.

17. Aristotle, *Prior Analytics* I, § 46, 51b32.

18. For Aristotle's treatment of obversion, see *On Interpretation* 10. For more detailed accounts, see Parsons, "The Traditional Square of Opposition," pp. 33–36; and M. Soreth, "Zum infiniten Prädikat im zehnten Kapitel der Aristotelischen Hermeneutik," *Islamic Philosophy and the Classical Tradition: Essays Presented by His Friends and Pupils to Richard Walzer*, ed. S. M. Stern, A. Hourani, and Vivian Brown (Columbia: University of South Carolina Press, 1972), pp. 389–424. On the difficulties raised by the "particular proposition," see Jacques Brunschwig, "La proposition particulière et les preuves de non-concluance chez Aristote," *Cahiers pour l'analyse* 10 (1969), pp. 3–26.

19. On the doctrine of "immediate consequences," see Jules Lachelier, *Études sur le syllogisme, suivies de l'Observation de Platner et d'une Note sur le "Philèbe"* (Paris: F. Alcan, 1907), pp. 3–39.

20. Aristotle, *De interpretatione* X, 19b9.

CHAPTER FOUR: VARIETIES OF INDEFINITENESS

1. Thucydides, *Thucydidis Historiae*, ed. Stuart Jones and J. E. Powell (Oxford: Clarendon Press, 1942), I.139.2. For the first translation, see *History of the Peloponnesian War*, trans. J. M. Dent (New York, E. P. Dutton, 1910); for the second, see *The English Works of Thomas Hobbes of Malmsbury* (London: Bohn, 1843). Lexicographers comment that the exact meaning of the adjective in this setting is "debatable."

2. Harry Austryn Wolfson, "Infinite and Privative Judgments in Aristotle, Averroes and Kant," *Philosophy and Phenomenological Research* 8. 2 (1947), pp. 173–87, rpt. in *Studies in the History of Philosophy and Religion*, ed. Isadore Twersky and George H. Williams (Cambridge, MA: Harvard University Press, 1973–77), vol. 2, p. 542. For a more recent study of Aristotle's theory of "negations," see Allan T. Bäck, *Aristotle's Theory of Predication* (Leiden/Boston/Cologne: E. J. Brill, 2000), pp. 199–227.

3. For Alexander's commentary, see *Alexandri Aphrodiensis in Aristotelis Metaphysica Commentaria* (=*Commentaria in Aristotelem graeca* 1), ed. Michael Hayduck (Berlin: Reimer, 1891), p. 327, 18–20; English in Alexander of Aphrodisias, *On Aristotle's Metaphysics* IV, trans. Arthur Madigan (Ithaca, NY: Cornell University Press, 1993), p. 122. The commentary refers to *Metaphysics* IV, 2, 1004a 10–16.

4. See Aristotle, *Categories* X, 10a 26–12 b 5.

5. See Aristotle's discussion of privation in *Metaphysics* V, 1022b22–1022b32.

6. In this sense, privation is, as Aristotle famously remarks, like an "idea": see *Physics* B 183 b18–20. Cf. Heidegger, "Vom Wesen und Begriff der Φύσις," in *Gesamtausgabe* I, vol. 9: *Wegmarken* (Frankfurt am Main: V. Klostermann, 1976), pp. 294–95.

7. Aristotle, *Categories* X, 12a26–27.

8. Wolfson, *Studies in the History of Philosophy and Religion*, vol. 2, p. 543.

9. *Metaphysics* V 1022b 22–1022b32; an English translation can be found in *The Complete Works of Aristotle*, ed. Jonathan Barnes (Princeton: Princeton University Press, 1984), vol. 2, p. 78.

10. Aristotle, *Metaphysics* V 1023a 2–3; English in *The Complete Works of Aristotle*, vol. 2, p. 79.

11. *Ibid.*, 1023a4–5; English in *The Complete Works of Aristotle*, vol. 2, p. 79.

12. See Wolfson, *Studies in the History of Philosophy and Religion*, vol. 2, p. 554.

13. *Metaphysics* V, 1022b33-4.

14. Pseudo-Magentius, *On Aristotle's De interpretatione* 10 19b19 (*CAG* vol. 4.5, p. xliv.11–14 Busse); 87C in *Theophrastus of Eresus: Sources for his Life, Writings, Thought, and Influence*, ed. William W. Fortenbaugh, Pamela M. Huby, Robert W. Sharples, and Dimitri Gutas (Leiden and New York: E. J. Brill, 1992), vol. 1, pp. 150–51.

15. For the terminology, see the remarks in F. W. Zimmermann, *Al-Farabi's Commentary and Short Treatise on Aristotle's "De Interpretatione"* (Oxford: Oxford University Press, 1981), pp. lxiii–lxvii.

16. Theophrastus 87C, in *Theophrastus of Eresus*, p. 151.

17. Theophrastus 87D, in *Ibid.*: *he dia to metatithesthai ten hou' arnēsin ek tou 'esti' tritou proskatēgoroumenou epi ton katēgoroumenon.*

18. Theophrastus 87B, in *Theophrastus of Eresus*, pp. 149–51. As the editors remark in a note, the diagram at issue has been lost (p. 151 n. 1).

19. *Ammonius in Aristotelem De Interpretatione Commentarius* (=*Commentaria in Aristotelem Graeca*, vol. IV), ed. Adolf Busse (Berlin: Reimer, 1897), p. 41.18–20; English in Ammonius, *On Aristotle's "On Interpretation" 1–8*, ed. David Blank (Ithaca, NY: Cornell University Press, 1996), p. 50.

20. *Ammonius*, p. 42.1–8; English in *On Aristotle's "On Interpretation" 1–8*, p. 50.

21. The qualification is important, for it allows one to avoid the fallacious conclusion that, by virtue of the law of the excluded middle, if it is false that "The wall is blind," it must be true that "The wall is not blind." Such an inference would be valid only if "blind" could be predicated of anything whatsoever; but the field of application of such a predicate is limited to such subjects as could, by nature, be said to possess the corresponding positive predicate ("seeing").

22. *De Interpretatione* 3, 16b 15–16; English in Barnes, *The Complete Works of Aristotle*, vol. 1, p. 3. See L. M. De Rijk, "The Logic of Indefinite Names in Boethius, Abelard, Duns Scotus and Radulphus Brito," in *Aristotle's Peri hermeneias in the Latin Middle Ages: Essays on the Commentary Tradition*, ed. H. A. G. Braakhuis and C. H. Kneepkens (Groningen: Ingenium Publishers, 2003), pp. 207–33, esp. pp. 213–16.

23. Raffaella Petrilli, *Temps et détermination dans la grammaire et la philosophie anciennes* (Munster: Nodus Publikationen, 1997), p. 26.

24. On the commentaries, see James Shiel, "Boethius's Commentaries on Aristotle," *Mediaeval and Renaissance Studies* 4 (1958), pp. 217–44, esp. pp. 228–34.

25. Anicius Manlius Severinus Boethius, *Commentarii in librum Aristotelis Peri hermeneias*, ed. Karl Meiser (Leipzig: Teubner, 1877–80), vol. 1, p. 52.15.

26. Boethius, *Commentarii in librum Aristotelis Peri hermeneias*, vol. 2, p. 62, 14–16.

27. This translation follows Migne's edition, rather than Meiser's, as confirmed by a reading of the manuscript proposed by H. A. G. Braakhuis: see De Rijk "The Logic of Indefinite Names," p. 212.

28. *Ibid.*, p. 62, 11.

29. *Ibid.*, p. 62, 21–29.

30. *Ibid.*, p. 62, 16–18: *omne enim nomen . . . definite id significant quod nominatur.*

31. *Ibid.*, p. 63, 13–14.

32. In his *Introductio ad Syllogismos Categoricos* and his *De Syllogismo categorico*, Boethius uses the term *indefinitum* to render *aprosdioristos* and *adioristos*. The statement is "indefinite," in this sense, when its subject is not distributed, or lacks a "quantifier," such as "every" or "some." See Cristina Thomsen Thörnqvest, ed., *Anicii Manlii Severini Boethii De Syllogismo Categorico: Critical Edition with Introduction, Translation, Notes, and Indexes* (Gothenburg: University of Gothenburg, 2008) and *Anicii Manlii Severinii Boethii Introductio ad Syllogismos Categoricos: Critical Edition with Introduction, Commentary, and Indexes* (Gothenburg: University of Gothenburg, 2008). On the development of Boethius's logical doctrine, see L. M. De Rijk, "On the Chronology of Boethius' Works on Logic I," *Vivarium* 2. 1 (1964), pp. 1–149 and "On the Chronology of Boethius' Works on Logic II," *Vivarium* 2. 2 (1964), pp. 125–62.

33. In the *De Hypotheticis Syllogismis*, by contrast, Boethius presents a theory of the categorical syllogism that takes account of infinite terms. See Arthur N. Prior, "The Logic of Negative Terms in Boethius," *Franciscan Studies* 13 (1953), pp. 1–6; cf. Christopher J. Martin, "The Logic of Negation in Boethius," *Phronesis* 36. 3 (1991), pp. 277–304.

CHAPTER FIVE: AN IMPORTED IRREGULARITY

1. Henri Hugonnard-Roche, "L'Organon. Tradition syriaque et arabe," in *Dictionnaire des philosophes antiques*, ed. Richard Goulet, preface by Pierre Hadot (Paris: CNRS, 1989–), vol. 1: *Abam(m)on à Axiothéa*, pp. 502–507, at p. 502.

2. See F. W. Zimmermann, *Al-Farabi's Commentary and Short Treatise on Aristotle's De Interpretatione* (Oxford: Oxford University Press, 1981), pp. lxviii–lxix.

3. *Ibid.*, p. lxix. This is the form attested today by an eleventh-century copy in Paris.

4. Al-Fārābī, *Kitāb al-ḥurūf*, ed. Muḥsin Mahdī (Beirut: Dār al-Mashriq, 1970), § 156; English translation in Muhammad Ali Khalidi, *Medieval Islamic Philosophical Writings* (Cambridge: Cambridge University Press, 2005), p. 25.

5. Al-Fārābī, *Kitāb al-ḥurūf* §155; *Medieval Islamic Philosophical Writings*, pp. 24–25.

6. Al-Fārābī, *Kitāb al-ḥurūf* § 156; *Medieval Islamic Philosophical Writings*, p. 25. As evidence, Al-Farabi evokes the rendition of the Greek word for "element," *stoikheion*, by *istaqsis*, which, although "very strange" in Arabic, resembles the Greek in sound.

7. See Charles H. Kahn, "On the Terminology for Copula and Existence," in *Essays on Being* (Cambridge: Cambridge University Press, 2009), pp. 41–61.

8. Al-Fārābī, *Kitāb al-ḥurūf* § 82.

9. *Ibid.*

10. Al-Fārābī, *Kitāb al-ḥurūf* § 83.

11. Respectively Aristotle, *Categories* X, 12a, 31–33; *De interpretatione* X, 19b, 27–28 and 28. See Wolfson, *Studies in the History of Philosophy and Religion*, vol. 1, p. 387.

12. *Ibid.*

13. Al-Farabi evokes the possibility of employing either *huwa* or *mawjūd* for the missing particle. See Al-Fārābī, *Kitāb al-ḥurūf*, § 82–86.

14. Avicenna argues that if, in a statement, the negative particle precedes the copula (as in *Zayid laysa huwa baṣīran*), the proposition will be negative; if, by contrast, the copula precedes the negative particle (as in *Zayid huwa ghayr baṣīr*), it will be indefinite. In such cases, however, the Arabic thinker resorts to two morphologically and etymologically distinct particles of negation. See Ibn Sīnā, *Al-Ishārāt wa-al-tanbīhāt*, ed. Sulaymān Dunyā (Cairo: Dār al-maʿarif fī Maṣr, 1971), vol. 1, 242; *Remarks and Admonitions, Part One: Logic*, trans. Shams Constantine Inati (Toronto: Pontifical Institute of Mediaeval Studies, 1984), p. 84.

15. Wolfson, *Studies in the History of Philosophy and Religion*, vol. 2, p. 547.

16. *Ibid.*, vol. 1, p. 391.

17. See W. Kutsch, "Muḥaṣṣal, Ghair muḥaṣṣal," *Mélanges de l'Université Saint Joseph* 27. 9 (1947–1948), pp. 169–76; Zimmerman, *Al-Farabi's Commentary and Short Treatise*, p. lxiii. For a fuller study, see Soreth, "Zum infiniten Prädikat."

18. Zimmermann, *Al-Farabi's Commentary and Short Treatise*, xlviii–xlix.

19. *Ibid.*, 39, p. 222.

20. *Ibid.* Zimmermann adds: "The text can hardly be correct, but as I see no obvious emendation I follow the reading."

21. *Short Treatise* 70, in Zimmermann, *Al-Farabi's Commentary and Short Treatise*, p. 240.

22. *Ibid.*, 32, p. 20.

23. *Ibid.*, 39, p. 222.

24. See Deborah L. Black, "Aristotle's *Peri hermeneias* in Medieval Latin and Arabic Philosophy: Logic and the Linguistic Arts," *Canadian Journal of Philosophy* 21 (supplement 1) (1991), pp. 25–83, at p. 63.

25. Zimmermann, *Al-Farabi's Commentary and Short Treatise*, 38, p. 28. The comments bear on the indefinite name, rather than the indefinite verb; but the structure of "non-definition" remains the same.

26. *Ibid.*, 38, p. 29.

27. *Ibid.*, 68, p. 238; Arabic in *Al-Mantiq 'ind Al-Fārābī*, vol. 3, 57B, p. 154. Zimmermann evokes the technical meaning of *rafaʻa* as an example of "Al-Farabi's Hellenizing jargon": "*rafaʻa* (pass. *irtafaʻa*) 'to lift,' opp. *waḍaʻa* 'to put,' for *anaireō*, opp. *títhēmi*, in the sense of 'to ablate, eliminate' opp. 'to posit'" (*Al-Farabi's Commentary and Short Treatise*, p. cxxx n. 2).

28. *Ibid.*, 68, p. 238.

29. *Ibid.*, p. 239.

30. *Ibid.*, p. 238. Cf. Petrilli, *Temps et détermination*, pp. 107–11 and, more recently, Paul Thom, "Al-Fārābī on Indefinite and Privative Names," *Arabic Sciences and Philosophy* 18 (2008), pp. 189–209.

31. See Black, "Aristotle's *Peri hermeneias* in Medieval Latin and Arabic Philosophy," pp. 65–70.

32. See Black's summary, *ibid.*, pp. 67–68.

33. Avicenna, *Al-Ibara: Commentary on Aristotle's De interpretatione: Part One and Part Two*, ed. and trans. Allan Bäck (Munich: Philosophia, 2013), 12.6–13.7, p. 38.

34. Avicenna, *Remarks and Admonitions, Part One: Logic*, p. 83.

35. Averroes, *Commentaire moyen sur le De interpretatione*, ed. and trans. Ali Benmakhlouf and Stéphane Diebler (Paris: Vrin, 2000), p. 83.

36. Averroes, *Epitome of De interpretatione*, 1, 2, p. 41 I, Latin and English in Wolfson, *Studies in the History of Philosophy and Religion*, vol. 1, pp. 391–92.

37. See Zimmermann, *Al-Farabi's Commentary and Short Treatise*, 69, p. 239.

38. Averroes's Middle Commentary was translated in two versions; the first has been traditionally attributed to Wilhelmus of Luna, the second to Jacob Mantinus. See *Averroes, Commentarium medium super libro Peri hermeneias Aristotelis, Translatio Wilhelmo de Luna attribuita*, ed. Roland Hissette (Louvain: Peeters, 1996); *Aristotelis Opera cum Auerrois commentariis* (Venice, 1562–74), vol. 1, part 1 (1562): *Aristotelis De interpretatione liber primus et liber secundus, Severino Boetho interprete, cum Averrois Cordubensis Expositione et Leui Ghersonidis Annotationibus omnibus nunc primum a Iacob Mantino Hebraeo Medico in Latinum conuersis*, fol. 68–106 (rpt. Frankfurt, 1962).

39. Black, "Aristotle's *Peri hermeneias* in Medieval Latin and Arabic Philosophy," pp. 62–71.

40. *Alberti Magni Opera Omnia*, ed. Auguste and Émile Borgnet (Paris: Ludovic Vivès, 1890–99), vol. I, *Logica, Liber I Perihermeneais*, II, V, pp. 391; English in Hans Arens, ed. and trans., *Aristotle's Theory of Language and its Tradition: Texts from 500 to 1750* (Amsterdam and Philadelphia: John Benjamins, 1984), pp. 361–62.

41. Simon of Faversham, *Quaestiones super libro Perihermeneias*, in *Magistri Simonis Anglici sive de Faverisham Opera omnia*, vol. 1, *Opera logica,* ed. Pasquale Mazzarella (Padua: CEDAM, 1957), q. 4, 152.27–153.3. See Black, "Aristotle's *Peri hermeneias* in Medieval Latin and Arabic Philosophy," pp. 43–44.

For a study of Averroës and the indefinite proposition, see Ali Benmakhlouf, "Averroès et les propositions indéfinies," in Philippe Büttgen, Stéphane Diebler and Marwan Rashed, eds., *Théories de la phrase et de la proposition de Platon à Averroès* (Paris: École normale supérieure, 1999), pp. 269–79.

CHAPTER SIX: WAYS OF INDETERMINACY

1. On *aoriston* in ancient grammar, see Petrilli, *Temps et détermination*, esp. 159–93.

2. *Ibid.*, p. 172. For the distinction between sense and reference, see Gottlob Frege, "Über Sinn und Bedeutung," *Zeitschrift für Philosophie und philosophische Kritik*, NF 100 (1892), pp. 25–50; English in "On Sense and Reference," trans. Max Black, in *Translations from the Philosophical Writings of Gottlob Frege*, ed. Peter Geach and Max Black (Oxford: Basil Blackwell, 1960), pp. 56–78. For the notion of "virtual" reference, see Jean-Claude Milner, *Introduction à une science du langage* (Paris: Éditions du Seuil, 1989), pp. 332–36.

3. Varro, *De lingua latina* VIII, 45.

4. *Ars Minor*, 357, in Louis Holtz, *Donat et la tradition de l'enseignement grammatical: Étude sur l'Ars Donati et sa diffusion (IVe–IXe siècle) et édition critique* (Paris: Centre National de la Recherche Scientifique, 1981), p. 585.

5. *Ars Minor*, p. 379.

6. GL IV, 410, 2–16; see commentary in Petrilli, *Temps et détermination*, pp. 173–74.

7. Priscian, *Institutiones grammaticarum libri XVIII*, ed. Martin Hertz (Leipzig: Teubner, 1855), vol. I, Book II, p. 131, 3–6.

8. *Ibid.*, vol. I, Book II, p. 55, 14–19.

9. L. M. De Rijk, ed. *Logica Modernorum: A Contribution to the History of Early Terminist Logic* (Assen: Van Gorcum, 1962), vol. 2, part 2, 312.6. On these "names," see Klaus Jacobi's "*Nomina transcendentia*. Untersuchungen von Logikern des 12. Jahrhunderts über transkategoriale Terme," in *Die Logik des Transcendentalen: Festschrift für Jan A. Aertsen*, ed. Martin Pickavel (Berlin and New York: W. de Gruyter, 2003), pp. 23–36. Cf. Luisa Valente,

"Names That Can Be Said of Everything: Porphyrian Tradition 'Transcendental' Terms in Twelfth-Century Logic," *Vivarium* 45. 2/3 (2007), pp. 298–310.

10. On the so-called *Ars Meliduna* and its contents, see De Rijk, *Logica Modernorum*, pp. 264–390. A complete edition of the treatise has yet to be published. In his essay, Jacobi draws on Yukio Iwakuma's forthcoming edition; see *"Nomina transcendentia,"* p. 27 n. 22.

11. De Rijk has edited the commentary on Priscian in *Logica Modernorum*, II, 1, pp. 234–55; for this passage, see p. 243.

12. On pronouns in medieval theories of signification, see Peter Thomas Geach, *Reference and Generality: An Examination of Some Medieval and Modern Theories* (1962, 3rd ed., Ithaca, NY: Cornell University Press, 1980), pp. 136–90; on relative pronouns in particular, cf. Irène Rosier, "Relatifs et relatives dans les traités des XIIe et XIIIe siècles," *Vivarium* 23. 1 (1983), pp. 1–22, and *Vivarium* 24. 1 (1986), pp. 1–21.

13. Jacobi, "Nomina transcendentia," pp. 26–27 (Latin cited in n. 22).

14. See, for instance, Aristotle, *Metaphysics* III, 2, 998 b 22.

15. Aristotle, *Categories* IV, 1b25–2a5. The translation cited is that of Barnes: *The Complete Works of Aristotle*, vol. 1, p. 3.

16. On "equivocation," see De Rijk, *Logica Modernorum*, II, 1, pp. 475–78.

17. Jacobi, *"Nomina transcendentia,"* p. 27 n. 22.

18. On the *Dialectica Monacensis*, see De Rijk, *Logica Modernorum*, II, 1, pp. 49–54; 408–15; Jacobi, *"Nomina transcendentia,"* pp. 31–34.

19. Jacobi, *"Nomina transcendentia,"* p. 34.

20. See Henri Pouillon, "Le Premier Traité des proprieties transcendentales. La 'Summa de bono' du Chancelier Philippe," *Revue néoscolastique de philosophie* 42 (1939), pp. 40–77, at p. 42.

21. For the adage, see Jorge J. E. Gracia, "The Transcendentals in the Middle Ages: An Introduction" (*Topoi* 11 [1992], pp. 113–20, n. 10), who notes that "Averroes and Avicenna seem to have used this formula only for being and unity."

22. Jacobi, *"Nomina transcendentia,"* p. 35.

23. *Ibid.*

24. *Ibid.*, p. 25.

25. The text can be found in De Rijk, *Logica Modernorum* II, 2, 34.29–35.2.

26. For the *Tractatus Anagnani*, see De Rijk, *Logica Modernorum*, II, 2, VI, pp. 215–332. For the cited statement, see p. 312.6. As Jacobi notes (*"Nomina transcendentia,"* p. 25), they restate this rule elsewhere, in the same words: see p. 313.3.

27. De Rijk, *Logica Modernorum*, II, 2, p. 312.7.

28. Garlandus Compotista, *Dialectica: First Edition of the Manuscript*, ed. L. M. De Rijk (Assen: Van Gorcum, 1959), p. 62. See the discussion in Kneepkens, "Infinite Sophismata," p. 71.

29. Robert of Paris, *Summa 'Breve sit'*, in C. H. Kneepkens, ed., *Het iudicium construc-tionis: het leerstuk van de construction in de 2de helft van de 12de eeuw* (Nijmegen: Ingenium Publishers, 1987), vol. 2, p. 47, 22–27. Robert also argues that the "infinite names" of gram-mar cannot be "infinitized."

30. Kneepkens, "Infinite Sophismata," p. 72.

31. See Nikolaus von Kues, *De non aliud: Nichts Anderes*, ed. Klaus Reinhardt, Jorge M. Marchetta, and Harald Schwaetzer (Munster: Aschendorff, 2011); English in Nicholas of Cusa, *On God Considered as Not-Other*, ed. and trans. Jaspar Hopkins (University of Min-nesota, 1979); Johann Gottlieb Fichte, *Gesamtausgabe der Bayerischen Akademie der Wissen-schaften*, ed. Reinhard Lauth and Hans Jacob (Stuttgart-Bad Cannstatt: Fromann Verlag, 1962–2012); partial English translation in *The Science of Knowledge, with the First and Second Introductions*, ed. and trans. Peter Heath and John Lachs (Cambridge: Cambridge Univer-sity Press, 1982); Samuel Beckett, *Collected Shorter Plays* (London: Faber, 1984), pp. 204–23; Jacques Lacan, *Télévision* (Paris: Éditions du Seuil, 1973); English in *Television*, trans. Denis Hollier, Rosalind Krauss, and Annette Michelson, and *A Challenge to the Psychoanalytic Establishment*, trans. Jeffrey Mehlman, ed. Joan Copjec (New York: Norton, 1990).

CHAPTER SEVEN: FROM EMPTY WORDS

1. The expression is Leo Spitzer's: see his "Parole vuote (A proposito di 'Blittri')," *Lingua nostra*, 16. 1 (1955), p. 1.

2. On both words, see Wolfram Ax, *Laut, Stimme und Sprache: Studien zu drei Grundbe-griffen der antiken Sprachtheorie* (Göttingen: Vandenhoeck & Ruprecht, 1986), pp. 197–99.

3. Diogenes Laertius, *De Claroroum philosophorum vitis* 7.57.

4. Galen, *De differentia pulsuum*, in *Opera Omnia*, ed. Karl Gottlob Kühn (Leipzig: C. Cnobloch, 1821–33), vol. VIII, p. 662.

5. Sextus Empiricus, *Adversus Mathematicos*, 8. 133.

6. Ammonius, *In Arist. Anal. Prior.* I, ed. M. Wallies (=CAG 4/6) (1891), 1, 6ff.

7. Syrianus, *In Metaphysica Commentaria* (=*Commentaria in Aristotelem graeca*, vol. VI, 1), ed. Wilhelm Kroll (Berlin: Reimer, 1902), p. 84.16; English in Syrianus, *On Aristotle's Metaphysics, 13–14*, trans. John Dillon and Dominick O'Meara (London: Bloomsbury, 2006), p. 36, l. 17.

8. Boethius, *Commentaria in librum Aristotelem perihermeneias*, ed. Meiser, vol. 2, p. 54, 5–7.

9. Joh. Versor, *Comm. In Petri Hispani Summuals* (1572), 7r. On medieval accounts of nonsense words, see Jordan Kirk, "Theories of the Nonsense Word in Medieval England" (PhD dissertation, Princeton University, 2013), esp. chapters 1 and 2.

10. Jean Leclerc, *Ontologia, sive De ente, in genere*, in *Opera philosophica in quattuor volumina digesta* (Amsterdam: Apud Georgium Gallet, 1698), vol. I., p. 407.

11. Gottfried Wilhelm Leibniz, *Essais de théodicée*, §76, in C. I. Gerhardt, *Die philosophischen Schriften* (Berlin: Weidmann, 1875–90), vol. 6, p. 95: *Les anciennes écoles appelloient Scindapsus ou Blityri . . . des paroles vuides de sens.*

12. Gottfried Wilhelm Leibniz, *Opuscules et fragments inédits*, ed. Louis Couturat (Paris: Alcan, 1903), p. 255. See also *ibid.*, p. 512. On ancient, medieval, and modern *blityri*, see also S. Meier-Oeser and W. Schröder, "Skindapsos," in *Historisches Wörterbuch der Philosophie*, ed. Joachim Ritter and Karlfried Gründer (Basel: Schwabe, 1971–2007), vol. 9: *Se–Sp*, pp. 974–76; Giancarlo Carabelli, "Blictri: Una parola per Arlecchino," in *Eredità dell' illuminismo: Studi sulla cultura europea fra Settecento e Ottocento*, ed. Antonio Santucci (Bologna: Mulino, 1979), pp. 231–57; Piero Camporesi, "Biltri, Blittri," *Lingua nostra* 13. 1 (1952), pp. 70–72.

13. Alexander Fidora, "Dominicus Gundissalinus and the Introduction of Metaphysics into the Latin West," *The Review of Metaphysics* 66 (June 2013), pp. 691–712, at p. 693.

14. On the Arabic usage, see Fidora, "Gundissalinus and the Introduction of Metaphysics," p. 695.

15. For the corresponding Boethian classification see Boethius, *In Isagogen Porphyrii commenta*, ed. Samuel Brandt, 1st ed. (Vienna: Tempsky, 1906), p. 8: "*tres sint speculativae partes, naturalis . . . mathematica . . . theologica.*"

16. See Dominicus Gundissalinus, *De divisione philosophiae: Über die Einteilung der Philosophie*, ed. and trans. Alexander Fidora and Dorothée Werner (Freiburg im Breisgau: Herder, 2007), p. 68.

17. Pierre Aubenque, "Aristotle et le problème de la métaphysique," in *Problèmes aristotéliciens* (Paris: Vrin, 2009–11), vol. 1: *Philosophie théorique*, pp. 117–29, at p. 121.

18. Aristotle, *Metaphysics* I, 983a 21; 996b 3; 955a 24.

19. Leibniz, "De emendatione primae philosophiae et notione substantiae," in *Die Philosophischen Schriften*, vol. 4, pp. 468–73, at p. 468.

20. Avicenna, *Al-Shifāʾ al-ṭabiʿīyāt*, ed. Ibrāhīm Madkūr and Saʿīd Zāyid (Cairo: Hayʾah al-Miṣrīyah al-ʿĀmmah lil-Kitāb, 1983), bk. I, ch. 2, 12.8; for the Latin text, see *Liber de philosophia prima, sive, Scientia divina*, ed. Simon van Riet, introduction by Gérard Verbeke (Louvain: E. Peeters/Leiden: E. J. Brill, 1977–83), vol. 1, bk. I, ch. 2, line 12.

21. See Albert Zimmermann, *Ontologie oder Metaphysik? Die Diskussion der Metaphysik im 13. und 14. Jahrhundert: Texte und Untersuchungen* (1965, Louvain: Peeters, 1998).

22. *Ibid.*, pp. 156–84.

23. *Ibid.*, pp. 185–222.

24. *Ibid.*, pp. 223–50. There are, however, major doctrinal differences among those who espouse this position, the most important of which being the sense of God's "being," which could either be "analogous" or "univocal" with respect to that of created things.

25. See G. A. Wilson, ed., *Henrici de Gandavo Opera Omnia* (Leiden: E. J. Brill, 1979–91), vol. ɪɪ: *Quodlibet VII*, ed. G. A. Wilson, qu. 1 and 2, pp. 26–27.

26. Jean Paulus, *Henri de Gand: Essai sur les tendances de sa métaphysique* (Paris: Vrin, 1938), p. 32.

27. Jean-François Courtine, *Suarez et le système de la métaphysique* (Paris: Vrin, 1990), p. 184.

28. The double etymology appears for the first time only a few decades before Henry. It can also be found in Bonaventure: see *S. Bonaventurae Opera Omnia* (Qua-racchi: Ex Typographia Collegii S. Bonaventurae, 1882–1902), vol. ɪ, dist. 25, dub. III, p. 446b. See Jacqueline Hamesse, "*Res* chez les auteurs philosophiques des 12e et 13e siècles ou le passage de la neutralité à la spécificité," in *Res, III Colloquio Internazionale del Lessico Intellettuale Europeo*, ed. M. Fattori and M. Bianchi (Rome: Edizioni dell'Ateneo, 1982), pp. 285–96, esp. pp. 91–104, and Pasquale Porro, "Res a reor reris/Res a ratitudine: Autour d'Henri de Gand," in *Mots médiévaux offerts à Ruedi Imbach*, ed. I. Atucha, D. Calma, C. König-Pralong, and I. Zavattero (Porto: Fédération internationale des Instituts d'études médiévales, 2011), pp. 617–28.

29. For the goat-stag, see Aristotle, *De interpretatione* I, 16a13–18; *Prior Analytics* I, 38, 49 a 24; *Posterior Analytics* II, 7, 92 b 7; *Physics* IV, 1, 208 a 30. See Giovanna Sillitti, *Tragfelaphos. Storia di una metafora e di un problema* (Naples: Bibliopolis, 1980).

30. Avicenna, *Al-Shifā' al-ṭabi'iyāt*, I, V, 29–36; *Liber de philosophia prima*, 31–42. For an English translation and commentary, see Michael Marmura, "Avicenna on Primary Concepts: The *Metaphysics* of his al-Shifā'," in *Logos Islamikos: Studia Islamica in honorem Georgii Michaelis Wickens*, ed. Roger M. Savory and Dionisius A. Agius (Toronto: Pontifical Institute of Mediaeval Studies, 1984), pp. 219–39.

31. Avicenna, *Al-Shifā' al-ṭabi'iyāt* I, V, 31.10–32.2; *Liber de philosophia prima*, 35–36.

32. On Avicenna's understanding of existence, see Deborah L. Black, "Mental Existence in Thomas Aquinas and Avicenna," *Medieval Studies* 61. 1 (1999), pp. 45–71, esp. pp. 47–61.

33. Avicenna, *Al-Shifā' al-ṭabi'iyāt*, I, V, 30. 12; *Liber de philosophia prima*, 34.

34. Avicenna, *Al-Shifā' al-ṭabiʿīyāt*, 31.10–32.11; *Liber de philosophia prima*, 35–37.

35. Avicenna, *Al-Shifā' al-ṭabiʿīyāt*, I, V, 32.13–16; *Liber de philosophia prima*, 36–37. See the remarks in Marmura, "Avicenna on Primary Concepts," pp. 228–32.

36. Al Fārābī, *Kitāb al-ḥurūf*, ed. Mahdī, p. 128, §104.

37. *Ibid.*

38. See the discussions in Jean Jolivet, "Aux origins de l'ontologie d'Ibn Sīnā," in *Philosophie médiévale arabe et latine* (Paris: Vrin, 1995), pp. 227–28, and the fuller treatment in Robert Wisnovsky, "Notes on Avicenna's Concept of Thingness (*Šayʾiyya*)," *Arabic Sciences and Philosophy* 10 (2000), pp. 181–221, esp. pp. 182–200. Cf. also Marmura, "Avicenna on Primary Concepts."

39. See Qur'ān 16:40 (*inna-mā qawlunā li-šayʾin ida aradnāhu an naqūla lahu kun fa-yakūnu*) and 36:82 (*inna-mā amruhu ida arāda šayʾan an yaqūla kun fa-yakūnu*).

40. Jolivet, "Aux origins de l'ontologie d'Ibn Sīnā," p. 229, basing himself on Al-Rāzī, ʿAbd al-Jabbār ibn Aḥmad al-Asadābādī, *Muhaṣṣal afkār al-mutaqaddimīn min al-ʿulamāʾ wa-al-mutakallimīn* (Cairo: Maktabat al-kullīyāt al-Azharīyah, 1978), pp. 37–38.

41. Al-Ḥasan ibn Aḥmad Ibn Mattawayh, *al-Tadhkirah fī aḥkām al-jawāhir wa-al aʿrāḍ*, ed. Sāmi Naṣr Luṭtf and Fayṣal Badīr ʿAwn (Cairo: Dār al-Thaqāfah, 1975), p. 75.

42. ʿAbd al-Jabbār ibn Aḥmad al-Asadābādī, *al-Mughnī fī abwāb al-tawḥīd wa-al-ʿadl*, ed. Muṣṭafā Ḥilmi and Abū al-Wafā al-Janīmī, dir. Ṭaha Ḥussayn (Cairo: Wizāfat al-Thaqāfah wa-al-Iršād al-Qawmī, n.d.), vol V, p. 252.10–11.

43. Ahmed Alami, *L'ontologie modale: Étude sur la théorie des modes d'Abū Hāšim al-Gubbāʾi* (Paris: Vrin, 2001), p. 36.

44. Expressions such as *rem auguere*, "to increase one's thing, or possessions," and *in rem alicui esse*, "to be an advantage to something," as well as the elaborate taxonomy of "things" (*res*) as the objects of legal claims in the Roman code all testify to this fact. See Jean-François Courtine, "Res," *Historisches Wörterbuch der Philosophie*, vol. 8: R–Sc, pp. 892–901, at p. 892. Courtine also remarks that in the rhetorical tradition, *res* designates the "matter" that is treated in a discourse. Cf. Isidore of Seville, *Etymologiae* I, V, XXV, 2, in *Isidori Hispalensis episcopi Etymologiarum sive originum libri XX*, ed. W. M. Lindsay (Oxford: Clarendon Press, 1911), vol. 1: *Res sunt que in nostro jure consistunt.*

45. Lucius Anneaus Seneca, Book VI, Letter 58, 15. Latin in *Lettere a Lucilio*, ed. Umberto Boella (Turin: UTET, 1995), p. 322. This translation is indebted to Jacques Brunschwig, "The Stoic Theory of the Supreme Genus and Platonic Ontology," in *Papers in Hellenistic Philosophy*, trans. Janet Lloyd (Cambridge: Cambridge University Press, 1994), pp. 92–157, p. 112.

46. See Plotinus *Enneads* VI, I, 25. For an analysis of the letter, see Brunschwig, "The Stoic Theory of the Supreme Genus," pp. 110–15.

47. See the classic study by Émile Bréhier, *La théorie des incorporels dans l'ancien stoïcisme* (Paris: A. Picard, 1908).

48. Sanctus Aurelius Augustinus, *De vera religione*, ed. Joseph Martin and Klaus-Detlef Daur (Turnhout: Brepols, 1962), I, 5, p. 9.1–4.

49. Anselm of Canterbury, *Epistola de incarnatione verbi*, ed. Franciscus Salasius Schmitt (Bonn: P. Hanstein, 1931), II, p. 10.10–11, 14.

50. See in particular the long discussions in *Glosae super Peri ermeneias*, in *Peter Abaelards philosophische Schriften*, ed. Bernhard Geyer (Munster: W. Aschendorff, 1919), vol. 1, part 2, 365–70, and *Dialectica: First Complete Edition of the Parisian Manuscript*, ed. L. M. de Rijk (1956, 2nd ed., Assen: Van Gorcum, 1970), pp. 157–60.

51. Abelard, *Glosae super Peri ermeneias*, 18. 9–12.

52. Jean Jolivet, "Notes de lexicographie abélardienne," *Pierre Abélard, Pierre le Vénérable: Les Courants philosophiques, littéraires et artistiques en Occident au milieu du XIIe siècle* (Paris: CNRS, 1975), pp. 531–45, esp. pp. 534–38. For a different perspective on these notions and terms, see John Marenbon, *The Philosophy of Peter Abelard* (Cambridge: Cambridge University Press, 1997), pp. 202–209.

53. Abelard, *Glossae super Predicamenta Aristotelis*, in *Peter Abaelards philosophische Schriften*, vol. 1, part 2, p. 242, 23–24.

54. Rijk, *Logica Modernorum*, vol. 2, 2, 35.3–4: *Ad quod dicendum est non posse converti propositiones habentes terminus omnia continentes.*

55. Philip the Chancellor, *Summa de bono*, ed. Nikolaus Wicki (Bern: Francke, 1985), vol. 1, p. 4.

56. Jan A. Aertsen, "'Res' as Transcendental: Its Introduction and Significance," in *Le problème des transcendantaux du XIVe au XVIIe siècle*, ed. Graziella Federici-Vescovini (Paris: Vrin, 2002), pp. 139–56, at p. 139.

57. Thomas Aquinas, Aquinas, *Opera Omnia*, vol. 22: *De veritate* (Rome: Commissio Leonina/1970), q 1, a 1, pp. 3–8.

58. Aertsen, "Res as Transcendental," p. 146. Cf. Sylvio Ducharme, "Note sur le transcendantal 'res' selon Saint Thomas," *Revue de l'Université d'Ottawa* 10 (1940), pp. 85*–99*.

59. See Franciscus de Marchia, *Quodlibet cum quaestionibus selectis ex commentario in librum sententiarum*, ed. Nazareno Mariani (Rome: Editiones Collegii S. Bonaventurae ad Claras Aquas, 1997), q. 3, pp. 71–104.

60. Sabine Folger-Fonfara, *Das 'Super'-Transzendentale und die Spaltung der Meta-*

physik: Der Entwurf des Franziskus von Marchia (Leiden/Boston: E. J. Brill, 2008), pp. 30–31.

61. Franciscus de Marchia, *Quodlibet,* quodlibet 3, a2, 3, in Mariani, p. 99.

62. *Ibid.*, Quodlibet 3, a. 2, 1, ed. Mariani, p. 94. See the commentary in Folger-Fanfana, *Das 'Super'-Transzendentale und die Spaltung der Metaphysik*, pp. 60–62.

CHAPTER EIGHT: TOWARD THE OBJECT IN GENERAL

1. Lorenzo Valla, *Dialectical Disputations*, ed. and trans. Brian P. Copenhaver and Lodi Nauta (Cambridge, MA: Harvard University Press, 2012), vol. 1, Book 1, ch. 2, p. 19.

2. *Ibid.*, pp. 23–23.

3. *Ibid.*, pp. 18–19.

4. *Ibid.*, pp. 26–27.

5. Fosca Mariana Zini, "Lorenzo Valla et la réflexion sur la *Res*," *Penser entre les lignes: Philologie et philosophie au Quattrocento*, ed. Fosca Mariani Zini (Lille: Presses Universitaires du Septentrion, 2001), pp. 275–91, p. 288.

6. Valla, *Dialectical Disputations*, vol. 1, Book 1, ch. 2, pp. 18–19.

7. On Al-Khwārizmī's invention of "algebra," see Roshdi Rashed, "L'Idée de l'Algèbre selon Al-Khwārizmī," *Fundamenta Scientiae* 4. 1 (1983), pp. 87–100.

8. Pierre Costabel and Pietro Redondi, "Contribution à la sémantèse de *res/cosa/cossa* dans la langue scientifique du XVIe siècle," in *Res: III Colloquio internazionale del lessico intelletuale europeo*, ed. Marta Fattori and Massimo Bianchi (Rome: Edizioni dell'Ateneo, 1982), pp. 179–96, p. 187.

9. Luca Pacioli, *Summa de arithmetica geometria proportioni et proportionalita* (Venice, 1494), 57r.

10. Giovanni Crapulli, "'Res' e 'cosa' ('cossa') nella terminologia algebrica del sec. XVI," in Fattori and Bianchi, *Res*, pp. 151–78, p. 154.

11. See for instance, Roshdi Rashed, "Mathématiques et philosophie chez Avicenne," in *Études sur Avicenne*, ed. Jean Jolivet and Roshdi Rashed (Paris: Les Belles Lettres, 1984), pp. 29–39, esp. 34–35.

12. Francisco Suárez, *Disputationes metaphysicae*, d. 1, s. 1, n. 26, in Francisco Suárez, *Opera Omnia*, ed. Charles Berton (Paris: L. Vivès, 1856–78), vol. 25, p. 11.

13. See John P. Doyle, "Suárez on the Reality of the Possibles," *The Modern Schoolman* 45 (1967), pp. 29–48.

14. *Disputationes metaphysicae*, d. 54, s. 1, n. 6, in Suárez, *Opera Omnia*, vol. 26, p. 106.

15. *Disputationes metaphysicae*, d. 54, s. 4, n. 10, in *ibid.*., p. 1031.

16. For a treatment of Suárez's theory of *entia rationis*, see John P. Doyle, "Suárez on Beings of Reason and Truth (1)," *Vivarium* 25. 1 (1987), pp. 47–75, and "Suárez on Beings of Reason and Truth (2)," *Vivarium* 26. 1 (1988), pp. 51–72.

17. Aristotle, *Metaphysics* IV, 2, 1003 b 10.

18. See *Disputationes metaphysicae*, d. 54, s. 5, n. 16, in Suárez, *Opera Omnia*, vol. 26, p. 1035. For a commentary, see Doyle, "Suárez on Beings of Reason and Truth (1)," pp. 61–62.

19. *Disputationes metaphysicae*, d. 54, s. 1, n. 4.

20. *Disputationes metaphysicae*, d. 54, s. 1, n. 9, in Suárez, *Opera Omnia*, vol. 26, p. 1017.

21. Walter Burleigh, *De Puritate artis logicae tractatus longior, with a Revised Edition of the Tractatus Brevior*, ed. Philotheus Boehner (St. Bonaventure, NY: Franciscan Institute, 1955), Tr. 1, p. 3, p. 59; cf. H. Shapiro, "Walter Burley's *De Ente*," *Manuscripta* 7 (1963), pp. 103–108, esp. p. 108.

22. John P. Doyle, "Supertranscendent Being: On the Verge of Modern Philosophy," in *Meeting of the Minds: The Relations between Medieval and Classical Modern European Philosophy*, ed. Stephen F. Brown (Turnhout: Brepols, 1998), pp. 297–315, at p. 301.

23. Domingo de Soto, *Summae,* ed. Wilhelm Risse (Hildesheim and New York: G. Olms, 1980), c. 6, n. 4, fol. 10r.

24. Pedro Fonseca, S. J., *Institutionum dialecticarum libro octo*, I, c. 28 (1575), in *Pedro da Fonseca: Instituiçiones dialécticas*, ed. J. Ferreira Gomes (Coimbra: Universidade de Coimbra, 1964), 1, 82.

25. Doyle, "Supertranscendental Being," p. 307.

26. *Ibid.*, pp. 308–309.

27. Jean Salabert, *Les Addresses du parfait raisonnement, Où l'on découvre les thrésors de la Logique Françoise, & les ruses de plusieurs Sophismes* (Paris: Claude Collet, 1638).

28. *Ibid.*, pp. 53–54.

29. See John P. Doyle, "Supertranscendental Nothing: A Philosophical Finisterre," *Medioevo* 24 (1998), pp. 1–30, esp. pp. 13–30.

30. Sylvester Mauro, *Quaestiones philosophicae, Summulae seu Logica brevis*, ed. Matteo Liberatore (Paris: Bloud & Barral, 1876), vol. I, ch. 2, pp. 16–17.

31. Luis de Lossada, *Institutiones dialecticae, vulgo Summulae* (Salamanca: Ex Typographia Francisci Garcia Onorato et San Miguel, 1721), d. 4, ch. 3, s. 6, n 35, p. 67.

32. José Aguilar, *Summulae* tr. 1, sect. 9, n. 214, in *Cursus philosophicus dictatus Limae* (Seville: Ex. Offc. Joannis Francisci de Blas, 1701), vol. I, p. 32.

33. Richard Lynch, *Universa philosophia Scholastica* (Leyden: n. p., 1654), vol. 1: *Dialectica*, 50, 3, Tr. 3, ch. 2, 85.

34. Antonio Bernaldo de Quiros, *Opus philosophicum, seu selectae disputationes philo-sophicae* (Lyon: Philippe Borde, 1666), *Logica*, tract 1, disp. 2, sect. 4, p. 14.

35. For a summary and analysis, see Doyle, "Supertranscendental Nothing," pp. 16–29.

36. Miguel de Viñas, *Philosophia Scholastica* (Genoa: Typis Antonii Casamarae, 1709), vol. 1, Laurea 1, Pars 1, Lib. 2, Controv. 2, Exam VIII, Punct. 2, n. 10, p. 162.

37. *Ibid.*

38. *Ibid.*

39. Doyle, "Supertranscendental Nothing," pp. 29–30.

40. *Ibid.*, p. 30.

41. Clemens Timpler, *Metaphysicae systema methodicum, Libri quinque*, 1, c. 1, problema 4 (Hanover: Atonius, 1612), pp. 6–7. On Timpler, see Jean-François Courtine, *Suarez et le système de la métaphysique*, pp. 419–30 and Jan A. Aertsen, *Medieval Philosophy as Transcendental Thought: from Philip the Chancellor (ca. 1225) to Francisco Suárez* (Leiden: Brill, 2012), pp. 639–41.

42. On Goclenius and "ontology," see Courtine, *Suarez et le système de la métaphysique*, pp. 408–12.

43. Gottfried Wilhelm Leibniz, "Introductio ad Encyclopediam Arcanam," in *Sämtliche Schriften und Briefe*, ed. Deutsche Akademie der Wissenschaften (Darmstadt: Akademie-Verlag, 1923–), series VI, vol. 4, p. 528.

44. Kant, *Kritik der reinen Vernunft*, A290/B346; English in *Critique of Pure Reason*, trans. and ed. Paul Guyer and Allan Wood (Cambridge: Cambridge University Press, 1998), p. 382.

45. See Ernst Vollrath, "Kants These über das Nichts," *Kant-Studien* 61 (1970), pp. 50–65, esp. 54–55.

46. Alexander Gottlieb Baumgarten, *Metaphysica* (1757, Halle: H. Hemmerde, 1779), I, I §8, p. 3.

47. Kant, *Kritik der reinen Vernunft*, A290/B346, English in *Critique of Pure Reason*, p. 382.

48. Kant, *Gesammelte Werke*, ed. Königlich Preußische [later Deutsche] Akademie der Wissenschaften (Berlin: G. Reimer; later, De Gruyter, 1900), vol. 18: *Metaphysik, Zweiter Teil*, Refl. 5726, pp. 336–37, at p. 336. Cf. the commentary in Courtine, *Suarez et le système de la métaphysique*, p. 425.

49. John T. Doyle has argued this point in several publications. See in particular "Supertranscendental Nothing" and "Between Transcendental and Transcendental: The Missing Link?" *Review of Metaphysics* 50. 4 (1997), pp. 783–815.

50. Duns Scot, Quodlibet III, in *Cuestiones cuodlibetales*, ed. Felix Alluntis (Madrid: Biblioteca de autores cristianos, 1968), p. 92. See the helpful commentary in Olivier

Boulnois, *Être et representation: Une généalogie de la métaphysique moderne à l'époque de Duns Scot, XIIIe–XIVe siècle* (Paris: Presses Universitaires de France, 1999), pp. 446–52.

51. Baumgarten, *Metaphysica*, Caput I, section 1, § 8 (p. 3): "Nonnihil est aliquid: repraesentabile, quicquid non inuoluit contradictionem, quicquid non est A et non-A."

CHAPTER NINE: THE INFINITE JUDGMENT

1. Kant, *Kritik der reinen Vernunft*, A VII; English in *Critique of Pure Reason*, p. 99.

2. *Ibid.*, Ax; English in *Critique*, p. 100.

3. *Ibid.*, Axiii; English in *Critique*, p. 101.

4. *Ibid.*, Axvii, English in *Critique*, p. 103.

5. *Ibid.*, Axxi; English in *Critique*, pp. 104–105.

6. *Ibid.*, Bxvi; English in *Critique*, p. 110.

7. The term *Leitfaden* appears in the titles of sections nine and ten of the Transcendental Analytic.

8. Baumgarten, *Metaphysica*, § 36, pp. 11–12.

9. Meier, *Metaphysik* §46, 48, quoted in Anneliese Maier, *Kants Qualitätskategorien* (Berlin: Pan-Verlag Kurt Metzner, 1930), p. 15.

10. Kant, *Kritik der reinen Vernunft*, A80/B106; English in *Critique*, p. 212.

11. Béatrice Longuenesse, *Kant and the Capacity to Judge: Sensibility and Discursivity in the Transcendental Analytic of the* Critique of Pure Reason, trans. Charles T. Wolfe (Princeton: Princeton University Press, 1998), pp. 293–94.

12. Kant, *Kritik der reinen Vernunft*, A571/B597; English in *Critique*, p. 553.

13. See C. S. Peirce, "The Logic of Quantity," in *Collected Papers of Charles Sanders Peirce*, ed. Charles Hartshorne and Paul Weiss (Cambridge, MA: Harvard University Press, 1931–58), vol. 4: *The Simplest Mathematics*, p. 98.

14. Amos Funkenstein, *Theology and the Scientific Imagination: From the Middle Ages to the Seventeenth Century* (Princeton: Princeton University Press, 1986), pp. 347–48.

15. *Ibid.*

16. Christian Wolff, *Philosophia prima, sive ontologia* (Frankfurt and Leipzig: Prostat in officina Libraria Rengeriana, 1730), § 226, p. 189.

17. Wolff, *Philosophia prima*, § 227.

18. Maier, *Qualitätskategorien*, p. 19.

19. Kant, *Kritik der reinen Vernunft*, A571–72/B 599–600; English in *Critique*, p. 553.

20. *Ibid.*, A 572/B600; English in *Critique*, p. 553–54. On Kant's distinction between the principle of contradiction and the principle of thoroughgoing determination, see Nicholas

F. Stang, "Kant on Complete Determination and Infinite Judgment," *British Journal for the History of Philosophy* 20. 6 (2012), pp. 1117–39.

21. Kant, *Kritik der reinen Vernunft*, A 573/ B 601; English in *Critique*, p. 554.

22. *Ibid.*

23. *Ibid.*, A579–80/B606–7; English in *Critique*, p. 557.

24. *Ibid.*, A577/B605; English in *Critique*, p. 556.

25. *Ibid.*

26. *Ibid.*, A577–78/B605–606; English in *Critique*, p. 557.

27. *Ibid.*, A580/B608; English in *Critique*, p. 558.

28. *Ibid.*, A582–83/B660–61; English in *Critique*, p. 559.

29. *Ibid.*, A593/B661; English in *Critique*, p. 559.

30. For a helpful overview of the pertinent "Reflexions," see *Critique*, p. 746 n. 87.

31. Kant, *Gesammelte Werke*, vol. 24.2, 929–30; English in *Lectures on Logic*, trans. J. Michael Young (Cambridge: Cambridge University Press, 1992), p. 370 (translation modified).

32. *Ibid.*

33. *Ibid.*

34. Kant, *Gesammelte Werke*, ed. Königlich Preußische [later Deutsche] Akademie der Wissenschaften (Berlin: G. Reimer; later, De Gruyter, 1900), vol. 9, §22, pp. 103–104; English in *Lectures on Logic*, p. 600.

35. Erdmann's prints *"nichtsterblich"* as a single word: see Kant, *Gesammelte Werke*, vol. 3, p. 88, and vol. 4, p. 61.

36. *Ibid.*, vol. 24.2, p. 930; English in *Lectures on Logic*, p. 370.

37. *Ibid.*, vol. 9, pp. 103–104; English in *Lectures on Logic*, p. 600.

38. The recent translators of the Cambridge University Press edition (*Critique*, p. 207) have made this passage difficult to perceive, for they have translated *"Die Seele ist nicht sterblich"* (which Erdmann, for his part, prints as *"Die Seele ist nichtsterblich"*) as "The soul is not mortal." The syntax of the German is ambiguous: the sentence could be translated as either "The soul is not mortal" or "The soul is non-mortal." But the context leaves little doubt as to the meaning of the proposition that Kant puts before his reader; it is clearly an infinite judgment, which corresponds to the Latin *anima est non mortalis.* Cf. Stang, "Kant on Complete Determination," p. 1123.

39. Kant, *Kritik der reinen Vernunft*, A72/B97; English in *Critique*, p. 207.

40. *Ibid.*, A72–73/B97–98; English in *Critique*, pp. 207–208.

41. *Ibid.*, Bviii; English in *Critique*, p. 106.

42. Johann Micraelius, *Lexicon Philosophicum Terminorum* (1661), p. 448, cited by Albert Menne, "Das unendliche Urteil Kants," *Philosophia Naturalis* 19 (1982), pp. 151–62, p. 156.

43. Christian Wolff, *Philosophia rationalis sive logica* (1728, 3rd ed. Leipzig and Frankfurt: Prostat in officina libraria Rengeriana, 1740), § 208, p. 221; § 209, p. 221.

44. See the summary in Fumiyasu Ishikawa, *Kants Denken von einem Dritten: Das Gerichtshof-Modell und das unendliche Urteil in der Antonomienlehre* (Frankfurt and New York: Peter Lang, 1990), pp. 38–51.

45. Friedrich Christian Baumeister, *Philosophia definitive* (Vienna, 1775), p. 27, cited in Ishikawa, *Kants Denken von einem Dritten*, p. 42.

46. Hermann Friedrich Kahrel, *Denckkunst* (Herborn, 1755), § 145, p. 75, in Ishigawa, *Kants Denken von einem Dritten*, p. 45.

47. Kant, *Kritik der reinen Vernunft*, A72/B97; English in *Critique*, p. 207.

48. Cf. Kant's remarks in the "Introduction" to the *Critique*: A55/B79–A57/B82. On Kant's claims for "general logic," see John MacFarlane, "Frege, Kant, and the Logic in Logicism," *The Philosophical Review* 111. 1 (2002), pp. 25–65.

49. Willem van der Kuijlen, "Infinite Judgment in Kant's *Critique of Pure Reason*," *Proceedings of the International Workshop 'Logical Kant-Studies'* 4 (Kaliningrad: Kaliningrad State University, 1998), pp. 199–215, at p. 203.

50. Johann Heinrich Lambert, *Anlage zur Architectonic, oder Theorie des Einfachen und des Ersten in der philosophischen und mathematischen Erkenntnis* (Riga: Johann Friedrich Hartknoch, 1771), vol. 1, §257, p. 231.

51. See Ishikawa, *Kants Denken von einem Dritten*, p. 73. Ishikawa draws on Ernst Marcus, *Logik. Die Elementar lehre zur allgemeinen und die Grundzüge der transzendentalen Logik. Einführung in Kants Kategorienlehre* (1906, 2nd ed. Herford: W. Menckhoff, 1911). p. 84.

52. "Reflexion 3065," in Kant, *Gesammelte Werke*, vol. 16, p. 639. Cf. the *Jäsche Logic*, where the passage appears in almost the same form, with one striking difference: the "infinite somewhere," in the *Jäsche Logic*, is defined as belonging to a sphere (*Gesammelte Werke*, vol. 9, pp. 103–104; *Lectures on Logic*, p. 600).

53. Kant, *Gesammelte Werke*, vol. 9, p. 103; English in *Lectures on Logic*, p. 600.

54. *Ibid.*

55. Kant, "Reflexion 3063," in *ibid.*, vol. 16, p. 638; English in *Notes and Fragments*, p. 62.

56. Longuenesse, *Kant and the Capacity to Judge*, p. 296.

57. Kant, "Reflexion 3063," in *Gesammelte Werke*, vol. 16, p. 638; English in *Notes and Fragments*, p. 62.

58. See Gilles Deleuze, *Logique du sens* (Paris: Éditions du Minuit, 1969), pp. 342–34;

English in *The Logic of Sense*, trans. Mark Lester with Charles Stivale, ed. Constantin V. Boundas (London: Athlone Press, 1990), pp. 295–96.

59. Kant, *Kritik der reinen Vernunft*, A80/B106; English in *Critique*, p. 212. On Kant's terminology of *Limitation, Einschränkung* and *Beschränkung*, see Maier, *Kants Qualitätskategorien*, pp. 38–72.

60. Kant, *Kritik der reinen Vernunft*, A577/B605; English in *Critique*, p. 556.

61. Arthur Schopenhauer, "Kritik der Kantischen Philosophie," in *Die Welt als Wille und Vorstellung* (Zurich: Diogenes, 1977), vol. 2, p. 528; English in *The World as Will and Idea*, trans. R. B. Haldane and John Kemp (London: Tübner & Co., 1883–86), vol. 2, p. 23.

62. Schopenhauer, *Die Welt als Wille und Vorstellung*, vol. 2, p. 558; English in *World as Will and Idea*, vol. 2, p. 58.

63. C. S. Peirce, "Limitative," in James Mark Baldwin, ed. *Dictionary of Philosophy and Psychology* (New York: Macmillan, 1902), vol. 2: *Le–Z*, p. 6.

64. Norman Kemp Smith, *A Commentary to Kant's Critique of Pure Reason* (Atlantic Highlands, NJ: Humanities Press, 1918), p. 192.

65. Jonathan Bennett, *Kant's Analytic* (Cambridge: Cambridge University Press, 1966), p. 78.

66. See Ishikawa, *Kants Denken von einem Dritten*, p. 34 n. 15.

67. Kant, *Gesammelte Werke*, vol. 8, p. 137; English in Kant, *Religion and Rational Theology*, ed. and trans. Allen W. Wood and George Di Giovanni (Cambridge: Cambridge University Press, 1996), p. 11.

68. Kant, *Gesammelte Werke*, vol. 8, p. 137; English in *Religion and Rational Theology*, p. 10.

69. *Ibid.*, p. 138; English in *Religion and Rational Theology*, p. 11.

70. *Ibid.* See the discussion in Paul W. Franks, *All or Nothing: Systematicity, Transcendental Arguments, and Skepticism in German Idealism* (Cambridge, MA: Harvard University Press, 2005), pp. 69–79.

71. Kant, *Gesammelte Werke*, vol. 21, p. 603; English in *Opus Postumum*, ed. Eckart Förster, trans. Eckart Förster and Michael Rosen (Cambridge: Cambridge University Press, 1993), p. 96 (translation modified).

72. Kant, *Gesammelte Werke*, vol. 22, p. 73. On the "ether deduction" in the *Opus Postumum*, see among others, Burckhard Tuschling, "Apperception and Ether: On the Idea of a Transcendental Deduction of Matter in Kant's *Opus postumum*," in *Kant's Transcendental Deductions: The "Three Critiques" and the "Opus postumum,"* ed. Eckart Förster (Palo Alto, CA: Stanford University Press, 1989), pp. 193–216; Eckart Förster, "Kant's *Selbstsetzungslehre*," in *ibid.*, pp. 217–38; Paul Guyer, "Kant's Ether Deduction and the Possibility of

Experience," in *Kant's System of Nature and Freedom: Selected Essays* (Oxford: Oxford University Press, 2005), pp. 74–85; Michael Friedman, *Kant and the Exact Sciences* (Cambridge, MA: Harvard University Press, 1992), pp. 290–342. On thoroughgoing determination in the *Opus Postumum*, see Peter Rohs, "Kants Prinzip der durchgängigen Bestimmung alles Seienden," *Kant-Studien* 69. 2 (1978), pp. 170–80.

73. Kant, *Gesammelte Werke*, vol. 22, p. 85; English in *Opus Postumum*, p. 191.

CHAPTER TEN: ZERO LOGIC

1. Letter of January 5, 1795, in Georg Wilhelm Friedrich Hegel, *Briefe an und von Hegel*, ed. Johannes Hoffmeister (Hamburg: Meiner Verlag, 1952–60), vol. 1, p. 14; English in *Hegel: The Letters*, trans. Clark Butler and Christiane Seiler, commentary by Clark Butler (Bloomington: Indiana University Press, 1984), p. 29.

2. Karl Leonhardt Reinhold, *Beyträge zur Berichtigung bisheriger Missverständnisse der Philosophen* (Jena: Johann Michael Manke, 1790–94), vol. 1, p. 167.

3. See Manfred Frank, ed., Gottlob Ernst Schulze, *Aenesidemus, oder, über die Fundamente der von dem Herrn Professor Reinhold in Jena gelieferten Elementar-Philosophie. Nebst einer Vertheidigung des Skepticismus gegen die Anmassungen der Vernunftkritik* (Hamburg: Meiner, 1996).

4. Friedrich Heinrich Jacobi, *Werke* (Leipzig: Gerhard Fleischer, 1812–25), vol. 2, p. 304.

5. Salomon Maimon, Letter to Kant of April 7, 1789, in Kant, *Gesammelte Werke*, vol. 11, pp. 15–16; English in *Correspondence*, ed. and trans. Arnulf Zweig (Cambridge: Cambridge University Press, 1999), p. 293.

6. Salomon Maimon, *Versuch über die Transsendentalphilosophie, mit einem Anhang über die symbolische Erkenntnis und Anmerkungen* (Berlin: Bei Christian Friedrich Voss und Sohn, 1790), rpt. in *Gesammelte Werke*, ed. Valerio Verra (Hildesheim: G. Olms, 1965–76), vol. 2, p. 557. See also the recent edition by Florian Ehrensperger, *Versuch über die Transzendentalphilosophie* (Hamburg: Meiner, 2004). Subsequent page numbers are to the 1790 German edition. English in *Essay on Transcendental Philosophy*, trans. Nick Midgley, Henry Somers-Hall, Alistair Welchman, and Merten Reglitz (New York: Continuum, 2010), p. xi.

7. German in Kant, *Gesammelte Werke*, vol. 11, p. 15; English in *Correspondence*, p. 292.

8. German in Kant, *Gesammelte Werke*, vol. 11, p. 49; English in *Correspondence*, pp. 311–12.

9. Johann Gottlieb Fichte, *Gesamtausgabe der Bayerischen Akademie der Wissenschaften*, vol. 3, part 2, p. 282; English in Frederick Beiser, "Maimon and Fichte," in Gideon Freudenthal, ed., *Salomon Maimon: Rational Dogmatist, Empirical Skeptic: Critical Assessments* (Dordrecht: Kluwer, 2003), pp. 233–48, at p. 233.

10. Salomon Maimon, *Kritische Untersuchungen über den menschlichen Geist, oder das höhere Erknenntnis- und Willensvermögen* (Leipzig: Bei Gerhard Fleischer dem Jüngern, 1797), p. 7 (rpt. in *Gesammelte Werke*, vol. 7).

11. Samuel Hugo Bergman, *The Philosophy of Solomon Maimon*, trans. Noah J. Jacobs (Jerusalem: Magnes Press, 1967), p. 24.

12. Samuel Atlas, *From Critical to Speculative Idealism: The Philosophy of Solomon Maimon* (The Hague: Martinus Nijhoff, 1964), pp. 40–41; cf. Bergman, *Philosophy of Solomon Maimon*, p. 25.

13. Bergman, *Philosophy of Solomon Maimon*, p. 25; cf. Atlas, *From Critical to Speculative Idealism*, pp. 40–41.

14. See Atlas, *From Critical to Speculative Idealism*, p. 43.

15. See Bergman, *Philosophy of Solomon Maimon*, p. 27.

16. Maimon, *Kritische Untersuchungen*, in *Gesammelte Werke*, vol. 7, p. 65.

17. Maimon, *Versuch über die Transsendentalphilosophie*, in *Gesammelte Werke*, vol. 2, p. 104; English in *Essay*, p. 59.

18. Maimon, *Versuch über die Transsendentalphilosophie*, in *Gesammelte Werke*, vol. 2, p. 210; English in *Essay*, p. 111.

19. Nathan Rotenstreich, *Experience and Its Systematization: Studies in Kant* (1965, 2nd ed. The Hague: Martinus Nijhoff, 1972), p. 7.

20. Bergman, *Philosophy of Solomon Maimon*, p. 93.

21. See the illuminating analysis in Rotenstreich, *Experience and Its Systematization*, pp. 14–21.

22. Salomon Maimon, *Versuch einer neuen Logik oder Theorie des Denkens, nebst ange- hängten Briefen des Philaletes an Aenesidemus* (Berlin: Bei Ernst Felisch, 1794), pp. xxi–xxii, rpt. in *Gesammelte Werke*, vol. 5.

23. Maimon, *Kritische Untersuchungen*, in *Gesammelte Werke*, vol. 7, pp. 178–79.

24. Kant, *Kritik der reinen Vernunft*, A107; English in *Critique of Pure Reason*, p. 232.

25. Kant, *Kritik der reinen Vernunft*, B131–32; English in *Critique of Pure Reason*, p. 246.

26. Maimon, *Kritische Untersuchungen*, in *Gesammelte Werke*, vol. 7, pp. 114–15.

27. *Ibid.*, p. 146.

28. *Ibid.*, p. 200. On the principle of determinability, see Friedrich Kuntze, *Die Philos- ophie Salomon Maimons* (Heidelberg: C. Winter, 1912), pp. 48–69; Bergman, *The Philosophy of Salomon Maimon*, pp. 93–115; Martial Guéroult, *La Philosophie transcendentale de Salomon Maïmon* (Paris: Alcan, 1929), pp. 41–49; Atlas, *From Critical to Speculative Idealism*, pp. 146–67; Sylvian Nacht-Eladi, "Aristotle's Doctrine of the Differentia Specifica and Maimon's Law

of Determinability," *Scripta Hierosolymitana* 6 (1960), pp. 222–48; Oded Schechter, "The Logic of Speculative Philosophy and Skepticism in Maimon's Philosophy: *Satz der Bestimmbarkeit* and the Role of Synthesis," in Gideon Freudenthal, *Salomon Maimon: Rational Dogmatist, Empirical Skeptic: Critical Assessments* (Dordrecht: Kluwer, 2003), pp. 18–53.

29. Maimon, *Versuch über die Transsendentalphilosophie*, in *Gesammelte Werke*, vol. 2, pp. 90–91; English in *Essay*, p. 52.

30. For Kant's definition, see *Kritik der reinen Vernunft*, A6/B10; English in *Critique of Pure Reason*, p. 141. On Maimon, mathematics, and synthetic judgments, see Atlas, *From Critical to Speculative Idealism*, esp. 219–48; David Rapport Lachterman, "Mathematical Construction, Symbolic Cognition and the Infinite Intellect: Reflections on Maimon and Maimonides," *Journal of the History of Philosophy*, 30. 4 (1992), pp. 497–522; and Gideon Freudenthal, "Maimon's Subversion of Kant's *Critique of Pure Reason:* There Are No a Priori Synthetic Judgments in Physics," in Freudenthal, *Salomon Maimon*, pp. 144–75.

31. Maimon, *Versuch über die Transsendentalphilosophie*, in *Gesammelte Werke*, vol. 2, pp. 84–85; English in *Essay*, p. 49.

32. Bergman, *Philosophy of Solomon Maimon*, p. 98.

33. Maimon, *Versuch über die Transsendentalphilosophie*, in *Gesammelte Werke*, vol. 2, pp. 377–78; English in *Essay*, p. 194.

34. Maimon, *Kathegorien des Aristoteles*, in *Gesammelte Werke*, vol. 6, p. 150.

35. *Ibid.*

36. *Ibid.*, p. 151. The example would have a long life: see J. D. Mabbott's argument, without reference to Maimon, that "'Virtue is square' is a Turkey carpet judgment," "Negation," *Proceedings of the Aristotelian Society* Supplementary vol. 9 (1929) pp. 67–79, p. 68.

37. *Ibid.*

38. Maimon, *Versuch einer neuen Logik*, in *Gesammelte Werke*, vol. 5, p. 69.

39. Maimon, *Kathegorien des Aristoteles*, in *Gesammelte Werke*, vol. 6, p. 151.

40. *Ibid.*, p. 152. Cf. *ibid.*, p. 225. For Kant's corresponding example, see "Versuch, den Begriff der negativen Größen in die Weltweisheit einzuführen," in *Gesammelte Werke*, vol. 2, *Vorkritische Schriften II: 1757–1777*, pp. 165–204, esp. pp. 177–78; English in "Attempt to Introduce the Concept of Negative Magnitudes into Philosophy," in Kant, *Theoretical Philosophy: 1755–1770*, trans. and ed. David Walford (Cambridge: Cambridge University Press, 2003), pp. 207–41, pp. 216–17.

41. Maimon, *Kathegorien des Aristoteles*, in *Gesammelte Werke*, vol. 6, pp. 152–53.

42. *Ibid.*, p. 224.

43. *Ibid.*, pp. 224–25.

44. Atlas, *From Critical to Speculative Idealism*, p. 160.

45. English in Maimonides, *The Guide of the Perplexed*, trans. Shlomo Pines, with an introduction by Leo Strauss (Chicago: University of Chicago Press, 1963), vol. 1, 56, p. 130; Arabic in Mūsā ibn Maimūn al-Quṭubī al-Andalusī, *Dalālat al-ḥā'irīn*, ed. Hüseyin Atay (Ankara: Maṭba'ah Jāmi'at Anqara, 1974), pp. 137-38. See Shlomo Pines, "Dieu et l'être selon Maïmonide: Exégèse d'Exode 3, 14 et doctrine connexe," in *Celui qui est: Interprétations juives et chrétiennes d'Exode 3, 14*, ed. Alain de Libera and Emilie Zum Brunn (Paris: Éditions du Cerf, 1986), pp. 15-24, rpt. in *The Collected Works of Shlomo Pines*, vol. 5: *Studies in the History of Jewish Thought*, ed. Warren Zev Harvey and Moshe Idel (Jerusalem: Magnes Press, 1997), pp. 447-56.

46. English in *Guide*, vol. 1, chapter 56, p. 131; Arabic in *Dalālat al-ḥā'irīn*, p. 138.

47. English in *Guide*, vol. 1, chapter 58, p. 136; Arabic in *Dalālat al-ḥā'irīn*, p. 143.

48. English in *Guide*, vol. 1, chapter 58, p. 136; Arabic in *Dalālat al-ḥā'irīn*, p. 143.

49. See Wolfson, "Maimonides on Negative Attributes," *Studies in the History of Philosophy and Religion*, vol. 2, pp. 195-230, esp. pp. 219-20.

50. English in *Guide*, vol. 1, chapter 58, p. 137; Arabic in *Dalālat al-ḥā'irīn*, p. 143.

51. On Maimon's Maimonides commentaries, see Maurice-Ruben Hayoun's introduction to Salomon Maïmon, *Commentaires de Maïmonide*, preface by Jean Jolivet, ed. and trans. Maurice-Ruben Hayoun (Paris: Éditions du Cerf, 1999), pp. 7-63.

52. Salomon Maimon, *Lebensgeschichte*, in *Gesammelte Werke*, vol. 1, part 2, p. 54.

53. *Ibid*, p. 55.

54. Salomon Maimon, *Giv'at ha-more*, ed. Hugo Bergman and Nathan Rotenstreich (Jerusalem: ha-Akademyah ha-le'umit ha-Yiśre'elit le mada'im, 726 [1965]), ch. 56, pp. 83-84; English in Bergman, *Philosophy of Solomon Maimon*, pp. 98-99.

55. Maimon, *Versuch einer neuen Logik*, in *Gesammelte Werke*, vol. 5, p. 157.

56. Kunzte, *Die Philosophie Salomon Maimons*, p. 231.

CHAPTER ELEVEN: NON-I AND I

1. Johann Gottlieb Fichte, *Sämmtliche Werke*, ed. J. H. Fichte (Berlin: Veit, etc., 1844-46), vol. 1, p. 29.

2. *Ibid.*, p. 91; English in Johann Gottlieb Fichte, *The Science of Knowledge,*, p. 93.

3. Fichte, *Sämmtliche Werke*, vol. 1, p. 116; English in *Science of Knowledge*, p. 114.

4. *Ibid.*

5. *Ibid.*

6. See Dieter Henrich, "Fichtes urpsrüngliche Einsicht," in *Subjektivität und*

Metaphysik, Festschrift für Wolfgang Cramer, ed. Dieter Henrich and Hans Wagner (Frankfurt am Main: Vittorio Klostermann, 1966), pp. 188–232.

7. Fichte, *Sämmtliche Werke*, vol. 1, p. 117; English in *Science of Knowledge*, p. 115.

8. Fichte, *Sämmtliche Werke*, vol. 1, p. 118; English in *Science of Knowledge*, p. 115.

9. On Kant's doctrine of existence as the "absolute positing of a thing," see Martin Heidegger, "Kants These über das Sein," in *Gesamtausgabe*, vol. 9: *Wegmarken* (Frankfurt am Main: Vittorio Kostermann, 1976), pp. 445–80.

10. Wolfgang Janke, "Thetisches Urteil—Spekulativer Satz. Fichte und Hegel über die Ausdrucksform der Grundsetzung 'Ich bin—Ich,'" in *Entgegensetzungen: Studien zu Fichte-Konfrontationen von Rousseau bis Kierkegaard* (Amsterdam: Rodopi, 1994), pp. 47–68, p. 55.

11. Werner Hamacher has explored this "depositional" structure of Fichte's primal positing from a different perspective. See his "Position Exposed: Schlegel's Poetological Transposition of Fichte's Absolute Proposition," in *Premises: Essays on Literature and Philosophy from Kant to Celan*, trans. Peter Fenves (Cambridge, MA: Harvard University Press, 1996), pp. 222–60.

12. Fichte, *Sämmtliche Werke*, vol. I, 117; English in *Science of Knowledge*, p. 115.

13. Hegel, *The Difference Between Fichte's and Schelling's System of Philosophy*, trans. H. S. Harris and Walter Cerf (Albany: State University of New York Press, 1977), p. 82.

14. Fichte, *Sämmtliche Werke*, vol. I, 117; English in *Science of Knowledge*, p. 115.

15. *Ibid.*

16. Friedrich Wilhelm Joseph Schelling, *Historisch-kritische Ausgabe*, ed. Hans Michael Baumgartner et al. (Stuttgart: Frommann-Holzboog, 1976–), series 1: *Werke*, vol. 2, Preface, pp. 70–71; English in Schelling, *The Unconditional in Human Knowledge: Four Early Essays, 1794-1796*, ed. and trans. Fritz Marti (Lewisburg, PA: Bucknell University Press, 1980), p. 64.

17. Schelling, *Werke*, vol. 2, §1, 85; English in *Unconditional in Human Knowledge*, p. 71.

18. Schelling, *Werke*, vol. 2, §3, p. 89; English in *Unconditional in Human Knowledge*, p. 74.

19. Schelling, *Werke*, vol. 2, pp. 90–91; English in *Unconditional in Human Knowledge*, p. 75 (translation modified).

20. Schelling, *Werke*, vol. 2, §4, p. 93; English in *Unconditional in Human Knowledge*, p. 77.

21. Schelling, *Werke*, vol. 2, p. 94; English in *Unconditional in Human Knowledge*, p. 77.

22. *Ibid.*

23. Schelling, *Werke*, vol. 2, §6, p. 100; English in *Unconditional in Human Knowledge*, p. 81.

24. Schelling, *Werke*, vol. 2, §16, p. 146; English in *Unconditional in Human Knowledge*, p. 110.

25. On the reasons to translate *nicht-ich* by "non-I," rather than "not-I," see George J. Seidel, *Fichte's Wissenschaftslehre of 1794: A Commentary on Part 1* (West Lafayette, IN: Purdue University Press, 1993), p. 89.

26. Schelling, *Werke*, vol. 2, §16, p. 150; English in *Unconditional in Human Knowledge*, p. 113.

27. Schelling, *Werke*, vol. 2, §16, pp. 150–51; English in *Unconditional in Human Knowledge*, p. 113.

28. Schelling, *Werke*, vol. 2, §16, p. 151; English in *Unconditional in Human Knowledge*, p. 113.

29. Jean-Christophe Lemaitre, "La réévaluation des rapports entre logique formelle et logique transcendentale dans l'idéalisme allemand: Le cas du jugement infini chez Kant et chez Schelling," in *La question de la logique dans l'idéalisme allemand: Actes du colloque de Bruxelles, 7–9 avril 2011*, ed. Guillaume Lejeune (Zurich: Georg Olms, 2013), pp. 125–40, at pp. 136–37.

CHAPTER TWELVE: COLLAPSING SENTENCES

1. Georg Wilhelm Friedrich Hegel, *Gesammelte Werke, Deutsche Forschungsgemeinschaft* (Hamburg: F. Meiner, 1957–2015), vol. 21: *Wissenschaft der Logik*, ed. Friedrich Hogemann and Walter Jaeschke (Hamburg: Meiner, 1985), p. 32; English in *The Science of Logic*, trans. and ed. George Di Giovanni (Cambridge: Cambridge University Press, 2010), p. 28.

2. Hegel, *Gesammelte Werke*, vol. 21, p. 34; *Science of Logic*, p. 29.

3. *Ibid.*

4. *Ibid.*

5. *Ibid.*, p. 32; *Science of Logic*, p. 27.

6. *Ibid.*, p. 37; *Science of Logic*, p. 32. On Hegel's allusions to the inorganic state of traditional logic, see Robert Pippin, *Hegel's Idealism: The Satisfactions of Self-Consciousness* (Cambridge: Cambridge University Press, 1989), p. 236.

7. Hegel, *Gesammelte Werke*, vol. 9: *Die Phänomenologie des Geistes*, ed. Wolfgang Bonsiepen and Reinhard Heede (Hamburg: Meiner, 1980), p. 35; English in *Phenomenology of Spirit*, trans. A. V. Miller (Oxford: Oxford University Press, 1977), §47, p. 27. Cf. Jean Hyppolite, *Logique et existence: Essai sur la logique de Hegel* (Paris: Presses Universitaires de France, 1953), pp. 213–14. Cf. Georges Noël, *La Logique de Hegel* (Paris: Alcan, 1897), p. 88.

8. Hegel, *Gesammelte Werke*, vol. 21, p. 11; *Science of Logic*, p. 12.

9. *Ibid.*

10. *Ibid.* Hegel takes this principle to be true to different degrees, depending on the

language; in a parenthetical remark, he observes that "the Chinese language has apparently not advanced far culturally" in this respect.

11. Hyppolite, *Existence et logique*, p. 221.

12. *Ibid.*, pp. 221–22.

13. Béatrice Longuenesse, *Hegel's Critique of Metaphysics*, trans. Nicole J. Simek (Cambridge: Cambridge University Press, 2007), p. 203.

14. Hegel, *Gesammelte Werke*, vol. 12: *Wissenschaft der Logik*, ed. Friedrich Hogemann and Walter Jaeschke (Hamburg: Meiner, 1978), pp. 17–18; *Science of Logic*, p. 515.

15. Hegel, *Gesammelte Werke*, vol. 12, pp. 22–23; *Science of Logic*, pp. 519–20.

16. Hegel, *Gesammelte Werke*, vol. 12, p. 27; *Science of Logic*, p. 524.

17. On the spurious etymology of *Urteil* as *Ur-Teil*, see Manfred Frank, *The Philosophical Foundations of Early German Romanticism*, trans. Elizabeth Millán-Zaubert (Albany: SUNY Press, 2004), pp. 103–104. For Hölderlin and judgment, see above all Friedrich Hölderlin, "Urteil und Seyn," *Sämtliche Werke*, ed. Friedrich Beissner (Stuttgart: Cotta, 1946–85), vol. 4: *Der Tod des Empedokles; Aufsätze*, pp. 226–27. The literature on this text is abundant. Among others, see Dieter Henrich, "Hölderlin über Urteil und Sein: Eine Studie zur Entstehungsgeschichte des Idealismus," *Hölderlin-Jahrbuch* 14 (1965–66), pp. 73–96.

18. Hegel, *Gesammelte Werke*, vol. 12, p. 55; *Science of Logic*, p. 552. On *Urteil* and concept, see also *Gesammelte Werke*, vol. 12, p. 52; *Science of Logic*, p. 549; *Ibid.*, vol. 20: *Enzyklopädie der philosophischen Wissenschaften im Grundrisse (1830)*, ed. Wolfgang Bonsiepen and Hans Christian Lucas (Hamburg: Meiner, 1992), §166, p. 182; English in *Encyclopedia of the Philosophical Sciences in Basic Outline, Part One: Science of Logic*, ed. and trans. Klaus Brinkmann and Daniel O. Dahlstrom (Cambridge: Cambridge University Press, 2010), p. 244.

19. Longuenesse, *Hegel's Critique of Metaphysics*, p. 210.

20. Hegel, *Gesammelte Werke*, vol. 4: *Jenaer kritische Schriften*, ed. Hatmut Buchner and Otto Pöggeler (Hamburg: Meiner, 1968), pp. 326–27; English in Hegel, *Faith and Knowledge*, trans. Walter Cerf and H. S. Harris (Albany: SUNY Press, 1977), p. 69.

21. For a commentary on this passage, see Longuenesse, *Hegel's Critique of Metaphysics*, pp. 182–88.

22. Hegel, *Gesammelte Werke*, vol. 12, p. 57; *Science of Logic*, p. 554.

23. Hegel, *Gesammelte Werke*, vol. 12, p. 60; *Science of Logic*, pp. 557–58.

24. Hegel, *Gesammelte Werke*, vol. 12, p. 61; *Science of Logic*, p. 558.

25. Hegel, *Gesammelte Werke*, vol. 12, p. 62, *Science of Logic*, p. 559.

26. Hegel, *Gesammelte Werke*, vol. 12, p. 64; *Science of Logic*, p. 561.

27. Hegel, *Gesammelte Werke*, vol. 12, p. 65; *Science of Logic*, p. 562.

28. Hegel, *Gesammelte Werke*, vol. 12, p. 66; *Science of Logic*, p. 564.

29. Hegel, *Gesammelte Werke*, vol. 12, p. 67; *Science of Logic*, pp. 564–65.

30. Hegel, *Gesammelte Werke*, vol. 12, *Science of Logic*, p. 565.

31. Hegel, *Gesammelte Werke*, vol. 12, pp. 67–68; *Science of Logic*, p. 565. Cf. Aristotle's argument that when something becomes "white," it does so from the "non-white," understood not as "*any* non-white" (such as "musical"), but "rather from black or some intermediate": *Physics* I, 188a32–188b3. See also Storrs McCall, "Contrariety," *Notre Dame Journal of Formal Logic* 8. 1–2 (1976), pp. 121–32, and, for a discussion that puts Hegel's account in relation to theories in which "negation presupposes affirmation," Horn, *A Natural History of Negation*, pp. 64–65.

32. Hegel, *Gesammelte Werke*, vol. 12, p. 69; *Science of Logic*, p. 567.

33. *Ibid.*

34. *Ibid.*

35. Hegel, *Gesammelte Werke*, vol. 12, pp. 69–70; *Science of Logic*, p. 567.

36. Hegel, *Gesammelte Werke*, vol. 12, p. 70; *Science of Logic*, p. 567.

37. *Ibid.*

38. *Ibid.*

39. *Ibid.*

40. Hegel, *Gesammelte Werke*, vol. 12, p. 70; *Science of Logic*, pp. 567–68.

41. Hegel, *Gesammelte Werke*, vol. 14, part 1: *Naturrecht und Staatswissenschaft im Grundrisse, Grundlinien der Philosophie des Rechts*, ed. Klaus Grotsch and Elisabeth Weisser-Lohmann (Hamburg: Meiner, 2009–11), §95, p. 89; English in *Outlines of the Philosophy of Right*, trans. T. M. Knox, rev. Stephen Houlgate (Oxford: Oxford University Press, 2008), p. 98. For the juridical infinite judgment, see also *Ibid.*, §295 and §53.

42. Hegel, *Gesammelte Werke*, vol. 20, §173, p. 187; English in *Encyclopedia of the Philosophical Sciences*, p. 247.

43. Hegel, *Gesammelte Werke*, vol. 20, §173, p. 187; *Encyclopedia of the Philosophical Sciences*, p. 248.

44. Hegel, *Gesammelte Werke*, vol. 7: *Jenaer Systementwurfe II*, ed. Rolf-Peter Horstmann and Johann Heinrich Trede (Hamburg: Meiner, 1971), p. 80; English in *The Jena System 1804–5: Logic and Metaphysics*, ed. and trans. John W. Burbidge and George di Giovanni, introduction by H. S. Harris (Montreal: McGill/Queens University Press, 1986), p. 84.

45. Hegel, *Gesammelte Werke*, vol. 7, p. 87; *Jena System*, p. 91.

46. Hegel, *Gesammelte Werke*, vol. 7, pp. 87–88; *Jena System*, p. 92.

47. Hegel, *Gesammelte Werke*, vol. 7, p. 88; *Jena System*, p. 92.

48. *Ibid.*

49. *Ibid.*

50. *Ibid.*

51. Hegel, *Gesammelte Werke*, vol. 7, p. 89; *Jena System*, p. 93.

52. Stanley Rosen, *The Idea of Hegel's Science of Logic* (Chicago: University of Chicago Press, 2014), p. 429. Cf. the different treatments in G. R. G. Mure, *A Study of Hegel's Logic* (Oxford: Clarendon Press, 1950), pp. 178–80; André Léonard, *Commentaire littérale de la Logique de Hegel* (Louvain and Paris: Éditions de l'institut supérieur de philosophie de Louvain/Vrin, 1974), pp. 361–62.

53. Hermann Schmitz, *Hegel als Denker der Individualität* (Meisenheim and Glan: Anton Hain, 1957), p. 115. On Hegel and the infinite judgment, see also Günter Wohlfart, "Das unendliche Urteil. Zur Interpretation eines Kapitels aus Hegels *Wissenschaft der Logik*," *Zeitschrift für philosophische Forschung* 39.1 (1985), pp. 85–100; Thomas Sören Hoffmann, *Die absolute Form: Modalität, Individualität und das Prinzip der Philosophie nach Kant und Hegel* (Berlin and New York: De Gruyter, 1991), pp. 115–30; Hans Lenk, *Kritik der logischen Konstanten: Philosophische Begründungen der Urteilsformen vom Idealismus bis zur Gegenwart* (Berlin: De Gruyter, 1968), pp. 359–61.

54. Georg Wilhelm Friedrich Hegel, *Jenenser Logik, Metaphysik und Naturphilosophie*, ed. Georg Lasson (Hamburg: Meiner, 1923), p. 33.

55. *Ibid.*, pp. 26, 28.

56. Hegel, *Gesammelte Werke*, vol. 4, p. 359; English in *Faith and Knowledge*, p. 113.

57. *Ibid.*, p. 401; *Faith and Knowledge*, p. 172.

58. Schmitz, *Hegel als Denker*, pp. 117–18.

59. Hegel, *Gesammelte Werke*, vol. 12, p. 70; *Science of Logic*, p. 568.

60. *Ibid.*

61. Hegel, *Lectures on Logic: Berlin 1831*, transcribed by Karl Hegel, trans. Clark Butler (Bloomington: Indiana University Press, 2008), p. 186.

62. *Ibid.*

63. Hegel, *Gesammelte Werke*, vol. 21, p. 16; *Science of Logic*, p. 18.

64. *Ibid.* In an as yet unpublished paper on Hegel's Logic, "Das Nicht im Satz (der Identität)," Werner Hamacher has given a far-reaching account of the consequences of Hegel's reliance on such a "dash" in the statement of identity.

65. Hegel, *Gesammelte Werke*, vol. 20, §173, p. 187; English in *Encyclopedia*, p. 247.

66. Hegel, *Gesammelte Werke*, vol. 9, p. 137; English in *Phenomenology* §232, p. 139. Cf. also 138, and 141.

67. Hegel, *Gesammelte Werke*, vol. 9, p. 138; *Phenomenology* §242, p. 146.

68. On Hegel, physiognomy and phrenology, see Mladen Dolar, "The Phrenology of Spirit," in *Supposing the Subject*, ed. Joan Copjec (London: Verso, 1994), pp. 64–83; Lambros Kordelas, *Geist und caput mortuum: Hegels Kritik der Lehre Galls in der "Phänomenologie des Geistes"* (Würzburg: Königshausen & Neumann, 1998), esp. pp. 183–231.

69. Hegel, *Gesammelte Werke*, vol. 9, p. 189; *Phenomenology* §340, p. 206.

70. Hegel, *Gesammelte Werke*, vol. 9, p. 192; *Phenomenology*, §346, p. 210.

71. Hegel, *Gesammelte Werke*, vol. 9, p. 190; *Phenomenology*, §346, p. 208.

72. Hegel, *Gesammelte Werke*, vol. 9, p. 191; *Phenomenology*, § 344, p. 209.

73. Cf. Pierre-Jean Labarrière, *Structures et mouvement dialectique dans la Phénoménologie de l'esprit de Hegel* (1968, 2nd ed., Paris: Aubier, 1985), p. 104.

74. Hegel, *Gesammelte Werke*, vol. 9, p. 423; *Phenomenology* §790, pp. 480–81.

75. Hegel, *Gesammelte Werke*, vol. 9, p. 423; *Phenomenology*, §791, p. 481.

76. *Ibid.*

77. Hegel, *Gesammelte Werke*, vol. 9, pp. 44–45; *Phenomenology* §63–64, p. 39.

78. Hegel, *Gesammelte Werke*, vol. 9, pp. 42–44; *Phenomenology* §60, pp. 36–37.

79. Hegel, *Gesammelte Werke*, vol. 9, p. 43; *Phenomenology* §60, p. 37.

80. Hegel, *Gesammelte Werke*, vol. 9, p. 44; *Phenomenology* §62, p. 38.

81. Hegel, *Gesammelte Werke*, vol. 9, p. 44; *Phenomenology* §62, p. 39.

82. Hegel, *Gesammelte Werke*, vol. 9,. p. 44; *Phenomenology* §61, p. 38.

83. Hegel, *Vorlesungen über die Ästhetik*, ed. Eva Moldenhauer and Karl Markus Michel (Frankfurt am Main: Suhrkamp Verlag, 1970), vol. 1, p. 21; English in *Aesthetics: Lectures on Fine Art*, I, II, trans. by T. M. Knox (New York: Oxford University Press, 1975), vol. 1, p. 8.

84. Hegel, *Vorlesungen über die Ästhetik*, vol. 3, p. 527; *Aesthetics*, vol. 2, p. 1199.

85. Werner Hamacher, "(The End of Art with the Mask)," trans. Kelly Barry, in *Hegel after Derrida*, ed. Stuart Barnett (New York: Routledge, 1998), pp. 105–30, p. 105.

CHAPTER THIRTEEN: THE SPRINGBOARD PRINCIPLE

1. On the fragment in German Romanticism, see, among others, Philippe Lacoue-Labarthe and Jean-Luc Nancy, *L'absolu littéraire: Théorie de la littérature du romantisme allemand* (Paris: Seuil, 1978), pp. 57–80.

2. See Alexis Philonenko, *L'École de Marbourg: Cohen — Natorp — Cassirer* (Paris: Vrin, 1989), p. 7.

3. See Ernst Cassirer, "Hermann Cohen und die Erneuerung der Kantischen Philosophie," *Kantstudien* 17. 1–3 (1912), pp. 252–73, p. 253.

4. Eduard Zeller, "Über Bedeutung und Aufgabe der Erkenntnistheorie: Vortrag bei Eröffnung der Vorlesungen über Logik und Erkenntnistheorie," in *Vorträge und Abhandlungen. Zweite Sammlung* (Leipzig: Fries, 1877), p. 490; Otto Liebmann, *Kant und die Epigonen: Eine kritsche Abhandlung* (Stuttgart: C. Schober, 1865), p. 85.

5. Hermann Cohen, *Kants Theorie der Erfahrung* (1871, 2nd ed., Berlin: F. Dümmler, 1885), p. 268; cf. Hermann Cohen, *Logik der reinen Erkenntnis* (1902, 3rd ed., Berlin: Bruno Cassirer, 1922), p. xi.

6. See Wolfgang Marx, *Transzendentale Logik als Wissenschaftstheorie: Systematisch-kritische Untersuchungen zur philosophischen Grundlegungsproblematik in Cohens 'Logik der reinen Erkenntnis'* (Frankfurt am Main: Klostermann, 1977), p. 18.

7. Paul Natorp, *Die logischen Grundlagen der exakten Wissenschaften* (Berlin and Leipzig: B. G. Teubner, 1910), p. 14.

8. Hermann Cohen, *Kants Theorie der Erfahrung* (Berlin: F. Dümmler, 1871), p. 3.

9. Cohen, *Kants Theorie der Erfahrung* (1871), p. 7.

10. *Ibid.*, pp. 15–16.

11. Kant, *Kritik der reinen Venunft*, B xviii; English in *Critique of Pure Reason*, p. 111. See Cohen, *Kants Theorie der Erfahrung* (1871), p. 12.

12. Cohen, *Kants Theorie der Erfahrung* (1871), p. 104.

13. Alan W. Richardson, "Conceiving, Experiencing, and Conceiving Experiencing: Neo-Kantianism and the History of the Concept of Experience," *Topoi* 22 (2003), pp. 55–67, at p. 60.

14. Ernst Cassirer, *Substance and Function and Einstein's Theory of Relativity*, trans. William Curtis Swabey and Marie Collins Swabey (New York: Dover, 1953), p. 269.

15. Philonenko, *L'École de Marbourg*, p. 22.

16. Cohen, *Logik der reinen Erkenntnis*, p. 37.

17. *Ibid.*, p. 12.

18. *Ibid.*, p. 11.

19. Marx, *Transzendentale Logik*, p. 9. On Cohen's use of the term "pure," see Josef Solowiejczyk, *Das reine Denken und die Seinskonstituierung bei Hermann Cohen* (Berlin: Reuther & Reichard, 1932), p. 51; Andrea Poma, *La filosofia critica di Hermann Cohen* (Milan: Mursia, 1988), p. 92; Helmut Holzhey, *Cohen und Natorp: Die Geschichte der 'Marburger Schule' als Auseinandersetzung um die Logik des Denkens* (Basel: Schwabe, 1986), vol. 1: *Ursprung und Einheit*, pp. 175–78.

20. Holzhey, *Cohen und Natorp*, vol. 1, p. 175.

21. Poma, *La filosofia critica di Hermann Cohen*, p. 92.

22. Cohen, *Logik der reinen Erkenntnis*, pp. 12–13.

23. See Cohen, *Logik der reinen Erkenntnis*, p. 36, p. 19, commented in Poma, *La filosofia critica di Hermann Cohen*, p. 94.

24. Cohen, *Logik der reinen Erkenntnis*, p. 23.

25. *Ibid.*, p. 26.

26. *Ibid.*, p. 61.

27. *Ibid.*, p. 28.

28. *Ibid.*, p. 29.

29. *Ibid.*

30. *Ibid.*, p. 36.

31. *Ibid.*, p. 82.

32. *Ibid.*

33. *Ibid.*, p. 83.

34. *Ibid.*

35. *Ibid.*, p. 35.

36. *Ibid.*, p. 36.

37. Holzhey, *Cohen und Natorp*, vol. 1, pp. 182–83.

38. Cohen, *Kants Theorie der Erfahrung,* 790. Cf. Poma, *La filosofia critica di Hermann Cohen*, p. 104.

39. Cohen, *Logik der reinen Erkenntnis*, pp. 84–85.

40. *Ibid.*, p. 84.

41. *Ibid.*

42. *Ibid.*, pp. 85, 93, 104–12.

43. William W. Goodwin, *A Greek Grammar* (1892, rev. Boston: Ginn & Co. 1900), pp. 345–46. For a more recent account of the Greek negative particles, see A. C. Moorhouse, *Studies in the Greek Negatives* (Cardiff: University of Wales Press, 1959).

44. Cohen, *Logik der reinen Erkenntnis*, p. 93.

45. *Ibid.*, p. 89. For Lotze's treatment of the infinite judgment, see Hermann Lotze, *System der Philosophie, Erster Teil: Drei Bücher der Logik, vom Untersuchen und Erkennen* (Leipzig: S. Hirzel, 1874), § 40. Cf. Holzhey, *Cohen und Natorp*, vol. 1, p. 191, and, on Cohen and his nineteenth-century predecessors in logic more generally, Jakob Gordin, *Untersuchungen zur Theorie des unendlichen Urteils* (Berlin: Akademie-Verlag, 1929).

46. See Werner Hamacher, "Guilt History: Benjamin's Sketch 'Capitalism as Religion,'" trans. Kirk Wetters, *diacritics* 32. 3–4 (2002), pp. 81–106, esp. 100–101.

47. Cohen, *Logik der reinen Erkenntnis*, p. 90. On Cohen's account of continuity, see

Peter Fenves, *Arresting Language: From Leibniz to Benjamin* (Palo Alto, CA: Stanford University Press, 2001), pp. 186–91.

48. *Ibid.*, p. 91.

49. *Ibid.*, pp. 91–92.

50. Gordin, *Untersuchungen*, p. 99.

51. Cohen, *Logik der reinen Erkenntnis*, p. 92.

52. Cohen, *Das Princip der Infinitesimal-Methode und seine Geschichte: Ein Kapitel zur Grundlegung der Erkenntniskritik* (Berlin: F. Dümmler, 1883), pp. 57–58.

53. Natorp, *Grundlagen*, p. 219.

54. Cohen, *Logik der reinen Erkenntnis*, p. 124.

55. *Ibid.*, p. 125.

56. See Cohen, *Kants Theorie de Erfahrung* (1885), esp. pp. 422–38. On Cohen's account of the intensity of sensation, see Marco Giovanelli, "Grandezza intensiva e grandezza infinitesimale. Hermann Cohen e il principio kantiano delle *Anticipazioni della percezione*," *Annuario filosofico* 19 (2003), pp. 275–318; Jules Vuillemin, *L'héritage kantien et la révolution copernicienne: Fichte — Cohen — Heidegger* (Paris: Presses Universitaires de France, 1954), pp. 132–209. On Kant's doctrine of intensive magnitude, see also Catharine Elizabeth Diehl, "The Theory of Intensive Magnitudes in Leibniz and Kant" (PhD dissertation, Princeton University, 2012), esp. pp. 158–241.

57. Cohen, *Logik der reinen Erkenntnis*, p. 35.

58. Nicolai Hartmann, *Platos Logik des Seins* (Giessen: A. Töpelmann, 1909), p. 160. On this passage, see Marco Giovanelli, *Reality and Negation — Kant's Principle of Anticipations of Perception: An Investigation of Its Impact on the Post-Kantian Debate* (Dordrecht: Springer, 2011), pp. 205–207.

59. Franz Rosenzweig, *Der Mensch und Sein Werk: Gesammelte Schriften*, vol. 4: *Der Stern der Erlösung*, introduction by Reinhold Mayer (4th ed., Haag: Nijhoff, 1976), pp. 22–23; English in *Star of Redemption*, foreword by Micahel Oppenheim, introduction by Elliot R. Wolfson, trans. Barbara E. Galli (Madison: University of Wisconsin Press, 2005), pp. 27–28 (translation modified). On Rosenzweig and Cohen, see Reiner Wiehl, "Logik und Metalogik bei Cohen und Rosenzweig," in *Der Philosoph Franz Rosenzweig (1886–1929)*, vol. 2: *Das neue Denken und seine Dimensionen*, ed. Wolfdietrich Schmied-Kowarzik (Freiburg and Munich: Karl Albert, 1988), pp. 623–42; Robert Gibbs, *Correlations in Rosenzweig and Levinas* (Princeton: Princeton University Press, 1992), esp. 47–54; Pierfrancesco Fiorato and Hartwig Wiedebach, "Rosenzweig's Readings of Hermann Cohen's *Logic of Pure Cognition*," *The Journal of Jewish Thought and Philosophy* 12. 2 (2003), pp. 139–46; Wolfdietrich

NOTES TO PAGES 207-211

Schmied-Kowarzik, *Rosenzweig im Gespräch mit Ehrenberg, Cohen und Buber* (Freiburg/Munich: Alber, 2006), pp. 113–43.

60. Bergman, *The Philosophy of Solomon Maimon*, p. 268. Cf. Walter Kinkel, "Das Urteil des Ursprungs: Ein Kapitel aus einem Kommentar zu H. Cohens *Logik der reinen Erkenntnis*," *Kant-Studien* 17. 1–3 (1912), pp. 274–82, esp. pp. 280–82.

61. Cohen, *Logik der reinen Erkenntnis*, p. 123.

62. *Ibid.*, p. 224.

63. Hermann Cohen, "Charakteristik der Ethik Maimunis," in *Moses ben Maimon: Sein Leben, seine Werke und Sein Einfluss: Zur Erinnerung an den siebenhundertsten Todestag des Maimonides*, ed. Marcus Brann et al. (Leipzig: Gustav Fock, 1908–14), vol. 1, pp. 63–134, at p. 100; an English translation can be found in *Ethics of Maimonides*, trans. with commentary by Almut Sh. Bruckstein, foreword by Robert Gibbs (Madison: University of Wisconsin Press, 2004), p. 101.

64. Cohen, "Charakteristik," p. 101; English in *Ethics*, p. 103 (trans modified).

65. *Ibid.*, p. 102; English in *Ethics*, p. 104 (trans. modified).

66. Hermann Cohen, *Die Religion der Vernunft aus den Quellen des Judentums* (Leipzig: Gustav Fock, 1919), pp. 71–72; English in *Religion of Reason: Out of the Sources of Judaism*, trans. Simon Kaplan, introductory essay by Leo Strauss (New York: Frederick Ungar, 1972), p. 62.

67. Cohen, *Die Religion der Vernunft*, p. 73; *Religion of Reason*, p. 63.

68. *Ibid.*

69. *Ibid.*; *Religion of Reason*, p. 64 (trans. modified).

70. *Ibid.*, pp. 73–74; *Religion of Reason*, p. 64 (trans. modified). Cf. the account in Hermann Cohen, *Der Begriff der Religion im System der Philosophie* (Giessen: Alfred Töpelman, 1915), pp. 46–47.

71. Émile Bréhier, "Le concept de religion d'après Hermann Cohen," *Revue de Métaphysique et de Morale* 32. 3 (1925), pp. 359–72, at p. 365.

72. Herman Cohen, *Ethik des reinen Willens* (Berlin: Bruno Cassirer, 1904), p. 198. Fichte was in fact well aware of the ambiguous status that one might accord to the *non-I*: see Fichte, *Sämmtliche Werke*, vol. 1, pp. 503–505; English in *Science of Knowledge*, pp. 73–75.

73. Cohen, *Ethik des reinen Willens*, p. 198.

74. *Ibid.*

75. *Ibid.*, p. 201. On this discussion, see Philonenko, *L'École de Marbourg*, pp. 71–72; Poma, *La filosofia critica di Hermann Cohen*, pp. 211–13. On Cohen's ethics more generally, see Gibbs, *Correlations*, pp. 176–91.

76. Amos Funkenstein, "The Persecution of Absolutes: On the Kantian and Neo-Kantian Theories of Science," in *The Kaleidoscope of Science*, ed. Edna Ullmann-Margalit (Dordrecht and Boston: D. Reidel, 1986), pp. 39–63, at p. 55.

77. Cohen, *Logik der reinen Erkenntnis*, p. 395.

78. Bertrand Russell, *The Principles of Mathematics*, vol. 1 (Cambridge: Cambridge University Press, 1903), p. 338; p. 331. On Cohen's book, see pp. 338–45. Cohen's book did not go unnoticed. See also the reviews by Gottlob Frege in *Zeitschrift für Philosophie und philosophische Kritik* 87 (1885), pp. 324–29, and Georg Cantor, *Deutsche Literaturzeitung* 5 (1884), pp. 268–88.

79. Russell, *The Principles of Mathematics*, p. 329.

80. *Ibid.*, p. 330.

81. John Grier Hibben, Review of Cohen, *Logik der reinen Erkenntnis*, *The Philosophical Review* 13. 2 (1904), pp. 207–12, at p. 211.

82. Funkenstein, "The Persecution of Absolutes," p. 57. See also Marx, *Transzendentale Logik*, pp. 133–54.

83. Cohen, *Logik der reinen Erkenntnis*, p. 119.

84. *Ibid.*, pp. 84, 89.

85. *Ibid.*, p. 105.

86. *Ibid.*, p. 107.

87. *Ibid.*

88. Natorp, "Zu Cohens Logik," in Holzhey, *Cohen und Natorp*, vol. 2: *Der Marburger Neokantismus in Quellen*, pp. 6–40, at p. 23.

89. *Ibid.*, p. 23.

90. *Ibid.*, p. 24.

91. *Ibid.* On Natorp's critique of Cohen's logic, see Holzhey, *Cohen und Natorp*, vol. 1; Jürgen Stolzenberg, *Ursprung und System: Probleme der Bedeutung systematischer Philosophie im Werk Hermann Cohens, Paul Natorps und beim frühem Martin Heidegger* (Göttingen: Vandenhoeck & Ruprecht, 1995), pp. 61–121.

92. For a discussion of Cohen and "me-ontology," see Martin Kavka, *Jewish Messianism and the History of Philosophy* (Cambridge: Cambridge University Press, 2004), esp. pp. 66–127.

93. Cf. Jacques-Alain Miller's account of Frege's zero in the *Grundlagen der Arithmetik*, "Suture. Éléments de la logique du signifiant," *Cahiers pour l'analyse* 1 (1966), pp. 37–49, rpt. in *Un début dans la vie* (Paris: Gallimard, 2002), pp. 194–215.

94. Cohen, *Logik der reinen Erkenntnis*, p. 118.

95. In several early texts, Benjamin calls attention to the consequences of Cohen's failure to grant the "fact of language" its rightful place in transcendental method. See in particular "Über das Programm der kommenden Philosophie" and "Über die transzendentale Methode," in Walter Benjamin, *Gesammelte Schriften*, ed. Rolf Tiedemann and Germann Schweppenhäuser, 7 vols. (Frankfurt am Main: Suhrkamp, 1972-91), vol. II, pp. 157–68, esp. pp. 167–68, and vol. VI, pp. 52-53. On Benjamin's critique of Cohen, see Peter Fenves, *The Messianic Reduction: Walter Benjamin and the Shape of Time* (Palo Alto, CA: Stanford University Press, 2011), esp. pp. 152–86.

CHAPTER FOURTEEN: AFTER THE JUDGMENT

1. Aristotle, *De interpretatione* V, 17a 6–8.

2. Aristotle, *Prior Analytics* I, 3, 25b 32–26a.

3. Alexander of Aphrodisias, *In Aristotelem Analyticorum priorum librum I commentarium*, ed. Maximilian Wallies (Berlin: G. Reimer, 1883), 379.28-29. On the use of letters and schematic representations in ancient logic, see Barnes, *Truth Etc.*, pp. 292–359.

4. See Łukasiewicz, *Aristotle's Syllogistic*, pp. 15–19.

5. See Aristotle, *Prior Analytics*, I, 1, esp. 24a16.

6. For a summary of the emergence of quantificational notation, see Stanley Peters and Dag Westerstål, *Quantifiers in Language and Logic* (Oxford: Oxford University Press, 2006), pp. 21–52.

7. This presentation is indebted to Quine's account of bound variables. See "On What There Is," in Willard Van Orman Quine, *From a Logical Point of View: 9 Logico-Philosophical Essays* (Cambridge, MA: Harvard University Press, 1953), pp. 1–19.

8. Gottlob Frege, *Begriffsschrift: Eine der arithmetischen nachgebildete Formelsprache des reinen Denkens* (Halle: Louis Nebert, 1879), § 3, p. 4; English in *Conceptual Notation and Related Articles*, ed. and trans. Terrell Ward Bynum (Oxford: Clarendon Press, 1972), p. 113.

9. Frege, *Begriffsschrift*, §3, p. 2; English in *Conceptual Notation*, p. 112.

10. *Ibid.*, p. vii; English in *Conceptual Notation*, pp. 106–107.

11. Gottlob Frege, "Logik," in *Nachgelassene Schriften und wissenschaftlicher Briefwechsel*, ed. Hans Hermes, Friedrich Kambartel, and Friedrich Kaulbach (Hamburg: Felix Meiner, 1969-1976), vol. 1, pp. 137–63; English in "Logic" (1897) in Gottlob Frege, *Posthumous Writings*, ed. Hans Hermes, Friedrich Kambartel, and Friedrich Kaulbach, with the assistance of Gottfried Gabriel and Walburga Rödding, trans. Peter Long and Roger White, with the assistance of Raymond Hargreaves (Chicago: University of Chicago Press, 1979), pp. 26–151.

12. Gottlob Frege, "Ausführungen über Sinn und Bedeutung," *Nachgelassene Schriften*,

vol. 1, pp. 128–36, at p. 130; English in "Comments on Sense and Reference," *Posthumous Writings*, pp. 118–25, at p. 120.

13. Frege, *Begriffsschrift*, §3, p. 3; English in *Conceptual Notation*, pp. 112–13.

14. *Ibid.*, §4, p. 4; English in *Conceptual Notation*, p. 114. For Frege's full account of negation, see §7; cf. his later essay, "Die Verneinung—Eine logische Untersuchung," *Beiträge zur Philosophie des deutschen Idealismus* 1 (1918–19), pp. 143–57, rpt. in Frege, *Logische Untersuchungen*, ed. Günther Patzig, 5th ed. (1966, Göttingen: Vandenhoeck & Ruprecht, 2003), pp. 63–84; English in "Negation," in *The Frege Reader*, ed. Michael Beaney (Oxford: Blackwell, 1997), pp. 346–61.

15. Frege, *Begriffsschrift*, §4, p. 4; English in *Conceptual Notation*, p. 114.

16. Claude Imbert, "Le projet idéographique," *Revue internationale de philosophie* 33. 130 (1979), pp. 621–65, p. 653.

17. Frege, *Begriffsschrift*, §2, p. 2; English in *Conceptual Notation*, p. 112.

18. Frege, *Nachgelassene Schriften*, vol. 1, p. 200; *Posthumous Writings*, p. 184. On the judgment stroke, see, among others, P. T. Geach, "Assertion," in *Logic Matters* (Oxford: Blackwell, 1972), pp. 254–69; Wayne W. Martin, "The Judgment Stroke and the Truth Predicate: Frege, Heidegger, and the Logical Representation of Judgment," *The New Yearbook for Phenomenology and Phenomenological Research* 3 (2003), pp. 27–52.

19. Giuseppe Peano, "Review of Frege's *Grundgesetze* (1885)," trans. Victor Dudman *Southern Journal of Philosophy* 9 (1971), pp. 25–37, p. 29.

20. Ludwig Wittgenstein, *Werkausgabe* (Frankfurt: Suhrkamp, 1984), vol. 1: *Tractatus logico-philosophicus, Tagebücher 1914–1916, Philosophische Untersuchungen*, 4.442, p. 42; English in *Tractatus Logico-Philosophicus*, preface by Bertrand Russell (London: Kegan Paul, Trench, Trubner, 1922), p. 52.

21. Wittgenstein, *Tractatus* 4.001, in *Werke*, vol. 1, p. 25; English in *Tractatus*, p. 38 (trans. modified).

22. See Gilles Granger, "Wittgenstein et la métalangue," in *Wittgenstein et le problème d'une philosophie de la science*, ed. Gilles Granges (Paris: Éditions du Cerf, 1970), pp. 77–90.

23. Wittgenstein, *Tractatus* 5.631, in *Werke*, vol. 1, p. 67; English in *Tractatus*, p. 74 (trans. modified).

24. *Ibid.*, 4.0312, p. 29; English in *Tractatus*, p. 42.

25. *Ibid.*, 4.121, p. 33; English in *Tractatus*, p. 45.

26. See Claude Imbert, *Phénoménologies et langues formulaires* (Paris: Presses Universitaires de France, 1992).

27. Alfred Tarski, "The Concept of Truth in Formalized Languages," in *Logic*,

Semantics, Metamathematics: Papers from 1923 to 1938, trans. J. H. Woodger (Oxford: Clarendon Press, 1956), pp. 152–278, pp. 154–65.

28. Tarski, "The Concept of Truth," p. 158.

29. Bertrand Russell, *Our Knowledge of the External World as a Field for Scientific Method in Philosophy* (London: Open Court, 1914), p. 40.

30. *Ibid.*, pp. 41, 45.

31. *Ibid.*, p. 59.

32. Rudolf Carnap, "Die alte und die neue Logik," *Erkenntnis* 1 (1930–31), pp. 12–26, p. 13; English in "The Old Logic and the New Logic," trans. Isaac Levi, in *Logical Positivism*, ed. A. J. Ayer (New York: Free Press, 1959), pp. 133–46, p. 134.

33. *Ibid.*

34. Carnap, "Die alte und die neue Logik," p. 25; English in "The Old Logic and the New Logic," p. 145.

35. Edmund Husserl, *Husserliana: Gesammelte Werke*, ed. H. L. van Breda (The Hague: Nijhoff, 1950–), vol. 2: *Die Idee der Phänomenologie* (The Hague: Nijhoff, 1950), p. 23; English in Husserl, *The Idea of Phenomenology: A Translation of Die Idee der Phänomenologie Husserliana II*, trans. Lee Hardy (Dordrecht/Boston/London: Kluwer, 1999), p. 19.

36. Husserl, *Idee der Phänomenologie*, p. 24; English in *Idea of Phenomenology*, p. 20.

37. Husserl, *Husserliana*, vol. III-V: *Ideen zu einer reinen Phänomenologie und phänomenologischen Philosophie*, ed. Marly and Walter Biemel (The Hague: Nijhoff, 1950), vol. I, §3, p. 11; English in *Ideas Pertaining to a Pure Phenomenology and to a Phenomenological Philosophy*, trans. F. Kersten, Richard Rojcewicz, and André Schuwer (The Hague: Nijhoff, 1980-89), vol. I: *General Introduction to a Pure Phenomenology*, p. 10.

38. Husserl, *Ideen zu einer reinen Phänomenologie*, §94, p. 194; *Ideas Pertaining to a Pure Phenomenology*, pp. 227–28. Husserl had offered a different account of negation in the Sixth Logical Investigation: see Edmund Husserl, *Logische Untersuchungen* (1913, Tübingen: Max Niemeyer, 1968), vol. 2, part 2, VI, §39 pp. 122–27. On Husserl and negation, see Jocelyn Benoist, "La théorie phénoménologique de la négation, entre acte et sens," *Revue de métaphyisque et de morale* 30. 2 (2001), pp. 21–35.

39. Husserl, *Ideen zu einer reinen Phänomenologie*, §106, p. 218; *Ideas Pertaining to a Pure Phenomenology*, pp. 253–54.

40. Edmund Husserl, *Erfahrung und Urteil: Untersuchungen zur Genealogie der Logik*, ed. Ludwig Landgrebe (Prague: Akademia, 1939), §21, pp. 94–98, p. 97.

41. Martin Heidegger, *Gesamtausgabe*, vol. 1: *Frühe Schriften*, ed. Friedrich-Wilhelm von Herrmann (Frankfurt am Main: Vittorio Klostermann, 1978), p. 63.

42. Heidegger, *Frühe Schriften*, p. 64.

43. See Hugo Ott, *Martin Heidegger: Unterwegs zu seiner Biographie* (Frankfurt: Campus, 1988), pp. 85–86.

44. Martin Heidegger, *Sein und Zeit* (1927, 11th ed., Tübingen: Max Niemeyer, 1967), §2, p. 5; English in *Being and Time*, trans. John Macquarrie and Edward Robinson (Oxford: Blackwell, 1962), p. 25.

45. Martin Heidegger, *Gesamtausgabe*, vol. 26: *Metaphyische Anfangsgründe der Logik im Ausgang von Leibniz*, ed. Klaus Held (Frankfurt am Main: Vittorio Klostermann, 1978), p. 126. On Heidegger's deconstruction of logic, see Françoise Dastur, *Heidegger. La Question du logos* (Paris: Vrin, 2007), pp. 121–51.

46. Heidegger, *Sein und Zeit*, §33 p. 158; *Being and Time*, p. 201 (trans. modified).

47. *Ibid.*, §44, pp. 218–19; *Being and Time*, p. 261. Translation slightly modified.

48. Martin Heidegger, *Gesamtausgabe*, vol. 40: *Einführung in die Metaphysik*, ed. Petra Jaeger (Frankfurt am Main: Vittorio Klostermann, 1983), p. 129.

49. Martin Heidegger, *Gesamtausgabe*, vol. 7: *Vorträge und Aufsätze* (Frankfurt am Main: Vittorio Klostermann, 2000), ed. Friedrich-Wilhelm von Herrmann, "Logos (Heraklit, fragment 50)," pp. 211–34, esp. p. 216; English in *Early Greek Thinking: The Dawn of Western Philosophy*, trans. David Farrell Krell and Frank A. Capuzzi (New York: Harper & Row, 1975), pp. 39–78, p. 63.

50. Martin Heidegger, *Gesamtausgabe*, vol. 5: *Holzwege*, ed. Friedrich-Wilhelm von Herrmann (Frankfurt am Main: Vittorio Klostermann, 1977), p. 314; English in *Pathmarks*, ed. William McNeill (Cambridge: Cambridge University Press, 1998), p. 240.

51. Martin Heidegger, *Gesamtausgabe*, vol. 41: *Die Frage nach dem Ding. Zu Kants Lehre von den transzendentalen Grundsätze*, ed. Petra Jaeger (Frankfurt am Main: Vittorio Klostermann, 1984), p. 159.

52. Martin Heidegger, *Gesamtausgabe*, vol. 12: *Unterwegs zur Sprache*, ed. Friedrich-Wilhelm von Herrmann (Frankfurt am Main: Vittorio Klostermann, 1985), p. 150. On Heidegger's critique of symbolic logic, see Thomas A. Fay, *Heidegger: The Critique of Logic* (The Hague: Martinus Nijhoff, 1977), pp. 70–93.

53. Martin Heidegger *Gesamtausgabe*, vol. 14: *Zur Sache des Denkens*, ed. Friedrich-Wilhelm von Herrmann (Frankfurt am Main: Vittorio Klostermann, 2007), p. 9; English in *On Time and Being*, trans. Joan Stambaugh (New York: Harper & Row, 1972), pp. 4–5. On the syntax of such statements, see Imbert, *Phénoménologies et langues formulaires*, pp. 286–96.

54. Martin Heidegger, *Gesamtausgabe*, vol. 3: *Kant und das Problem der Metaphysik* (1929, Frankfurt: Vittorio Klostermann, 1991), pp. 278–79.

55. See Michael Friedman, *A Parting of the Ways: Carnap, Cassirer, and Heidegger* (Chicago: Open Court, 2000), pp. 7-9.

56. Rudolf Carnap, "Überwindung der Metaphysik durch logische Analyse der Sprache," *Erkenntnis* 2 (1932), pp. 219-41, at p. 219; English in "The Elimination of Metaphysics Through Logical Analysis of Language," trans. Arthur Pap, in Ayer, *Logical Positivism*, pp. 60-81, at p. 60.

57. Carnap, "Überwindung der Metaphysik," p. 229; "Elimination of Metaphysics," p. 69. Heidegger's name appears in note 2.

58. *Ibid.*

59. See Friedman, *A Parting of the Ways*, pp. 11-12.

60. Carnap, "Überwindung der Metaphysik," p. 232; "Elimination of Metaphysics," p. 72.

61. *Gesamtausgabe*, vol. 40: *Einführung in die Metaphysik*, pp. 227-28. Heidegger did not republish this passage in his 1953 edition of this course. See Friedman, *A Parting of the Ways*, pp. 22-23 (to which this translation is indebted).

62. Martin Heidegger, *Gesamtausgabe*, vol. 9: *Wegmarken* (Frankfurt am Main: Vittorio Klostermann, 1976), p. 308.

63. See Friedman, *A Parting of the Ways*, p. 156.

64. See Heidegger, *Frühe Schriften*, pp. 181-85, 228.

65. Heidegger, *Kant und das Problem der Metaphysik*, pp. 66-67, p. 243. On Heidegger's implicit critique of Cohen in this book, see Stephan Käufer, "On Heidegger on Logic," *Continental Philosophy Review* 34 (2001), pp. 455-76.

66. Heidegger, *Wegmarken*, p. 112; English in Martin Heidegger, *Basic Writings: From Being and Time (1927) to The Task of Thinking (1964)*, trans. David Farrell Krell (New York: Harper & Row, 1977), p. 103.

CHAPTER FIFTEEN: A PERSISTENT PARTICLE

1. For an argument against the obsolescence of traditional logic, see Fred Sommers, *The Logic of Natural Language* (Oxford: Clarendon Press, 1982).

2. Friedrich Adolf Trendelenburg, *Logische Untersuchungen* (1840, 3rd ed., Leipzig: S. Hirzel, 1870), vol. 2, p. 285. Trendelenburg took this as a strong argument against the infinite judgment.

3. George Boole, *An Investigation of the Laws of Thought, on Which Are Founded The Mathematical Theories of Logic and Probability* (London: Walton and Maberly, 1854), p. 48.

4. *Ibid.*

5. Ernst Schröder, Review of Frege, *Begriffsschrift*, *Zeitschrift für Mathematik und Physik*

25 (1880), pp. 81–94; English in Frege, *Conceptual Notation*, pp. 218–32, at p. 224. Schröder alludes here to Lotze's *Logic*.

6. For a later development of this theory of complimentary classes, see P. F. Strawson, *Introduction to Logical Theory* (London: Methuen & Co., 1963), pp. 102–24.

7. See Theodor Wiesengrund Adorno, *Negative Dialektik* (Frankfurt am Main: Suhrkamp, 1966). On the non-identical as "absolute," see p. 396; English in *Negative Dialectics*, trans. E. B. Ashton (London and New York: Routledge, 1973), p. 406.

8. Adorno, *Negative Dialektik*, p. 15; English in *Negative Dialectics*, p. 5 (trans. modified).

9. Adorno, *Negative Dialektik*, p. 159; English in *Negative Dialectics*, p. 158.

10. Adorno, *Negative Dialektik*, p. 163; English in *Negative Dialectics*, p. 163.

11. J. R. Searle, *Speech Acts: An Essay in the Philosophy of Language* (Cambridge: Cambridge University Press, 1969), pp. 32–33.

12. Gilles Deleuze, *Différence et répétition* (Paris: Presses Universitaires de France, 1968), p. 261; English in *Difference and Repetition*, trans. Paul Patton (New York: Columbia University Press, 1994), p. 202.

13. The example, drawn from Anatole France, is one of several discussed in Jacques Damourette and Édouard Pichon, *Des mots à la pensée. Essai de grammaire et de langue française* (Paris: Collection des linguistes contemporains, 1911–40), vol. I, § 115.

14. Deleuze, *Différence et répétition*, p. 261; English in *Difference and Repetition*, p. 202 (trans. modified).

15. Aristotle, *Metaphysics* IX, 1, 1046 a 29–35.

16. Martin Heidegger, *Gesamtausgabe*, vol. 33: *Aristoteles, Metaphysik Θ 1–3: Von Wesen und Wirklichkeit der Kraft* (Frankfurt am Main: Klostermann, 1981), p. 111; English in *Aristotle's Metaphysics Θ 1–3: On the Essence and Actuality of Force*, trans. Walter Brogan and Peter Warnek (Bloomington: Indiana University Press, 1995), p. 94 (trans. modified).

17. See Giorgio Agamben, *Homo Sacer: Sovereign Power and Bare Life*, trans. Daniel Heller-Roazen (Palo Alto, CA: Stanford University Press, 1998), pp. 44–48; "Bartleby, or On Contingency," in *Potentialities: Collected Essays in Philosophy*, ed. and trans. Daniel Heller-Roazen (Palo Alto, CA: Stanford University Press, 1999), pp. 243–74. Cf. Deleuze's essay on Melville's story: "Bartleby, ou la formule," in Gilles Deleuze, *Critique et clinique* (Paris: Éditions de Minuit, 1993), pp. 89–114; English in "Bartleby; or the Formula," *Essays Critical and Clinical*, trans. Daniel W. Smith and Michael A. Greco (Minneapolis: University of Minnesota Press, 1997), pp. 68–90.

18. Jacques Lacan, *Autres écrits* (Paris: Seuil, 2001), p. 516. The formula also appears in a number of Lacan's seminars, most famously XX, or *Encore*.

19. Ferdinand de Saussure, *Cours de linguistique générale*, ed. Tullio de Mauro (Paris: Payot, 1972), p. 317.

20. For a classic statement, see Noam Chomsky, *Aspects of the Theory of Syntax* (Cambridge, MA: MIT Press, 1965).

21. Roman Jakobson, *Six leçons sur le son et les sens*, preface by Claude Lévi-Strauss (Paris: Éditions de Minuit, 1976), p. 53.

22. For a statement of the first, see Paul Kiparsky, "Roman Jakobson and the Grammar of Poetry," in *A Tribute to Roman Jakobson, 1896–1982* (Berlin: Mouton, 1983), pp. 27–39, at p. 34. For a statement of the second hypothesis, see D. T. Langendoen and P. M. Postal, "Sets and Sentences," in *The Philosophy of Linguistics*, ed. Jerrold J. Katz (Oxford: Oxford University Press, 1985), pp. 227–48.

23. F. N. Robinson, ed., *The Complete Works of Geoffrey Chaucer* (Boston: Houghton Mifflin, 1933), *Boece*, Book 3, prose 5, line 19: *certes uppon thilke syde that power fayleth, which that maketh folk blisful, ryght on the same syde noun-power entreth undirnethe.*

24. John Algeo, "The Voguish Uses of Non," *American Speech* 46. 1–2 (1971), pp. 87–105, at p. 95.

25. *Ibid.*, p. 95.

26. *Ibid.*

27. John Milton, *The Doctrine and Discipline of Divorce* (1643, 2nd ed., London: T. P. and M. S., 1644), Book II, ch. IV.

28. Algeo, "The Voguish Uses," p. 94.

29. Clarence L. Barnhart, "Of Matters Lexicographical: Keeping a Record of New English, 1963–1972," *American Speech* 45. 1–2 (1970), pp. 98–107, at pp. 105–106. For further accounts of "affixal negation," see also Otto Jespersen, *Negation in English and Other Languages* (Copenhagen: A. F. Høst, 1917), esp. pp. 139–49; Karl Ernst Zimmer, *Affixal Negation in English and Other Languages: An Examination of Restricted Productivity* (London: W. Clowes, 1964); Horn, *A Natural History of Negation*, pp. 273–96, and, on *un-*, in particular, "Uncovering the Un-Word: A Study in Lexical Pragmatics," *Sophia linguistica* 49 (2002), pp. 1–64.

Bibliography

'Abd al-Jabbār ibn Aḥmad al-Asadābādī, *al-Mughnī fī abwāb al-tawḥīd wa-al-'adl*, ed. Muṣṭafā Ḥilmī and Abū al-Wafā al-Janīmī, dir. Ṭaha Ḥussayn (Cairo: Wizāfat al-Thaqāfah wa-al-Iršād al-Qawmī, n.d.).

Abelard, Peter, *Philosophische Schriften*, ed. Bernhard Geyer, 2 vols. (Munster: W. Aschendorff, 1919).

———, *Dialectica: First Complete Edition of the Parisian Manuscript*, ed. L. M. De Rijk (1956, 2nd ed., Assen: Van Gorcum, 1970).

Adorno, Theodor Wiesengrund, *Negative Dialektik* (Frankfurt am Main: Suhrkamp, 1966).

Aertsen, Jan A., "'Res' as Transcendental: Its Introduction and Significance," in *Le problème des transcendantaux du XIVe au XVIIe siècle*, ed. Graziella Federici-Vescovini, pp. 139–56 (Paris: Vrin, 2002).

———, *Medieval Philosophy as Transcendental Thought: From Philip the Chancellor (ca. 1225) to Francisco Suárez* (Leiden: Brill, 2012).

Agamben, Giorgio, *Homo Sacer: Sovereign Power and Bare Life*, trans. Daniel Heller-Roazen (Palo Alto, CA: Stanford University Press, 1998).

———, *Potentialities: Collected Essays in Philosophy*, ed. and trans. Daniel Heller-Roazen (Palo Alto, CA: Stanford University Press, 1999).

Aguilar, José, *Cursus philosophicus dictatus Limae*, 3 vols. (Seville: Ex. Offc. Joannis Francisci de Blas, 1701).

Alami, Ahmed, *L'ontologie modale: Étude sur la théorie des modes d'Abū Hāšim al-Ǧubbā'i* (Paris: Vrin, 2001).

Albert the Great, *Alberti Magni Opera Omnia*, ed. Auguste and Émile Borgnet, 38 vols. (Paris: Ludovic Vivès, 1890–99).

Alexander of Aphrodisias, *In Aristotelem Analyticorum priorum librum I commentarium*, ed. Maximilian Wallies (Berlin: G. Reimer, 1883).

———, *Alexandri Aphrodiensis in Aristotelis Metaphysica Commentaria* (=*Commentaria in Aristotelem graeca* 1), ed. Michael Hayduck (Berlin: Reimer, 1891).

———, *On Aristotle's Metaphysics* IV, trans. Arthur Madigan (Ithaca, NY: Cornell University Press, 1993).

Al-Farabi (=Abū Naṣr al-Fārābī), *Kitāb al-ḥurūf*, ed. Muḥsin Mahdī (Beirut: Dār al-Mashriq, 1970).

———, *Commentary and Short Treatise on Aristotle's De Interpretatione*, ed. and trans. F. W. Zimmermann (Oxford: Oxford University Press, 1981).

Algeo, John, "The Voguish Uses of Non," *American Speech* 46.1–2 (1971), pp. 87–105.

Al-Ḥasan ibn Aḥmad ibn Mattawayh, *Al-Tadhkirah fī aḥkām al-jawāhir wa-al a'rāḍ*, ed. Sāmi Naṣr Luṭf and Fayṣal Badīr 'Awn (Cairo: Dār al-Thaqāfah, 1975).

Ali Khalidi, Muhammad, *Medieval Islamic Philosophical Writings* (Cambridge: Cambridge University Press, 2005).

Al-Rāzī, Fakhr al-Dīn Muḥammad ibn 'Umar, *Muḥaṣṣal afkār al-mutaqaddimīn min al-'ulamā' wa-al-mutakallimīn* (Cairo: Maktabat al-kullīyāt al-Azharīyah, 1978).

Ammonius, *In Aristotelem "De Interpretatione" Commentarius* (=*Commentaria in Aristotelem Graeca*, vol. IV), ed. Adolf Busse (Berlin: Reimber, 1897).

———, *On Aristotle's "On Interpretation" 1–8*, ed. David Blank (Ithaca, NY: Cornell University Press, 1996).

Anselm of Canterbury, *Epistola de incarnatione verbi*, ed. Franciscus Salasius Schmitt (Bonn: P. Hanstein, 1931).

Apuleius, *Peri hermeneias V*, ed. and trans. David Londey and Carmen Johansen, in *The Logic of Apuleius: Including a Complete Latin Text and English Translation of the Peri Hermeneias of Apuleius of Madaura* (Leiden: E. J. Brill, 1987).

Arens, Hans, ed. and trans., *Aristotle's Theory of Language and Its Tradition: Texts from 500 to 1750* (Amsterdam/Philadelphia: John Benjamins, 1984).

Aristotle, *Aristotelis Opera cum Auerrois commentariis*, 14 vols. (Venice: 1562–74), vol. 1, part 1 (1562): *Aristotelis De interpretatione liber primus et liber secundus, Severino Boetho interprete, cum Averrois Cordubensis Expositione et Leui Ghersonidis Annotationibus omnibus nunc primum a Iacob Mantino Hebraeo Medico in Latinum conuersis* (rpt. Frankfurt, 1962).

———, *The Complete Works: The Revised Oxford Translation*, ed. Jonathan Barnes, 2 vols. (Princeton: Princeton University Press, 1984).

———, *De interpretatione*, ed. Hermann Weidemann (Berlin/Boston: De Gruyter, 2014).

Atlas, Samuel, *From Critical to Speculative Idealism: The Philosophy of Solomon Maimon* (The Hague: Martinus Nijhoff, 1964).

Aubenque, Pierre, *Problèmes aristotéliciens*, 2 vols. (Paris: Vrin, 2009–11).

Augustine, Sanctus Aurelius, *De doctrina christiana: De vera religione*, ed. Joseph Martin and Klaus-Detlef Daur (Turnhout: Brepols, 1962).

Austin, Norman, "Name Magic in the *Odyssey*," *California Studies in Classical Antiquity* 5 (1972), pp. 1–19.

Averroes (=Abū al-Walīd ibn Rušd), *Commentarium medium super libro Peri hermeneias Aristotelis, Translatio Wilhelmo de Luna attribuita*, ed. Roland Hissette (Louvain: Peeters, 1996).

———, *Commentaire moyen sur le De interpretatione*, ed. and trans. Ali Benmakhlouf and Stéphane Diebler (Paris: Vrin, 2000).

Avicenna (=Ibn Sīnā), *Al-Ishārāt wa-al-tanbīhāt*, ed. Sulaymān Dunyā, 4 vols. (Cairo: Dar al-maʿarif fī Maṣr, 1971).

———, *Liber de philosophia prima, sive, Scientia divina*, ed. Simon van Riet, introduction by Gérard Verbeke, 3 vols. (Louvain: E. Peeters/Leiden: E. J. Brill, 1977–83).

———, *Al-Shifāʾ al-ṭabiʿīyāt*, ed. Ibrāhim Madkūr and Saʿīd Zāyid (Cairo: Hayʾah al-Miṣ rīyah al-ʿĀmmah lil-Kitāb, 1983).

———, *Remarks and Admonitions, Part One: Logic*, trans. Shams Constantine Inati (Toronto: Pontifical Institute of Mediaeval Studies, 1984).

———, *Al-ʿIbārā: Commentary on Aristotle's De interpretatione: Part One and Part Two*, ed. and trans. Allan Bäck (Munich: Philosophia, 2013).

Ax, Wolfram, *Laut, Stimme und Sprache: Studien zu drei Grundbegriffen der antiken Sprachtheorie* (Göttingen: Vandenhoeck & Ruprecht, 1986).

Bäck, Allan T., *Aristotle's Theory of Predication* (Leiden/Boston/Cologne: E. J. Brill, 2000).

Barnes, Jonathan, *Truth, Etc.: Six Lectures on Ancient Logic* (Oxford: Clarendon Press, 2007).

Barnhart, Clarence L., "Of Matters Lexicographical: Keeping a Record of New English, 1963–1972," *American Speech* 45. 1–2 (1970), pp. 98–107.

Baumgarten, Alexander Gottlieb, *Metaphysica* (1757, Halle: H. Hemmerde, 1779).

Beckett, Samuel, *Collected Shorter Plays* (London: Faber, 1984).

Beiser, Frederick, "Maimon and Fichte," in *Salomon Maimon: Rational Dogmatist, Empirical Skeptic*, ed. Gideon Freudenthal, pp. 233–48 (Dordrecht: Kluwer, 2003).

Benardete, Seth, *The Bow and the Lyre: A Platonic Reading of the Odyssey* (New York: Rowman & Littlefield, 1997).

Benjamin, Walter, *Gesammelte Schriften*, ed. Rolf Tiedemann and Germann Schweppenhäuser, 7 vols. (Frankfurt am Main: Suhrkamp, 1972–91).

Benmakhlouf, Ali, "Averroès et les propositions indéfinies," in Philippe Büttgen, Stéphane

Diebler and Marwan Rashed, eds., *Théories de la phrase et de la proposition de Platon à Averroès* (Paris: École normale supérieure, 1999), pp. 269–79.

Bennett, Jonathan, *Kant's Analytic* (Cambridge: Cambridge University Press, 1966).

Benoist, Jocelyn, "La théorie phénomenologique de la négation, entre acte et sens," *Revue de métaphyisque et de morale* 30. 2 (2001), pp. 21–35.

Bergman, Samuel Hugo, *The Philosophy of Solomon Maimon*, trans. Noah J. Jacobs (Jerusalem: Magnes Press, 1967).

Bernaldo de Quirós, Antonio, *Opus philosophicum, seu selectae disputationes philosophicae* (Lyon: Philippe Borde, 1666).

Black, Deborah L., "Aristotle's *Peri hermeneias* in Medieval Latin and Arabic Philosophy: Logic and the Linguistic Arts," *Canadian Journal of Philosophy* 21 (supplement 1) (1991), pp. 25–83.

———, "Mental Existence in Thomas Aquinas and Avicenna," *Medieval Studies* 61. 1 (1999), pp. 45–79.

Boethius, Anicius Manlius Severinus, *Commentarii in librum Aristotelis Peri hermeneias*, ed. Karl Meiser, 2 vols. (Leipzig: Teubner, 1877–80).

———, *In Isagogen Porphyrii commenta*, ed. Samuel Brandt, 1st ed. (Vienna: Tempsky, 1906).

———, *De Syllogismo Categorico: Critical Edition with Introduction, Translation, Notes, and Indexes,* ed. and trans. Cristina Thomsen Thörnqvest (Gothenburg: University of Gothenburg, 2008).

———, *Introductio ad Syllogismos Categoricos: Critical Edition with Introduction, Commentary, and Indexes*, ed. Cristina Thomsen Thörnqvest (Gothenburg: University of Gothenburg, 2008).

Bonaventure, *Opera Omnia*, 10 vols. (Quaracchi: Ex Typographia Collegii S. Bonaventurae, 1882–1902).

Boole, George, *An Investigation of the Laws of Thought, on Which Are Founded the Mathematical Theories of Logic and Probability* (London: Walton and Maberly, 1854).

Boulnois, Olivier, *Être et representation: Une généalogie de la métaphysique moderne à l'époque de Duns Scot, XIIIe–XIVe siècle* (Paris: Presses Universitaires de France, 1999).

Bréhier, Émile, *La théorie des incorporels dans l'ancien stoïcisme* (Paris: A. Picard, 1908).

———, "Le concept de religion d'après Hermann Cohen," *Revue de Métaphysique et de Morale* 32. 3 (1925), pp. 359–72.

Brunschwig, Jacques. "La proposition particulière et les preuves de non-concluance chez Aristote," *Cahiers pour l'analyse* 10 (1969), pp. 3–26.

———, *Papers in Hellenistic Philosophy*, trans. Janet Lloyd (Cambridge: Cambridge University Press, 1994).

Burleigh, Walter, *De Puritate artis logicae tractatus longior, with a Revised Edition of the Tractatus Brevior*, ed. Philotheus Boehner (St. Bonaventure, NY: Franciscan Institute, 1955).

Camporesi, Piero, "Biltri, Blittri," *Lingua nostra* 13. 1 (1952), pp. 70–72.

Cantor, Georg, Review of Cohen, *Das Princip der Infinitesimal-Methode und seine Geschichte*, *Deutsche Literaturzeitung* 5 (1884), pp. 268–88.

Carabelli, Giancarlo, "Blictri: Una parola per Arlecchino," in *Eredità dell'illuminismo: Studi sulla cultura europea fra Settecento e Ottocento*, ed. Antonio Santucci, pp. 231–57 (Bologna: Mulino, 1979).

Carnap, Rudolf, "Die alte und die neue Logik," *Erkenntnis* 1 (1930–31), pp. 12–26.

———, "Überwindung der Metaphysik durch logische Analyse der Sprache," *Erkenntnis* 2 (1932), pp. 219–41.

———, "The Old Logic and the New Logic," trans. Isaac Levi, in *Logical Positivism*, ed. A. J. Ayer, pp. 133–46 (New York: The Free Press, 1959).

———, "The Elimination of Metaphysics Through Logical Analysis of Language," trans. Arthur Pap, in Ayer, *Logical Positivism*, pp. 60–81.

Cassirer, Ernst, "Hermann Cohen und die Erneuerung der Kantischen Philosophie," *Kantstudien* 17. 1–3 (1912), pp. 252–73.

———, *Substance and Function and Einstein's Theory of Relativity*, trans. William Curtis Swabey and Marie Collins Swabey (New York: Dover, 1953).

Chaucer, Geoffrey, *The Complete Works*, ed. F. N. Robinson (Boston and New York: Houghton Mifflin, 1933).

Chomsky, Noam, *Aspects of the Theory of Syntax* (Cambridge, MA: MIT Press, 1965).

Cohen, Hermann, *Kants Theorie der Erfahrung* (1871, 2nd ed., Berlin: F. Dümmler, 1885).

———, *Das Princip der Infinitesimal-Methode und seine Geschichte: Ein Kapitel zur Grundlegung der Erkenntniskritik* (Berlin: F. Dümmler, 1883).

———, *Logik der reinen Erkenntnis* (1902, 3rd ed., Berlin: Bruno Cassirer, 1922).

———, *Ethik des reinen Willens* (Berlin: Bruno Cassirer, 1904).

———, "Charakteristik der Ethik Maimunis," in *Moses ben Maimon: Sein Leben, seine Werke und Sein Einfluss: Zur Erinnerung an den siebenhundertsten Todestag des Maimonides*, ed. Marcus Brann et al., 2 vols., vol. 1, pp. 63–134 (Leipzig: Gustav Fock, 1908–14).

———, *Der Begriff der Religion im System der Philosophie* (Giessen: Alfred Töpelman, 1915).

———, *Die Religion der Vernunft aus den Quellen des Judentums* (Leipzig: Gustav Fock, 1919).

———, *Religion of Reason: Out of the Sources of Judaism*, trans. Simon Kaplan, introductory essay by Leo Strauss (New York: Frederick Ungar, 1972).

——, *Ethics of Maimonides*, trans. with commentary by Almut Sh. Bruckstein, foreword by Robert Gibbs (Madison: University of Wisconsin Press, 2004).

Costabel, Pierre and Pietro Redondi, "Contribution à la sémantèse de *res/cosa/cossa* dans la langue scientifique du XVIe siècle," in *Res: III Colloquio internazionale del lessico intelletuale europeo*, ed. Marta Fattori and Massimo Bianchi, pp. 179–96 (Rome: Edizioni dell'Ateneo, 1982).

Courtine, Jean-François, *Suarez et le système de la métaphysique* (Paris: Vrin, 1990).

——, "Res," *Historisches Wörterbuch der Philosophie*, ed. Joachim Ritter and Karlfried Gründer, vol. 8: *R–Sc*, pp. 892–901 (Basel: Schwabe & Co., 1971–2007).

Crapulli, Giovanni, "'Res' e 'cosa' ('cossa') nella terminologia algebraica del sec. XVI," in Marta Fattori and Massimo Bianchi, *Res*, eds., *Res, III Colloquio Internazionale del Lessico Intellettuale Europeo*, pp. 151–78 (Rome: Edizioni dell'Ateneo, 1982).

Damourette, Jacques, and Édouard Pichon, *Des mots à la pensée. Essai de grammaire et de langue française*, 6 vols. (Paris: Collection des linguistes contemporains, 1911–40).

Dastur, Françoise, *Heidegger. La question du logos* (Paris: Vrin, 2007).

De Lossada, Luis, *Institutiones dialecticae, vulgo Summulae ad primam partem philosophici cursus pertinentes* (Salamanca: Ex Typographia Francisci Garcia Onorato et San Miguèl, 1721).

De Rijk, L. M., ed. *Logica Modernorum: A Contribution to the History of Early Terminist Logic*, 2 vols. (Assen: Van Gorcum, 1962).

——, "On the Chronology of Boethius' Works on Logic I," *Vivarium* 2. 1 (1964), pp. 1–49 and *Vivarium* 2. 2 (1964), pp. 125–62.

——, "The Logic of Indefinite Names in Boethius, Abelard, Duns Scotus and Radulphus Brito," in *Aristotle's Peri hermeneias in the Latin Middle Ages: Essays on the Commentary Tradition*, ed. H. A. G. Braakhuis and C. H. Kneepkens, pp. 207–33 (Groningen: Ingenium Publishers, 2003).

Deleuze, Gilles, *Différence et répétition* (Paris: Presses Universitaires de France, 1968).

——, *Logique du sens* (Paris: Éditions du Minuit, 1969).

——, *The Logic of Sense*, trans. Mark Lester with Charles Stivale, ed. Constantin V. Boundas (London: Athlone Press, 1990).

——, *Critique et clinique* (Paris: Éditions de Minuit, 1993).

——, *Difference and Repetition*, trans. Paul Patton (New York: Columbia University Press, 1994).

——, *Essays Critical and Clinical*, trans. Daniel W. Smith and Michael A. Greco (Minneapolis: University of Minnesota Press, 1997).

Diehl, Catharine Elizabeth, "The Theory of Intensive Magnitudes in Leibniz and Kant" (PhD dissertation, Princeton University, 2012).

Dimrock, E., "The Name of Odysseus," *The Hudson Review* 9.1 (1956), pp. 52–70.

Dolar, Mladen, "The Phrenology of Spirit," in *Supposing the Subject*, ed. Joan Copjec, pp. 64–83 (London: Verso, 1994).

Dominicus Gundissalinus, *De divisione philosophiae: Über die Einteilung der Philosophie*, ed. Alexander Fidora and Dorothée Werner, eds. and trans. (Freiburg im Breisgau: Herder, 2007).

Doyle, John P., "Suárez on the Reality of the Possibles," *The Modern Schoolman* 45 (1967), pp. 29–48.

———, "Between Transcendental and Transcendental: The Missing Link?" *Review of Metaphysics* 50.4 (1997), pp. 783–815.

———, "Suárez on Beings of Reason and Truth (1)," *Vivarium* 25.1 (1987), pp. 47–75.

———, "Suárez on Beings of Reason and Truth (2)," *Vivarium* 26.1 (1988), pp. 51–72.

———, "Supertranscendent Being: On the Verge of Modern Philosophy," in *Meeting of the Minds: The Relations between Medieval and Classical Modern European Philosophy*, ed. Stephen F. Brown, pp. 297–315 (Turnhout: Brepols, 1998).

———, "Supertranscendental Nothing: A Philosophical Finisterre," *Medioevo* 24 (1998), pp. 1–30.

Ducharme, Sylvio, "Note sur le transcendantal 'res' selon Saint Thomas," *Revue de l'Université d'Ottawa* 10 (1940), pp. 85*–99*.

Duns Scot, *Cuestiones cuodlibetales*, ed. Felix Alluntis (Madrid: Biblioteca de autores cristianos, 1968).

Englebretson, George, "The Square of Opposition," *Notre Dame Journal of Formal Logic* 17.4 (1976), pp. 531–41.

Fay, Thomas A., *Heidegger: The Critique of Logic* (The Hague: Martinus Nijhoff, 1977).

Fenves, Peter, *Arresting Language: From Leibniz to Benjamin* (Palo Alto, CA: Stanford University Press, 2001).

———, *The Messianic Reduction: Walter Benjamin and the Shape of Time* (Palo Alto, CA: Stanford University Press, 2011).

Fichte, Johann Gottlieb, *Sämmtliche Werke*, ed. J. H. Fichte, 11 vols. (Berlin: Veit und comp., 1834).

———, *Gesamtausgabe der Bayerischen Akademie der Wissenschaften*, ed. Reinhard Lauth and Hans Jacob, 41 vols. (Stuttgart–Bad Cannstatt: Fromann Verlag, 1962–2012).

———, *The Science of Knowledge, with the First and Second Introductions*, ed. and trans. Peter Heath and John Lachs (Cambridge: Cambridge University Press, 1982).

Fidora, Alexander, "Dominicus Gundissalinus and the Introduction of Metaphysics into the Latin West," *The Review of Metaphysics* 66 (June 2013), pp. 691–712.

Fiorato, Pierfrancesco, and Hartwig Wiedebach, "Rosenzweig's Readings of Hermann Cohen's *Logic of Pure Cognition*," *The Journal of Jewish Thought and Philosophy* 12. 2 (2003), pp. 139–46.

Folger-Fonfara, Sabine, *Das 'Super'-Transzendentale und die Spaltung der Metaphysik: Der Entwurf des Franziskus von Marchia* (Leiden: E. J. Brill, 2008).

Fonseca, Pedro S. J., *Institutionum dialecticarum libro octo*, I, c. 28 (1575), in *Pedro da Fonseca: Instituições dialécticas,* ed. J. Ferreira Gomes, 2 vols. (Coimbra: Universidade de Coimbra, 1964).

Förster, Eckart, "Kant's *Selbstsetzungslehre*," in *Kant's Transcendental Deductions: The Three "Critiques" and the "Opus postumum,"* ed. Eckart Förster, pp. 217–38 (Palo Alto, CA: Stanford University Press, 1989).

Franciscus de Marchia, *Quodlibet cum quaestionibus selectis ex commentario in librum sententiarum* (Rome: Editiones Collegii S. Bonaventurae ad Claras Aquas, 1997).

Frank, Manfred, *The Philosophical Foundations of Early German Romanticism*, trans. Elizabeth Millán-Zaubert (Albany: SUNY Press, 2004).

Franks, Paul W., *All or Nothing: Systematicity, Transcendental Arguments, and Skepticism in German Idealism* (Cambridge, MA: Harvard University Press, 2005).

Frege, Gottlob, *Begriffsschrift: Eine der arithmetischen nachgebildete Formelsprache des reinen Denkens* (Halle: Louis Nebert, 1879).

———, Review of Cohen, *Das Prinzip der Infinitesimal-Methode und seine Geschichte*, *Zeitschrift für Philosophie und philosophische Kritik* 87 (1885), pp. 324–29.

———, "Über Sinn und Bedeutung," *Zeitschrift für Philosophie und philosophische Kritik*, NF 100 (1892), pp. 25–50.

———, *Translations from the Philosophical Writings of Gottlob Frege*, ed. Peter Geach and Max Black (Oxford: Basil Blackwell, 1960).

———, *Logische Untersuchungen*, ed. Günther Patzig, 5th ed. (1966, Göttingen: Vandenhoeck & Ruprecht, 2003).

———, *Nachgelassene Schriften und wissenschaftlicher Briefwechsel*, ed. Hans Hermes, Friedrich Kambartel, and Friedrich Kaulbach, 2 vols. (Hamburg: Felix Meiner, 1969–76).

———, *Conceptual Notation and Related Articles*, ed. and trans. Terrell Ward Bynum (Oxford: Clarendon Press, 1972).

————, *Posthumous Writings*, ed. Hans Hermes, Friedrich Kambartel, Fredrich Kaulbach, with the assistance of Gottfried Gabriel and Walburga Rödding, trans. Peter Long and Roger White, with the assistance of Raymond Hargreaves (Chicago: University of Chicago Press, 1979).

————, *The Frege Reader*, ed. Michael Beaney (Oxford: Blackwell, 1997).

Freudenthal, Gideon, "Maimon's Subversion of Kant's *Critique of Pure Reason:* There Are No a Priori Synthetic Judgments in Physics," in *Salomon Maimon: Rational Dogmatist, Empirical Skeptic: Critical Assessments*, ed. Gideon Freudenthal, pp. 144–75 (Dordrecht: Kluwer, 2003).

Friedman, Michael, *Kant and the Exact Sciences* (Cambridge, MA: Harvard University Press, 1992).

————, *A Parting of the Ways: Carnap, Cassirer, and Heidegger* (Chicago: Open Court, 2000).

Funkenstein, Amos, *Theology and the Scientific Imagination: From the Middle Ages to the Seventeenth Century* (Princeton: Princeton University Press, 1986).

————, "The Persecution of Absolutes: On the Kantian and Neo-Kantian Theories of Science," in *The Kaleidoscope of Science*, ed. Edna Ullmann-Margalit, pp. 39–63 (Dordrecht and Boston: D. Reidel, 1986).

Galen, *Opera Omnia,* ed. Karl Gottlob Kühn, 20 vols. (Leipzig: Cnobloch, 1821–33).

Garlandus Compotista, *Dialectica: First Edition of the Manuscript*, ed. L. M. De Rijk (Assen: Van Gorcum, 1959).

Goodwin, William W., *A Greek Grammar* (1892, rev. Boston: Ginn & Co. 1900).

Geach, Peter Thomas, *Reference and Generality: An Examination of Some Medieval and Modern Theories* (1962, 3rd ed., Ithaca, NY: Cornell University Press, 1980).

————, "Assertion," in *Logic Matters*, pp. 254–69 (Oxford: Blackwell, 1972).

Gibbs, Robert, *Correlations in Rosenzweig and Levinas* (Princeton: Princeton University Press, 1992).

Giovanelli, Marco, "Grandezza intensiva e grandezza infinitesimale. Hermann Cohen e il principio kantiano delle *Anticipazioni della percezione*," *Annuario filosofico* 19 (2003), pp. 275–318.

————, *Reality and Negation — Kant's Principle of Anticipations of Perception: An Investigation of Its Impact on the Post-Kantian Debate* (Dordrecht: Springer, 2011).

Gordin, Jakob, *Untersuchungen zur Theorie des unendlichen Urteils* (Berlin: Akademie-Verlag, 1929).

Gracia, Jorge J. E., "The Transcendentals in the Middle Ages: An Introduction," *Topoi* 11 (1992), pp. 113–20.

Granger, Gilles, "Wittgenstein et la métalangue," in *Wittgenstein et le problème d'une philosophie de la science*, ed. Gilles Granges, pp. 77–90 (Paris: Éditions du Cerf, 1970).

Guéroult, Martial, *La philosophie transcendentale de Salomon Maïmon* (Paris: Alcan, 1929).

Guyer, Paul, *Kant's System of Nature and Freedom: Selected Essays* (Oxford: Oxford University Press, 2005).

Hamacher, Werner, "Position Exposed: Schlegel's Poetological Transposition of Fichte's Absolute Proposition," in *Premises: Essays on Literature and Philosophy from Kant to Celan*, trans. Peter Fenves, pp. 222–60 (Cambridge, MA: Harvard University Press, 1996).

——, "(The End of Art with the Mask)," trans. Kelly Barry, in *Hegel after Derrida*, ed. Stuart Barnett, pp. 105–30 (New York and London: Routledge, 1998).

——, "Guilt History: Benjamin's Sketch 'Capitalism as Religion,'" trans. Kirk Wetters, *diacritics* 32. 3–4 (2002), pp. 81–106.

——, "Das Nicht im Satz (der Identität)," (unpublished article).

Hamesse, Jacqueline, "*Res* chez les auteurs philosophiques des 12e et 13e siècles ou le passage de la neutralité à la spécificité," in *Res, III Colloquio Internazionale del Lessico Intellettuale Europeo*, ed. Mata Fattori and Massimo Bianchi, pp. 285–96 (Rome: Edizioni dell'Ateneo, 1982).

Hartmann, Nicolai, *Platos Logik des Seins* (Giessen: A. Töpelmann, 1909).

Hegel, Georg Wilhelm Friedrich, *Jenenser Logik, Metaphysik und Naturphilosophie*, ed. Georg Lasson (Hamburg: Meiner, 1923).

——, *Briefe an und von Hegel*, ed. Johannes Hoffmeister, 4 vols. (Hamburg: Meiner Verlag, 1952–60).

——, *Gesammelte Werke*, vol. 4: *Jenaer kritische Schriften*, ed. Hatmut Buchner and Otto Pöggeler (Hamburg: Meiner, 1968).

——, *Vorlesungen über die Ästhetik*, ed. Eva Moldenhauer and Karl Markus Michel, 3 vols. (Frankfurt am Main: Suhrkamp Verlag, 1970).

——, *Gesammelte Werke*, vol. 7: *Jenaer Systementwurfe II*, ed. Rolf-Peter Horstmann and Johann Heinrich Trede (Hamburg: Meiner, 1971).

——, *Aesthetics: Lectures on Fine Art*, I, II, trans. by T. M. Knox, 2 vols. (New York: Oxford University Press, 1975).

——, *The Difference Between Fichte's and Schelling's System of Philosophy*, trans. H. S. Harris and Walter Cerf (Albany: State University of New York Press, 1977).

——, *Faith and Knowledge*, trans. Walter Cerf and H. S. Harris (Albany: State University of New York Press, 1977).

——, *Gesammelte Werke*, vol. 9: *Die Phänomenologie des Geistes*, ed. Wolfgang Bonsiepen and Reinhard Heede (Hamburg: Meiner, 1980).

——, *Gesammelte Werke*, vol. 12: *Wissenschaft der Logik 1816*, ed. Friedrich Hogemann and Walter Jaeschke (Hamburg: Meiner, 1978).

——, *The Letters*, trans. Clark Butler and Christiane Seiler, commentary by Clark Butler (Bloomington: Indiana University Press, 1984).

——, *Gesammelte Werke, Deutsche Forschungsgemeinschaft* (Hamburg: F. Meiner, 1957–2015), vol. 21: *Wissenschaft der Logik*, ed. Friedrich Hogemann and Walter Jaeschke (Hamburg: Meiner, 1985).

——, *The Jena System 1804–5: Logic and Metaphysics*, ed. and trans. John W. Burbidge and George di Giovanni, introduction by H. S. Harris (Montreal: McGill/Queens University Press, 1986).

——, *Gesammelte Werke*, vol. XX: *Enzyclopädie der philosophischen Wissenschaften im Grundrisse (1830)*, ed. Wolfgang Bonsiepen and Hans Christian Lucas (Hamburg: Meiner, 1992).

——, *Outlines of the Philosophy of Right*, trans. T. M. Knox, rev. Stephen Houlgate (Oxford: Oxford University Press, 2008).

——, *Lectures on Logic: Berlin 1831*, transcribed by Karl Hegel, trans. Clark Butler (Indianapolis: Indiana University Press, 2008).

——, *Gesammelte Werke*, vol. 14, part 1: *Naturrecht und Staatswissenschaft im Grundrisse, Grundlinien der Philosophie des Rechts*, ed. Klaus Grotsch and Elisabeth Weisser-Lohmann, 3 vols. (Hamburg: Meiner, 2009–11).

——, *The Science of Logic*, trans. and ed. George Di Giovanni (Cambridge: Cambridge University, Press, 2010).

——, *Encyclopedia of the Philosophical Sciences in Basic Outline, Part One: Science of Logic*, ed. and trans. Klaus Brinkmann and Daniel O. Dahlstrom (Cambridge: Cambridge University Press, 2010).

Heidegger, Martin, *Sein und Zeit* (1927, 11th ed., Tübingen: Max Niemeyer, 1967).

——, *Being and Time*, trans. John Macquarrie and Edward Robinson (Oxford: Blackwell, 1962).

——, *On Time and Being*, trans. Joan Stambaugh (New York: Harper & Row, 1972).

——, *Early Greek Thinking: The Dawn of Western Philosophy*, trans. David Farrell Krell and Frank A. Capuzzi (New York: Harper & Row, 1975).

——, *Gesamtausgabe*, vol. 9: *Wegmarken* (Frankfurt am Main: Vittorio Klostermann, 1976).

——, *Gesamtausgabe*, vol. 5: *Holzwege*, ed. Friedrich-Wilhelm von Herrmann (Frankfurt am Main: Vittorio Klostermann, 1977).

————, *Basic Writings: From Being and Time (1927) to The Task of Thinking (1964)*, trans. David Farrell Krell (New York: Harper & Row, 1977).

————, *Gesamtausgabe*, vol. 1: *Frühe Schriften*, ed. Friedrich-Wilhelm von Herrmann (Frankfurt am Main: Vittorio Klostermann, 1978).

————, *Gesamtausgabe*, vol. 26: *Metaphysische Anfangsgründe der Logik im Ausgang von Leibniz*, ed. Klaus Held (Frankfurt am Main: Vittorio Klostermann, 1978).

————, *Gesamtausgabe*, vol. 33: *Aristoteles, Metaphysik Θ 1–3: Von Wesen und Wirklichkeit der Kraft*, ed. Heinrich Huni (Frankfurt am Main: Vittorio Klostermann, 1981).

————, *Gesamtausgabe*, vol. 40: *Einführung in die Metaphysik*, ed. Petra Jaeger (Frankfurt am Main: Vittorio Klostermann, 1983).

————, *Gesamtausgabe*, vol. 41: *Die Frage nach dem Ding. Zu Kants Lehre von den transzendentalen Grundsätze*, ed. Petra Jaeger (Frankfurt am Main: Vittorio Klostermann, 1984).

————, *Gesamtausgabe*, vol. 12: *Unterwegs zur Sprache*, ed. Friedrich-Wilhelm von Herrmann (Frankfurt am Main: Vittorio Klostermann, 1985).

————, *Gesamtausgabe*, vol. 3: *Kant und das Problem der Metaphysik* (1929, Frankfurt: Vittorio Klostermann, 1991).

————, *Pathmarks*, ed. William McNeill (Cambridge: Cambridge University Press, 1998).

————, *Aristotle's Metaphysics Θ 1–3: On the Essence and Actuality of Force*, trans. Walter Brogan and Peter Warnek (Bloomington: Indiana University Press, 1995).

————, *Gesamtausgabe*, vol. 7: *Vorträge und Aufsätze*, ed. Friedrich-Wilhelm von Herrmann (Frankfurt am Main: Vittorio Klostermann, 2000).

————, *Gesamtausgabe*, vol. 14: *Zur Sache des Denkens*, ed. Friedrich-Wilhelm von Herrmann (Frankfurt am Main: Vittorio Klostermann, 2007).

Henrich, Dieter, "Hölderlin über Urteil und Sein: Eine Studie zur Entstehungsgeschichte des Idealismus," *Hölderlin-Jahrbuch* 14 (1965–66), pp. 73–96.

————, "Fichtes ursprüngliche Einsicht," in *Subjektivität und Metaphysik, Festschrift für Wolfgang Cramer*, ed. Dieter Henrich and Hans Wagner, pp. 188–232 (Frankfurt am Main: Vittorio Klostermann, 1966).

Henry of Ghent, *Henrici de Gandavo Opera Omnia*, vol. XI: *Quodlibet VII*, ed. G. A. Wilson (Leiden: E. J. Brill, 1979–91).

Heubeck, Alfred, and Arie Hoekstra, *A Commentary on Homer's Odyssey*, vol. 2: *Books IX–XVI* (Oxford: Clarendon Press, 1989).

Hibben, John Grier, Review of Cohen, *Logik der reinen Erkenntnis*, *The Philosophical Review* 13. 2 (1904), pp. 207–12.

Hobbes, Thomas, *The English Works of Thomas Hobbes of Malmsbury* (London: Bohn, 1843).

Hoffmann, Thomas Sören, *Die absolute Form: Modalität, Individualität und das Prinzip der Philosophie nach Kant und Hegel* (Berlin and New York: De Gruyter, 1991).

Hölderlin, Friedrich, *Sämtliche Werke*, ed. Friedrich Beissner, 8 vols. (Stuttgart: Cotta, 1946–85).

Holtz, Louis, *Donat et la tradition de l'enseignement grammatical: Étude sur l'Ars Donati et sa diffusion (IVe–IXe siècle) et édition critique* (Paris: Centre National de la Recherche Scientifique, 1981).

Holzhey, Helmut, *Cohen und Natorp: Die Geschichte der 'Marburger Schule' als Auseinandersetzung um die Logik des Denkens*, 2 vols. (Basel: Schwabe, 1986).

Homer, *The Odyssey*, trans. Richmond Lattimore (New York: Harper Perennial, 1963).

Horn, Lawrence R., *A Natural History of Negation* (1989, reissue ed. Stanford: CSLI, 2001).

——, "Uncovering the Un-Word: A Study in Lexical Pragmatics," *Sophia linguistica* 49 (2002), pp. 1–64.

Hugonnard-Roche, Henri, "L'Organon. Tradition syriaque et arabe," in *Dictionnaire des philosophes antiques*, ed. Richard Goulet, preface by Pierre Hadot (Paris: CNRS, 1989–), vol. 1: *Abam(m)on à Axiothéa*, pp. 502–507.

Humberstone, Lloyd, "Note on Contraries and Subcontraries," *Nous* 37. 4 (2003), pp. 690–705.

Husserl, Edmund, *Erfahrung und Urteil: Untersuchungen zur Genealogie der Logik*, ed. Ludwig Landgrebe (Prague: Academia, 1939).

——, *Husserliana: Gesammelte Werke*, ed. H. L. van Breda (The Hague: Nijhoff, 1950–), vol. 2: *Die Idee der Phänomenologie* (The Hague: Nijhoff, 1950).

——, *Husserliana*, vols. III–V: *Ideen zu einer reinen Phänomenologie und phänomenologischen Philosophie*, ed. Marly and Walter Biemel, 3 vols. (The Hague: Nijhoff, 1950–52).

——, *Logische Untersuchungen*, 2 vols. (1913, Tübingen: Max Niemeyer, 1968).

——, *Ideas Pertaining to a Pure Phenomenology and to a Phenomenological Philosophy*, trans. F. Kersten, Richard Rojcewicz, and André Schuwer, 3 vols. (The Hague: Nijhoff, 1980–89).

——, *The Idea of Phenomenology: A Translation of Die Idee der Phänomenologie Husserliana II*, trans. Lee Hardy (Dordrecht/Boston/London: Kluwer, 1999).

Hyppolite, Jean, *Logique et existence: Essai sur la logique de Hegel* (Paris: Presses Universitaires de France, 1953).

Imbert, Claude, "Le projet idéographique," *Revue internationale de philosophie* 33. 130 (1979), pp. 621–65.

——, *Phénoménologies et langues formulaires* (Paris: Presses Universitaires de France, 1992).

Irvine, Martin, *The Making of Textual Culture: 'Grammatica' and Literary Theory 350–1100* (Cambridge: Cambridge University Press, 1994).

Ishikawa, Fumiyasu, *Kants Denken von einem Dritten: Das Gerichtshof-Modell und das unendliche Urteil in der Antonomienlehre* (Frankfurt and New York: Peter Lang, 1990).

Isidore of Seville, *Isidori Hispalensis episcopi Etymologiarum sive originum libri XX*, ed. W. M. Lindsay, 2 vols. (Oxford: Clarendon Press, 1911).

Jacobi, Friedrich Heinrich, *Werke*, 6 vols. (Leipzig: Gerhard Fleischer, 1812–25).

Jacobi, Klaus, "*Nomina transcendentia*. Untersuchungen von Logikern des 12. Jahrhunderts über transkategoriale Terme," in *Die Logik des Transcendentalen: Festschrift für Jan A. Aertsen*, ed. Martin Pickavel, pp. 23–36 (Berlin and New York: W. de Gruyter, 2003).

Jakobson, Roman, *Six leçons sur le son et les sens*, preface by Claude Lévi-Strauss (Paris: Éditions de Minuit, 1976).

Janke, Wolfgang, "Thetisches Urteil—Spekulativer Satz. Fichte und Hegel über die Ausdrucksform der Grundsetzung 'Ich bin—Ich,'" in *Entgegensetzungen: Studien zu Fichte-Konfrontationen von Rousseau bis Kierkegaard*, pp. 47–68 (Amsterdam: Rodopi, 1994).

Jespersen, Otto, *Negation in English and Other Languages* (Copenhagen: A. F. Høst, 1917).

Jolivet, Jean, "Notes de lexicographie abélardienne," in *Pierre Abélard, Pierre le Vénérable: Les Courants philosophiques, littéraires et artistiques en Occident au milieu du XIIe siècle*, pp. 531–45 (Paris: CNRS, 1975).

——, *Philosophie médiévale arabe et latine* (Paris: Vrin, 1995).

Kahn, Charles H., "On the Terminology for Copula and Existence," in *Essays on Being*, pp. 41–61 (Cambridge: Cambridge University Press, 2009).

Kant, Immanuel, *Gesammelte Werke*, ed. Königlich Preußische [later Deutsche] Akademie der Wissenschaften (Berlin: G. Reimer; later, De Gruyter, 1900–).

——, *Lectures on Logic*, trans. J. Michael Young (Cambridge: Cambridge University Press, 1992).

——, *Opus Postumum*, ed. Eckart Förster, trans. Eckart Förster and Michael Rosen (Cambridge: Cambridge University Press, 1993).

——, *Religion and Rational Theology*, ed. and trans. Allen W. Wood and George Di Giovanni (Cambridge: Cambridge University Press, 1996).

——, *Critique of Pure Reason*, trans. and ed. Paul Guyer and Allan Wood (Cambridge: Cambridge University Press, 1998).

——, *Correspondence*, trans. and ed. Arnulf Zweig (Cambridge: Cambridge University Press, 1999).

———, *Theoretical Philosophy: 1755–1770*, trans. and ed. David Walford (Cambridge: Cambridge University Press, 2003).

Käufer, Stephan, "On Heidegger on Logic," *Continental Philosophy Review* 34 (2001), pp. 455–76.

Kavka, Martin, *Jewish Messianism and the History of Philosophy* (Cambridge: Cambridge University Press, 2004).

Kinkel, Walter, "Das Urteil des Ursprungs: Ein Kapitel aus einem Kommentar zu H. Cohens *Logik der reinen Erkenntnis*," *Kant-Studien* 17. 1–3 (1912), pp. 274–82.

Kiparsky, Paul, "Roman Jakobson and the Grammar of Poetry," in *A Tribute to Roman Jakobson, 1896–1982*, pp. 27–39 (Berlin and New York: Mouton, 1983).

Kirk, Jordan, "Theories of the Nonsense Word in Medieval England" (PhD dissertation, Princeton University, 2013).

Kneepkens, C. H., ed., *Het iudicium constructionis: Het leerstuk van de construction in de 2de helft van de 12de eeuw*, 4 vols. (Nijmegen: Ingenium Publishers, 1987).

Kordelas, Lambros, *Geist und caput mortuum: Hegels Kritik der Lehre Galls in der "Phänomenologie des Geistes"* (Würzburg: Königshausen & Neumann, 1998).

Kuntze, Friedrich, *Die Philosophie Salomon Maimons* (Heidelberg: C. Winter, 1912).

Kutsch, W., "Muḥassal, Ghair muḥassal," *Mélanges de l'Université Saint Joseph* 27. 9 (1947–48), pp. 169–76.

Labarrière, Pierre-Jean, *Structures et mouvement dialectique dans la Phénoménologie de l'esprit de Hegel* (1968, 2nd ed., Paris: Aubier, 1985).

Lacan, Jacques, *Télévision* (Paris: Éditions du Seuil, 1974).

———, *Television*, trans. Denis Hollier, Rosalind Krauss, and Annette Michelson, and *A Challenge to the Psychoanalytic Establishment*, trans. Jeffrey Mehlman, ed. Joan Copjec (New York: Norton, 1990).

———, *Autres écrits* (Paris: Seuil, 2001).

Lachelier, Jules, *Études sur le syllogisme, suivies de l'Observation de Platner et d'une Note sur le "Philèbe"* (Paris: F. Alcan, 1907).

Lachterman, David Rapport, "Mathematical Construction, Symbolic Cognition and the Infinite Intellect: Reflections on Maimon and Maimonides," *Journal of the History of Philosophy* 30. 4 (1992), pp. 497–522.

Lacoue-Labarthe, Philippe and Jean-Luc Nancy, *L'absolu littéraire: Théorie de la littérature du romantisme allemand* (Paris: Seuil, 1978).

Lambert, Johann Heinrich, *Anlage zur Architectonic, oder Theorie des Einfachen und des Ersten in der philosohischen und mathematischen Erkenntnis*, 2 vols. (Riga: Johann Friedrich Hartknoch, 1771).

Langendoen, D. T., and P. M. Postal, "Sets and Sentences," in *The Philosophy of Linguistics*, ed. Jerrold J. Katz, pp. 227–48 (Oxford: Oxford University Press, 1985).

Leclerc, Jean, *Opera philosophica in quattuor volumina digesta*, 4 vols. (Amsterdam: Apud Georgium Gallet, 1698).

Leibniz, Gottfried Wilhelm, *Die philosophischen Schriften*, ed. C. I. Gerhardt, 7 vols. (Berlin: Weidmann, 1875–90).

———, *Opuscules et fragments inédits*, ed. Louis Couturat (Paris: F. Alcan, 1903).

Lemaitre, Jean-Christophe, "La réevaluation des rapports entre logique formelle et logique transcendentale dans l'idéalisme allemand: Le cas du jugement infini chez Kant et chez Schelling," in Guillaume Lejeune, ed., *La question de la logique dans l'idéalisme allemand: Actes du colloque de Bruxelles, 7–9 avril 2011* (New York: Georg Olms, 2013), pp. 125–40.

Lenk, Hans, *Kritik der logischen Konstanten: Philosophische Begründungen der Urteilsformen vom Idealismus bis zur Gegenwart* (Berlin: De Gruyter, 1968).

Léonard, André, *Commentaire littérale de la Logique de Hegel* (Louvain and Paris: Éditions de l'institut supérieur de philosohie de Louvain/Vrin, 1974).

Liebmann, Otto, *Kant und die Epigonen: Eine kritsche Abhandlung* (Stuttgart: C. Schober, 1865).

Longuenesse, Béatrice, *Kant and the Capacity to Judge: Sensibility and Discursivity in the Transcendental Analytic of the "Critique of Pure Reason,"* trans. Charles T. Wolfe (Princeton: Princeton University Press, 1998).

———, *Hegel's Critique of Metaphysics*, trans. Nicole J. Simek (Cambridge: Cambridge University Press, 2007).

Lotze, Hermann, *System der Philosophie*, 2 vols. (Leipzig: S. Hirzel, 1874).

Łukasiewicz, Jan, *Aristotle's Syllogistic from the Point of View of Modern Formal Logic* (2nd ed., Oxford: Clarendon Press, 1957).

Lynch, Richard, *Universa philosophia Scholastica*, 3 vols. (Leyden: n. p., 1654).

Mabbott, J. D., "Negation," *Proceedings of the Aristotelian Society* Supplementary vol. 9 (1929), pp. 67–79.

MacFarlane, John, "Frege, Kant, and the Logic in Logicism," *The Philosophical Review* III. 1 (2002), pp. 25–65.

Maier, Anneliese, *Kants Qualitätskategorien* (Berlin: Pan-Verlag Kurt Metzner, 1930).

Maimon, Salomon, *Gesammelte Werke*, ed. Valerio Verra, 7 vols. (Hildesheim: G. Olms, 1965–76).

——, *Giv'at ha-more*, ed. Hugo Bergman and Nathan Rotenstreich (Jerusalem: ha-Akademyah ha-le'umit ha-Yiśre'elit le mada'im, 726 [1965]).

——, *Commentaires de Maïmonide*, preface by Jean Jolivet, ed. and trans. Maurice-Ruben Hayoun (Paris: Éditions du Cerf, 1999).

——, *Versuch über die Transzendentalphilosophie*, ed. Florian Ehrensperger (Hamburg: Meiner, 2004).

——, *Essay on Transcendental Philosophy*, trans. Nick Midgley, Henry Somers-Hall, Alistair Welchman, and Merten Reglitz (New York: Continuum, 2010).

Maimonides, *The Guide of the Perplexed*, trans. Shlomo Pines, with an introduction by Leo Strauss, 2 vols. (Chicago: University of Chicago Press, 1963).

——. (=Mūsā ibn Maimūn al-Qurṭubī al-Andalusī), *Dalālat al-ḥā'irīn*, ed. Hüseyin Atay (Ankara: Maṭba'ah Jāmi'at Anqara, 1974).

Marcus, Ernst, *Logik. Die Elementarlehre zur allgemeinen und die Grundzüge der transzendentalen Logik. Einführung in Kants Kategorienlehre* (1906, 2nd ed. Herford: W. Menckhoff, 1911).

Marenbon, John, *The Philosophy of Peter Abelard* (Cambridge: Cambridge University Press, 1997).

Marmura, Michael, "Avicenna on Primary Concepts: The *Metaphysics* of His al-Shifā'," in *Logos Islamikos: Studia Islamica in honorem Georgii Michaelis Wickens*, ed. Roger M. Savory and Dionisius A. Agius, pp. 219–39 (Toronto: Pontifical Institute of Mediaeval Studies, 1984).

Martin, Christopher J., "The Logic of Negation in Boethius," *Phronesis* 36. 3 (1991), pp. 277–304.

Martin, Wayne W., "The Judgment Stroke and the Truth Predicate: Frege, Heidegger, and the Logical Representation of Judgment," *The New Yearbook for Phenomenology and Phenomenological Research* 3 (2003), pp. 27–52.

Marx, Wolfgang, *Transzendentale Logik als Wissenschaftstheorie: Systematisch-kritische Untersuchungen zur philosophischen Grundlegungsproblematik in Cohens 'Logik der reinen Erkenntnis'* (Frankfurt am Main: Klostermann, 1977).

Mauro, Sylvester, *Quaestiones philosophicae, Summulae seu Logica brevis*, ed. Matteo Liberatore, 3 vols. (Paris: Bloud & Barral, 1876).

McCall, Storrs, "Contrariety," *Notre Dame Journal of Formal Logic* 8. 1–2 (1976), pp. 121–32.

Meier-Oeser, S. and W. Schröder, "Skindapsos," in *Historisches Wörterbuch der Philosophie*, ed. Joachim Ritter and Karlfried Gründer, 13 vols. (Basel: Schwabe & Co., 1971–2007), vol. 9: *Se–Sp*, pp. 973–76.

Menne, Albert, "Das unendliche Urteil Kants," *Philosophia Naturalis* 19 (1982), pp. 151–62.

Miller, Jacques-Alain, "Suture. Éléments de la logique du signifiant," in *Un début dans la vie*, pp. 94–115 (Paris: Gallimard, 2002).

Milner, Jean-Claude, *Introduction à une science du langage* (Paris: Éditions du Seuil, 1989).

Milton, John, *The Doctrine and Discipline of Divorce* (1643, 2nd ed., London: T. P. and M. S., 1644).

Moorhouse, A. C., *Studies in the Greek Negatives* (Cardiff: University of Wales Press, 1959).

Mure, G. R. G., *A Study of Hegel's Logic* (Oxford: Clarendon Press, 1950).

Nacht-Eladi, Sylvian, "Aristotle's Doctrine of the Differentia Specifica and Maimon's Law of Determinability," *Scripta Hierosolymitana* 6 (1960), pp. 222–48.

Natorp, Paul, *Die logischen Grundlagen der exakten Wissenschaften* (Berlin and Leipzig: B. G. Teubner, 1910).

Nicholas of Cusa, *On God Considered as Not-Other*, ed. and trans. Jaspar Hopkins (University of Minnesota, 1979).

——, *De non aliud: Nichts Anderes*, ed. Klaus Reinhardt, Jorge M. Marchetta, and Harald Schwaetzer (Munster: Aschendorff, 2011).

Ott, Hugo, *Martin Heidegger: Unterwegs zu seiner Biographie* (Frankfurt: Campus, 1988).

Pacioli, Luca, *Summa de arithmetica geometria proportioni et proportionalita* (Venice: n. p., 1494).

Parsons, Terence, "The Traditional Square of Opposition — A Biography," *Acta Analytica* 18 (1997), pp. 23–49.

Paulus, Jean, *Henri de Gand: Essai sur les tendances de sa métaphysique* (Paris: Vrin, 1938).

Peano, Giuseppe, "Review of Frege's *Grundgesetze* (1885)," trans. Victor Dudman *Southern Journal of Philosophy* 9 (1971), pp. 25–37.

Peirce, Charles Sanders, "Limitative," in *Dictionary of Philosophy and Psychology*, ed. James Mark Baldwin, 3 vols., vol. 2: *Le–Z*, p. 6 (New York and London: Macmillan, 1902).

——, *Collected Papers*, ed. Charles Hartshorne and Paul Weiss, 8 vols. (Cambridge, MA: Harvard University Press, 1931–58).

Peradotto, John, *Man in the Middle Voice: Name and Narration in the Odyssey* (Princeton: Princeton University Press, 1990).

Peters, Stanley, and Dag Westerstål, *Quantifiers in Language and Logic* (Oxford: Oxford University Press, 2006).

Petrilli, Raffaella, *Temps et détermination dans la grammaire et la philosophie anciennes* (Munster: Nodus Publikationen, 1997).

Philip the Chancellor, *Summa de bono*, ed. Nikolaus Wicki, 2 vols. (Bern: Francke, 1985).

Philonenko, Alexis, *L'École de Marbourg: Cohen — Natorp — Cassirer* (Paris: Vrin, 1989).

Pines, Shlomo, "Dieu et l'être selon Maïmonide: Exégèse d'Exode 3, 14 et doctrine connexe," in *The Collected Works of Shlomo Pines*, vol. 5: *Studies in the History of Jewish Thought*, ed. Warren Zev Harvey and Moshe Idel, pp. 447–56 (Jerusalem: Magnes Press, 1997).

Pippin, Robert, *Hegel's Idealism: The Satisfactions of Self-Consciousness* (Cambridge: Cambridge University Press, 1989).

Poma, Andrea, *La filosofia critica di Hermann Cohen* (Milan: Mursia, 1988).

Porro, Pasquale, "Res a reor reris/Res a ratitudine: Autour d'Henri de Gand," in *Mots médiévaux offerts à Ruedi Imbach*, ed. I. Atucha, D. Calma, C. König-Pralong, I. Zavattero, pp. 617–28 (Porto: Fédération internationale des Instituts d'études médiévales, 2011).

Pouillon, Henri, "Le Premier Traité des proprieties transcendentales. La 'Summa de bono' du Chancelier Philippe," *Revue néoscolastique de philosophie* 42 (1939), pp. 40–77.

Prior, Arthur N., "The Logic of Negative Terms in Boethius," *Franciscan Studies* 13 (1953), pp. 1–6.

Priscian, *Institutiones grammaticarum libri XVIII*, ed. Martin Hertz, 2 vols. (Leipzig: Teubner, 1855).

Quine, Willard Van Orman, "On What There Is," in *From a Logical Point of View: 9 Logico-Philosophical Essays*, pp. 1–19 (Cambridge, MA: Harvard University Press, 1953).

Rashed, Roshdi, "L'idée de l'algèbre selon Al-Khwārizmī," *Fundamenta Scientiae* 4. 1 (1983), pp. 87–100.

———, "Mathématiques et philosophie chez Avicenne," in *Études sur Avicenne*, ed. Jean Jolivet and Roshdi Rashed, pp. 29–39 (Paris: Les Belles Lettres, 1984).

Reinhold, Karl Leonhardt, *Beyträge zur Berichtigung bisheriger Missverständnisse der Philosophen*, 2 vols. (Jena: Johann Michael Manke, 1790–94).

Richardson, Alan W., "Conceiving, Experiencing, and Conceiving Experiencing: Neo-Kantianism and the History of the Concept of Experience," *Topoi* 22 (2003), pp. 55–67.

Rohs, Peter, "Kants Prinzip der durchgängigen Bestimmung alles Seinden," *Kant-Studien* 69. 2 (1978), pp. 170–80.

Rosen, Stanley, *The Idea of Hegel's Science of Logic* (Chicago: University of Chicago Press, 2014).

Rosenzweig, Franz, *Der Mensch und Sein Werk: Gesammelte Schriften*, vol. 4: *Der Stern der Erlösung*, introduction by Reinhold Mayer (4th ed., Haag: Nijhoff, 1976).

——, *Star of Redemption*, foreword by Michael Oppenheim, introduction by Elliot R. Wolfson, trans. Barbara E. Galli (Madison: University of Wisconsin Press, 2005).

Rosier, Irène, "Relatifs et relatives dans les traités des XIIe et XIIIe siècles," *Vivarium* 23. 1 (1983), pp. 1–22, and *Vivarium* 24. 1 (1986), pp. 1–21.

Rotenstreich, Nathan, *Experience and Its Systematization: Studies in Kant* (1965, 2nd ed. The Hague: Martinus Nijhoff, 1972).

Russell, Bertrand, *The Principles of Mathematics*, vol. 1 (Cambridge: Cambridge University Press, 1903).

——, *Our Knowledge of the External World as a Field for Scientific Method in Philosophy* (London: Open Court, 1914).

Salabert, Jean, *Les Addresses du parfait raisonnement, Où l'on découvre les thrésors de la Logique Françoise, & les ruses de plusieurs Sophismes* (Paris: Claude Collet, 1638).

Sanford, David H., "Contraries and Subcontraries," *Nous* 2. 1 (1968), pp. 95–96.

Saussure, Ferdinand de, *Cours de linguistique générale*, ed. Tullio de Mauro (Paris: Payot, 1972).

Schechter, Oded, "The Logic of Speculative Philosophy and Skepticism in Maimon's Philosophy: *Satz der Bestimmbarkeit* and the Role of Synthesis," in *Salomon Maimon: Rational Dogmatist, Empirical Skeptic*, ed. Gideon Freudenthal, pp. 18–53 (Dordrecht: Kluwer, 2003).

Schein, Seth L., "Odysseus and Polyphemus in the *Odyssey*," *Greek, Roman and Byzantine Studies* 11. 2 (1970), pp. 73–83.

Schelling, Friedrich Wilhelm Joseph, *Historisch-kritische Ausgabe*, ed. Hans Michael Baumgartner et al. (Stuttgart: Frommann-Holzboog, 1976–).

——, *The Unconditional in Human Knowledge: Four Early Essays, 1794–1796*, ed. and trans. Fritz Marti (Lewisburg, PA: Bucknell University Press, 1980).

Schmied-Kowarzik, Wolfdietrich, *Rosenzweig im Gespräch mit Ehrenberg, Cohen und Buber* (Freiburg and Munich: Alber, 2006).

Schmitz, Hermann, *Hegel als Denker der Individualität* (Meisenheim and Glan: Anton Hain, 1957).

Schopenhauer, Arthur, *The World as Will and Idea*, trans. R. B. Haldane and John Kemp, 2 vols. (London: Tübner & Co., 1883–86).

——, *Die Welt als Wille und Vorstellung*, 2 vols. (Zurich: Diogenes, 1977).

Schröder, Ernst, Review of Frege, *Begriffsschrift*, *Zeitschrift für Mathematik und Physik* 25 (1880), pp. 81–94.

Schulze, Gottlob Ernst, *Aenesidemus, oder, über die Fundamente der von dem Herrn Professor Rein-hold in Jena gelieferten Elementar-Philosophie. Nebst einer Vertheidigung des Skepticismus gegen die Anmassungen der Vernunftkritik*, ed. Manfred Frank (Hamburg: Meiner, 1996).

Searle, J. R., *Speech Acts: An Essay in the Philosophy of Language* (Cambridge: Cambridge University Press, 1969).

Seidel, George J., *Fichte's Wissenschaftslehre of 1794: A Commentary on Part 1* (West Lafayette, IN: Purdue University Press, 1993).

Seneca, Lucius Anneaus, *Lettere a Lucilio*, ed. Umberto Boella (Turin: UTET, 1995).

Shapiro, H., "Walter Burley's *De Ente*," *Manuscripta* 7 (1963), pp. 103–108.

Shiel, James, "Boethius's Commentaries on Aristotle," *Mediaeval and Renaissance Studies* 4 (1958), pp. 217–44.

Sillitti, Giovanna, *Tragelaphos. Storia di una metafora e di un problema* (Naples: Bibliopolis, 1980).

Simon of Faversham, *Quaestiones super libro Perihermeneias,* in *Magistri Simonis Anglici sive de Faverisham Opera omnia*, vol. 1, *Opera logica*, ed. Pasquale Mazzarella (Padua: CEDAM, 1957).

Simpson, Michael, "*Odyssey* 9: Symmetry and Paradox in Outis," *The Classical Journal* 68. 1 (1972), pp. 22–25.

Smith, Norman Kemp, *A Commentary to Kant's Critique of Pure Reason* (Atlantic Highlands, NJ: Humanities International, 1918).

Solowiejczyk, Josef, *Das reine Denken und die Seinskonstituierung bei Hermann Cohen* (Berlin: Reuther & Reichard, 1932).

Sommers, Fred, *The Logic of Natural Language* (Oxford: Clarendon Press, 1982).

Soreth, M. "Zum infiniten Prädikat im zehnten Kapitel der Aristotelischen Hermeneu-tik," *Islamic Philosophy and the Classical Tradition: Essays Presented by His Friends and Pupils to Richard Walzer*, ed. S. M. Stern, A. Hourani, and Vivian Brown, pp. 389–424 (Columbia: University of South Carolina Press, 1972).

Soto, Domingo de, *Summulae*, ed. Wilhelm Risse (Hildesheim and New York: G. Olms, 1980).

Spitzer, Leo, "Parole vuote (A proposito di 'Blittri')," *Lingua nostra* 16. 1 (1955), p. 1.

Stanford, William Bedell, *Ambiguity in Greek Literature* (London and New York: Johnson Reprint Corp., 1972).

Stang, Nicholas F., "Kant on Complete Determination and Infinite Judgment," *British Journal for the History of Philosophy* 20. 6 (2012), pp. 1117–39.

Stolzenberg, Jürgen, *Ursprung und System: Probleme der Bedeutung systematischer Philosophie im Werk Hermann Cohens, Paul Natorps und beim frühem Martin Heidegger* (Göttingen: Vandenhoeck & Ruprecht, 1995).

Strawson, P. F., *Introduction to Logical Theory* (London: Methuen & Co., 1963).

Suárez, Francisco, *Opera Omnia*, ed. Charles Berton, 20 vols. (Paris: L. Vivès, 1856–78).

Syrianus, *In Metaphysica Commentaria* (=*Commentaria in Aristotelem graeca*, vol. 6, 1), ed. Wilhelm Kroll (Berlin: Reimer, 1902).

———, *On Aristotle's Metaphysics, 13–14*, trans. John Dillon and Dominick O'Meara (London: Bloomsbury, 2006).

Tarski, Alfred, "The Concept of Truth in Formalized Languages," in *Logic, Semantics, Metamathematics: Papers from 1923 to 1938*, trans. J. H. Woodger, pp. 152–278 (Oxford: Clarendon Press, 1956).

Theophrastus of Eresus, *Theophrastus of Eresus: Sources for his Life, Writings, Thought, and Influence*, ed. William W. Fortenbaugh, Pamela M. Huby, Robert W. Sharples, and Dimitri Gutas, 2 vols. (Leiden and New York: E. J. Brill, 1992).

Thom, Paul, "Al-Fārābī on Indefinite and Privative Names," *Arabic Sciences and Philosophy* 18 (2008), pp. 189–209.

Thomas Aquinas, *Opera Omnia*, 34 vols., vol. 22: *De veritate* (Rome: Commissio Leonina/1970).

Thucydides, *History of the Peloponnesian War*, trans. J. M. Dent (London and New York, E. P. Dutton, 1910).

———, *Thucydidis Historiae*, ed. H. Stuart Jones and J. E. Powell, 2 vols. (Oxford: Clarendon Press, 1942).

Timpler, Clemens, *Metaphysicae systema methodicum, Libri quinque* (Hanover: Atonius, 1612).

Trendelenburg, Friedrich Adolf, *Logische Untersuchungen*, 2 vols. (1840, 3rd ed., Leipzig: S. Hirzel, 1870).

Tuschling, Burckhard, "Apperception and Ether: On the Idea of a Transcendental Deduction of Matter in Kant's *Opus postumum*," in *Kant's Transcendental Deductions: The Three "Critiques" and the "Opus postumum,"* ed. Eckart Förster, pp. 193–216 (Palo Alto, CA: Stanford University Press, 1989)..

Valente, Luisa, "Names That Can Be Said of Everything: Porphyrian Tradition 'Transcendental' Terms in Twelfth-Century Logic," *Vivarium* 45. 2–3 (2007), pp. 298–310.

Valla, Lorenzo, *Dialectical Disputations*, ed. and trans. Brian P. Copenhaver and Lodi Nauta, 2 vols. (Cambridge, MA: Harvard University Press, 2012).

Van der Kuijlen, Willem, "Infinite Judgment in Kant's *Critique of Pure Reason*," *Proceedings of the International Workshop 'Logical Kant-Studies'* 4, pp. 199–215 (Kaliningrad: Kaliningrad State University, 1998).

Viñas, Miguel de, *Philosophia Scholastica*, 3 vols. (Genoa: Typis Antonii Casamarae, 1709).

Vollrath, Ernst, "Kants These über das Nichts," *Kant-Studien* 61 (1970), pp. 50–65.

Vuillemin, Jules, *L'Héritage kantien et la révolution copernicienne: Fichte — Cohen — Heidegger* (Paris: Presses Universitaires de France, 1954).

Wiehl, Reiner, "Logik und Metalogik bei Cohen und Rosenzweig," in *Der Philosoph Franz Rosenzweig (1886–1929)*, vol. 2: *Das neue Denken und seine Dimensionen*, ed. Wolfdietrich Schmied-Kowarzik, pp. 623–42 (Freiburg and Munich: Karl Albert, 1988).

Wisnovsky, Robert, "Notes on Avicenna's Concept of Thingness (*Šay'iyya*)," *Arabic Sciences and Philosophy* 10 (2000), pp. 181–221.

Wittgenstein, Ludwig, *Tractatus Logico-Philosophicus*, preface by Bertrand Russell (London: Kegan Paul, Trench, Trubner, 1922).

———, *Werkausgabe*, 8 vols. (Frankfurt: Suhrkamp, 1984).

Wohlfart, Günter, "Das unendliche Urteil. Zur Interpretation eines Kapitels aus Hegels *Wissenschaft der Logik*," *Zeitschrift für philosophische Forschung* 39. 1 (1985), pp. 85–100.

Wöhrmann, Jürgen, "Noch enimal: Utis — Odysseus," *Gymnasium* 70. 6 (1963), p. 549.

Wolff, Christian, *Philosophia rationalis sive logica* (1728, 3rd ed. Leipzig and Frankfurt: Prostat in officina libraria Rengeriana, 1740).

———, *Philosophia prima, sive ontologia* (Frankfurt and Leipzig: Prostat in officina Libraria Rengeriana, 1730).

Wolfson, Harry Austryn, *Studies in the History of Philosophy and Religion*, ed. Isadore Twersky and George H. Williams, 2 vols. (Cambridge, MA: Harvard University Press, 1973–77).

Zeller, Eduard, *Vorträge und Abhandlungen. Zweite Sammlung* (Lepizig: Fries, 1877).

Ziegler, Konrat, "Odysseus — Utuse — Utis," *Gymnasium* 69 (1962), pp. 396–98.

Zimmer, Karl Ernst, *Affixal Negation in English and Other Languages: An Investigation of Restricted Productivity* (London: W. Clowes, 1964).

Zimmermann, Albert, *Ontologie oder Metaphysik? Die Diskussion der Metaphysik im 13. und 14. Jahrhundert: Texte und Untersuchungen* (1965, Louvain: Peeters, 1998).

Zini, Fosca Mariana, "Lorenzo Valla et la réflexion sur la *Res*," *Penser entre les lignes: Philologie et philosophie au Quattrocento*, ed. Fosca Mariani Zini, pp. 75–91 (Lille: Presses Universitaires du Septentrion, 2001).

Index

doctrine of being, 171; doctrine of the
concept, 171–74; doctrine of essence, 171;
Encyclopedia of the Philosophical Sciences,
170–71, 178, 185; *Faith and Knowledge*, 174,
181; infinite judgment, 170–71, 177–85,
187–90, 203; *Jena System*, 179; on judgment,
170–91; on language and grammar, 169–70;
Lectures on Aesthetics, 190; *Lectures on Logic*,
184; *Lectures on the Philosophy of Right*,
178; *Phenomenology of Spirit*, 167, 169–70,
186–90; *Science of Logic*, 167–74, 178–79, 181–
85, 187, 190–91; speculative logic, 167–69,
171–72, 180.
Heidegger, Martin, 228–37, 239–40, 242–43,
300 n.57, 300 n.61; *Being and Time*, 228–29,
255; *Duns Scotus' Doctrine of Categories and
Meaning*, 235; *Introduction to Metaphysics*,
230, 233–34; *Kant and the Problem of Meta-
physics*, 231; "Letter on Humanism," 230;
The Metaphysical Foundations of Logic,
229; *Theory of Judgment in Psychologism*,
228; *Time and Being*, 231; *On the Way to
Language*, 230; "What Is Metaphysics?",
232–33, 235–37.
Henry of Ghent, 80–81, 85, 89, 95, 103.
Herz, Marcus, 133–34.
Hibben, John Grier, 212.
Hobbes, Thomas, 33.
Hölderlin, Friedrich, 230.
Holzhey, Helmut, 197, 200.
Homer, 7–11.
Horn, Lawrence R., 30.
Hume, David, 133, 194.
Ḥunayn ibn Isḥāq, 45.
Husserl, Edmund, 227–28; *Experience
and Judgment*, 228; *Ideas Pertaining
to a Pure Phenomenology*, 227.
Hyppolite, Jean, 171.

I, 155, 157, 160–61, 164–65, 172, 188, 211, 255.
I am, 154–58, 160, 165.
Ibn Muttawayh, 83.
Ideas Pertaining to a Pure Phenomenology
(Husserl), 227.
Identity, law of (Hegel), 185.
Imbert, Claude, 224.
Indefinite expressions, 40–42, 47–54, 57–58,
61, 71–72, 77, 245, 249–50, 254–56. *See also
Non-*.

Infinite affirmation, 119.
Infinite judgment, 239, 245, 300 n.2; Cohen,
199, 201–204, 206, 208–209, 211, 218, 255;
Fichte, 165–66; Hegel, 170–71, 177–85, 187–
90, 203; Kant, 10, 117–26, 128, 156–57, 163–66,
170, 180–81, 235, 255, 278 n.38; Maimon,
143–46, 150–51, 156; Schelling, 159, 163–66,
203. *See also* Judgment of origin; Thetic
judgment.
Infinite names, 28, 42, 50, 54–56, 59, 61, 68–69,
71–72, 88, 100, 105, 219, 235, 250, 269 n.29.
Infinite propositions, 120, 128–29, 143–44,
176, 191.
Infinite verbs, 41–42, 55, 104–105.
Infinite words, 55, 61–63, 68, 71–73, 86.
Infinitization (*infinitatio*), 68–71, 86, 95,
98–100, 245, 256.
Infinitude, grammatical, 62, 71.
Intelligible, the, 95, 97–101, 105.
Institutio logica (Galen), 25.
Introductio ad Syllogismos Categoricos
(Boethius), 264 n.32.
Introductiones Montane minores, 69.
Introduction to Metaphysics (Heidegger),
230, 233–34.
Introduction to a Secret Encyclopedia
(Leibniz), 101.
Investigation into the Laws of Thought
(Boole), 240.
*Investigations into the Theory of the Infinite
Judgment* (Gordin), 204.
Irrational number, 113.
Isḥāq ibn Ḥunayn, 45.
Ishikawa, Fumiyasu, 121.

JACKENDORFF, RAY, 30.
Jacobi, Friedrich Heinrich, 132–33.
Jakobson, Roman, 244–45.
Janke, Wolfgang, 157.
Jargon, 50, 75–76. *See also* Empty words.
Jäsche Logic (Kant), 118.
Jena System (Hegel), 179.
Jespersen, Otto, 30.
John of Seville, 93.
John of St. Thomas, 96.
Jolivet, Jean, 85.
Judgment: algebraic expression of, 142–43,
174–75, 199–200; of the concept, 173;
of determination, 122–23, 150, 177;

Zone Books series design by Bruce Mau
Typesetting by Meighan Gale
Image placement and production by Julie Fry
Printed and bound by Maple Press